THE NEW PATH

THE NEW PATH

RUSKIN AND THE AMERICAN PRE-RAPHAELITES

Linda S. Ferber
William H. Gerdts

THE BROOKLYN MUSEUM
SCHOCKEN BOOKS INC.

Published for the exhibition
The New Path:
Ruskin and the American Pre-Raphaelites

The Brooklyn Museum
New York
March 29–June 10, 1985

Museum of Fine Arts
Boston, Massachusetts
July 3–September 8, 1985

Research and publication of the catalogue for
The New Path: Ruskin and the American Pre-Raphaelites are made possible in part by a grant
from The Luce Fund for Scholarship in
American Art, a program of the Henry Luce
Foundation, Inc.

Front cover:
William Trost Richards
In the Woods 1860
Oil on canvas
15⅝ × 20 in. (39.7 × 50.8 cm.)
Collection: Bowdoin College Museum of Art, Brunswick, Maine
Cat. no. 73

Frontispiece:
Charles Herbert Moore
Winter Landscape, Valley of the Catskills 1866
Oil on canvas
7 × 10 in. (17.8 × 25.4 cm.)
Collection: The Art Museum, Princeton University, gift of Frank Jewett Mather, Jr.
Cat. no. 47

Back cover:
John William Hill
Pineapples *circa* 1864
Watercolor on paper
10½ × 15⅛ in. (26.6 × 38.4 cm.)
Collection: The Brooklyn Museum, purchased with funds given by Mr. and Mrs. Leonard L. Milberg
Cat. no. 29

Designed and published by The Brooklyn Museum, Eastern Parkway, Brooklyn, New York 11238. Printed in the U.S.A. by CLR, Inc., New York.

Exclusively distributed to the trade by Schocken Books Inc., 62 Cooper Square, New York, New York 10003.

Library of Congress Cataloging in Publication Data

Ferber, Linda S.
  The new path.

  Catalogue of an exhibition held at the Brooklyn Museum, New York, Mar. 29–June 10, 1985 and at the Museum of Fine Arts, Boston, July 3–Sept. 8, 1985.
  Bibliography: p.
  Includes index.
  1. Preraphaelitism–United States–Exhibitions.
2. Painting, American–Exhibitions. 3. Painting, Modern–19th century–United States–Exhibitions.
4. Ruskin, John, 1819–1900–Influence–Exhibitions.
5. Preraphaelites–United States–Exhibitions.
I. Ruskin, John, 1819–1900. II. Gerdts, William H.
III. Brooklyn Museum. IV. Museum of Fine Arts, Boston.
V. Title.
ND210.5.P67F47 1985   759.13'074'014461   85-5730
ISBN 0-87273-100-6
ISBN 0-8052-0780-5 (Schocken Books)

PHOTO CREDITS
Brenwasser: cat. no. 83
Geoffrey Clements: cat. nos. 22, 25, 27
Helga Photo Studios: cat. nos. 1, 4, 10, 14, 28, 32, 33, 70, 91, 97
Scott Hyde: cat. nos. 23, 24, 35, 60, 65, 75, 79, 85, 87, 94, 96, 103, 106, 122
Gerald Kraus: cat. no. 114
Edwin S. Roseberry: cat. no. 93
Joseph Szaszfai: cat. no. 105
Steven Tucker: cat. no. 44

Contents

Preface

The Brooklyn Museum has a tradition of pioneering exhibitions in the field of nineteenth-century American paintings. The Museum presented the first modern reappraisals of William Sidney Mount, John Quidor, Theodore Robinson, James Hamilton, John F. Peto, Eastman Johnson, and William T. Richards. All have inspired further research, contributing to the growing body of scholarship dealing with the rich and complex history of American art.

We are now proud to add to this distinguished list *The New Path: Ruskin and the American Pre-Raphaelites*, an exhibition which reintroduces a cast of characters and a body of work largely overlooked in past surveys of mid-nineteenth-century American painting. The exhibition offers the opportunity to discover familiar works in a different, sometimes startling, context, stimulating fresh energy in the continuing dialogue of scholarly inquiry.

We are pleased to share this exhibition with the Museum of Fine Arts, Boston. The splendid support of the Luce Fund for Scholarship in American Art was fundamental for the realization of this important publication; the support of the National Endowment for the Arts, which has made the exhibition and related programs possible, was also key to the Museum's undertaking the project.

ROBERT T. BUCK
Director
The Brooklyn Museum

Facing page:
Plate 1
Henry Roderick Newman
Italy 1883
Watercolor on paper, 39½ × 26⅜ in. (100.3 × 66.9 cm.)
Collection: Mr. and Mrs. Leonard L. Milberg
Cat. no. 63

THE NEW PATH: RUSKIN AND THE AMERICAN PRE-RAPHAELITES

Foreword

Despite the rapid rise and fall of the American Pre-Raphaelite movement, a remarkable number of documents recording their brief heyday remain—the *Minutes* of the Association for the Advancement of Truth in Art, twenty-four issues of *The New Path*, rich deposits of personal correspondence, and commentary in the contemporaneous press and literature. All of these are vital to the investigation of the artists who were at the core of the movement—Thomas C. Farrer, John Henry Hill, John William Hill, Charles Herbert Moore, Henry Roderick Newman, and William T. Richards. There is, however, a peculiar lacuna in this rich web: the majority of the drawings, watercolors, and paintings of the American Pre-Raphaelites are unlocated. While this situation presents an art historian's dilemma, particularly maddening for those organizing an exhibition, it also lends an excitement to the hunt as well as an expectation that this exhibition will provide information and stimulus to bring these lost works to light. Thus, *The New Path: Ruskin and the American Pre-Raphaelites* reopens a largely forgotten chapter, introducing a cast of characters and a body of work that must figure from now on in appraisals of mid-nineteenth-century American art history.

Many individuals and institutions acknowledged elsewhere have been helpful in the research and preparation of the exhibition and of this volume, and to all we extend our deep gratitude. We also wish to acknowledge the following for their special assistance: Alexander Acevedo; Lynn Addison; Karen Alexis; Kelley Anderson; Ada Bortoluzzi; Michael Batista; John I. H. Baur; Michael Botwinick; Mr. and Mrs. Robert L. Brandegee; Janice Buffington; Russell E. Burke; Gerald L. Carr; Mary Carver; Lady Clark; Janie Cohen; Thomas Colville; Larry Curry; Elaine Evans Dee; Rodney G. Dennis; Allison Eckardt; Rowland Elzea; Mr. and Mrs. Eugene D. Emigh; Trevor Fairbrother; Sarah C. Faunce; Stuart P. Feld; Gerald Fessenden; Ella Foshay; Wendell Garrett; Lord Glendevon; Susan Glover Godlewski; Edith Halley; Frederick D. Hill; James Berry Hill; Sylvia Hochfield; Michael Kan; Robert Kashey; Richard J. Koke; Conrad Kuchel; William McNaught; Paul Magriel; Janet and John Marqusee; Michael Martins; John Miller; M. P. Naud; Ellen Pearlstein; Glenn C. Peck; Patricia Pellegrini; Robert S. Persky; A. J. Phelan; Melanie Prejean; Robert Rainwater; Ira Spanierman; Natalie Spassky; Theodore E. Stebbins, Jr.; Miriam Stewart; Mrs. Robert L. Thompson; Stephen K-M. Tim; Carol Troyen; Lynn-Marie Villency; Robert Vose, Jr.; Joan Washburn; Gail Weinberg; Gerald Wunderlich; and Richard York.

As co-curators, we wish to acknowledge the Luce Fund for Scholarship in American Art for support of this publication and the National Endowment for the Arts for making the exhibition and related programs possible.

LINDA S. FERBER
WILLIAM H. GERDTS
Co-curators of the exhibition

Plate 2
Thomas C. Farrer
Mount Tom 1865
Oil on canvas, 16 × 24¼ in. (40.6 × 62.2 cm.)
Collection: Mr. and Mrs. Wilbur L. Ross, Jr.
Cat. no. 11

"Determined Realists": The American Pre-Raphaelites and the Association for the Advancement of Truth in Art

LINDA S. FERBER

Ripe for Revolution

"The Future of Art in America is not without hope," wrote Clarence Cook in the "Introductory" to the first issue of *The New Path*, a slender magazine that appeared in May 1863 (fig. 1) to announce that American art was ripe for revolution:

> The artists are nearly all young men; they are not hampered by too many traditions, and they enjoy the almost inestimable advantage of having no past, no masters and no schools. Add, that they work for an unsophisticated … public, which whatever else may stand in the way, will not be prevented from any prejudice or preconceived notions from accepting any really good work which may be set before it. These are solid advantages, hardly possessed by any other society, and make a good foundation on which to build well and beautifully for the future.

Historical parallels were located in medieval (that is, pre-Raphaelite) Europe and, even more distantly, in fifth-century Greece:

> The thirteenth century men had nothing of man's works behind them to awe them or make them ashamed; they worked their own will in glad unconsciousness of any standard but simple nature. They educated themselves and their work educated the people, and what is thus true of the thirteenth century is true of the Phidian age in Greece.

Both epochs—pre-Raphaelite Europe and Phidian Greece—had provided the foundations upon which great schools of painting, sculpture, and architecture had been developed. "Now," Cook continued,

> these conditions of a childish simplicity and ignorance in matters of Art coupled with a strong and wide interest in such matters—albeit, unformed, untrained—and perceptions naturally direct and true, are nowhere to be found today as pure as they are in America.[1]

Having thus articulated the belief in America as a virtual *tabula rasa* in the arts, *The New Path* surveyed the 1863 annual exhibition at the National Academy and made good the claim of "no past, no masters, no schools" by dismissing completely and irrevocably the work of the major figures of the first half of the century:

> They have done their work, and done it, no doubt, to the extent of their ability; our business is only to bid them 'Farewell,' while we turn to greet the young Americans who are to inaugurate the new day.[2]

Who were these "young Americans"? Chief among them were the members of the Association for the Advancement of Truth in Art, who were the writers and publishers of *The New Path*. The Association had been founded some eight months earlier, on January 27, in the Waverly Place studio of English expatriate artist Thomas Charles Farrer, by eight individuals—two artists, two architects, two geologists, and two lawyers.[3] They and like-minded friends who joined them at subsequent meetings organized in order to carry on a reform of American art and architecture. The architectural reform, which we shall refer to only briefly here, was committed to the Gothic Revival style current in England, where it was championed by John Ruskin, and in the United States, where Association members Peter B. Wight and Russell Sturgis were among its most dedicated practitioners.[4] The proposed reform of American art was based upon principles of truth to nature and programs of study that were expounded by Ruskin and, in the opinion of the Association, demonstrated in the paintings of the English Pre-Raphaelite Brotherhood, whose work the influential English critic had also championed.[5]

THE NEW PATH.

PUBLISHED BY THE

Society for the Advancement of TRUTH IN ART.

No. 1.] "Write the things which thou hast seen, and the things which are, and the things that shall be hereafter." [May, 1863.

THE future of Art in America is not without hope if looked at from certain points of view. The artists are nearly all young men; they are not hampered by too many traditions, and they enjoy the almost inestimable advantage of having no past, no masters and no schools. Add, that they work for an unsophisticated, and, as far as Art is concerned, uneducated public, which, whatever else may stand in the way, will not be prevented by any prejudice or preconceived notions from accepting any really good work which may be set before it. These are solid advantages, hardly possessed in such a degree by any other society, and make a good foundation on which to build well and beautifully for the future. All the omens are favorable, and the voices of the gods speak very plainly; nothing is wanting but that the priests fulfill their office worthily.

If we examine the list of the contributors to this year's Exhibition of the Academy, we shall find it set thick with the names of the young. The old names one by one disappear, and this, not because they represent superannuated, or feeble, or dead men, but because the breath of the new dawn which has already risen on our country blows too freshly and keenly for any but the young in spirit, in hope and courage, to breathe. It would be wanting in grace to speak harshly of men, the memory of whose works is fast disappearing from the minds of the people

as the works themselves are slowly leaving the walls of the Academy. They have done their work, and done it, no doubt, to the extent of their ability; our business is only to bid them "Farewell," while we turn to greet the young Americans who are to inaugurate the new day. It is no disgrace for the elders to have failed. Failure was foreordained. We cannot justly rebuke them, because, after forty years' uninterrupted labor they have given us not a single work which we care to keep, for they have worked under influences hostile to study and to the culture of Art, with no spur from within, and no friendly or sympathizing audience without. Good work has never been produced under such influences.

But for the younger men there is no such plea. The next generation may perhaps see a better time, but this is good enough. The old time was an era of political subsidence and stagnation. Hardly had we outgrown our colonial dependence; new-hatched as we were, many unseemly pieces of the old shells and straws from the nest still stuck to our feathers; the mother-hen, who did not know that she had hatched a swan, but thought us like herself, mere "tame, villatic fowl"—has even yet hardly ceased her admonitory cries and cluckings at our efforts to swim for ourselves, and, indeed, this reproach was fairly brought against us, that our literature and our Art were only copies,

Figure 1
Title page of *The New Path*, May 1863

Artist members of the Association, who included Farrer, John Henry Hill, John William Hill, Charles Herbert Moore, Henry R. Newman, and William T. Richards, adopted the English Brotherhood of 1848 as a model for their own defiance of convention in painting and as mentors in a strict attention to the appearance of objects out-of-doors which had produced the brilliant color and dazzling detail found in the early work of John Everett Millais (fig. 4) and William Holman Hunt (fig. 43) and had distinguished their paintings from the more subdued harmonies and painterly concerns of contemporaneous English painting. Since the primary concern of the American circle active in the 1850s, '60s, and '70s was directed to landscape and still-life subjects, the medieval revivalism of Dante Gabriel Rossetti's work—which fed later developments in England and here such as the Aesthetic and Arts and Crafts Movements—exercised far less influence upon American artists at mid-century than did the work of his fellow Brotherhood members Millais and Hunt, along with the work of those English artists of the 1850s and '60's who were strongly influenced by their meticulously detailed naturalism, like Arthur Hughes (fig. 40), John Brett (fig. 46), and John William Inchbold.[6] Members of the American Association for the Advancement of Truth in Art called themselves and were known variously as Realists, Naturalists, and, of course, Pre-Raphaelites.[7] The purpose and agenda of their reform were to be explained and promulgated by the Association's official organ, The New Path.

With its very first issue, The New Path began to earn a reputation for audacious criticism in its less than kind assessments of the works of the most distinguished figures in the American art establishment. In a review of the 1863 Artists' Fund Society exhibition, even Thomas Cole's paintings were dismissed as "three pieces of hopeless imbecility." "We rejoice," the reviewer (probably Cook) continued, "at their exhibition,"

> so that disinterested spectators might learn ... how empty are this man's much vaunted claims to high artistic rank. They cannot stand in the light of today, and in twenty-five years will not be worth the canvas they are painted on.[8]

These are strong terms for the acknowledged founder of the native school of landscape. Indeed, landscape, with a hybrid of still life and landscape elements, was the common specialty of artist members, and they ranged the territory Cole had established in the 1820s and 1830s as prime artist's ground: the Catskills and the Hudson Valley, the Adirondacks, and the White Mountains. Moore himself lived and painted during these years in the village of Catskill, New York, Cole's own home, and Farrer painted a view of the Hudson River from Cole's farm (cat. no. 9). The distinction lay in the different spirit motivating the artists' records of those hallowed subjects.

Cole's models, who were the models of his generation for interpretations of native scenery—the "wild Salvator Rosa, or the aerial Claude Lorrain"[9]—established in America a long-honored European landscape tradition originating in the seventeenth century. By 1863 this tradition was not only old-fashioned, but glorified precisely those artists John Ruskin set out to dethrone in Modern Painters, wherein he declared that these "professed landscape painters" were false to nature, not recording but betraying "the great verities of the material world."[10]

The New Path's prototypes and models for landscape were located in the realm of site-specific documentation and properly recorded natural history, with "the photograph" and the "topographical report" as standards of accuracy. The landscape of an American Pre-Raphaelite was to serve both science and art, conceived and rendered "in such a way that the poet, the naturalist and the geologist might have taken large pleasure from it."[11] Cole's landscape painting, therefore, came to represent the worst errors of the past school, and he himself was rejected by The New Path as a most unsuitable ancestor. The portrait and history painter John Trumbull was acknowledged as "a passably good Connecticut giotto," but in landscape no one—not even Asher B. Durand—of the older generation was tolerated.[12]

This is more surprising in the case of Durand, whose son John had founded and co-edited The New Path's precursor, The Crayon, with artist-journalist William James Stillman. The latter, hailed by the Association as the first American Pre-Raphaelite (see cat. no. 120),[13] was probably responsible for the appearance of the senior Durand's famous "Letters on Landscape Painting" in The Crayon. Presaging the program that would be outlined by The New Path, Durand urged the student "to attain as minute portraiture as possible" of objects in nature in order to gain "a knowledge of their subtlest truths and characteristics."[14] Durand's own response to Ruskin in the late 1840s is reflected in a more energetic production of careful outdoor studies from nature (cat. nos. 98 and 99) and a new commitment to a more natural, uncomposed appearance in his studio paintings; both approaches were a powerful influence on the development of plein-air practice and habits of close observation among American artists. However, Durand also shared the ideals of Cole's generation, which still admired and often emulated in studio productions the wilderness and pastoral landscape conventions based ultimately upon those of Salvatore Rosa and Claude Lorraine. Furthermore, Durand respected the traditional distinction between outdoor study and studio production, writing in the "Letters," "this excessively minute painting is valuable, not so much for itself as for the knowledge and facility it leads to"[15]—unlike the Association, for whom the study, as we shall see, was an acceptable end in itself. Most important, perhaps, for *The New Path* was the fact that Durand had served as President of the National Academy from 1845 to 1861 and so represented the embodiment of academic practice in landscape to a faction who declared that "the Academies... have done harm, and only harm, to the sacred cause of true Art."[16] *The New Path's* declared anti-academic stance was underlined in an 1864 review of Daniel Huntington's *The Republican Court* (1861, The Brooklyn Museum), in which the reader was pointedly informed that "this is the President of the National Academy of Design, whose picture is on exhibition." The reviewer concluded, in the course of a long, negative opinion, that the large history painting was in fact of value and should be seen "by daylight,—say at half price,—that all the young painters in the land might be induced to go and see what to avoid."[17]

The New Path gloried in the controversy such opinions stirred:

> We exist for the purpose of stirring up strife; of breeding discontent; of pulling down unsound reputations; of making the public dissatisfied with the work of most of the artists, and, better still, of making the artists dissatisfied with themselves.[18]

Statements like this one were probably responsible for the "curious fact," noted by Wight, "that very few artists allowed their names to go [on] the subscription book, but that a certain number of them were regular purchasers of single copies."[19]

Most feared among the critics contributing to the magazine was Clarence Cook, who by the spring of 1864 was notorious for his articles in the *New York Daily Tribune* which reviewed the exhibition shown at the New York Metropolitan Fair wholly in the spirit of *The New Path*. Reiterating his assessment of the condition of American painting that had appeared in the introductory editorial to *The New Path* a year earlier, Cook wrote of the impending "great revolution in art," dismissing the work of major figures like Leutze, Durand, and Huntington as representative of an art belonging "to a past age, and a dead system."[21] That Ruskinian enthusiasm fueled the "savage critic," as Whittredge recalled him,[22] is left in no doubt by Cook's response to a letter in which Farrer compared Cook's *Tribune* articles to the writings of the "Oxford graduate." "I am not vain enough to see any likeness," Cook responded with modesty:

> Ruskin is a discoverer, a genius, an altogether exceptional man. I am merely an educated man with some talent, very much interested in Art and trying to present what I have learned from him to my small audience. Think of the difference between Ruskin's works which are read by two nations and teach two, and set them thinking, and my six or seven articles in the Tribune which were scarcely read out of New York City. My dear, you are green! ... Not that I by any means think my work unimportant. Oh, by no manner of means! On the contrary, very important. And I mean to keep at it.[23]

The Prophet: Ruskin in America

For the past two decades, Ruskin had advocated what *The New Path* termed "the earnest loving study of God's work of nature" as the basis for the reform of painting, both in his widely read and influential books, *Modern Painters* and *The Elements of Drawing*, and in many lectures and articles.[24] In addition to the American editions of his books, Ruskin's writings were available to the American art community from 1855 to 1861 in *The Crayon*, which frequently printed excerpts, letters, and articles by and about Ruskin and the English Pre-Raphaelites.

Although Ruskin had no personal contact with the English Pre-Raphaelites until 1851, the first two volumes of *Modern Painters* (1843 and 1846) had been important in shaping the initial goals of the Brotherhood. Ruskin came to their defense in 1851 with two letters to the London *Times* and a pamphlet, "Pre-Raphaelitism," in which he pointed out the merit in their work, claiming that the Pre-Raphaelites were demonstrating in their paintings the practice of careful and devoted study from nature he had called for and receiving for their efforts "the most scurrilous abuse which I ever recollect seeing issue from the public press."[25] This defense firmly identified him with the movement in both England and the United States. Ruskin was closely associated in the public mind not only with the Pre-Raphaelites but also with J.M.W. Turner, the great English landscape painter; Ruskin's defense of Turner against charges of untruthfulness in his interpretations of nature had inspired *Modern Painters*.

Stillman recalled that the first volume of *Modern Painters* had been "one of the sensation-books of the time" in America,[26] where Ruskin's ideas about nature and landscape were received enthusiastically, largely because they reinforced and corroborated indigenous ideas and attitudes. Roger Stein writes that the fundamental importance of Ruskin's writings in America was "his identification of the interest in art with morality and religion as well as with the love of nature, his ability to build a loose but convincing system where art, religion, and nature were inextricably intertwined."[27] These ideas, expressed in Ruskin's eloquent and highly descriptive prose, struck a responsive chord in America, where a domestic Wordsworthian tradition, an attitude of reverence toward nature, already existed. In 1855, Clarence Cook confirmed in his own words the powerful response of Americans to the English critic's writings. "We love Ruskin's glowing style," Cook wrote, "we love his love of nature, we love his love of God. He carries us along with him by his enthusiasm."[28] Later, the Association's debt to Ruskin would be not only openly and repeatedly acknowledged but also celebrated, and his famous conclusion to *Modern Painters*—"that the right course for young artists is faithful and loving representation of nature, 'selecting nothing and rejecting nothing'"—became the manifesto of the Association.[29]

The foundation of artists' societies and associations outside the official academic structure was not in itself novel in America. The National Academy of Design had itself been founded in 1825 in protest against the policies of the American Academy of Fine Arts. By the 1860s, however, the National Academy had enjoyed four decades of nearly undisputed hegemony. Art associations and academies founded in other cities were no challenge to the New York institution but a response to growing interest in native production. Only the Pennsylvania Academy of the Fine Arts, established in 1805, rivaled the New York organization in age and esteem. While New York-based, the Academy's wider ambitions and influence were implied in its choice of a name, and, indeed, the National Academy of Design was the most prestigious American artists' organization, with an honorary body of academicians, the most important exhibition space, and a long-established school.

All of the major artists of the Association, with the exception of Newman, were, in fact, members of the Academy when they launched their reform. The organization of the Association for the Advancement of Truth in Art was the culmination of the activity and interests of a circle whose personal interaction began in the 1850s. These American Pre-Raphaelites should be understood as a radical manifestation, among a small group of artists, architects, and critics, of the pervasive influence of Ruskin's ideas in this country—ideas that had touched other artists as well, though less profoundly.

Worthington Whittredge, although not himself among the rebels, testified in his *Autobiography* to both the power and the most persistent criticism of Ruskin's impact upon the artist community:

> Ruskin, in his "Modern Painters," just out then and in every landscape painter's hand, had told these tyros nothing could be too literal in the way of studies, and many of them believed Ruskin. The consequence was that many of them made carefully painted studies of the most commonplace subjects without the slightest choice or *invention*, and exhibited them as pictures.[30]

Whittredge himself, however, was not entirely immune to certain Ruskinian influences, as his 1867 still life *Apples* (cat. no. 121) suggests.

Each major artist who became a member of the Association had undergone a radical change of style—commonly experienced as a kind of conversion—under the impact of Ruskin's ideas about truth to nature in painting. John William Hill received his inspiration around 1855 from reading *Modern Painters* and presumably passed his revelation on to his son John Henry Hill.[31] William T. Richards' major catalyst seems to have been Pre-Raphaelite works studied in the 1857-58 Exhibition of English Art that travelled in America.[32] Letters suggest that Charles H. Moore and Henry R. Newman were won over by Thomas C. Farrer,[33] who had received instruction in drawing in London from Ruskin himself.

Many records exist on which to base a study of the Association and its ideas and opinions: the fifty-seven-page minute book (Ryerson Library, Art Institute of Chicago), the twenty-four issues of *The New Path*, reports and reviews in the contemporary press, letters, memoirs, and monographic studies of a number of the artists. However, the major documents for a study of artist-members—the paintings themselves—remain, even for the major figures, elusive. Nevertheless, enough work has surfaced in the last decade to begin an investigation of this topic. Central to our discussion and to the exhibition are not only the works of artist-members themselves, but also those of a larger circle, contemporaneous or slightly earlier, whose works demonstrate closely parallel interests. These peripheral figures include William J. Stillman, Aaron D. Shattuck, Henry Farrer, Fidelia Bridges, Robert Brandegee, George B. Wood, and J.B. Duffey. Many of the names mentioned are not represented in the exhibition or discussed at length simply because, although documented in the records—sometimes extensively, as is the case with Robert J. Pattison (cat. no. 65) and Casimir C. Griswold—their works still remain unlocated. The artist-members and their immediate circle are complemented in the exhibition by a selection of still-life, landscape, and figure paintings by artists generally better known today—such as William Mason Brown, George C. Lambdin, Asher B. Durand, Frederic E. Church, Martin Johnson Heade, Albert Bierstadt, and John G. Brown—whose work was demonstrably touched by some of the same Ruskinian impulses and influences, although their commitment to stringent investigation and patient recording of detail did not persist or did not satisfy the stern criteria of *The New Path*. From the perspective of historical distance, a visual survey of these works nevertheless reveals a strong community of interests—sometimes documented, sometimes not—which argues that the botanical and geological specificity, brilliant palette, and sharp focus associated with the Ruskinian approach had wider influence on mid-nineteenth-century American painting than the American Pre-Raphaelites or their opponents might have recognized or acknowledged.

The Evangelist: Thomas Charles Farrer

It was an especial devotion and enthusiasm that galvanized the inner circle in the late 1850s, beginning in all likelihood with the arrival of Thomas Farrer from London and his drawing classes with Ruskin at the Working Men's College.[34] Farrer served as the dynamo energizing a group of American artists, architects, critics, and collectors already highly sympathetic to the Ruskinian point of view; Wight recalled him as "a self-made man who had the natural instincts of an artist."[35]

Farrer must have been among Ruskin's more talented students, for he was an excellent draftsman, as his fascinating *Self-portrait*, probably of 1859, reveals (fig. 2). His pencil studies of plants (cat. nos. 6 and 7) also demonstrate the care and detail that would have made his work attractive to the Hills. Their friendship and common enthusiasm is documented in his portrait drawing of the elder Hill, probably also of 1859 (cat. no. 5), showing his sitter quietly pensive in a studio setting and inscribed "A Lover of Ruskin Drawn by Ruskin's Pupil." Distinguishable among the pictures indicated in the background are the crisp profile of an American mountain range at the lower left and a Turnerian landscape composition beyond the sitter's right shoulder, representing, perhaps, the twin poles of the Ruskinian vision. This and the *Self-portrait* are two in a series of extraordinary figure drawings, all probably informal portraits, that were widely admired at the time (cat. nos. 2-4). Farrer's close association with the Hill family was natural, since John William, affectionately known as "Poppy," was an early dedicated convert to the new path, abandoning his landscape style, which had been grounded in the early nineteenth-century conventions practiced by his own father, John Hill, for an approach to both landscape and still life that was inspired by Ruskin (cat. nos. 27-43). The younger Hill followed his father's lead (cat. nos. 13-36). Early

Figure 2
Thomas Charles Farrer
Self-portrait Sketching *circa* 1859
Pencil with Chinese white on paper prepared with cream ground
10½ × 7⅝ in. (26.7 × 19.4 cm.)
Private collection
Cat. no. 1

letters convey a strong, if still informal, sense of fraternity several years before formation of the Association, and it is evident that the English Brotherhood of 1848 was already a model for the Americans, who felt themselves to be, and, indeed, took a measure of pride in being, outside the mainstream of the contemporary art establishment and practice.[36]

Farrer's role as persuasive spokesman was soon established, as he widened his circle of acquaintance among the young artists of New York. John Henry Hill wrote early in 1860, "I saw Charlie Moore he said you had been down to see him and staid till one O'clock and had a good talk, I hope you talked him over to preraphaelitism."[37] Moore's enthusiastic response is recorded in a letter to Farrer expressing his eagerness to carry on a correspondence on "art topics." "Do give me a provocation," he wrote, "and I will send my defense."[38] The impact on Moore of these exchanges is evident. Moving from early competent but unremarkable efforts such as In Berkshire County (circa 1859, The New-York Historical Society)— a landscape much in the manner of Durand's vertical forest compositions—Moore had the power by 1861 to produce The Catskills in Spring (cat. no. 44), which is painted with a brisk, controlled touch and infused with a startlingly convincing plein-airism. Abandoning the framing devices of rocks and trees, this modern little panoramic landscape is very much akin to John William Hill's bright and fresh little oil of 1859, Bridge at Androscoggin (cat. no. 27). Within a very few years, both eschewed even this limited painterliness, developing a much tighter surface control while maintaining the brilliance of plein-air effect that made them champions of the Pre-Raphaelite style in landscape. There is presently no evidence to indicate that the circle was aware of or used the English Pre-Raphaelite technique of painting in minute touches of color over a wet white ground which so enhanced the brilliance of Hunt's and Millais' landscapes.[39] However, the stipple technique, related in its application of broken color on a white paper surface, was used extensively in the watercolors of the circle as dictated by Ruskin in The Elements of Drawing (1857) and discussed below by Kathleen Foster. John W. Hill's View from High Tor, Haverstraw, New York of circa 1866 and Henry R. Newman's Mount Everett from Monument Mountain in April of 1867 (pl. 8) are panoramic watercolor landscapes whose prismatic brilliance and crisp detail is due to the skilled exercise of this painstaking technique. In the 1860s watercolor was a major medium for the Hills; the few early works known by Newman are watercolors (pls. 8 and 14), and Farrer's work in the medium, though still unknown, was praised. Early examples of watercolor works by Moore (cat. no. 45) and Richards (cat. no. 71) demonstrate the same meticulous application, which may have influenced their handling of the oil medium. Certainly John W. Hill's small oil painting Hunter and Dog of circa 1867 (pl. 9) owes a debt in its vivid palette and violet-blue cast shadows to the artist's mastery of the watercolor medium as well as to plein-air observation. In the main, however, American Pre-Raphaelites heightened local color, minimized shadow, and suppressed painterly qualities in their oils in order to achieve the static brilliance and linear clarity which characterizes their landscapes. Completion or near completion of work out-of-doors was also—as with the English Pre-Raphaelites—a major commitment of the American circle. Moore's Winter Landscape: Valley of the Catskills (frontispiece), a favorite subject transformed by snow, depicts a remarkable Pre-Raphaelite accumulation of detail bathed in winter light and blue shadow. Parallels in touch and use of colored shadows in Farrer's Mount Tom of about 1866 (pl. 2) suggest that artist's influence in the evolution of Hill's and Moore's mature Pre-Raphaelite manners. William T. Richards, apparently working independently in Philadelphia, began to investigate Pre-Raphaelitism in 1858 and by 1860 had mastered the approach in brightly colored and detailed oils like Landscape (cat. no 72) and In the Woods (cover), which were probably known to the New York circle prior to their direct contact with the artist. The intensity of palette and fixation on detail in David Johnson's Natural Bridge, Virginia of 1860 (pl. 12) and Martin J. Heade's Lake George of 1862 (pl. 11) suggest that other American artists were also experimenting with that approach in the early 1860s. Their mutual emphasis upon geological phenomena might have been inspired not only by the long descriptive passages on the earth's structure in Modern Painters but also by such pictorial models as Ruskin's Fragment of the Alps of 1854-56 (pl. 5) and John Brett's first Alpine tour de force, The Glacier of Rosenlaui, of 1857 (fig. 46), both of which were shown in the English Exhibition of 1857-58.

Farrer maintained some contact with his English mentor and, apparently, sought to introduce Ruskin to the American circle's work, prompting Moore's comment, "I am glad to hear that Ruskin speaks well of John's drawings."[40] This is probably a reference to the younger Hill, whose contact with Ruskin over the years is documented in letters and in *Lake George* (cat. no. 25), a watercolor study of 1873 bearing Ruskin's annotations and comments. Farrer may have carried American works with him on his return to England in the summer of 1860, when one of his missions was to make careful copies of works by Turner to bring back to New York. John Henry Hill urged him to study all the English work he saw; relieved to learn that Farrer was indeed to return to New York, Hill was moved to offer "three cheers for the Pre-Raphaelite cause in America."[41]

The Association for the Advancement of Truth in Art

When Farrer returned from England late in 1860, most of the key figures in the American Pre-Raphaelite circle were acquainted and, perhaps, already holding the "informal meetings" recalled by Wight "to talk over those art matters which were of so much interest to them."[42] The beginning of the Civil War in 1861 did not seem to dampen interest in "art matters" in general. In New York, in fact, Whittredge later recalled, Wight's Gothic Revival National Academy building was built "chiefly during the war" and "painters sold their pictures readily and native art flourished more conspicuously than now."[43] The war was reflected in subjects of several paintings of the circle: Richards exhibited the *Recruiting Station (Bethlehem)* in 1862 (unlocated); Hennessy's *Mon Brave*, 1870 (cat. no. 112), is a reprise of an earlier Civil War theme, and Farrer's *April 1861*, *circa* 1865 (unlocated), depicted the departure of New York's Seventh Regiment in a painting that, from its description in *The New Path*, was close to the format of *Gone! Gone!* (pl. 6).[44] Farrer himself served in the Union Army but was back in New York by October 1862 when Richards issued an eager invitation to visit Germantown in company with dealer Samuel P. Avery, surely to discuss their mutual interests.[45]

Meetings continued in New York, and at one of them Farrer suggested that the circle organize and form a society "to advocate the reforms which, as individuals they were all striving to effect."[46] The first such meeting was held at his Waverly Place studio in January 1863, and the proceedings were duly recorded. Farrer opened the meeting, explaining "the object that had called the present company together, ... the desirability of forming an association ... the object it should have in view, and the probable sphere of usefulness." A committee was appointed—Sturgis, Farrer, and geologist Clarence King—to prepare articles of organization "embracing ideas expressed by Messrs. Farrer, Moore and others." Discussions continued at three successive meetings, during which membership expanded to include the Hills and Clarence Cook in addition to a following of general sympathizers, some undoubtedly collectors, whose Ruskinian activities remain to be investigated.[47] The Articles of Organization were discussed, amended, and drafted at four preliminary meetings and then adopted and signed on February 18 at the first regular meeting, held at Wight's. The slate of elected officers presented a balanced profile of the interests of the Association: President, artist John William Hill; Vice President, critic Clarence Cook; Secretary, geologist Clarence King; and Treasurer, architect Peter B. Wight.

During February and March, meetings were held weekly at the residences and studios of members and friends. In April, a room was rented for Association use at 32 Waverly Place, Farrer's studio address. The first issue of *The New Path* appeared in May. After this busy three-month period, the major energies of the membership, which numbered about twenty-six, were evidently directed to production of its magazine; the Association met formally only twice more—in October 1863 and March 1864—and the latter meeting was devoted to the dissolution of the organization itself. *The New Path*, however, appeared regularly during this period and afterwards, effectively bringing the opinions and programs of the reformers to public attention.

In the second article of organization, the founders enumerated "our objects in forming this association":

> to secure for ourselves encouragement and mutual instruction;—to assist meritorious artists who may need
> help—to develop latent artistic ability, especially among the class of mechanics;—and to educate the public to
> a better understanding of the representative arts.

An agenda followed, outlining the program for realizing these objects and including "holding meetings for exchange of ideas, discussion, and exhibition of members' work." Recorded business meetings, which numbered only ten, seem to have alternated with non-official "Literary" evenings. Letters indicate that members' work was indeed brought to meetings for criticism and, since guests seem to have attended, perhaps in the hope of sales. Moore wrote from Catskill of his intention to send a current plein-air study "down to the Society—and perhaps someone will appreciate the subject," quizzing Farrer, on another study, "How does the P.R.B. like the 'Mandrakes'?"[48] In November, Newman thanked Farrer for the positive reception of drawings sent the month before from Vermont: "Being the first work I ever offered for criticism . . . I was naturally very anxious to hear from [the Association]."[49]

Farrer and Sturgis each apparently also acquired one of Newman's studies, in keeping with the Association's commitment "to commission and to purchase work of unusual merit" and otherwise "assist pecuniarily" young men of promise. A circle of devoted collectors—some of them members—also purchased and, on occasion, commissioned works; their small numbers and seemingly exclusive enthusiasm for Ruskinian work drew the charge from "scoffers" that "the American Pre-Raphaelites bought their own pictures."[50] The Association intended to "educate the public" through an ambitious program that included holding competitions in the visual arts, manufacture and design, and architecture, and by organizing exhibitions and public lectures. Not surprisingly, these varied activities seem to have proven to be beyond the capacity of the Association, most of whose energies ultimately focused upon realization of the final and, in retrospect, most important item on the agenda, to "conduct a journal or magazine for general circulation. . . . "

Such was the idealistic and highly ambitious program set by this small organization, whose treasury depended solely upon "voluntary contributions," and whose membership never seems to have exceeded twenty-seven. Reform, however, as Wight recalled, "can only be effected by reformers, and reformers must be enthusiasts."[51]

The New Path

At a special meeting on March 28, 1863, Clarence Cook, who had succeeded John William Hill as President of the Association, called for "an expression of opinion as to the propriety of at once beginning the publication of a journal." The organ of the English Brotherhood, *The Germ*, published briefly in 1850, might have been known to the American circle and, if so, was a prototype for their own publication.[52] Each issue was to be planned at a special monthly meeting at which manuscripts of articles, essays, and poems were to be read aloud by the editor and discussed, with the final content selected and approved by a majority of the members present. While the new journal, published by the Home Printing Company, appeared first in May 1863 and monthly thereafter, the Association apparently did not meet again formally until October; since the artist members regularly decamped for the summer—only Moore corresponding and contributing material regularly—the major responsibility for content and production was most likely left from the beginning in the hands of Cook (who served as editor), Sturgis, and Wight.

Over the two-and-a-half-year period from May 1863 to December 1865, twenty-four issues of *The New Path* were published in two volumes. Number one of each volume began with a statement of purpose and printed a recent letter of support from Ruskin.[53] An eight-page issue averaged three lengthy articles or reviews. This pattern altered in the last issues, from July to December 1865, when a number of extracts were also published, supplementing regular content and perhaps reflecting the increasing difficulty in meeting the quota of original copy necessary to fill each issue.

Equal attention was given to the other major concerns of the Association besides painting: architecture, sculpture, and design in the decorative arts. In the first four issues, a series of lengthy articles by Sturgis explained the Articles of Organization, and Farrer undertook to satisfy critics in "A Few Questions Answered." With issue five, Wight commenced a four-part survey of architectural history that ran concurrently with a four-part history of sculpture, perhaps by Cook. Obviously *The New Path* intended to meet the Association's first priority: to educate the public. Painting notices and reviews appeared regularly, covering major events such as the Academy Annual and the Artists' Fund Society as well as gallery exhibitions of American and foreign works and the special receptions promoting large popular works, such as Bierstadt's *The Rocky Mountains* (1863, The Metropolitan Museum of Art), Huntington's *The*

Republican Court (1861, The Brooklyn Museum), and Inness's *The Sign of Promise* (1863).[54] A long, detailed review of Millais' illustrations for *The Parables of Our Lord and Savior Jesus Christ* (1864) suggests the important role such graphics played as models in the absence of original English works.[55] Cook was undoubtedly responsible for many unsigned articles and retained the title of editor through the life of the magazine;[56] however, it seems clear that he and Sturgis shared this function and that the latter was the single most prolific contributor to *The New Path*.

Most consistent and enthusiastic among the artist-contributors was Moore, and because he himself was a practicing Pre-Raphaelite painter, his articles command special attention. "Fallacies of the Present School," his discussion and criticism of the current theory and practice of his own specialty, landscape, was to be followed by a sequel, never published. "I've been writing an article upon American Landscape Art as it has been and *ought* no more to be," he wrote to Farrer, "in which I've considered the case of Cole and Church and one or two others of our old school."[57]

John Henry Hill's contribution took the form of a series of letters written late in 1864 during his London sojourn, describing what he saw of English painting. In keeping with Ruskin's recommendation of models in *The Elements of Drawing*, he admired the watercolors of William Henry Hunt as "exquisite" (fig. 19) and those of John Frederick Lewis as "a marvel of elaboration." Hill also observed that Pre-Raphaelite follower Thomas Seddon's *Jerusalem and the Valley of Jehosaphat from the Hill of Evil Counsel* (1854-55; Tate Gallery, London) was "very like Farrer." Hill dwelt at length upon his experience of studying and copying the works of Turner—again according to the advice of Ruskin and Farrer—and urged his addressee to tell the latter "that I am not disappointed in Turner."[58]

The New Path assigned an exalted role to criticism and, indeed, the "new critic" was to play a key role in the "systematic effort" of reform advocated by the Association. In "A Few Questions Answered," Farrer bemoaned the current situation:

> The critics and Art public generally, used to coarse, bad work, and having had their natural right feeling for delicate drawing, fine colors, and beautiful forms, deadened by an artificial and long continued admiration of false work, when they see artists doing their simplest duty and drawing leaves or trees [so] that you can really tell ... whether it is an Oak, an Elm, or a Pine, and painting rocks [so] that you can ... see the difference between Trap Granite and red Sandstone—"What!" say the discerning public, "are painters to become botanists and geologists!" ... instead of receiving these with ... joy and gladness, receive them with a howl of scorn and disdain, and the works ... are characterized as finished with the "painful fidelity of the Pre-Raphaelites" ... "agonizing fidelity" ... "cold, remorseless fidelity." [These are] literal quotations from some of the best Art criticism that New York has yet produced. Poor, weak critics, how it must shake their delicate nerves to see honesty and truth![59]

The ideal critic, according to *The New Path*, was modeled on Ruskin, a prophetic figure who could interpret the new, honest, and truthful vision for both the artist and the public. Russell Sturgis's "Art Criticism," the lead article in the April 1864 issue, established the importance of the critic, defining the nature of and need for criticism, its purpose, and its conduct and requirements. "Criticism," wrote Sturgis, "is not only a natural consequence of all art but it is a necessary concomitant to good art."[60] Fellow critic James Jackson Jarves, although objecting to the Pre-Raphaelite interpretation of truth to nature, nevertheless agreed, in *The Art Idea* (1864), on "the special disadvantages to American art arising from false criticism" consisting of "high-sounding phrases and wanton praise" issuing from an "indiscriminating press."[61] Sturgis proposed a discipline termed a "science of art," listing the bodies of knowledge required of a "true" critic, which included a "practical" and a "scientific" knowledge of nature, including geology, botany, anatomy, and physics. Of particular importance was a knowledge and grasp of the critical vocabulary itself. "The critic," Sturgis declared, "is as a botanist with pictures for plants," stressing the serious, disciplined nature of the undertaking—an attitude embodied in Farrer's portrait drawing of Clarence Cook (fig. 3) at work in a Gothic Revival study adorned with icons of art history and of the English Pre-Raphaelites.

In this portrait, Cook, a prophetic bearded figure despite his youth, bends to his task, using a quill pen with all the serious concentration of a medieval scribe in a cell. The lintel bears the names of Ruskin's idols, Rossetti and Turner, while on the wall at the left hangs an engraving of Holman Hunt's *The Light of the World*; in the center, poised directly above Cook's head, is Dürer's famous engraving *Melancholia*,

Figure 3
Thomas Charles Farrer
Portrait of Clarence Cook *circa* 1861
Pencil on paper (?), size unknown
Location unknown

and hanging at the right, below Turner's name, is an unidentified portrait; below this is a globe, and to the right is a cast of the Venus de Milo. The crowded tabletop and the figure dominate the foreground, which is tightly contained in an arched format that compresses space into a claustrophobic melange of objects suggesting projections of Cook's mental process as he writes, with the quill overlapping head and hand and thus providing the visual link between the mind and the hand that guides the pen, translating thoughts about art into written words.

Although its extreme position provoked controversy, *The New Path's* efforts to establish a serious and informed art criticism in America did not go unnoticed or unapplauded. *The Independent* commented about "this keen edged periodical":

> Not assenting to half we find in these successive sprightly numbers, we nevertheless cannot join in the outcry against this adventurous journal ... We are confident that the great discussions opened by this journal will prove salutary to the best growth of American art.

The Boston *Daily Advertiser* judged the magazine "the only periodical in the country that ventures to have an independent opinion about art."[62] Nevertheless, circulation remained limited, and early in 1864 it was already clear that the expenses of publishing *The New Path* had proven too much for the Association. Extreme measures were necessary. Debts would be paid not only by draining the treasury but also by taxing the membership and "appropriating and selling all articles belonging to the Society." At the meeting of March 29, 1864, the Association terminated its sponsorship of the magazine, and *The New Path* was formally turned over to the trio whose energies had sustained the project from the first. This "change in management," the reader was assured, indicated "no change in the position of *The New Path*."[63] In fact, it marked the cessation of formal activity on the part of the Association, since no further meetings are recorded.

Group activity in the months following that March meeting centered around beginning Volume Two by producing issues for May, June, and July. Then, after fifteen months of steady activity, publication was suspended for nine months. This was due, according to the minutes of The New Path Association, to "want of means, of time and of ... experience in the publishing business." Cook, a major force on the magazine, was confined to Staten Island by the illness of his wife. Writing to Farrer in August, he also implied a measure of tension that may have played a role in the hiatus:

> I have not seen nor heard anything of the men since I came down ... you know I am not in love with any of them. How the "New Path" fares, I am entirely ignorant. I cannot write for it anymore than for anything else, and I dare say they are very willing I should not.[64]

Cook's energies were also diverted by his appointment that spring as art critic on the *New York Daily Tribune*. Of "the men," Wight must have been preoccupied with the completion of the National Academy building. Moore, the artist who, after Farrer, was most involved in the magazine, was, as usual, at Catskill. Farrer himself had been recently married (to Annie McLane, an Association member and artist whose works are unknown) and was in Gorham, New Hampshire.[65]

On his return to the city that fall, Farrer, obviously anxious to bring his flock back into the fold, wrote to Moore in Catskill about a meeting. While Farrer must have been reassured by Moore's report that he was at work on a "heretical essay," the latter declined his invitation to a New York "Pow-wow," citing the pressure of work.[66] Finally, in February 1865, the regulars met again to form The New Path Association and to raise funds to complete Volume Two, to be published by James Miller. Publication resumed in April 1865, with Cook again elected to editorship, but only four more issues appeared.

Didactic in tone and unremittingly serious, *The New Path* proclaimed itself "a plain-spoken, meddling asker of unanswerable questions, or, not-to-be answered questions," going on to declare:

> We do not care to be attractive; we have no famous contributors; nobody is paid anything to write for us, and nobody will be, and we make no effort to cater to the love of amusement ... If you like us ... you must like us because we are in earnest, because we *are* iconoclasts, because we will not budge from the stand we have taken, and because it is plain that we have made up our minds to be heard.[67]

This insistent, strident voice distinguishes *The New Path* from its precursor, *The Crayon*, as an American promoter of Ruskin's point of view and of the work of the English Pre-Raphaelites. Small in size, provocative in tone, without advertisements and offering no remuneration to contributors or "amusement" to readers, *The New Path* seems to have been limited enough in circulation to be considered already a rare item in 1884,[68] and it is hardly surprising that it did not prosper financially. Nevertheless, contemporary response concurs with Wight's recollections that *The New Path* enjoyed a measure of respect in some quarters and much notoriety in others, suggesting an influence and impact far beyond what might be expected from confessedly amateur management, irregular publication, and a short lifespan.

Determined Realists: The Artists at Work

In 1864, the cultural magazine *The Round Table* took exception to *The New Path*'s extremism, pointing out that "the great discussion" on Pre-Raphaelitism had been opened some years earlier and the movement "largely accepted in this country":

> With the purposes of the society and journal we have no quarrel, but we must express our surprise that both have ignored the fact of the existence here of that with which they intend to inoculate the body of American art.[69]

However, the Association argued that the current state of public taste had not been perceptibly improved by the Pre-Raphaelite pioneers of the 1850s and was not only "ignorant" of their principles but actively destructive to the development of the artist. *The New Path* called attention to the "wrecks of reputations"—artistic talents that had once showed promise, now lost—going on to observe that "the greater number of them have been destroyed by nothing else but the greediness of their owners for praise and money, and the fatal facility with which the critics and the public have given them their reward."[70] Bierstadt was cited as a prime example of the possessor of an endangered talent, encouraged by the current system to attempt a work as large as *The Rocky Mountains* (1863, The Metropolitan Museum of Art) so early in his career, before committing at least "ten years of study" to the subject. The artist, apparently undaunted by *The New Path*'s criticism, went on to produce *A Storm in the Rocky Mountains, Mount Rosalie* (1866, The Brooklyn Museum), a work on a scale equal to the painting of 1863. Nevertheless, Bierstadt's sharpened focus on foreground vegetation in particular may indicate that he was not entirely heedless of *The New Path*'s advice. The majority of Bierstadt's paintings, including his oil studies (cat. nos. 82 and 83), however, did not conform in their painterly energy to the Association's notion of proper finish.

Times were perilous for the American Pre-Raphaelite as well, for precisely opposite reasons—not adulation but neglect. The public did not yet "understand the superior value . . . of perfect work":

> We can hardly be sure how many of our own men have been ruined by want of due appreciation and reward for their most faithful work.[71]

In addition, Moore lamented the "misfortune" of the "dreadfully slow" pace of producing "perfect work." Writing to Farrer in 1864, he complained, "My work now costs *me* more than I can expect it to be worth to anyone else. I hope to gain facility after a while that will enable me to work somewhat faster, but I hope I shall never work any less thoroughly." The little-known J.B. Duffey, whose *October* (cat. no. 96) is the sole known example of the "little pre-Raphaelite sketches" he sent to Avery, also mentioned the negative economics of such a labor-intensive method. "I paint incredibly slow," he wrote to the dealer, "so that the price I receive for a painting is scarcely more than a nominal one, considering the time spent."[72]

Without doubt, the programs outlined in *The New Path* and the artist experience reported in letters demanded a level of artist commitment that discouraged all but the most devoted disciples. The emphasis upon direct and prolonged study from nature placed Association members and followers within the context of a long-standing strong American interest in the accurate depiction of native scenery. The practice of such selfless replication was perceived as a first step for the novice, and a vitally important corrective for the poorly schooled artist, in a system of training that formed the heart of the Pre-Raphaelite program and philosophy. Put simply, all future success in conceiving and executing transcriptional or imaginative subjects depended upon a knowledge of external nature gained from years of obsessive on-the-spot study.

"Naturalism and Genius," in the October 1863 issue of *The New Path*, outlined three stages of artist development, offering examples of each drawn from English painting.[73] The literal transcript from nature, designated as "naturalism," formed the first concern of the "young painter," whose duty was "to constantly copy nature" as "the one essential work which he must do, or be lost to art." Illustrating this initial phase was Ruskin's own *Fragment of the Alps* (pl. 5), exhibited as *Study of a Block of Gneiss, Valley of Chamouni, Switzerland* in the English exhibition of 1857–58, and, since 1858, in the collection of Charles Eliot Norton. A long, detailed description of its attention to every detail of appearance concluded that "direct copying of nature could not be carried further. The great boulder is, as it were, photographed in color." The reader was reminded, however, that this tour de force was not "great art" but "only a study, being one lesson in the course of study which Mr. Ruskin has followed and is by a man who is not a professional artist."

The writer of "Naturalism and Genius" then invited the reader to consider another English work as an example of the next grade of artistic development—a work "of genius, not of the highest order, but true and right." This was Millais' painting of 1852 *The Huguenot Lover*, "known to some of us in the original; to all of us by the engraving" (fig. 4). As a Pre-Raphaelite, the writer argued, Millais was grounded in the faithful study from nature recommended above. He had achieved the technical maturity and possessed the talent to exercise his powers of invention to recreate in his painting a moment in sixteenth-century France. The distinction between *Fragment of the Alps* and *The Huguenot Lover* was the distinction between the "study" and the "picture," the latter of which demanded more than "faithful work":

> A painter of pictures should be a thinker on canvas . . . and a picture should be thought on canvas.

Millais, then, was a "thinker on canvas" in whose painting "we find the imagination creating something not seen by the eye." *The Huguenot Lover*, probably the best known of Millais' early works, appears as an engraving on the wall in paintings by T.C. Farrer and Shattuck (figs. 5 and 6), where it offered comment

Figure 4
Thomas O. Barlow after Sir John Everett Millais
The Huguenot: Eve of St. Bartholomew's Day, 1572 1857
Engraving and mezzotint, 21½ × 17½ in. (69.8 × 44.5 cm.)
Collection: Yale Center for British Art, Paul Mellon Fund

Figure 5
Thomas Charles Farrer
Gone! Gone! 1860
Oil on canvas, 20 × 14 in. (50.8 × 33.0 cm.)
Private collection
Cat. no. 8

Figure 6
Aaron Draper Shattuck
Shattuck Family with Grandmother, Mother, and Baby William 1865
Oil on canvas, 20 × 16 in. (50.8 × 40.6 cm.)
*Collection: The Brooklyn Museum, given in memory of Mary and
John D. Nodine by Judith and Wilbur Ross*
Cat. no. 119

on the themes of the paintings and also served as an emblem of the artists' allegiance to the practice of Pre-Raphaelitism.

There was yet another degree of imaginative and creative achievement "in the course of study" advocated by Ruskin, accessible only to those artists possessed of "genius of the highest order," and which was demonstrated in the work of Ruskin's idol, Turner, "the most imaginative of landscape artists." The reader was informed, however, that Turner's inventiveness and creative genius had been disciplined by the same study procedures, the same "faithful transcript" recommended for the American novice:

> diligent work ... had also something to do with his greatness. Not that even his vast knowledge and skill without genius could have made him the painter he was; but then, neither would his genius without his work.

"The imagination," the student was reminded, "does not act without materials. Turner's was free to act, for his material was as inexhaustible as Nature's resources," precisely because of his lifelong habit of study.

In America, the program of study that might eventually produce a Millais or even a Turner was just beginning. However, the landscape artist of the "true school" was already distinguished from his unenlightened fellow artist by the way each studied from nature during the annual pilgrimage to sketching grounds in the Catskills, the Adirondacks, and beyond. The artist of the "False School" remained in his studio "until it becomes too warm to live in the city":

> then he ... makes all sorts of inquiries as to the most suitable place. The very finest scenery in the country must be placed before him before he will deign to put brush to canvas ... at the end of six weeks [of constant touring] he is home again—his portfolio enriched with numerous large sheets of coarse tinted paper, covered with scribbled outlines of subjects and several broad oil sketches from which he will manufacture an endless number of pictures ... for the next nine months.[74]

The artist of the "True School" had left his studio weeks earlier, and did not tour or devote much energy to selection of subjects conforming to current ideals of "the very finest scenery." Rather, "believing every subject worthy," he began to draw or paint immediately from some humble or non-picturesque subject, lavishing weeks and months on its completion on the spot—"and on this if it be a pencil drawing he may work not less than six weeks; if an oil study, about three months." Such had been the case with the early converts to the Pre-Raphaelite program. Inspired by *Modern Painters*, John William Hill "applied himself with unremitting zeal to working in the open air from morning til night, all through the hot Summer days."[75] In 1858, Richards spent the summer painting "a blackberry bush in the open air" (fig. 11).[76] At Factory Point, Vermont, in October 1863, Newman was inspired by reading "Naturalism and Genius" in *The New Path* to commence the first exercise recommended in the article, abandoning his oil studies to spend days working in watercolor, like Ruskin in the Alps, "trying to get acquainted with a fragment of flint rock."[77] In July 1863, John Henry Hill spent "nearly every afternoon in the month" painting *Study of Trap Rock* (cat. no. 17), "the most elaborately literal study from nature I ever made."[78] As a tribute to the program and a sign of his on-site labor, Hill painted himself at work in the lower right-hand corner.

The difficulties in pursuing this Pre-Raphaelite vision of nature were readily conceded. "It requires a great deal of resolution and patience," declared *The New Path*, "to sit out in the burning July sun from six or seven in the morning until six or seven in the evening, using every minute of time, and letting nothing escape, working as hard as you possibly can. This is not pleasant. This is not easy."[79] At work on a summer view of the Catskill Valley (unlocated), Moore complained to Farrer: "My work has ... progressed very slowly ... I cover about as much canvass as I could cover with the end of my thumb in a forenoon of three hours work."[80] In August, the lament continued: "I get on dreadfully slow. The picture ... is not now more than half done and I've been working all summer upon it ... It is *faithful* but I am not sure that it is *successful*."[81]

In describing one product of such obsessive study, "a pencil drawing by one of the true men, not more than six inches long and four wide," *The New Path* declared that "the amount of truth that is crowded on this small piece of paper might shame any of the old school men who yearly cover the walls of the Academy with canvasses six or eight feet long":

In the upper left hand corner in less than two inches of space are drawn the trunks of about ten forest trees, lichen covered and various in light and shade; ... No words can describe the myriad facts and marvelous delicacy and decision of hand and eye that has followed every little clover leaf with a loving care, and rendered the whole truth of every patch of lichen on the tree stems—in the foreground ... This drawing was made entirely out of doors.[82]

This description could apply with equal ease to the pencil achievements of Farrer's *May in the Woods* of 1864 (fig. 7), Richards' *Corner of the Woods* of 1864 (cat. no. 76), or Brandegee's *Anemones* of 1867 (fig. 8)—each a textbook example of "faithful work."

Working long hours for weeks to produce drawings like these, as well as oils and watercolors of a similar nature, was not only a physical strain but, from the standpoint of making a living during the "long apprenticeship" of the student of Pre-Raphaelitism, impractical as well, as we can see in the complaints of Moore and Duffey. These realities certainly weighed heavily not only in discouraging the faint-hearted from adopting such a strenuous regimen, but in the ultimate abandonment of the systematic effort of the Association to impose its program of education upon American artists.

Equally discouraging must have been the qualified response, beyond the small circle of enthusiasts, to the "faithful" works produced. Whittredge was typical in his observation that the Ruskinians "exhibited as pictures" works that conventional opinion saw only as "commonplace subjects without the slightest choice or *invention*."[83] Such selfless transcription, in the eyes of critics, reduced the artist to a mechanical duplicator of natural facts. Henry T. Tuckerman, in his 1867 *Book of the Artists*, found the Pre-Raphaelite work of Richards "interesting" and "the perfection of the minutiae enjoyable" and appears to have recognized and appreciated such work as a phase of study, noting that "such power for reproducing the details, added to an equal grasp of general effect, equips a landscape-painter for the most authentic work." But ultimately he rejected "the principle upon which they are executed" and doubted "the ultimate triumph of a literalness so purely imitative."[84] *The Round Table* also recognized in the work of Richards "the practical results of a special and would-be dominant theory of representation of nature"; these landscapes, however, remained "a painted text book of summer or autumn," "essentially mechanical," and not "great creative art."[85] Newman received his criticism firsthand at Factory Point in 1864, when a "Gentleman from Chicago" and "some N.Y. Ladies" examined his portfolio:

The Gentleman wanted me to do some work for him but after looking over my studies concluded that I was *to* [sic] *Pre Raphaelite*. The lady said she could see why I work in watercolor,—it was so much easier to work minutely than in oil. She said my work showed that I drew my inspiration from Ruskin.[86]

The artist concluded the report of this dubious tribute to his dual allegiance with the observation to Farrer that "I find that Pre-Raphs are not fashionable here 'they are so ultra.'"[87]

Newman's quip referred to the extreme position of the Pre-Raphaelites in their dedication to what the "N.Y. Lady" referred to as "minute" work. The paintings, watercolors, and drawings of Moore and Newman, with those of their fellow members, were, indeed, highly detailed. This characteristic alone, however, did not distinguish their work from mainstream figures like Durand, Church, and Bierstadt, who also worked with attention to detail for an audience whose preference for highly finished work provoked critic James Jackson Jarves to complain in 1864 that nearly all American landscapes were "realistic to a disagreeable degree."[88] However, the linear clarity and static brilliance of Pre-Raphaelite landscapes were universally recognized as a unique and controversial interpretation of realism. Jarves himself championed an alternative in expressing his admiration for the Barbizon-inspired landscape paintings of George Inness, a more painterly interpretation of nature dismissed by *The New Path* as "disgracefully bad."[89] The Association and its magazine, insisting upon a transcription of appearance deemed radical even by current American standards, opened a dialogue on the meaning of truth to nature just at a moment when a shift in taste was beginning to be perceptible—when the detailed landscape vision of the native school was being challenged by a more painterly and personal interpretation of nature.

The New Path, taking an extreme position, found even Jarves's "disagreeably realistic" landscapes disappointing. James Hart's *Morning in the Berkshires* (not located) came "very near the truth, but always stops a little short"; Church, an artist of "large capacity," misused his "great powers by frequent slightness

Top:
Figure 7
Thomas Charles Farrer
May in the Woods 1864
Pencil on paper, size unknown
Location unknown

Bottom:
Figure 8
Robert Brandegee
Anemones 1867
Pencil on paper, 4¼ × 6⅝ in. (10.8 × 16.8 cm.)
Collection: The Brooklyn Museum, Charles S. Smith Memorial Fund
Cat. no. 84

of work and recklessness of form," and his major rival for landscape laurels during the 1860s also fell short: "It would have been all well enough," *The New Path* wrote of Bierstadt's *The Rocky Mountains*, "if the marks of the brush had, by dextrous handling, been made to stand for scarp and fissure, crag and cranny, but as it is, we have only too little geology and too much bristle."[90] Yet for Jarves, artistic surrender to the absolute facts of the "extreme Pre Raphaelites" yielded not "truth" but "barren externalism and dry-bones literalism."[91]

The central dilemma lay in opposing definitions of realism and idealism. "He has good ideas in very many respects," Moore wrote of Jarves to Farrer, "but his chief error ... is that he separates the ideal from the real. He speaks of idealists and realists as though they were distinct necessarily."[92] "The true ideal," wrote Moore, "is based upon and grows out of the real":

> It is the artist's first duty to be true to the real ... The true and noble ideal comes of that penetrating perception which, by love and long discipline, sees at once the most essential qualities of things and records these with emphasis.[93]

In his article "The Office of the Imagination," Moore went on to address the charge of Jarves, Tuckerman, and others that such "long discipline" robbed art (and the artist) of feeling and creative freedom. "The truly imaginative mind," he wrote, "is a *deep seer*,"

> and it only differs from an ordinary healthy mind in being a more exquisitely sensitive instrument. It also differs from the falsely imaginative mind in that it is always controlled by knowledge. It never disobeys natural laws.

Expanding the metaphor of the "sensitive instrument," he paraphrased Ruskin's 1855 letter to *The Crayon*:

> The artist is a telescope—very marvelous in himself, as an instrument—And the best artist is he who has the clearest lens, and so makes you forget every now and then that you are looking through him.[94]

This perception translated into Moore's own *Winter Landscape* of 1866 (frontispiece), and Newman's *Mt. Everett from Monument Mountain in April* of 1867 (pl. 8)—paintings and watercolors of the greatest detail, brilliant color, and polished surface, allowing no hint of painterliness to suggest the artist's presence and disturb the clarity of the Ruskinian lens. Such was the pristine vision rejected by Jarves as "barren externalism," by Tuckerman as "purely imitative," by *The Round Table* as "essentially mechanical," and by Newman's "Gentleman from Chicago" as "too Pre-Raphaelite."

With their emphasis upon accuracy and dedicated pedagogical zeal, it is not surprising that the members of the Association should fix upon photography as "the only reliable medium" for disseminating "their ideas" to a wider public. Whether the choice of medium also suggests a recognition of some rivalry between the artist as a Ruskinian lens and the camera itself offers an interesting subject for speculation. The January 1864 issue of *The New Path* announced a project that had been planned for a year:

> The want of proper illustration of what we so often allude to as "faithful study from nature" has been so long felt that the proprietors of this journal propose to publish a series of ten photographs from drawings and paintings by men of the Realist School, provided a sufficient number of subscriptions are received.[95]

By April, enough subscriptions at ten dollars a set were in hand for Maurice Stadfeldt to prepare the photographs, which were to include three subjects by Farrer, two each by Moore and Richards, and single examples by Newman, Pattison, and John Henry Hill. While no example of the listed titles has been located, two of Farrer's contributions are known: the painting *Gone! Gone!* (fig. 5) and *May in the Woods*, which is certainly the pencil study of anemones illustrated in Edward Cary's article of 1906 (fig. 7). We may also assume with confidence that Moore's pen drawing of a *Cedar Tree* was close to his work of 1868 (cat. no. 48) and that Hill's *Mulleins* was not far in appearance from his pen plant studies of 1866 (cat. no. 21). Although Richards' work was not among the titles finally issued in June (it was replaced by two Farrer drawings), early photographs in the artist's papers of unlocated Pre-Raphaelite paintings such as *And Some Fell Among Thorns* of *circa* 1863 (fig. 9), were probably taken for the project.

Figure 9
William T. Richards
And Some Fell Among Thorns *circa* 1863
Oil on canvas, size unknown
Location unknown

Figure 10
Fidelia Bridges
Milkweeds 1876
Watercolor on paper, 16 × 9½ in. (40.6 × 24.1 cm.)
Collection: Munson-Williams-Proctor Institute
Cat. no. 90

While the disappearance of this set of photographs has led one author to speculate that they were never actually distributed,[96] letters of the time indicate that, in fact, the project seems to have been a success. Demand must have been stimulated by Sturgis's article in the July issue, "Pictures and Studies," which served as a text or manual to accompany the photographs, and which left no doubt of the pedagogical intent of the series ("We are glad to be able to give to our readers ... examples so perfect of the way in which our young painters ought to study nature"), describing the works as "studies undertaken for self improvement ... by men who are determined realists."[97] Their usefulness as models of self-instruction is suggested in the close parallels in subject, medium, and treatment between Robert Brandegee's drawing *Anemones* of 1867 (fig. 8) and Farrer's *May in the Woods* (fig. 7). Although Richards' work was not included among the final selection, one wonders whether Fidelia Bridges might have had reference to his *And Some Fell Among Thorns* (fig. 9) when she painted *Milkweeds* in 1876 (fig. 10). Both the motif and the point of view are strongly reminiscent of Richards' botanical parable, which itself strongly echoes the "weeds and fruitless corn" in the corner of Hunt's *The Light of the World* (fig. 43).

The pedagogical energy of the Pre-Raphaelite circle, which continued after the formal organization had disbanded, also inspired John Henry Hill's *Sketches From Nature*, published by the artist in 1867, in which etched plates of landscape and still-life subjects operated like *The New Path*'s photographs as easily duplicated and distributed models for the student. The considerable private teaching activity of members, culminating in Farrer and Moore's unrealized effort to establish a school in 1868, is discussed by William H. Gerdts.

While general critical and patron response to the "determined realism" of the American Pre-Raphaelites was negative or qualified, the final issue of *The New Path* detected signs of progress in their reform:

> Many of the painters whose works come before the people of New York paint more carefully now than they did when the New Path began its work, more than two years ago. Many of them have gained greater skill, better execution, profounder knowledge. Some have taken the great step from carelessness to care.[98]

Cook, writing two years later in the *Tribune*, noted the "tendency of all our younger artists to give us nothing but isolated studies"—an observation suggesting that the program of artist training recommended by *The New Path* was indeed underway:

> As, just now we need studies and students more than high art, at least as the majority of artists understand that term, and shall never get a real "high art" until we have had a long preparation of study, we are willing to bear with the monotony for a few years.[99]

Some artists active at this time, such as J.B. Duffey, whose *October* (cat. no. 96) closely parallels the contemporaneous all-foreground subjects of Richards (cat. nos. 68–71), Fidelia Bridges (cat. no. 90), and George B. Wood (cat. nos. 122 and 123), recognized their limitations and did not aspire to "high art." "I can paint what I see," the artist wrote to Avery in 1866, "but my imaginative faculty lacks the retentive power required to go much beyond a tolerably faithful transcript of Nature ... I do best in little pre-Raphaelite sketches such as you have."[100] Moore also affirmed the value of Pre-Raphaelite study in an 1866 letter to Charles Eliot Norton:

> Plain faithful recording is infinitely delightful to me and I think it possible that I may never do anything else. I think it is worthwhile "to spend a life" in doing this, especially when popular art is in such condition as at present.[101]

Nevertheless, the Association was anxious to demonstrate the more advanced stage of the Pre-Raphaelite program, and Farrer—English by birth, taught by Ruskin himself, and the organizer of the American movement—seemed the logical candidate. His drawings (cat. nos. 1–7) and oil studies (none of which we know) were held up as models of Pre-Raphaelite practice. It was not surprising, therefore, to find Sturgis counseling him in a letter of September 1863 to direct his energies toward "a large picture" rather than "drawings and studies which make no impression save on the initiated."[102]

Farrer seemed to have heeded Sturgis's advice, for in November Moore inquired from Catskill, "How does the big picture get on?"[103] When Moore saw the painting some months later, however, his reaction was one of unqualified dismay, and he opened a long letter of criticism with the plea "*not to exhibit it*":

> It is not at all worthy of you, and will be a great injury both to your own reputation, and the cause of "truth in Art" if shown to the public.

After this ominous beginning, Moore went on to compile a relentless catalogue of faults, concluding with the advice "to put it out of sight for a year and then after that, I am sure you will want to destroy it." Moore urged his friend to retreat from attempting to compose a picture to the safety of his "thoroughly beautiful" drawings and studies:

> I am sure none as fine have ever been done in this country before. Why on Earth don't you show these and your thorough *out-door* landscape work instead of this large canvass?[104]

The irony of Sturgis's urging him to advance beyond these studies for the good of the "Cause" and Moore's warning to retreat for the same reason cannot have been lost on Farrer and, in fact, constituted his apparent dilemma as an artist and the leader of the American Pre-Raphaelites. In 1865, the final issue of *The New Path* offered only the most qualified praise for another major effort, *Northampton* (pl. 15). "We heartily admire Mr. Thos. C. Farrer's picture," the reviewer (probably Cook) began, "and yet it is to us, rather a disappointment than a delight":

> All that there has been good in Mr. Farrer's landscapes of the last three years is bettered in this, but much that has been deficient or faulty is as bad or worse than ever. We cannot but feel, we repeat, less hopeful of Mr. Farrer's future as a landscape painter, than we felt before seeing this last, most powerful, most impressive of the pictures he has exhibited.[105]

Cook's opinion of Farrer's incapacity to progress beyond the primary stages of Pre-Raphaelite study remained unchanged two years later when he wrote in the *Tribune*, "so far as poetry, imagination, power to compose, power to color, are concerned Mr. Farrer, judging him by his pictures, stands today precisely where he stood in the beginning."[106] Farrer surely found Cook's opinion more bitter than sweet, and we are reminded of Ruskin's own uneasy realtionships as critic-adviser to Stillman, Brett, and Inchbold.

It seemed that Farrer had attempted in 1865 what was still impossible, for Cook wrote elsewhere in the same review,

> There is an ideal of landscape art which perhaps has never been reached by human work ... That ideal is the *perfect* union of detail and general effect.

There was, however, one landscape in the same exhibition at which *Northampton* appeared that made "the attainment of the ideal seem not so far in the future as it would seem without it." This was Moore's *Winter Study in the Catskills*, certainly close to if not identical with the work in this exhibition entitled *Winter Landscape* (frontispiece). Moore's painting succeeded, in Cook's opinion, precisely where Farrer's had failed: "in color, and in gradation of light and shade," as well as in "delicate and subtle truth of drawing." In the final issue of *The New Path*, then, the American Pre-Raphaelites found their champion in Moore, who, working exceedingly slowly and on a consistently small scale, demonstrated the potential for realizing the ultimate goals of Pre-Raphaelite study—the accommodation of detail and general effect. That achievement, the reviewer concluded, lay "more nearly within his reach than that of any other painter who exhibits in New York or Boston or Philadelphia, far as it may be yet beyond the reach of all."[107]

The mention of Philadelphia undoubtedly referred to Moore's rival for Pre-Raphaelite laurels, William T. Richards, whom *The Round Table* had identified early in 1864 as foremost among the American brotherhood, "the ablest man in the country in practically showing us the beauty of a certain system of work."[108] Indeed, Richards, older than the other artist members (with the exception of John William Hill), and among the early American adherents to Pre-Raphaelitism, was the best-known artist of the circle when the Association was founded. By 1862, Farrer and Richards were acquainted, and the Englishman had acquired Richards' *Scene from Nature* (unlocated).[109] In 1863, however, Richards' nomination by Farrer for membership, at the March 5 meeting, seems to have met with some resistance: the Philadelphian's name was brought up for discussion twice more before the April 7 meeting, when Wight "read a letter from Mr. W.T. Richards" in which we may assume the artist declared his Pre-Raphaelite allegiance. Wight then "made a few remarks in favor of admitting Mr. Richards," as did Farrer, and he was finally elected to membership. The opposition most certainly came from Cook, who would write a year later in the *Tribune* that Richards, who had spent several months in 1856 in Germany, was not a true Pre-Raphaelite, and that the source of his detailed style was German, a school the critic disliked intensely:

> It is from Düsseldorf, and not from London, that he draws his inspiration; he is the only American who has been permanently mastered by that school, but he has found himself in most entire sympathy with it.[110]

Cook's resistance, though obviously countered by Farrer and Wight, may well have accounted for the withdrawal of Richards' work from the photograph series, for the paucity of mention of him in *The New Path*, and for the fact that Richards was not listed among the members at the Association's demise. Nevertheless, his status as the best-known American Pre-Raphaelite remained intact, and in 1867 Tuckerman singled Richards out as the "most remarkable" artist of the school.[111]

By that date, however, the "school" was largely a thing of the past. The Association had long since disbanded, *The New Path* had ceased publication, and the collective energy of the organized Pre-Raphaelite reform movement was on the wane, although individual artists like the Hills and Newman would continue on "the new path" for many years. Their ambitious reform had failed and may, in fact, be interpreted in a wider sense as a kind of last stand for traditional American allegiance to the importance of subject and finish in painting in the face of rising preoccupation on the part of artists, critics, and patrons with an art in which formal and painterly considerations weighed more heavily than the specifics of subject and object. Nevertheless, the ideas and issues discussed in *The New Path*, and especially the effort to introduce a disciplined and serious criticism into American art life, had a lasting influence. Cook and Sturgis, for example, went on to long careers as distinguished critics and art historians. It is also apparent from this survey that, while their heyday was short and their numbers small, a distinctive body of work was created by the American Pre-Raphaelites—a body of work which was both a part of and apart from the mainstream, which attracted equally articulate and passionate champions and critics, and whose significance and influence must now figure in reappraisals of mid-nineteenth-century American painting.

1. Clarence Cook, "Introductory," *The New Path* 1, no. 1 (May 1863), pp. 1–2.
2. Ibid.
3. Present were lawyers Eugene Gardner and James E. Munson, the latter also a painter; geologists James F. Gardner and Clarence King; and Farrer and Charles Herbert Moore, artists (The Association for the Advancement of Truth in Art, Minutes, p. 3. Ryerson Library, The Art Institute of Chicago, hereafter cited as Minutes).
4. Karin M.E. Alexis, "Russell Sturgis: A Search for the Modern Aesthetic—Going Beyond Ruskin," *Athanor III*, 1983, pp. 31–39; Sarah B. Landau and John Zukowsky, *P.B. Wight: Architect, Contractor, and Critic, 1838–1925* (exhibition catalogue, Burnham Library of Architecture, The Art Institute of Chicago, January 22–July 31, 1981), pp. 9–59.
5. Allen Staley, *The Pre-Raphaelite Landscape* (Oxford: Oxford University Press, 1973), pp. 15–19, passim. Staley's study, which deals in detail with Pre-Raphaelite naturalism, is the major reference consulted on the English movement.
6. Although his work did not provide models for the landscape and still-life painters of the American circle, Rossetti, whom Ruskin identified as the leader of the English Pre-Raphaelites and "the greatest of English painters now living" in his 1863 letter to *The New Path* (p. 10), was mentioned repeatedly in the pages of the magazine. His poem "The Blessed Damozel" was printed in the December 1863 issue and read aloud by Sturgis at the March 5 meeting. Rossetti's name is enshrined with Turner's in Farrer's portrait of Cook (fig. 3) and his example may have inspired that artist to undertake figure subjects with medieval themes in addition to the modern-life subjects so far located. Cook referred to a Farrer "drawing of 'Arthur,'" commenting that "the head of the queen . . . was not up to your mark nor Rossetti's was it?" In the same letter, Cook urged Farrer to go to Cambridge "and see Mr. Norton's 'Rossettis'. . . . I am very anxious to have you see these drawings—The two by Rossetti and the one by his wife [Elizabeth Siddal]." In 1863, Sturgis had written Farrer about a visit to Norton, promising to "tell you all about the Rossettis" and to report on the content of "recent and intimate letters from Ruskin & D.G. Rossetti." Clarence Cook to Thomas C. Farrer, Marshland, Staten Island, August 21, 1864; Russell Sturgis to Thomas C. Farrer, New York, September 4, 1863. Both GLF/NYPL.

7. Wight wrote in 1884 that "the American reformers never called themselves Pre-Raphaelites. . . . They preferred to be called only 'Realists.'" *The Development of New Phases of the Fine Arts in America. From The Inland Architect and Builder of November and December 1884* (Chicago, 1884), p. 22, hereafter cited as Wight (1884). However, as early as 1856 (?), in a letter to Farrer, John William Hill referred to "we P.R.G.'s," a curious variation of P.R.B. whose exact translation is not known but whose intentional parallel to the English Brotherhood is unmistakable. John William Hill to Thomas C. Farrer, August 17, 1856 (?), GLF/NYPL.
8. "The Artists' Fund Society, Fourth Annual Exhibition," *The New Path* 1, no. 8 (December 1863), p. 98. These paintings were no. 76, *Catskill Creek*, belonging to Robert L. Stuart (The New-York Historical Society); no. 160, *The Titan's Goblet*, belonging to John M. Falconer (The Metropolitan Museum of Art); and no. 191, *An Italian Autumn*, belonging to the estate of A. Baker.
9. Thomas Cole, "Essay on American Scenery," *American Monthly Magazine*, n.s. 1 (January 1836), pp. 1–12; reprinted in John W. McCoubrey, *American Art, 1700–1960: Sources and Documents* (Englewood Cliffs, New Jersey: Prentice-Hall, Inc., 1965), p. 99.
10. Ruskin, *Modern Painters* 1, p. 170.
11. J.S., "Art as a Record," *The New Path* 1, no. 4 (August 1863), p. 43; "Notices of Recent Pictures. Bierstadt's 'Rocky Mountains,'" *The New Path* 1, no. 12 (April 1864), p. 162.
12. "Mr. Street's Gift to Yale College, The Yale School of Fine Arts," *The New Path* 2, no. 9 (September 1865), p. 149.
13. "The Work of the True and the False School," *The New Path* 1, no. 7 (November 1863), p. 87.
14. Asher B. Durand, "Letters on Landscape Painting. No. V," *The Crayon* 1, no. 10 (March 7, 1855), p. 145.
15. Ibid.
16. "A Letter to a Subscriber," *The New Path* 1, no. 9 (January 1863), p. 114.
17. "Mr. Huntington's 'Republican Court in the Time of Washington,'" *The New Path* 2, no. 11 (November 1865), pp. 177–178.
18. "A Letter to a Subscriber," *The New Path* 1, no. 9 (January 1864), p. 114.
19. Wight (1884), p. 20.
20. "The Exhibition of Pictures at the Metropolitan Fair," *New York Daily Tribune*, April 9, 1864, p. 12; "Exhibition of Pictures at

the Sanitary Fair," *New York Daily Tribune*, April 16, 1864, p. 12. These reviews are extensively quoted and discussed in John P. Simoni, "Art Critics and Criticism in Nineteenth Century America" (Ph.D. dissertation, Ohio State University, 1952), in the chapter "Clarence Cook on Painting and Sculpture," pp. 231–348, where his association with *The New Path* is also discussed at length; hereafter cited as Simoni (1952).

21. "Exhibition of Pictures at the Sanitary Fair," *New York Daily Tribune*, April 16, 1864, p. 12; quoted in Simoni (1952), p. 250.

22. Worthington Whittredge, "The Autobiography of Worthington Whittredge, 1820–1910," edited by John I.H. Baur, *Brooklyn Museum Journal*, 1942, p. 54.

23. Clarence Cook to Thomas C. Farrer, August 12, 1864. GLF/NYPL.

24. Clarence Cook, "Introductory," *The New Path* 1, no. 1 (May 1863), p. 2. The best overview of Ruskin's influence in the United States is found in Rober B. Stein, *John Ruskin and Aesthetic Thought in America, 1840-1900* (Cambridge: Harvard University Press, 1967).

25. Ruskin's comment is quoted in Staley, *The Pre-Raphaelite Landscape*, p. 18. The role played by Ruskin and *Modern Painters* in the origin and early development of the English movement is discussed on pp. 1–30.

26. William James Stillman, review of John Ruskin, "Modern Painters V," *Atlantic Monthly* (August 1860), p. 239.

27. Stein, *John Ruskin*, p. 41.

28. Clarence Cook, "The Modern Architecture of New York," *New York Quarterly* 4 (April 1855), pp. 105–110; quoted in Simoni (1954), p. 169.

29. Minutes, p. 12. The Articles of Organization were published in "Association for the Advancement of Truth in Art," *The New Path* 1, no. 1 (May 1863), pp. 11–12.

30. Whittredge, *Autobiography*, p. 55.

31. John Henry Hill, *John William Hill: An Artist's Memorial* (New York, 1888), p. 5.

32. Linda S. Ferber, "William Trost Richards (1833–1905): American Landscape and Marine Painter" (Ph.D. dissertation, Columbia University, 1980), pp. 139–142; published (New York: Garland Publishing, Inc., 1980).

33. John Henry Hill to Thomas C. Farrer, Nyack, New York, January 19, 1860; Henry R. Newman to Thomas C. Farrer, Factory Point, Vermont, October 13, 1863; both letters GLF/NYPL.

34. Wight (1884), p. 13. Farrer may have been in the United States by the summer of 1856 if the final digit on a letter from John William Hill can indeed be interpreted as a "6." John William Hill to Thomas C. Farrer, Nyack, New York, August 17, 1856 (?), GLF/NYPL. He was certainly here by the fall of 1857 when, as William H. Gerdts has noted, he was in correspondence with Samuel P. Avery.

35. Ibid.

36. The younger Hill commiserated with Farrer about their "misfortunes in the art world." His father, in much the same tone, wrote hoping Baltimore collector William T. Walters would give Farrer "a commission worth having but it is hardly to be expected in as much as we P.R.G.s are not yet at all notorious." John Henry Hill to Thomas C. Farrer, Nyack, New York, February 20, 1860; John William Hill to Thomas C. Farrer, Nyack, New York, August 17, 1856 (?), both letters, GLF/NYPL.

37. John Henry Hill to Thomas C. Farrer, Nyack, New York, January 19, 1860, GLF/NYPL.

38. Charles Herbert Moore to Thomas C. Farrer, Studio Building, New York, February 19, 1860, GLF/NYPL.

39. The relation of brilliant local color and minute detail to the technique of working upon a white ground—sometimes wet in emulation of fresco technique—is discussed in Staley, *Pre-Raphaelite Landscape* (pp. 5, 12, 27), where he also traces the evolution of the practice into a hallmark of Pre-Raphaelitism.

40. Charles Herbert Moore to Thomas C. Farrer, Studio Building, New York, March 4, 1860, GLF/NYPL.

41. John Henry Hill to Thomas C. Farrer, Nyack, New York, July 1860, GLF/NYPL.

42. Wight (1884), p. 14.

43. Whittredge, *Autobiography*, p. 43. Cook, in his *Tribune* articles commented upon "a kind of picture mania" during the War:

"Pictures are selling daily at what would have been regarded as fabulous prices in the flush times before the Rebellion. . . ." "Another Artists' Reception," *New York Daily Tribune*, April 14, 1863, p. 2, quoted in Simoni (1952), p. 240.

44. Richards, PAFA, 1862, no. 519. J.L. Claghorn; Farrer's *April 1861*, exhibited at the National Academy of Design, 1865, no. 161, was discussed in "National Academy of Design—Fortieth Annual Exhibition," *The New Path* 2, no. 6 (June 1865), p. 93.

45. William T. Richards to Thomas C. Farrer, Germantown, Pennsylvania, October 22 and December 26, 1862. Miscellaneous Papers, Manuscripts and Archives Division, The New York Public Library.

46. Wight (1884), p. 14.

47. The Minutes of the final meeting of the Association on March 29, 1864, at which Henry R. Newman was elected to membership, include a list of members: John Matthews Jr.—manufacturer; Clarence Cook—writer and teacher; Eugene T. Gardener—lawyer; James F. Gardner—geologist; J. Henry Hill—painter; Thomas C. Farrer—painter; Clarence R. King—geologist; Charles H. Moore—painter; Eastborne Hastings—architect; R.J. Pattison—painter; P.B. Wight—architect; James E. Munson—lawyer and reporter; Russell Sturgis, Jr.—architect; J. Lyman Van Buren—lawyer and soldier; Eugene Schuyler—lawyer; Mary L. Booth—writer; Annie R. McLane; Louisa W. Cook; Sarah M. Barney. In his 1884 memoir, Wight brought the reader up to date on the activities of the former members during the ensuing two decades (pp. 20–22).

48. Charles Herbert Moore to Thomas C. Farrer, Catskill, New York, October 26, 1863, GLF/NYPL.

49. Henry R. Newman to Thomas C. Farrer, Factory Point, New York, November 8, 1863, GLF/NYPL.

50. Wight (1884), p. 17.

51. Wight (1884), p. 24.

52. The title, according to the Minutes of the April 7 meeting, "was suggested by Mrs. Cook, moved by Mr. Wight and seconded by Mr. Pattison" (p. 44). The name may have been inspired by Ruskin's lectures published in 1859 as *The Two Paths*, which he described in the preface as an effort to illustrate "the dependence of all noble design, in any kind, on the sculpture or painting of Organic Form." The "acceptance of that truth," Ruskin wrote, forced upon the student "responsibility for choice . . . between two modes of study, which involve ultimately the development, or deadening, of every power he possesses. . . . Let him pause at the parting of *The Two Paths*." Ruskin, *The Two Paths* 16, pp. 253–254. On *The Germ* see: Lawrence Wodehouse, "'New Path' and the American Pre-Raphaelite Brotherhood," *College Art Journal* 25 (Summer 1966), pp. 351–354.

53. "A Letter from Mr. Ruskin," *The New Path* 1, no. 1 (May 1863), pp. 9–10; "Retrospective and Prospective," *The New Path* 2, no. 1 (May 1864), pp. 1–3.

54. "Notices of Recent Pictures. Bierstadt's 'Rocky Mountains,'" *The New Path* 1, no. 8 (December 1863), pp. 160–162; "Mr. Huntington's 'Republican Court in the Time of Washington,'" *The New Path* 1, no. 11 (March 1865), pp. 176–178; "Pictures on Exhibition. George Inness' *The Sign of Promise*, Snedecor's Gallery," *The New Path* 1, no. 8 (December 1863), pp. 99–101.

55. "Millais' 'Parables,'" *The New Path* 1, no. 11 (March 1864), pp. 142–152.

56. Cook was elected editor at the meeting of April 3, 1863, and again on February 23, 1865, at the only recorded meeting of The New Path Association.

57. Charles Herbert Moore to Thomas C. Farrer, Catskill, New York, August 7, 1864, GLF/NYPL.

58. John Henry Hill, "Letter from J.H.H.," *The New Path* 2, no. 5 (May 1865), pp. 73–74; "Another English Letter," *The New Path* 2, no. 8 (August 1865), pp. 127–129.

59. Thomas C. Farrer, "A Few Questions Answered," *The New Path* 1, no. 2 (June 1863), pp. 13–18.

60. Russell Sturgis, "Art Criticism," *The New Path* 1, no. 12 (April 1864), pp. 153–157.

61. James Jackson Jarves, *The Art Idea* (1864), ed. Benjamin D. Rowland, Jr. (Cambridge, Mass.: Belknap Press, 1960), pp. 152–153, hereafter cited as Jarves, *The Art Idea*.

62 Both reviews are quoted in Wight (1884), p. 20.

63. "Retrospective and Prospective," *The New Path* 2, no. 1 (May 1864), p. 1.
64. Clarence Cook to Thomas C. Farrer, Marshland, Staten Island, August 21, 1864, GLF/NYPL.
65. Farrer wrote to a Mr. Sperry from Gorham, Maine, on August 18, 1864, GLF/NYPL.
66. Charles Herbert Moore to Thomas C. Farrer, Catskill, New York, November 5, 1864, GLF/NYPL.
67. "A Letter to a Subscriber," *The New Path* 1, no. 9 (January 1864), pp. 114-115.
68. Wight recalled that the "circulation never was large," and that by 1884, there were "in all probability, but few copies of *The New Path* in existence, and it is now considered a rare and scarce book" (pp. 17, 18).
69. "Recent Art Criticism: 'The New Path,'" *The Round Table* 1 (January 2, 1864), p. 42.
70. "Recent Exhibitions, Sales, Etc.: The Mutual Art Association. Bierstadt's Mount Hood," *The New Path* 2, no. 5 (May 1865), p. 75.
71. "The Essential Difference between the True and Popular Art Systems," *The New Path* 2, no. 3 (July 1864), pp. 35-36.
72. Charles Herbert Moore to Thomas C. Farrer, Catskill, New York, August 7, 1864; John B. Duffey to Samuel P. Avery, Woodbury, New Jersey, September 10, 1866, Avery Autograph Collection, Art Reference Library, The Metropolitan Museum of Art. I am grateful to May Brawley Hill and William H. Gerdts for this reference.
73. J.S. (possibly Russell Sturgis), "Naturalism and Genius," *The New Path* 1, no. 6 (October 1863), pp. 64-70.
74. "The Work of the True and the False Schools," *The New Path* 1, no. 7 (November 1863), p. 85.
75. Hill, *An Artist's Memorial*, p. 5.
76. Harrison S. Morris, *Masterpieces of the Sea: William T. Richards, A Brief Outline of His Life and Art* (Philadelphia: J.P. Lippincott Co., 1912), pp. 10-11; quoted in Ferber (1980), p. 137.
77. Henry R. Newman to Thomas C. Farrer, Factory Point, Vermont, October 22, 1863, GLF/NYPL.
78. John Henry Hill to Metropolitan Museum of Art, May 14, 1911, The Metropolitan Museum of Art Archives, quoted in Natalie Spassky et al., *American Paintings in the Metropolitan Museum of Art, II: A Catalogue of Works by Artists Born between 1816 and 1845.*
79. "National Academy of Design: Fortieth Annual Exhibition," *The New Path* 2, no. 6 (June 1865), pp. 88-89.
80. Charles Herbert Moore to Thomas C. Farrer, Catskill, New York, July 10, 1864, GLF/NYPL.
81. Charles Herbert Moore to Thomas C. Farrer, Catskill, New York, August 7, 1864, GLF/NYPL.
82. "The Work of the True and the False Schools," *The New Path* 1, no. 7 (November 1863), pp. 85-86.
83. Whittredge, *Autobiography*, p. 55.
84. Henry T. Tuckerman, *Book of the Artists* (New York: G.P. Putnam and Son, 1867), p. 524.
85. "Art: Three Pictures by W. T. Richards," *The Round Table* 1 (February 20, 1864), p. 153.
86. Henry R. Newman to Thomas C. Farrer, Factory Point, Vermont, September 11, 1864, GLF/NYPL.
87. Ibid.
88. Jarves, *The Art Idea*, p. 193.
89. "Pictures on Exhibition. George Inness' *The Sign of Promise*, Snedecor's Gallery," *The New Path* 1, no. 8 (December 1863), p. 100. The review discusses not only the painting, later repainted as *Peace and Plenty* in 1865 (The Metropolitan Museum of Art, New York) but also the pamphlet with statements by Inness and Jarves which accompanied the painting.
90. "Pictures on Exhibition. J.M. Hart, A Summer's Memory of Berkshires. Knoedler's Gallery," *The New Path* 1, no. 8 (December 1863), p. 100; "Notices of Recent Pictures. Bierstadt's 'Rocky Mountains,'" *The New Path* 1, no. 12 (April 1864), p. 161; "Pictures on Exhibition. George Inness' *The Sign of Promise*, Snedecor's Gallery," *The New Path* 1, no. 8 (December 1863), p. 101.
91. Jarves, *The Art Idea*, p. 199.
92. Charles Herbert Moore to Thomas C. Farrer, Catskill, New York, December 11, 1864, GLF/NYPL.
93. Charles Herbert Moore, "Fallacies of the Present School," *The New Path* 1, no. 6 (October 1863), p. 61.
94. Charles Herbert Moore, "The Office of the Imagination," *The New Path* 1, no. 7 (November 1863), pp. 77-78.
95. "Advertisement," *The New Path* 1, no. 9 (January 1864), p. 120. Plans for photographing works by the circle were afoot even before the formal establishment of the Association. Two weeks before the meeting at Farrer's studio, Moore wrote to the latter that Wight "wants something of mine to *photograph* and I am led to think from his letter that it might be important to send him something . . . won't you send the Mandrakes. I think they would be the *best thing* to publish (Catskill, New York, January 13, 1863, GLF/NYPL). Minutes of the March 10, 1863, meeting record an "informal discussion . . . on the results of photographing colored objects, and the effects of different colors on photographic pictures" (p. 33).
96. Frank Jewett Mather, *Charles Herbert Moore: Landscape Painter* (Princeton, New Jersey: Princeton University Press, 1957), p. 20. A survey of photography archives, dealers, and scholars in connection with this exhibition has failed to locate a set or single example of the "Photographs of Studies from Nature."
97. Russell Sturgis, "Pictures and Studies," *The New Path* 2, no. 3 (July 1864), p. 43.
98. "The Sixth Annual Exhibition of the Artists' Fund Society," *The New Path* 2, no. 12 (December 1865), p. 191.
99. Clarence Cook, "The National Academy of Design," *New York Daily Tribune*, June 14, 1867, p. 2. I am grateful to William H. Gerdts and May Brawley Hill for making this reference available to me.
100. John B. Duffey to Samuel P. Avery, Woodbury, New Jersey, September 10, 1866, Avery Autograph Collection, Art Reference Library, The Metropolitan Museum of Art.
101. Charles Herbert Moore to Charles Eliot Norton, Catskill, New York, April 8, 1866, New York State Museum, quoted in Mather, *Moore*, p. 26.
102. Russell Sturgis to Thomas C. Farrer, Brattleboro, Vermont, September 17, 1863, GLF/NYPL.
103. Charles Herbert Moore to Thomas C. Farrer, Catskill, New York, November 15, 1863, GLF/NYPL.
104. Charles Herbert Moore to Thomas C. Farrer, Catskill, New York, April 25, 1864, GLF/NYPL.
105. "The Sixth Annual Exhibition of the Artists' Fund Society," *The New Path* 2, no. 12 (December 1865), p. 193.
106. "Art Criticism," *New York Daily Tribune*, July 8, 1867, p. 3. I am grateful to William H. Gerdts and May Brawley Hill for making this reference available to me.
107. "The Sixth Annual Exhibition of the Artists' Fund Society," *The New Path* 2, no. 12 (December 1865), pp. 192-193.
108. "Recent Art Criticism: 'The New Path'," *The Round Table* 1 (January 2, 1864), p. 42.
109. PAFA, 1862, no. 495.
110. Clarence Cook, "Exhibition of Pictures at the Sanitary Fair," *New York Daily Tribune*, April 16, 1864, p. 12, quoted in Simoni (1952), pp. 250-251.
111. Tuckerman, *Book of the Artists*, p. 524.

Plate 3
John William Hill
Bird's Nest and Dogroses 1867
Watercolor on paper, 10¾ × 13⅞ in. (27.3 × 35.2 cm.)
Collection: The New-York Historical Society
Cat. no. 31

Through a Glass Brightly:
The American Pre-Raphaelites
and Their Still Lifes and Nature Studies

WILLIAM H. GERDTS

American Pre-Raphaelite painters, unlike their more renowned English counterparts, whose subjects were primarily figurative, specialized in landscape, still life, and the "nature study." An in-between area of foreground landscape treated as still life, the nature study was not a new thematic contribution nor was it conceived as a distinct one. Yet "Nature" was paramount for these artists, and their devotion to rendering it faithfully blurred the distinctions among their subjects.

Fifteen years ago I introduced my earliest discussion of American Pre-Raphaelite still life with a quotation from Henry T. Tuckerman's *Book of the Artists*, published in 1867, at the peak of the American Pre-Raphaelite movement: "A few also earnestly develop the minute and graphic practice of the Pre-Raphaelites, by the most patient and conscientious rendering of the details of nature; among them Henry Farrer, Henry Newman, Charles Moore, Miss McDonald, Miss Adams, S.W. Hill [sic], whose fruit-pieces, rocks, trees, grasses, and scenery offer instructive exemplars, not without their inspiring as well as controversial influence."[1]

Tuckerman might have expanded the American Pre-Raphaelite circle to include another half-dozen painters and draftsmen as well as a number of artists who subscribed briefly or partially to the movement. Yet American Pre-Raphaelitism was not only short-lived but it was practiced by a rather obscure company of talented men and women. Miss Adams remains unidentified, though she may be the Eliza, or Elizabeth, Adams of Boston who exhibited briefly in the 1860s and 1870s. Miss McDonald is certainly Margaret J. McDonald, about whose life and art there is growing data but for whom no paintings or drawings have come to light—a condition particularly applicable to the women artists connected with American Pre-Raphaelitism. No paintings have surfaced yet by Maria Nims and Annie McLane, while only a few landscapes and almost no still lifes exist by McLane's better known artist-husband, Thomas Farrer, despite his one-man show in 1865 at Knoedler Galleries in New York.

To compound this irony, during their heyday from about 1857 to 1867, the American Pre-Raphaelites "enjoyed" critical exposure far beyond the size and scope of their efforts. Their works tended to be relatively few in number, small in size, and often confined to what critics considered the "lesser" media of watercolor and the graphic arts. In part, this attention was caused by the emergence of professional art criticism just as English Pre-Raphaelitism was exerting influence on American painting, and it stems from the same intellectual and philosophic milieu—the art writing and art criticism of John Ruskin. Indeed, the first great American art critic, Clarence Cook, was an intimate of the American Pre-Raphaelite artists, such as Thomas Farrer, Charles Moore, and John William and John Henry Hill, father and son. The rigor of Cook's art criticism, however, boded even greater ill for those artists he ostensibly admired, such as Farrer, than for the more traditional, "idealist," painters whose art he detested, such as Emanuel Leutze, William Beard, and John La Farge. Cook not only imbibed Ruskin's moral imperative in art criticism but he donned Ruskin's mantle even more single-mindedly than his model. Cook became the scourge of the American art world, not sparing his Pre-Raphaelite colleagues, particularly after he became the art critic of the *New-York Tribune* in 1864.

Other writers of the 1860s also fell under Ruskin's influence to some degree, and, along with Cook, they introduced professional art criticism in America. Russell Sturgis began to write the art columns in the newly founded *Nation* in 1865, and James Jackson Jarves' independent volumes of art criticism, history, and theory, as well as his periodical columns, began to appear in the mid-1850s. Jarves, particularly, saw the value of Pre-Raphaelitism early and in 1865 became a member of the New Path Association in an attempt to continue *The New Path*, the most radically Pre-Raphaelite periodical in this country. But almost from the start Jarves recognized the limitations of Pre-Raphaelitism, bringing on himself the wrath of the magazine's artist-writers and ultimately defining the aesthetic split that spelled the demise of the movement in this country.

Jarves wrote of Pre-Raphaelitism as early as 1860 in *Art Studies*, a book dedicated to Ruskin's closest American friend, Charles Eliot Norton: "The miscalled Pre-Raphaelites of our time, exaggerating the law of fidelity in parts, and losing sight of the broader principle of effect by which particulars are absorbed into large masses, protrude upon the sight with microscopic clearness the near and the distant, delineating the tiniest flower in a wide landscape, of which, in nature, it would form, at their point of sight, but an uncertain speck of color. . . ."[2]

Jarves' comments gave Charles Herbert Moore a rationale to vindicate the Pre-Raphaelite aesthetic in perhaps the most famous single article in *The New Path*, "Fallacies of the Present School." In the October 1863 issue, quoting Jarves at length, Moore acknowledged that "the revival of the Pre-Raphaelite principles is only beginning to dawn, and therefore much that is awkward must be expected. . . ." But upholding the sword of moral truth in art, he stated that "nature is not *all* we believe in, but we know it must come first. . . . By the mercy of God, Ruskin has been sent to open our eyes and loose the seals of darkness. He has shown us the truth and we thank him and give God the glory; and the truth once clearly shown becomes ours if we will receive it. It also becomes our imperative duty to proclaim it."[3] Hardly subdued, Jarves moved from denigration on purely aesthetic grounds to challenge on more spiritual ones. In *The Art-Idea* of 1864 he saw in Pre-Raphaelite works the "tendency to subordinate great laws to lesser, and to exalt the common and integumental above the intellectual and spiritual"; he recognized that "nature is not to be exhausted by the utmost diligence of exploration . . . because life or spirit is something more than color and form. These are mediums only. . . . So far, therefore, as Pre-Raphaelitism robs art of her poetry in order to give the literal facts of nature, it may subserve exact science by way of illustration, but it subverts noble art." Jarves, however, followed Ruskin's ultimately dichotomous path: "Pre-Raphaelitism in the keeping of genius, uniting Turnerian breadth and freedom to its legitimate spirituality of vision and scientific accuracy, offers a possibility of progress as exhaustless as the pure principles and noble aspirations which are or should be the basis of its theory of painting."[4]

Although by 1864 Jarves was already familiar with the American Pre-Raphaelites, his remarks referred only to the work of the original band of English painters, whom he named—John Everett Millais, William Holman Hunt, and Dante Gabriel Rossetti. By 1869, in *Art Thoughts*, Jarves spoke specifically of the Americans Charles Moore and Thomas Farrer, calling them "exact literalists, having a conscientious regard for their specific motive, and doing their work with a thoroughness of touch and study which affords example to others." Yet "their art thus far relies too much on its local truth of design and hue, and topographical exactitude of representation, and too little on the sentiment of nature or on the language of color, the strong points of the idealists. It is based on a misconception of high art, which has a deeper purpose in view than mere truthful representation of external nature, though it demands that."[5] By this time Jarves had located his ideal of spirituality in John La Farge, whom Clarence Cook had excoriated for totally ignoring those qualities implicit in Pre-Raphaelitism. Thus by 1870 the critical lines were clearly drawn.

Some confusion may arise in distinguishing the influence of Ruskin himself from that of the English Pre-Raphaelite painters on American artists. Ruskin's vital championing of Pre-Raphaelite principles was enunciated in his monograph *Pre-Raphaelitism* of 1851, and Americans became aware of Ruskin's writings and the art of the Pre-Raphaelites concurrently in the late 1840s, and then far more emphatically in the later 1850s. Particularly in regard to still-life painting, Pre-Raphaelitism might seem more a matter of technique, while Ruskin's influence might seem to partake of aesthetics and even moral philosophy. But this distinction is complicated by his own role as an artist who not only used his work to demonstrate his principles but exhibited in the first show of English Pre-Raphaelite art in America, in New York, Philadelphia, and Boston in 1857–58.

Technically, Pre-Raphaelitism in America meant above all a heightened meticulousness and specificity of detail in rendering observed, as opposed to "composed," nature. This may seem almost inconceivable given the factually oriented landscape art of the mid-nineteenth-century Hudson River School. Works of this school, usually sketched in pen and pencil in natural surroundings but composed in the studio, were indeed "composites," rearrangements, or in the words of their Pre-Raphaelite detractors, "conventionalities," actually *untrue* to nature.

Pre-Raphaelites on both sides of the Atlantic abolished dark shadows, in which detail was lost, and made the range of prismatic color more brilliant, another hallmark of their art. To the more traditional artist and critic this was at the expense of tonal harmony. The brilliant hues often found complementary reflections in colored shadows: the red of a cherry reflected in the blue of a neighboring plum, coloristic qualities precursive to later Impressionism. This aesthetic coincidence was underscored in the watercolor technique of the Pre-Raphaelites. They abandoned the more single-toned washes, usually within a linear outline, of the pioneering British watercolorists, and substituted the techniques of hatching and stippling that previously were confined to miniature watercolor portraits. The Pre-Raphaelites also devoted considerable technical attention to independent watercolors and drawings, not only to preparatory studies for more ambitious oil paintings. This shift in emphasis was especially innovative in America, and it became most evident in the formation of the American Society of Painters in Watercolors in 1866. This was a very conscious action at the acme of Pre-Raphaelite activity among American artists, and American Pre-Raphaelites contributed strongly to the Society's first show at the National Academy of Design in winter 1867–68. These artists had already made unprecedented contributions to the November 1866 show of the New York Artists' Fund Society and the summer 1867 exhibition inaugurating the Yale University Art Gallery.

Less recognized is the innovative role of these artists in the "etching revival" here, though, unlike Europe, America had no tradition to revive. John Henry Hill, Henry Farrer, and Charles Herbert Moore pioneered the investigation of etching in America in the late 1860s, which led to the formation of the New York Etching Club in 1877 and the writing of Sylvester Koehler. "Humble" media assumed a new importance that coincided with the untraditional dignity given to hitherto despised or dismissed subject matter: the transcriptional landscape, the still life, and the study from nature.

The "Study from Nature" began to appear with increasing regularity in American exhibitions during the 1850s, painted by artists of various aesthetic persuasions. Landscape artists always had "studied in" and "sketched from" nature, whether viewed as subject or background; but only in the mid-1850s was a distinction made between the "sketch" and the "study," validating the "study" and making it acceptable for exhibition and even acquisition. This was stated most clearly in an early article in the Ruskin-inspired and -influenced journal *The Crayon*, in March 1855. Its author, probably the artist-editor William J. Stillman, noted that instead of broad sketches made outdoors "the true method of study is to take small portions of scenes, and thereto explore perfectly, and with the most insatiable curiosity, every object presented, and to define them with the carefulness of a topographer. . . . To make a single study of a portion of landscape in this way, is more worth than a summer's sketching. Young artists should never *sketch*, but always *study*, and especially never make studio sketches."[6]

The importance of the study was emphasized eight years later, when the American Pre-Raphaelites had become a more codified group under the inspiration and tutelage of Thomas Farrer. In August 1863, Farrer wrote in *The New Path*:

> Those who have visited artists' studios, will remember little canvasses, on which are painted bits of vines, groups and clusters of leaves, single and picked flowers. These are for the subsequent manufacture from them of all sorts of foregrounds, to be made up in the studio during the winter. The visitors have also seen hundreds of oil sketches called studies, and have sometimes felt these to be better than the finished, exhibited and sold pictures by the same hand. The pictures are made from the studies, the studies, with some altering on the spot, from nature. Of course an artist who works in that way, can never hope to give us representations of natural scenes and objects. . . . The men who wish to record truths of nature, paint what they undertake to paint from the thing itself. . . . And if any of them ever paint anything from studies, it is copied exactly from these studies, which, being faithful beyond peradventure, are to a great extent nature itself.[7]

And a very long article in the July 1864 issue entitled "Pictures and Studies" defined in detail the distinction between the two and the multiple purposes of the study to perfect the power of the hand, the eye, and the memory, without hurry or slovenliness, concentrating only on the chosen motif: "If, for instance, an artist . . . sit down to make a study of a blackberry bush, he should not spend one moment on accessories. . . . Studies, then, are the means; pictures, the end. Studies are the preparation, pictures the result. Studies are the aspiration and the beginning, pictures the achievement and the end."[8]

Acknowledging the truthful recording of nature as the highest artistic goal reversed the traditional hierarchy of genres. This hierarchy was enunciated by the French Academy in the mid-1600s, and it governed Sir Joshua Reynolds' influential *Discourses*. Again in America in 1827, Daniel Fanshaw gave history painting the place of primacy.[9] Landscape was inferior to the depiction of man, God's noblest creation, but "composed" landscape was superior to transcriptional, recorded landscape. Thus still life—primarily of natural growth—transcriptionally rendered and without noble implications was the least worthy theme. Such was the academic doctrine that was completely overturned in Ruskin's theories: "The so-called historical or 'high art' painter is a person infinitely inferior to the painter of flowers or still life. He is, in modern times, nearly always a man who has great vanity without pictorial capacity, and differs from the landscape or fruit painter merely in misunderstanding and overestimating his own powers."[10] Ruskin's validation of still-life painting proved crucial to its overall development in American art.

Not unlike his American counterpart Ralph Waldo Emerson, Ruskin saw the macrocosm in the microcosm: "Paint the leaves as they grow! If you can paint *one* leaf, you can paint the world."[11] Not only does this summarize his still-life aesthetic but it also obliterates any clear distinction between still-life and landscape painting. Leaves—especially in Ruskinian iconography—are a still-life subject; leaves grow on trees; and thus the growing leaf is part of the landscape.

Reviewing the 1857 Royal Academy exhibition in London, Ruskin wrote: "I believe the most beautiful position in which flowers can possibly be seen is precisely their most natural one—low flowers relieved by grass or moss, and tree blossoms relieved against the sky. How it happens that no flower-painter has yet been moved to draw a cluster of boughs of peach blossom, or cherry blossom, or apple blossom just as they grow, with the deep blue sky between every bud and petal, is more than I can understand. . . ."[12] And, reviewing the 1858 Academy exhibition, he predicted that:

> even the best of the quiet, accessible, simple fits of Nature are yet to come. How strange that among all this painting of delicate detail there is not a true one of English spring!—that no Pre-Raphaelite has painted a cherry-tree in blossom, dark-white against the twilight of April; nor an almond-tree rosy on the blue sky; nor the flush of the apple-blossom, nor a blackthorn hedge nor a wild-rose hedge; nor a wood-ground of hyacinths; no, nor even heather yet, nor a rock spotted richly with mosses; nor gentians, nor Alpine roses, nor white oxtails in the woods, nor anemone hermorosa, nor even so much as the first springing leaves of any tree in their pale, dispersed, delicate sharpness of shape. Everything has to be done yet; and we must not think quite so much of ourselves till we have done it. . . .[13]

His prescription was followed almost instantaneously; if he called for apple blossoms in 1857, then the American still-life specialist George Henry Hall would depict a spray of them that year.

Ruskin's preference for the natural over the artful setting and for the humble and commonplace met tremendous response in America in still lifes by both Pre-Raphaelite and more conventional artists. He wrote long and often about grasses, leaves and ferns, weeds and lichens, and plants such as mulleins and burdocks. Ruskin was fascinated by the botanical specimen as a tool for drawing and above all as the revelation of God's infinite creativity. He wrote of this in spring 1842: "I made, by mere accident, my first drawing of leafage in natural growth—a few ivy leaves round the stump in the hedge of the Norwood road, under Tulse Hill. . . . I never (in my drawings, however much in my writings) *imitated* anybody any more after that one sketch was made: but entered at once on the course of study which enabled me afterwards to understand Pre-Raphaelitism."[14]

In August 1847, Ruskin wrote his father of an experience in the Scottish landscape that is almost a catalogue of the still-life and nature interests that inspired the Americans two decades later:

> I came on a little bit of quiet lake among the rocks, all belled about with heather and fresh with fern, birch trunks over it, and ash, and silky beech, and on the other side a copse of dark, slight-pointed, close-set pines, and the water divided between water-lilies and blue sky. Then I got among some fallen rocks with such fantastic Scotch firs growing out of them that they looked as if they had been to Dunsinane and back again; and then I saw some leaves that I thought were not such as I was used to see grouped with pine, and what should this be but a Spanish chestnut—and presently another; and after that, at the bottom of a crag, and forming a dark foil to a knob of birches, another tree which made me start again from its strange look in such a place, and behold a great laurel—a laurel as big as those in the Isola Madre—and ever so many bluebells just over it, and then some oxalis not half so large in leaf as the Swiss, but as beautiful, and all put together with a freedom and sentiment beyond everything—a peculiar softness and wildness mixed, like the finest Scotch music—and an intense melancholy too.[15]

Leaves especially were beloved by Ruskin, who recommended them to art students of nature. A whole section of the last volume of *Modern Painters* was entitled "Of Leaf Beauty"; earlier, in 1857, the study of leaves was important in *The Elements of Drawing*, published in conjunction with his teaching at the Working Men's College. Ruskin recognized the whole in the smallest part and urged this vision on his students and readers: "In the leaf is the strength of the tree itself . . . the leaves *are* the tree itself. Its trunk sustains; its fruit burdens and exhausts; but in the leaf it breathes and lives." With leaves, so with rocks. In 1857 Ruskin advised his students: "So a stone may be round or angular, polished or rough, cracked all over like an ill-glazed teacup, or as united and broad as the breast of Hercules. It may be as flaky as a wafer, as powdery as a field puffball; it may be knotted like a ship's hawser, or kneaded like hammered iron, or knit like a Damascus sabre, or fused like a glass bottle, or crystalized like hoar-frost, or veined like a forest leaf: look at it, and don't try to remember how anybody told you to 'do a stone'."[16] Ruskin was fascinated by the geological rock forms he found in the Alps in 1854, and his best-known example, the *Block of Gneiss*, painted and exhibited in America in 1857–58, inspired artists here in the 1860s and 1870s to record with loving precision the rocks and boulders from the mountains and the shores of rivers, lakes, and ocean. Subject matter alone is enough to identify Ruskin-inspired landscapes, still lifes, and nature studies by American artists from the mid-1850s to the mid-1870s. Many of these works have disappeared but are known through their titles and through descriptions by critics and reviewers. One such work, a *Study of Rocks* by Aaron Draper Shattuck, was exhibited as early as 1856 at the National Academy of Design and at the Brooklyn Art Association, presumably the same picture.

"Grass and moss, and parsley and fern, have each their own delightfulness," wrote Ruskin, and grass and moss and parsley and fern entered the iconography of American still-life and nature painting.[17] Shattuck exhibited a *Study of Grass and Flowers* at the National Academy in 1856, along with the rock study, and presumably that same oil appeared at the Boston Athenaeum that year, at the Pennsylvania Academy in 1857, and at the Troy Young Men's Association exhibition of 1859. The little-known American Pre-Raphaelite, Robert J. Pattison, showed a *Study of Leaves and Grasses* at the National Academy in 1866, and Margaret McDonald a *Bunch of Grass* at the American Water Color Society in New York in 1873. Fidelia Bridges' *Study of Moss and Ferns* was shown at the Brooklyn Art Association in 1866. Ferns were a particular favorite among the Ruskin-oriented Americans, and Shattuck did several paintings of women among ferns about 1857–58. Bridges adopted the motif at least as early as 1863 for a show in Brooklyn, for another in Philadelphia in 1864 to support the United States Sanitary Commission, for the Artists' Fund Society of New York in 1866, and another at the Pennsylvania Academy in 1868. Her mentor, William Trost Richards, exhibited a watercolor *Study of Ferns* in Troy in 1862, and his oil shown there in 1878 may be the work in the present exhibition (cat. no. 68); his interest in ferns may well have led Bridges to use the theme. In October 1863, Henry Roderick Newman sent a pencil drawing of ferns to Thomas Farrer in New York, and Farrer himself exhibited *Young Ferns* at the Brooklyn Art Association in March 1863, presumably the work also shown that year at the Pennsylvania Academy. A watercolor drawing of ferns, of about 1867, by Farrer's young pupil, Robert Brandegee, is known today.

Similar subjects were no less popular among Ruskin-inspired artists. William Hart showed pictures of weeds at Brooklyn in 1856 and at the National Academy in 1858, where John Henry Hill had exhibited a *Study of Weeds* in 1857; an example by Thomas Farrer was at Brooklyn in 1863 and at the National Academy the following year, while Newman's *Milkweed* appeared there in 1865. In 1868, Mrs. Eliza Bisbee Duffey's *Ducks and Water Weeds* was exhibited at the Pennsylvania Academy, and in 1872 Fidelia Bridges showed her *Pickerel Weed* at the Water Color Society.

Detailed, close-up studies of leaves were first exhibited by the Moravian naturalist-artist, Rufus Grider, at the Pennsylvania Academy in 1854, but the theme was used abundantly by American Pre-Raphaelites in the 1860s. One of the earliest was Robert Pattison, whose *Autumn Leaves* appeared in 1862 in New York at the Artists' Fund Society; in 1866 he showed both a *Strawberry Leaves* and a *Study of Leaves and Grasses* at the National Academy. Arthur Parton, briefly identified with Pre-Raphaelitism, exhibited an *Autumn Leaves* at the Pennsylvania Academy in 1863, as well as a companion, *Spring Leaves*, in 1864 at the National Academy in New York. Nina Moore seems to have specialized in the leaf theme, beginning with her watercolor, *Autumn Leaves*, shown in 1857 and again in 1866 at the National Acad-

Figure 11
William T. Richards
Blackberry Bush 1858
Oil on canvas, 14¾ × 12½ in. (37.5 × 31.8 cm.)
Private collection
Cat. no. 66

emy, at the Pennsylvania Academy in 1867, at the Water Color Society in 1869, and in Davenport, Iowa, in 1876. But perhaps the quintessential example is that by the mysterious John B. Duffey of Woodbury, New Jersey, who showed his *Nothing But Leaves*, at the Artists' Fund Society in New York, in 1866.

Among ordinary leafy plants, Ruskin was intrigued by the burdock, and burdock is prominent in nature studies and foreground depictions by Pre-Raphaelite artists as well as others. For Ruskin "the principal business of that plant being clearly to grow leaves wherewith to adorn foregrounds. . . . When a leaf is to be spread wide, like the Burdock, it is supported by a framework of extending ribs like a Gothic roof."[18] Jervis McEntee did drawings of burdock as early as 1857, and Jasper Cropsey painted it in foreground studies; Stephen Shaughnessey showed a burdock study at the Artists' Fund Society in New York in 1864; and a *Study of Burdocks* was in the John F. Kensett estate sale in 1873. *Burdocks* was in John Henry Hill's landmark etching portfolio of 1867.

All these themes were new to American art. Our still-life tradition had been based on the common themes of fruit and flowers, though flowers were a more recent interest. The American Pre-Raphaelites also depicted the usual fruit subjects of their more conventional colleagues and predecessors. One fruit subject especially associated with the Pre-Raphaelites was blackberries, even though Ruskin wrote rela-

Figure 12
George Henry Hall
Raspberries in a Leaf 1861
Oil on canvas, 12½ × 15½ in. (31.8 × 39.4 cm.)
Collection: William Nathaniel Banks
Cat. no. 108

tively little about the blackberry. Artists attracted to this subject may have followed the precedent of William Trost Richards, who became the best known of the American Pre-Raphaelites and whose in-volvement with Ruskinian themes and Pre-Raphaelite style was first manifested in his *Blackberry Bush* (fig. 11) of 1858. Created immediately after the first exhibition of English Pre-Raphaelitism in America—in New York in 1857 and in Philadelphia early in 1858—this painting announced Richards' conversion when it was shown at the National Academy in 1859. *Blackberry Bush* appeared at the Royal Academy in London in 1860 and again in this country at the Sanitary Fair in Albany, New York, in 1864. Although *Blackberry Bush* is a landscape, not a still life, it is a typically Pre-Raphaelite foreground study of tremen-dous detail and particularity, painted outdoors in summer. Richards returned to the subject, exhibiting *Golden Rod and Blackberry* at the National Academy. In 1860 he took on Fidelia Bridges as a student, and a decade later Bridges exhibited her own *Study of a Blackberry Bush* at the Academy. In 1871 she showed a *Blackberry Bushes* at the Brooklyn Art Association, and in 1875 a similarly titled picture at the American Water Color Society. By February 1860, John Henry Hill wrote Thomas Farrer that "East-bourn has taken . . . a small drawing of a blackberry briar which I believe I was making when you were up here last."[19] Henry Roderick Newman exhibited a still life of *Raspberries and Blackberries* at the inaugural of the Yale University Art Gallery in 1867, and John William Hill showed still lifes of blackberries in 1875 at the American Water Color Society and at the Philadelphia Centennial. Nina Moore showed a picture of a *Blackberry Vine and Rocks* at the Water Color Society's first exhibition late in 1867.

Inspired by Ruskin, the American Pre-Raphaelites developed a new, more profound interpretation of fruit subjects. The traditional "setting" for such subjects was on "supports," usually defined as tabletops; they were consciously and pictorially arranged indoors on a horizontal tabletop, or shelf, or ledge, or board, either left bare or covered with a cloth or some other "softening" and sometimes decorative element. American Pre-Raphaelites occasionally painted this kind of picture in the 1860s, as we know from reviews, though few have come to light. And certainly it remained a viable form and format of still life in the hands of the conventional specialist. From the 1860s, a very different format appeared that combined the still life and the nature study: still life in a natural setting, in a nook or glade of intimate nature, close-up concentrations of fruit on the earth ground, or softened by leaves and grasses. This was the fruit equivalent of Ruskin's growing flowers springing from the earth or set against the blue sky. Smaller fruits were preferred, presented in multiples—especially berries and cherries. And this "Ruskinian" format was adopted by more conventional artists as well as by the Pre-Raphaelites. George Hall might paint his favored raspberries in a china bowl on a polished tabletop, or they might appear cupped in a large rhubarb leaf that protected them from the rocky ground (fig. 12).

Flower subjects, traditional in European still lifes as were fruits and other edibles, were more of an innovation in America in the late 1840s and usually were formal bouquets, set on tabletops. This mode, from Dutch seventeenth-century prototypes, was the floral mode Ruskin railed so vehemently against. Influenced by Ruskin's writings and English Pre-Raphaelite work of the 1850s, the American Pre-Raphaelites usually chose to depict more casual blooms in their still lifes and nature studies. Following Ruskin, these were often wild flowers, and nature studies of growing wild flowers were exhibited as early as 1856 at the Pennsylvania Academy by William Hart, one of the first artists associated with Pre-Raphaelitism in America. Studies of wild flowers became a feature among the women artists of the movement here: Nina Moore and Margaret McDonald both exhibited paintings of this subject in American Water Color Society exhibitions, and Fidelia Bridges made it her specialty, not only at the Society, but at the National Academy, the Boston Athenaeum, and the Brooklyn Art Association. John Henry Hill showed his *Wild Flowers* at the National Academy in 1878; another by his father appeared in Troy that year; and Henry Roderick Newman exhibited *Wild Flowers* at the Brooklyn Art Association in January 1884.

More specific titles were chosen by many artists who featured the wild flower, the casual wayside growth. *Marigolds*, exhibited by John William Hill at the National Academy in 1858, is among the earliest of these; presumably the same work was shown in 1859 at the Pennsylvania Academy, followed by *Buttercups and Daisies* at the National Academy in 1860. Hill showed a *Marsh Mallows* at the National Academy and at the Boston Athenaeum in 1863, *Morning Glories* at the Brooklyn Art Association in 1867, and *Lady Slippers* at the Louisville Industrial Exposition in 1878.

Hill's son, John Henry Hill, seems less attracted to the subject of field flowers than was his father, though his delicate watercolors *Dandelions* (1858, fig. 13) and *Fringed Gentians* (circa 1867, pl. 4) are in the present exhibition. Many other members of the Pre-Raphaelite group were, however. Violets were painted by Fidelia Bridges and Charles Herbert Moore; Bridges' were shown at the National Academy in 1863 and the Pennsylvania Academy in 1866 and Moore's at the New York Watercolor Society in 1872. Such subjects were common in Bridges' art from the mid-1860s: she showed columbine in Brooklyn in 1867, daisies in Brooklyn in 1870 and two years later at the Water Color Society, marsh flowers at the Society in 1875, and wild morning glories in Brooklyn in 1877.

Although no still-life paintings by Thomas Farrer have surfaced yet, he also employed this theme in the 1860s. His *Study of a Dandelion* appeared at the National Academy in 1865 and again in 1867; his *Study of Columbine* was shown in Brooklyn in 1867 and at the Academy in 1868; and his *Study of Laurel* in Brooklyn in 1868. Farrer's pupil Margaret McDonald showed nasturtiums at Brooklyn in 1867 and primroses at the Philadelphia Centennial in 1876. Another pupil, Robert Brandegee, who worked in a Pre-Raphaelite mode for a few years in the late 1860s, exhibited laurel at the National Academy in 1868 and morning glories at the Water Color Society in 1869. While depictions of autumn leaves seem to have

Figure 13
John Henry Hill
Dandelions 1858
Watercolor on paper, 6 in. diameter (15.2 cm.)
Lent anonymously
Cat. no. 13

Above:
Figure 14
John William Hill
Apple Blossoms *circa* 1874
Watercolor on paper, 15⅞ × 8⅞ in. (39.0 × 22.3 cm.)
Collection: The Brooklyn Museum
Cat. no. 39

Facing page:
Figure 15
Robert Brandegee
Apple Blossoms *circa* 1869
Watercolor on paper, 4¾ × 4¾ in. (12.0 × 12.0 cm.)
Anonymous loan
Cat. no. 87

been a specialty of the sparsely documented, rather mysterious, Nina Moore, the casual flower theme also attracted her. She showed arbutus at the first Water Color Society exhibition in 1867, morning glories in 1868, and laurel as well as columbine in 1869.

Ruskin's special recommendation of the flowering branch, of apple blossoms in particular, was taken up by American Pre-Raphaelites later than by their more traditional colleagues. John William Hill first exhibited the subject in Brooklyn in 1867, perhaps the *Apple Blossoms* in the present exhibition (fig. 14), and showed this or a similar picture in Troy, New York, in 1878. Hill's example may have inspired the small watercolor of 1867 by Robert Brandegee (fig. 15), and Hill himself painted *Peach Blossoms* in 1874 (cat. no. 40). Charles Herbert Moore exhibited apple blossoms in Chicago at the Interstate Industrial Exhibition in 1876. The theme became a specialty of Martin Johnson Heade as early as 1867, and is especially associated with him today in American art. But Heade's most renowned connection with Ruskinian still life is in his pulsating images of orchids growing in the Brazilian jungles. Yet Heade never adopts a Pre-Raphaelite technique in his still lifes.

A few other flower subjects fascinated the American Pre-Raphaelites. Although a cultivated flower, the hollyhock could be represented growing and climbing. John Henry Hill exhibited hollyhocks at the National Academy as early as 1861, as did his father in 1866 at the Artists' Fund Society, while Henry Farrer showed a work at the Brooklyn Art Association in 1871. Other Americans explored the subject, too. John La Farge's still lifes of hollyhocks are most remembered today, while Eastman Johnson featured them in several genre garden pictures of the 1870s.

In all its varieties, the lily was certainly the most popular flower of the Pre-Raphaelites. Again, very few works have surfaced. The earliest recorded example was shown by John William Hill at the Pennsylvania Academy in 1861; he also exhibited the subject at the Water Color Society in 1870 and in Troy in 1878. Thomas Farrer exhibited water lilies in Brooklyn in 1864, and other lily pictures at the National

Figure 16
Charles Herbert Moore
Lilies of the Valley *circa* 1861
Watercolor on paper, 4⅜ × 8⅛ in. (11.0 × 20.7 cm.)
Collection: The Art Museum, Princeton University, gift of
Frank Jewett Mather, Jr.
Cat. no. 45

Academy, the Water Color Society, and the inaugural show of the Yale Art Gallery in New Haven, Connecticut, all in 1867. The theme also was taken up by a number of his pupils—Frank Lathrop at the National Academy in 1865 and Margaret McDonald at the Water Color Society in 1867 as well as at the National Academy in 1873. The first Water Color Society show included a good many lily pictures by Pre-Raphaelites—by Thomas Farrer, McDonald, and John Henry Hill. Henry Roderick Newman showed lilies there and in Brooklyn in 1869, while Fidelia Bridges exhibited lilies in Brooklyn in 1872 and in 1874, and at the Water Color Society in 1873. Her *Calla Lily* of 1875 is in the present exhibition (cat. no. 89) as is Charles Herbert Moore's 1861 *Lilies of the Valley* (fig. 16).

One other thematic area introduced as well as explored by the American Pre-Raphaelites was the dead bird, a subject primarily associated with field sport and game pictures. Common enough in Europe, the theme was rare in America, until the arrival of English-born and -trained Arthur Fitzwilliam Tait in 1850. Tait painted more than two dozen hanging-game pictures during the ensuing decade. In the mid-1860s, John William Hill turned to the sporting-game theme in still life, though unlike Tait he depicted his hanging game in colorful detail against elaborate landscape backgrounds. As a still-life subject, however, its great popularity would begin in the 1880s with the trompe l'oeil tradition of William Michael Harnett. The Pre-Raphaelite approach of the 1860s was very different. Tender, compassionate renderings of small birds, such as the titmouse, emphasized their frailness, and the starkness of death was heightened by specificity of technique. Both Farrers and both Hills depicted the subject. Thomas Farrer exhibited his work at the Artists' Fund Society in 1866 and Henry Farrer his at the National Academy and in New

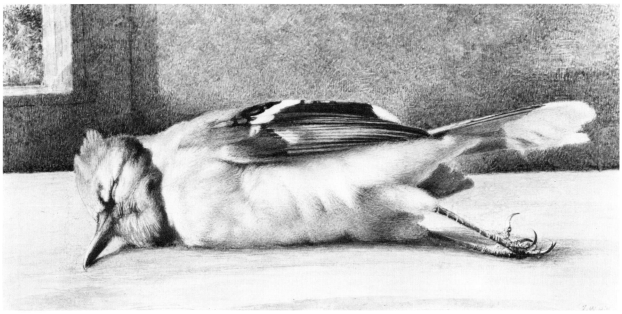

Figure 17
John William Hill
Dead Blue Jay *circa* 1865
Watercolor on paper, 5¾ × 12 in. (14.6 × 30.5 cm.)
Collection: The New-York Historical Society
Cat. no. 30

Figure 18
John Henry Hill
Black Capped Titmouse *circa* 1866
Etching on white paper
Plate: 4¾ × 7½ in. (12.0 × 19.0 cm.)
Image: 2½ × 5¾ in. (6.1 × 14.5 cm.)
*The New York Public Library, Astor, Lenox,
and Tilden Foundations, Print Collection*
Cat. no. 19

Figure 19
William Henry Hunt
Hedge-Sparrow's Nest with Primroses and Violets *circa* 1840–50
Watercolor on paper, 7½ × 9⅝ in. (19.0 × 24.5 cm.)
Collection: David Daniels
Cat. no. 124

Haven in 1867. It is likely that John William Hill's *Dead Blue Jay* (fig. 17) was done at this time, as was his son's etching of a *Black Capped Titmouse* (fig. 18) that appeared in his publication *Sketches from Nature* in 1867. In *Sketches*, John Henry Hill specified that he used a real, not a stuffed, model.

This spate of depictions of dead birds offers evocative images of sadness and death, not totally unrelated in sentiment to Albert Pinkham Ryder's later, great *Dead Bird*. This emotional evocation and the allusion to life's temporality is further suggested by the bird's-nest theme, so associated with William Henry Hunt (fig. 19). Seldom painted in America earlier, the theme appeared often in the 1860s and early 1870s: John Williamson, a landscapist and occasional still-life painter, showed a bird's nest at the National Academy in 1860, and in 1864 the otherwise unknown Hannah Millard also showed one there. Whether these followed Ruskinian precepts is probable but unknown. Certainly that format was followed by Pre-Raphaelites such as Fidelia Bridges, who exhibited the theme at Brooklyn in 1863 and again in 1873, when she specified her subject as a *thrush's* nest. The thrush's smallness and plainness identified it with the weeds and wild flowers of everyday nature. John Henry Hill included a *Thrush's Nest* in his 1867 book of etchings (fig. 20), noting that the shadows on the right side of the thrush's eggs were cast by the fibers of the nest. In 1871 he exhibited a bird's-nest watercolor at Brooklyn, where his father had shown such

Figure 20
John Henry Hill
Thrush's Nest 1866
Pen and ink on paper, 16 × 12½ in. (40.7 × 31.2 cm.)
Collection: Mr. and Mrs. Leonard L. Milberg
Cat. no. 20

a subject in 1867, very possibly the work included in the present exhibition (pl. 3). From that time, too, is a watercolor drawing by Robert Brandegee of a bird's nest hanging in a tree. These nest pictures not only show the humble "homes" of the little birds but also depict the eggs inside, and, in concert with the images of dead birds, they refer to the course of life.

Ruskin's influence, however, was not just in the realm of subject matter and setting. He clearly supported the English Pre-Raphaelites, whose techniques the Americans emulated, and he provided formal examples in his own work. And his commitment to detailed rendering was unequivocal. He wrote to William Stillman, on May 14, 1855, that "as far as you can *see* detail, you should always paint it . . . in every picture intended for finished work, and intended to be seen near, the limit of detail is—visibility—and no other."[22] This became the keystone of Stillman's aesthetic philosophy during his editorship of *The Crayon* and is clearly expressed in his editorial, "Dii Majores ac Minores," published later in 1855:

> There is indeed a broad distinction to be drawn, not always, perhaps, to be clearly defined, but clearly enough to be readily followed, between facts and truths, the former being the individual instances exemplifying the law, the full expression of which constitutes the former. Thus the peculiar form of a single oak-leaf is a fact; but the universal angularity of oak-leaves, their general obedience to one law of formation is a truth; the lightness and

flexibility of a single leaf, a fact; the openness and looseness of foliage, as a mass, a truth. The presence of a certain kind of lichen on a particular rock, a fact; but when we learn that that lichen only occurs on that kind of rock, we have discovered a truth, and so through the whole range of Nature . . . . It is not indeed necessary that each oak-leaf should have its form studied out in a picture, or that the particular lichen which happens in Nature should be given to the particular rock, but it is absolutely so that oak-leaves should be felt as such entirely, and that the lichen of granite should never be attributed to the limestone; and the only sure way of arriving at the truths of creation is by carefully studying the *facts* which occur to our sight . . . . The particular form which a leaf may assume is, within certain limits, a matter of accident, and no two leaves will be precisely alike. Now, each leaf is a fact, and contains the essential statement of what an oak-leaf should be, excepting certain imperfections peculiar to the individual, and the result of accident; and the absolute truth of the oak-leaf is the form which gives all its essential characteristics without any of those accidental imperfections. If we could find a leaf absolutely perfect, it would be no less a fact, and would also express truth perfectly. It is thus that the aggregate of the facts express the truth, and thus that no man learns truth except from the very closest and most thoughtful study of facts.[23]

Ruskin experienced a major problem: he recognized that the minute recording of nature was not an end in itself. Like traditional aestheticians, he sought individual interpretation and he found it in Turner but could not find it in John Brett's great Pre-Raphaelite *Val d'Aosta* of 1858, for all its success in presenting natural history. He wrote in *Modern Painters*, "These sources of beauty . . . are not presented by any very great work of art in a form of pure transcript. They invariably receive the reflection of the mind under whose shadow they have passed, and are modified or colored by its image. This modification is the Work of Imagination."[24] This lack of personal interpretation constantly evoked the censure of American critics and eventually proved the undoing of the Pre-Raphaelite movement here. The ultimate failure of the American Pre-Raphaelite movement may be ascribed to a lack of emotional expressivity, heightened by obsessive detailing, in landscape and still life, a lack that troubled Ruskin himself. At the same time, he precipitated the rupture with traditional attitudes toward nature in America—his doctrine of the "pathetic fallacy." Ruskin attempted to deanthropomorphize pictorial attitudes toward nature by encouraging the understanding of a natural history worthy of its *own* expression, rather than one with imposed anthropocentric values. Beyond scientific identification, he lectured in 1870, "what we especially need at present for education purposes is to know, not the anatomy of plants, but their biography . . . ."[25] Ruskin introduced a new concept of history in pictorializing nature, one that made conventional landscape and still life appear generalized and even inaccurate. This sharpened the division of practitioners into "ideal" and "real" schools. The short-lived Pre-Raphaelite movement represented the "real" and the avant-garde.

What was Ruskin's rationale for this emphasis on the humble and the everyday? Excellent evidence for the answer is found in his justification before a parliamentary committee investigating the teaching procedures of the Working Men's College in 1860. Ruskin asked support to help inculcate a moral direction in the masses:

Nothing assists him [the working man] so much as having the moral disposition developed rather than the intellectual, after his work; anything that touches his feelings is good, and puts new life into him; therefore I want modern pictures, if possible, of that class which would ennoble and refine by their subjects. I should like prints of all times, engravings of all times; those would interest him with their variety of means and subject; and natural history of three kinds, namely shells, birds, and plants . . . whatever town he may be in, he may take some interest in the birds, and in the plants, or in the sea shells of his own country and coast. I should like the commonest of all our plants first, and most fully illustrated; the commonest of all our birds and of our shells; and men would be led to take an interest in those things wholly for their beauty and for their separate charm. . . .[20]

This emphasis on the commonplace underlay Ruskin's teaching, his *Elements of Drawing*, published to underscore his instruction, and his own natural history and art, passed on to his disciples and followers.

While the English Pre-Raphaelites did not offer their American counterparts examples of still life to emulate, *per se*, Ruskin himself created nature studies, such as the rocks and floral pieces in the present show. More significant was Ruskin's admiration for the still lifes of William Henry Hunt, who worked in a similar stippled and hatched watercolor technique, producing images of fruit and flowers in bright colors and great minutiae. Hunt's special theme earned him the appellation "Bird's Nest Hunt." His still lifes were known and admired early by Americans abroad and were later seen here. William Cullen Bryant wrote from London on July 7, 1849, of visiting a watercolor exhibition:

> That which appeared to me the most remarkable, though not in the highest department of art, were still-life pieces by Hunt. It seems to me impossible to carry pictorial illusion to a higher pitch than he has attained. A sprig of hawthorne flowers, freshly plucked, lies before you, and you are half-tempted to take it up and inhale its fragrance; those speckled eggs in the bird's nest, you are sure you might, if you pleased, take into your hand; that tuft of ivy leaves and buds is so complete an optical deception that you can hardly believe that it has not been attached by some process to the paper on which you see it.[21]

Hunt did not contribute still lifes to the influential British art exhibition held in America in 1857–58, although he exhibited a *Fruit* watercolor at the first American Water Color Society show in 1867 and another at the Boston Arts Club in 1873. But others working in a similar vein, often imitators of Hunt, were seen in New York, Philadelphia, and Boston in the historic British show.

It would be impossible to pinpoint precisely the first awareness of Ruskin and Pre-Raphaelitism among American artists, critics, and art lovers. It probably began to manifest itself by 1847, when volume one of the first American edition of Ruskin's *Modern Painters* appeared. American periodicals reviewed it extensively, and we know that writers such as Ralph Emerson and Walt Whitman read Ruskin's writings in 1847, though most earlier critics and reviewers (Emerson excepted) knew the author only as "a Graduate of Oxford," his designation on the title page. Certainly, Ruskin was known to Americans before they became aware of Pre-Raphaelite painters. Frederic Church was one of the earliest American painters involved with the Ruskinian aesthetic, although his extremely complex relationship to it needs further elucidation. Church's first pupil, William James Stillman, came across Ruskin's *Modern Painters* in winter 1848-49, an encounter that affected and directed Stillman's entire future career—from the first zealous enthusiasm to the later rueful disillusion. Stillman's recollections indicated his teacher's urging: Church's "mind seemed the camera obscura in which everything that passed before it was recorded permanently, but he added in the rendering of its record nothing which sprang from human emotion."[26] Stillman's critical comment became commonplace in reference to American Pre-Raphaelites during the 1860s.

Stillman arrived in England early in 1850, a fateful year for his career and for the ensuing course of American art. He met Turner, saw the English Pre-Raphaelite work, and then met Ruskin. Stillman later renounced the ensuing decade of association with Ruskin as "fatal to the career to which I was then devoted,"[27] but at the time his thinking, observations, and reactions were very close to those of his new spiritual mentor. Of his first summer in Kent, Stillman wrote, "The timid little forget-me-not bewildered the eye with its profusion of blue flowers springing in the green banks—the pansy—the daisy, thick springing with the red poppies in the grass of the meadows and hay-fields—and the wild hyacinth, profusely scattered in the borders of the fields, while in the shadowed nooks might be found some late violets."[28]

On his return to New York late in 1850, Stillman became active in the New York art world as a landscape painter: "My larger studies from nature (25 × 30 inches) had attracted attention and had been hung on the line, getting me the election of the Associateship of Design, and the appellation of the 'American Pre-Raphaelite'."[29] Stillman noted that his studies from nature had a fidelity and completeness unknown in conventional landscape painting of the time. His few still lifes known today were painted later in his career, when he had almost abandoned painting and certainly Pre-Raphaelite aesthetics and Ruskinian precepts. Still-life details, however, were painted with loving care and they abounded in his pictures. After seeing John Everett Millais' *Proscribed Royalist* in England, Stillman began a landscape that was primarily foreground and for it "transplanted a violet which I wanted in the near foreground . . . to be sure that it was in correct light and proportion . . . . On that study I spent such long hours of the day as the light served, for three months . . . ."[30] This was *The Forest Spring* of 1853, one of the painter's favorite canvases, exhibited at the National Academy in 1854, where critics praised the drawing of its foreground detail.

In 1855, Stillman founded *The Crayon*, one of the two earliest American art periodicals. During its first two years, under his editorship, it became a primary mouthpiece for Ruskinian principles. Stillman's own editorials, particularly those in the first volume, may constitute the most thorough discussion of those principles and may have influenced the growth of Pre-Raphaelitism in American art more significantly than the examples set by his own art. He summed up the basic Ruskinian philosophy in "The Artist as Teacher" on April 4:

> We must disclaim the position that Art is to take the chair of Science, and tell us simply of the facts of the outer world—that the meadow is studded with butter-cups, the rocks covered with lichens, or that the clouds are divided into their classes, and have their laws of construction. This, botany and meteorology will tell us much more concisely. . . . Very few of us could tell wherein the fractures of slate differ from those of gneiss, or the leaf of the maple from that of the oak . . . But the painter may know all these things and still be only a botanist or geologist in his feeling . . . he must go beyond this in order to teach us anything *as* Artist. He must pass from the merely actual into the ideal of Nature, and not only tell us that flowers exist, but that there is a perfect type of the flower, more fully beautiful than any which we see—free from all imperfection of accident and circumstance.[31]

Stillman turned *The Crayon* over to his partner John Durand after 1856, and while the magazine's Ruskinian bias continued, it was not unqualified. In 1860 Stillman returned to England, and to Ruskin, with *Bed of Ferns*, a large nature study done on Saranac Lake which suggests the Ruskinian predilection investigated by many Americans. With Stillman were Joseph Ames and George Fuller, members of an informal "Brooklyn School" in the 1850s that centered around the sculptor Henry Kirke Brown. Later in 1860, Ames and Fuller met Ruskin in Switzerland when he was traveling with Stillman and attempting to exert even greater influence on Stillman's landscape painting.

The 1850s were the formative years of American Pre-Raphaelitism, the 1860s its maturity. Ruskin's publications were reviewed at length by American critics, who concentrated on formal identification of Pre-Raphaelite influences rather than on recognizing the reflection of Ruskin's writings and theories. Stillman was one of the first Americans to see English Pre-Raphaelite paintings, in London in 1850, although they were not shown here until later in the decade. Ruskin's pamphlet *Pre-Raphaelitism*, however, was published in New York by John Wiley in 1851, and by 1854 American critics had begun to describe Pre-Raphaelite art and to cite appropriate American examples. In reviewing the 1854 National Academy exhibition, the *New-York Tribune* critic mentioned artists working in the Pre-Raphaelite mode— Godfrey Frankenstein, James Hope, and Stillman—though he only commended the pictures by Stillman and Hope. *Putnam's Monthly* was even more enthusiastic over Stillman's "marvellous piece of greenery" in *The Forest Spring*, claiming that its "mosses, leaves, flowers and grasses are painted with wonderful delicacy and accuracy," and adding that "we have heard it called a pre-Raphaelite picture; but we should like to learn what pre-Raphaelite artist ever attempted any thing in this style."[32]

Many painters identified with Pre-Raphaelitism by the critics in the 1850s seem to have flirted with the movement only momentarily. Despite the vigorous support of Ruskin and that of America's major art magazine from 1855, the new aesthetic was difficult and time-consuming and may have made undue technical demands on some of the artists. Thus we hear no more of Frankenstein and Hope, though Hope's later paintings of Watkins Glen have a geological obsessiveness that a Pre-Raphaelite might envy. Instead, we read of James Hart, singled out in *The Crayon*, in 1855, by a writer who visited his Albany studio and saw "some of the most perfect studies of foreground material that I have ever seen, perfectly pre-Raphaelite in their delicacy of rendering of detail." At the National Academy of Design exhibition that year, the reviewer noted Samual Colman's "fine study from nature of a Pre-Raphaelite tendency" and James Hart's *In Olden Time*, which showed the Pre-Raphaelite distinction between an accurate study and a careless sketch.[33]

Although in the 1850s Pre-Raphaelitism was associated rather exclusively with landscape painting, it was becoming more specifically identified with the detailed study of natural foreground, as especially emphasized in landscape or with independent foreground studies. These were the basic constituents of the many "Studies from Nature" that began to proliferate in exhibitions of the later 1850s and the 1860s. Reviewing the Academy exhibition of 1856, the critic for *The Crayon* chided established landscapists such as Asher B. Durand and Frederic Church for the sameness of foreground foliage and the lack of distinction among the rocks in their pictures, and commended the studies from nature of both James and William Hart, while singling out Aaron Draper Shattuck. Shattuck's only previous entries at the

National Academy, the year before, were straightforward landscapes; this time, several were specifically labeled "studies" and one of these, a *Study of Grasses and Flowers*. The *Tribune* critic referred to it as "a perfect thing in its way," "a genuine reflection of nature" and said that "a geologist would know how to prize his *Study of Rocks*." *Grasses and Flowers* appeared again in Boston that year and at the Pennsylvania Academy a year later, and William Trost Richards mentioned the work in a letter to his wife that summer. Shattuck was identified early with Pre-Raphaelite principles. Ten years later Henry T. Tuckerman recalled that "this artist was one of the first of our landscape painters to render foregrounds with care and fidelity . . . ." And in a retrospective consideration of recent American art in 1864 in the *Round Table*, a sympathetic but not militant periodical, the writer observed that "people began to be interested in the grasses, the flowers, and the weeds of the fields" about seven years earlier. He listed Shattuck, Colman, and William Hart as the first artists involved, followed by William Trost Richards, but pointed out that the first three had abandoned the Pre-Raphaelite aesthetic rather quickly.[34]

John Henry Hill first attracted the attention of periodical critics about 1857 with works that were seen as "actual studies from nature . . . faithful transcripts of the objects attempted,"[35] including a *Study of Weeds*, *Study of a Hickory*, and *Study of a Pine*. Unlike Shattuck, Colman, and Hart, John Henry Hill and his father John William Hill became permanent converts to the Pre-Raphaelite aesthetic. The elder Hill had just abandoned his more fluid, conventional watercolor technique when he discovered Ruskin's writings about 1855. He began to create his studies from nature in 1856, in the Catskills, and by 1857 he was pursuing an even more brilliant and luminous watercolor palette. Ten years later, in the *Tribune*, Clarence Cook recalled that "there were two immediate promoters of this new phase, but they both had one inspiration. Mr. J.W. Hill, 'old Mr. Hill' as he is called, to distinguish him from his son J.H. Hill, was the first, and Thomas Charles Farrer was the second. Mr. Hill was taught by Ruskin through his books, Mr. Farrer was taught by Ruskin himself."[36] Charles Herbert Moore observed in 1888 that:

> among the subjects which he particularly enjoyed, and which he always treated with peculiar success, were weedy banks, and masses of garden flowers, wild flowers and grasses. These last he always portrayed in their natural growth, the work being done out of doors, just as was the case with his landscapes. This mode of treating flower subjects was at that time not so common as it has become—largely, no doubt, under Mr. Hill's influence. In winter, when the inclemency of the weather rendered working out of doors impossible, it was his habit to make studies of birds, fruit, and other still-life subjects.[37]

Thus John William Hill was the first American Pre-Raphaelite not only to treat individual natural forms with detailed emphasis in nature studies but also to work with intensity and great success in still life, as well as landscape. The correspondence of both Hills frequently mentions their involvement with still life. The younger Hill wrote to Thomas Farrer in July 1860, "Father has been hard at work as usual painting fruit, cherries, currants, etc. he has moss rose with blue sky background which I know you would think was beautiful." In a letter from the father to Farrer that same year, John William Hill noted that "My garden study of squash blossoms is also advancing in installments," and that he had "just finished a drawing of some cucumbers . . . I have made two large drawing uprights out of doors one of Lillies in the field the other of Hollyhock in the garden not our garden but down at Greenbush and I shall go into plums on Monday in the house. . . ." Hill began to exhibit these subjects at the National Academy: in 1858, *Marigolds*; in 1860, a number of fruit pieces; in 1861, *Hollyhocks* and *Vegetables and Fruit*; and more still-life subjects in 1862 and 1863. He later deserted the Academy, Cook wrote in 1867, because his work was "hung high, low, in the dark, near big glazing oil painting daubs."

Russell Sturgis, writing of Hill in the *Nation* in 1866, distinguished three preferences for settings in the still-life painting of the time, two of them the special province of the Pre-Raphaelites. He clearly stated his preference: "a cut-off branch of fruit thrown upon the ground is not dignified . . . a poor subject cut flowers and plucked fruit must always remain. The orchard bough is better than the dinner table, and better than the ground beneath the tree . . ."[38] By this time, Hill invariably was compared to the Englishman William Henry Hunt. Later, Hill's obituary in the *New York Times* mentioned that "his fruit and flowers have been compared by critics of authority, in the depth and richness of their color, and in the refinement of their drawing, to the work of William Hunt."[40] Probably the still-life paintings of the Pre-Raphaelites were the most consistently appreciated by contemporary writers and critics.

John Henry Hill came to artistic maturity just as his father became an ardent convert to the radical new aesthetic. His subjects were similar to those of his father and they were painted with a similar Pre-Raphaelite fidelity. The precise relationship between the two artists and their work is difficult to determine. The son's preoccupation with close-up landscape studies and the specificity of natural history is suggested in studies of a hickory and a pine that bespeak Ruskinian involvement. These studies were shown at the National Academy in 1857 and again at the Pennsylvania Academy in 1858. In February 1860, he wrote Farrer that he had completed a drawing of a blackberry briar, and in August his father informed Farrer that "John has painted a study of Trumpet weeds on the creek which is beautiful in form."[41] A date of 1862 for the exhibition of his *Ruffled Grouse and Quail* at the National Academy suggests that he may have introduced the dead-game theme before it was taken up by his father. In 1870 he exhibited a picture of woodcocks and in 1871 one of a bird's nest. Both were shown at the Brooklyn Art Association, where he had begun to exhibit in 1866 and where both Hills enjoyed an association with Gordon Ford that was extremely advantageous in terms of exposure and patronage. Ford was the treasurer of the Association and the owner of the influential *Brooklyn Daily Union*, which commended the Pre-Raphaelites regularly, and a major patron of the movement.

Young Hill spent part of 1864–65 in England, and thus, unlike his father, he had extensive contact with contemporary English painting. The following year his long exhibition association with Brooklyn began. In 1867 his volume of twenty-five etchings was published as *Sketches from Nature*. Probably John Henry Hill's most distinctive contribution to American art, it was also one of the first American manifestations of the etching revival. Charles Herbert Moore started to work in the medium in 1866, and in 1868 Henry Farrer began to investigate it with great success. The earliest etching in Hill's volume, *Chestnut Tree*, was dated 1859, however, well before "official" involvement in the mid-1860s. In the letterpress introduction Hill defined his Ruskinian bias: "I have reason to believe that the illustrations in this book . . . may . . . fall into the hands of those who are working in the green fields, among the tender grass and lovely flowers, and who seek to impress upon their fellow men the infinite beauty of God's handiwork. . . . To all such I would say, drawing a single flower, leaf, or bit of rock thoroughly well is something better worth doing than conjuring up pictures in the studio without a bit of accurate drawing. . . ."[42] Most of the dated etchings were made in 1866 and most of these are landscapes, often with very accurately rendered foreground foliage. In *Green River*, Hill even noted that the foreground consisted of yellow water lilies. Four of the etchings are more specifically still lifes, and they conveniently sum up Pre-Raphaelite innovations within the theme. These are *Thrush's Nest* and *Burdocks* of 1866; *Wild Flowers*, specifically designated as "of the Genus Bidens"; and a *Black Capped Titmouse*, with Hill's note that "dead birds make excellent studies; many of W. Hunt's most beautiful water-color drawings are of dead game; do not waste time on stuffed specimens if you can get the real."

A comparison is instructive between the younger Hill's etching of a dead bird and his father's water-color of a *Dead Blue Jay* of about the same time. The setting for John Henry Hill's subject is far less specific than is his father's—the dead jay lies on a tabletop, with a wall and the corner of a picture in the background. The younger Hill's titmouse lies on its back amidst a dark tomb of cross-hatched lines, which thin out toward the corners. In *Thrush's Nest* and *Burdocks*, he deliberately vignettes—leaving the corners bare—concentrating totally on the specified subject. In these etchings, Hill emphasizes a centralized and circular composition that even holds true in *Wild Flowers*, where surrounding leaves fill the "spandrel" corners. Centralized, circular, and vortexual compositions were a feature of J.M.W. Turner's most experimental canvases of the 1840s, and vignetting a feature of many of Turner's famous book illustrations. The younger Hill, in 1864–65, had the opportunity of studying the work of Turner firsthand in England. Yet vignetting and emphatically centralized compositions can be found in John Henry Hill's work, such as his 1858 watercolor of *Dandelions*, painted before his first trip abroad. The work of the younger Hill tends to be somewhat more abstract than his father's. In their still lifes this is evident both in the treatment of settings and in the somewhat looser and freer application of stippling and hatched lines in watercolor. Still, this greater spontaneity, even if present in John Henry's earliest work, must have been reinforced by his experience with Turner's art.

John Henry Hill spent 1878–79 in Europe, following an itinerary set forth for him by Ruskin himself.

John William Hill died shortly before his son's return, and John Henry helped arrange a memorial section at the Brooklyn Art Association exhibition in December 1879, with many of the nineteen works lent by Gordon Ford, Alexander Forman, and Edward Cary. In 1888 a second folio volume was published by the younger Hill: *John William Hill. An Artist's Memorial*; obituaries from the *Times* and the *Tribune* were reprinted with an affectionate, thoughtful biographical essay by Charles Herbert Moore. The volume is illustrated with an engraved portrait of John William Hill by his son and etchings by both men, those by John Henry Hill after oils, watercolors, and pencil drawings by his father.

The major event of 1857 in the progress of Pre-Raphaelitism in America was the New York exhibition of contemporary British art. Susan Casteras has written of its significance elsewhere in this volume. The exhibition may have had an even greater impact early the next year in Philadelphia, because it gained the greatest American adherent of the Pre-Raphaelite movement, William Trost Richards. Other artists, such as Thomas Farrer, assumed a more evangelical role, while the Hills remained more fully committed to the aesthetic than Richards. But Richards rose to international prominence, as the New York-based artists did not, and his subscription to Pre-Raphaelitism has been best remembered by later historians of American art.

Richards' interest in Ruskinian principles had been aroused somewhat earlier, but it was immediately after the British exhibition that Richards painted his *Blackberry Bush*. The impression made by Richards' painting was not merely local, but a rare case of carrying back not coals to Newcastle but brambles to London. The picture was exhibited in 1860 at the Royal Academy, and English reviewers commented on it favorably.[43] For the next five years Richards exhibited similar landscapes that emphasized foreground detail in Philadelphia, New York, Boston, and Troy; the *Blackberry Bush* appeared in Albany in 1864. Moreover, in March 1862 a group of Richards' Pre-Raphaelite studies was shown at Knoedler's commercial gallery in New York; the *Tribune* reviewer commented on "five studies of forest scenery by W. T. Richards of Philadelphia, of such exquisite delicacy of finish, and such fidelity to nature, that a pre-Raphaelite might blush to examine them. They have everything in them to cheat the imagination but the fresh fragrance of the green-wood scenes they represent."[44]

By 1862 Richards had come into contact with Thomas Farrer, the leading Pre-Raphaelite evangelist in this country. Farrer already owned a *Scene from Nature* by Richards, which was lent to the Pennsylvania Academy annual, and the two artists were in correspondence by October. Richards invited Farrer to visit him in Germantown at the end of the year, and Farrer in turn proposed Richards as a member of the Association for the Advancement of Truth in Art.

While Richards was primarily a landscapist and not a still-life painter, many of his pictures are filled with still-life detail. Works like his oil of 1859 *Ferns in a Glade* introduce the most popular Pre-Raphaelite motifs in a distinctly still-life manner, the receding background only sketchily defined. George Sheldon, in 1879, described Richards' art by quoting Henry T. Tuckerman's comment of 1867, which doubtless referred to paintings such as *Blackberry Bush* and *Ferns in a Glade*: "So carefully finished are his leaves, grasses, grain-stalks, weeds, stones, and flowers that we seem not to be looking at a distant prospect, but lying on the ground, with the herbage and blossoms directly under our eyes. Marvellous in accurate imitation are these separate objects in the foreground of his pictures; the golden-rod seems to wave, and the blackberry to glisten."[45] *Red Clover, Butter-and-Eggs, and Ground Ivy* of 1860 is about as close as Richards came to pure still life, though even here the various plants still grow in an almost junglelike profusion; but now with no suggestion of background. Tuckerman praised Richards and found him the most obsessed "of our landscape-painters who, in the minuteness of their limning, carry out in practice the extreme theory of the Pre-Raphaelites," although he bemoaned the loss of aerial gradation and distance and questioned "the ultimate triumph of a literalness so purely imitative."[46] In the following decade Richards maintained his reputation as the leading representative of Pre-Raphaelitism in this country. His significance for the development of the movement lay not only in his works but also in his influence on other artists, especially in Philadelphia, where he had both students and followers. Among his pupils in 1860 were Arthur Parton, George Lambdin, and Fidelia Bridges, all of whom exhibited Pre-Raphaelite tendencies at one time or another. None of Parton's early work as a landscapist has surfaced, but his *Spring Leaves* was shown at the National Academy in 1863.

Fidelia Bridges' adherence to Pre-Raphaelitism under Richards' guidance was longer lasting and more completely in the realm of still life. She, too, was associated with the "Brooklyn School" in the mid-1850s, when she first became aware of Ruskin. In 1860, she was invited to Philadelphia by her friend and colleague, the sculptor Anne Whitney, to attend some lectures by Richards, and then she drew at the Pennsylvania Academy. The summers of 1860 and 1861 were spent with Richards in Bethlehem, Pennsylvania. She began to exhibit at the Academy in 1862, and at the National Academy and the Brooklyn Art Association the following year. Working primarily in watercolor, she specialized in meticulous renderings of foreground nature—growing grasses, flowers, weeds, and ferns—against flattened backgrounds, or no background, presenting a microcosm of nature. By 1865 she was winning critical acclaim for her rather distinctive Pre-Raphaelite painting, the only one of many women artists associated with Pre-Raphaelitism who rose out of obscurity. Named an Associate of the National Academy of Design in 1873, she had her diploma portrait painted by Oliver Lay, a portraitist who had studied with Thomas Hicks, whom Bridges had met in spring 1865. In 1871 she began to summer in Stratford, Connecticut, attracted there by her neighbor, Lay. A residual Pre-Raphaelite-oriented group that deserves further study seems to have developed in rural Connecticut. About 1873 Bridges began to add ornithological subjects to her nature studies and went on to investigate birds along a broad horizontal coastal expanse, a later interest of her mentor, Richards.

By the time Richards had begun to work in a Pre-Raphaelite manner, the movement was strengthened by the arrival of Thomas Farrer, who was to become the dynamic force in propagating Ruskinian principles in American art. Farrer provided a unified presence and solicited adherents to a cause that united moral fervor behind a unique aesthetic system. Ironically, that very moral drive revealed the limitations of both the Pre-Raphaelite aesthetic and Farrer's own artistry.

Farrer's early years are insufficiently documented. We know that he studied with Ruskin at the Working Men's College in London—a cooperative movement promoted by Frederick Denison Maurice which aimed at bringing within the reach of the working classes the same kind of education enjoyed by the upper classes. It saw in education a way of life as well as a livelihood. Soon after the College was founded in 1854 at Number 31, Red Lion Square, Ruskin volunteered to assume the teaching of art; at the same time, he was writing the third and fourth volumes of *Modern Painters*. Ruskin also enlisted Dante Gabriel Rossetti as a teacher. Ruskin, Rossetti, and Lowes Dickinson, one of the original founders, taught every Thursday evening, four terms a year, except from August to October. Beginning with the Easter 1855 term, classes were subdivided, and Rossetti taught the figure while Ruskin and Dickinson taught elementary and landscape classes. When Ruskin did not attend the summer term, students would come to his home at Denmark Hill to sketch. He taught until May 1858 and returned for a term in spring 1860.

Farrer's pupilage at the College suggests a comparatively humble background. There, he studied with Ruskin, presumably early in the history of the College. Farrer was in America by 1857, possibly a year earlier, and soon seems to have made contact with the Hills and the New York dealer Samuel Avery. By November 1857, he wrote to Avery about the hopeless state of his finances and his isolation in Rockland County outside of Nyack, New York, near the Hills. Avery attempted to promote Farrer's drawings with collectors, such as William T. Walters of Baltimore. Farrer found in the Hills two artists very much in sympathy with his Ruskinian training and Pre-Raphaelite aesthetic bent, and, from the wealth of letters preserved, it seems that he was taken into their household and treated as a son and brother. By 1860 he was proselytizing for Pre-Raphaelite principles. He successfully took on the very young Frank Lathrop as a pupil. Farrer spent the summer of 1860 in England, where he no doubt saw Richards' *Blackberry Bush* at the Royal Academy, though he probably knew Richards' work earlier.[48]

On his return to America, Farrer became increasingly identified with Pre-Raphaelitism. In 1861–62 he served for some months in the Union Army, at Baltimore and Harper's Ferry, but he stayed in contact with Samuel Avery and Clarence Cook. On his release from the Army, Farrer intensified his promotion of the artistic principles he had been practicing, through exhibition, publication, and teaching. At this time, probably 1862, his younger brother, Henry Farrer, joined him; unlike Thomas, Henry Farrer remained here and made substantial contributions to American art.

It was well that Thomas Farrer brought such concerted energy and moral fervor to the still-incipient

Pre-Raphaelite cause, for by the late 1850s critical reaction was beginning to turn against its novelty. Adam Badeau, in *The Vagabond*, of 1859, devoted a whole chapter to castigating Pre-Raphaelitism. He wrote in part, "If we want nothing more of painters than absolute representations of old buildings, or copies of oak trees and fern leaves, Pre-Raphaelitism is very well; but if artists are to awake emotions, to excite sentiments, to arouse feeling, then Pre-Raphaelitism is not well. . . . This fault I find with the Pre-Raphaelite brethren—that their doctrine leads directly to a worship of the material; to an ignoring of the ideal. . . ."

More serious was the criticism of Ruskin and Pre-Raphaelitism within *The Crayon* itself, now that William Stillman was no longer its editor. In June 1859 *The Crayon* noted that "Pre-Raphaelitism had done much mischief by giving undue importance to manipulation and to insignificant details; the result is to smother the artist's individuality, or, in other words, the subjective element of Art. External nature being material form, and therefore objective, when nature comes before us in Art reflected by human sentiment, it becomes subjectively visible to us, and, according to our view, more beautiful because radiant with charm of man's spirit."[50] In September 1860 all five volumes of Ruskin's *Modern Painters* were reviewed in the magazine. Again the reviewer severely qualified his enthusiasm:

> Take a summary of that part of *Modern Painters* which may be held as Mr. Ruskin's best directed labor, consisting of certain geological, botanical and atmospheric facts, the result of his own observation, and which, being recorded from an artistic point of view, may be accepted as original matter in art literature . . . in the last volume the chapters on the Bud, Leaf, Branch, Stem, and the part devoted to Clouds—he insists upon a study of details as leading to the highest ends of art. All very well as an honest opinion, provided such an opinion be not accompanied with contemptuous judgement of those who minister to another and a higher phase of beauty, and who are not conspicuous for "intense definition" in art. Ruskin seems to be insensible to this higher phase of Beauty, and to the works of artists who best express it.[51]

The Crayon ceased publication in 1861, an early casualty of the Civil War, which concentrated intellectual and moral fervor to preserve the Union. Growing reaction against Pre-Raphaelitism may have been caused in part by increasing antipathy toward British support for the South. In late January 1863, Farrer summoned a group of artists and sympathetic laymen to his studio at 32 Waverly Place to form the Association for the Advancement of Truth in Art, and two months later to consider founding a journal to express the aspirations of the group. The organization and its journal are discussed at length in this volume by Linda Ferber. A good number of artists were at these gatherings and thus identified as subscribers or converts to Pre-Raphaelitism, or at least sympathetic to the movement. Some of them, such as Robert Pattison, seem to have been quite active, but very few of their works have surfaced. Others are completely unknown today, including a significant number of women, such as Annie McLane, Mary L. Booth, Louisa W. Cook, Sarah Barney, Miss S.M. Hitchcock, Sarah S. Tuthill, and Miss E.C. Field. Some may have been amateurs, and others may not have been artists at all. Miss Field did exhibit in the 1860s, and Annie McLane, who married Farrer in 1864, was a painter from Brooklyn whose still lifes were collected by Gordon Ford, although marriage may have curtailed her professional activity. Mary Booth became the editor of *Harper's Bazaar*. A number of the young painters associated with the Association and *The New Path* in 1864 and 1865 did leave their marks on American art, such as Henry Roderick Newman and Farrer's pupil, Frank Lathrop, but only Newman remained a staunch Pre-Raphaelite.

Farrer certainly served to some degree as a mentor to Newman as he did for Charles Herbert Moore. During the years he led the Association he also was active as a persuasive if controversial teacher at the Woman's Art School of Cooper Union in New York. How Farrer received his appointment and exactly when he began to serve are unclear; but his friend, Clarence Cook, had taught architectural drawing at Cooper Union from 1859 to 1861 and, when he left, may well have proposed Farrer. Farrer seems to have assumed the elementary class by November 1861, when Principal Henrietta Field reported that his group of thirty-six pupils allowed her to reduce her own teaching. She acknowledged the "wisdom of that rigid *adherence to Nature* which is the main principle of his teaching."[52] A later report on Farrer's methodology translates directly into a Ruskinian emphasis on still life and nature studies, and, in 1863–64, Farrer taught "Drawing and Painting, Still Life." Another report, undated, states that "the system favored by Mr. Cook is that initiated by Mr. Farrer; a very excellent one as far as it goes. Mr. Farrer's method is to teach pupils to copy with the most literal fidelity small objects from Nature, such as mosses, flowers and shells. This is very pleasant work, but . . . *very easy*. . . . These studies are . . . the mere alphabet of the science." This report was probably inspired by periodic visits of outside artists invited to comment on the school's system and written at a time when objections to Farrer's teaching were growing. Cook seems to have written the principal in support of Farrer, and an October 1865 article in the *Round Table* (when Farrer no longer was teaching at Cooper Union) condemned the opposition to his Pre-Raphaelite teaching principles, pointing to the lack of vitality in the more traditional classes taught by McEntee, Henry Peters Gray, and Worthington Whittredge. Farrer's "system consisted in the total abandonment of the paraphernalia and machinery of drawing and painting academies—the plaster casts, the lithographic models—and in putting in their place whatever natural objects could be easily procured and conveniently employed. Single leaves, small twigs and boughs, a lichened branch or stone, small stuffed birds (employed as studies in color), an apple or a pear, a pine-cone or a cluster of acorns—were placed before the pupils, and they were set to copying them with all the accuracy possible to their unaccustomed hands."[53] Farrer's methodology should be compared with that instilled in him by his teacher, John Ruskin, who was described at Working Men's College as "always trying their powers at first with a round plaster ball pendant from a string, then going on to plaster casts of natural leaves (all of which were paid for by him). Also, he frequently brought drawings by various artists, belonging to him, for the purpose of showing how certain effects were got, *e.g.*, the rounding of a pear by William Hunt."[54]

The impact of Farrer's teaching at Cooper Union is impossible to estimate. His most significant pupil was Margaret J. McDonald, who went on to an active career in New York. Frequently, she substituted for Henry Roderick Newman, who assumed Farrer's class at Cooper Union in 1865–66. Newman was never in robust health, and the Cooper Union *Monthly Report* for April 2, 1866, noted that "Miss McDonald, a graduate of Mr. Farrer, is going to take the class. She is quite capable of doing so." Farrer's role as a proselytizing instructor did not cease with his separation from Cooper Union. In summer 1865, he painted landscapes and still lifes at Northampton, Massachusetts. Soon after, he moved to Ashfield, Massachusetts, for the winter, and early in 1866 he was teaching a free drawing class at the Ashfield Academy. Perhaps the following winter season, Farrer became the teacher of Robert Brandegee of Berlin, Connecticut, who had studied with one of the Hills in Nyack. While the Hills probably referred Brandegee to Farrer, Brandegee's initial impetus toward art came from his aunt, Sarah Tuthill, who almost certainly was the "Miss S.S. Tuthill" of Brooklyn, the Cooper Union student connected with the Association for the Advancement of Truth in Art. A Tuthill was also a patron of Thomas Farrer.[55]

Farrer's instructional methodology, even more than Ruskin's, was integrally related to still life. Of all the American Pre-Raphaelites of the 1860s, excepting perhaps John William Hill, Farrer was most involved with the production of still-life and still-life-related paintings. An ultimate irony is that so few of his works are known, and only two are still lifes. Ironic, too, is our considerable knowledge about his still lifes as well as his other work through *The New Path*, the very periodical he promoted, and through subsequent criticism of Clarence Cook and Russel Sturgis. Discussions of Farrer's work, and Pre-Raphaelite work in general, also were eagerly presented in the *Brooklyn Daily Union*. The newspaper was owned by the patron of the movement, Gordon Ford, who appointed Edward Cary as editor. In 1863, Cary, in turn, hired Farrer to write on the Brooklyn Art Association exhibitions. Cary and his daughter, Elisabeth Luther Cary, ultimately became keepers of the flame of American Pre-Raphaelitism.

Given the traditional denigration of still-life painting, *The New Path* became one of the first periodicals to give it serious attention in its exhibition reviews, articles, and editorials. Initial notices in the National Academy annual of 1863 enthusiastically reviewed Arthur Parton's *Spring Leaves*, Sarah Wenzler's *Fruit*, and James Scudder's *Dead Game* along with two works by John William Hill, one of them his *Marsh Mallows*.[57] Hill and Wenzler were deemed the only artists to really paint fruit, and Scudder's work was found exceedingly well drawn, painted for love of facts alone. In the August issue, "Art as a Record" seems to paraphrase, while Americanizing, Ruskin's *Academy Notes* of 1857 and 1858 on still life:

Who of our readers has seen the Rhodora in bloom? Who goes into New England woods in May? Why do none of our Artists go, and paint the flower for us? . . . Who has painted Thoreau's favorite plant, the "Poke Berry"? Who has painted a cherry tree in full bearing, or a branch of it, the red jewels set along the green ridge of each full-leafed branch? Who has painted our magnificent flowering shrubs as they look in May, the Spiraeas and the Hawthorns and the "Golden shower" of the Laburnum? Some one tried last spring to paint a bank of violets and liver leafs; we were grateful for the attempt, but it ought to be done again and much better done . . . Remember Mr. J.W. Hill's "Marsh Mallows," in the last Academy—that is the way it ought to have been done. . . .[58]

The New Path reviewer of the National Academy show in 1864 especially commended Thomas Farrer's pencil drawings of *Horseradish* and *Spring Weeds*, specifying the latter as American Hellebore, or Indian Poke, and admired a *Bird's Nest* by a Hannah Millard of Englewood, New Jersey, for being as carefully drawn as Farrer's work.[59]

Both of Farrer's drawings were among the set of ten photographs offered for distribution by *The New Path* that July, a working set of nature studies. Most were still lifes, and half were after pictures by Farrer: the pencil drawing, *Spring Weeds*, fifteen inches high, done by a brook behind the New Jersey Palisades in late spring 1863; his pencil drawing of a *Pumpkin Vine*, done the previous summer at Catskill, New York; *Horseradish*; *May in the Woods* of 1864, a more recent drawing of old blackberry vine stems with briars and new-sprung wild flowers with a foreground of large-lobed Bloodroot leaves, thickly growing anemones, white strawberry flowers and leaves, one blue and two or three white violets; and a sepia *Yellow Water Lily*. Among the other still lifes were Henry Roderick Newman's pencil drawing of *Ferns*; John Henry Hill's pen drawing of *Mulleins*, a tangle and confusion of wayside weeds; and Charles Herbert Moore's pencil drawing of *Mandrakes*, a foreground clump of mandrake plants before an open forest.

By spring 1864, Clarence Cook had become art critic for *The New-York Tribune*. His architect-colleague Peter B. Wight, in a reminiscence of Russell Sturgis, his former architectural partner, observed that "one cause of the discontinuance of *The New Path* was that its writers attracted the attention of publishers of journals of wide circulation. . . . " Sturgis left next to become "the art critic of 'The Nation' from its first appearance. . . ."[60] Cook's Pre-Raphaelite preferences soon surfaced in his multicolumned, serial reviews of the National Academy of Design exhibitions. Many of his *Tribune* columns featured one or two artists or even one or two works, sometimes praising, sometimes damning, but always with perception, intelligence, and fervor. Cook's consideration of Thomas Farrer on May 21, 1864, typically, dealt only with his landscapes, while on June 4 he mentioned Virginia Granbery's *Cherries* and Sarah Wenzler's *Currants*, the former more mature, the latter evincing more love, but he questioned the choice of lesser subjects. On May 21, 1864, however, Cook defended the Pre-Raphaelites and their nature studies. Referring to the works at the Academy by his associates, he told the public to "stop buying line engravings, copper-plates, etchings; buy these drawings from nature. More pleasure, and of a more enduring kind, more love of Nature, more understanding of the real uses of Art will flow to you out of one such drawing as this before us, of a spray of blackberry blossoms; or this of a daisy by John Henry Hill; this mullen, or this tree trunk by Farrer—simple drawings, all, in pen and ink—than from all the Raphael Morghens, or Stranges, or Marc Antonios, that were ever sold to deluded buyers."[61]

At this time the architect Peter Bonnett Wight was becoming prominent in the Association. He was engaged in constructing two notable art galleries: the National Academy of Design, at Fourth Avenue and 23rd Street in New York, begun in 1863 and opened in April 1865; and Street Hall at Yale University in New Haven, built from 1864 to 1866. Wight's National Academy was one of the finest embodiments of Ruskinian Gothic in America. Wight had fully imbibed Ruskin's principles of art and architecture, and he recognized them in the work of Thomas Farrer, to whom he wrote in August 1863: "Corn fields and meadows were not made to paint, they are God's work as man's improvements . . . God speaks to us in the mossy rocks, the trickling rivulet and the rustling leaves—you are the interpreter of that language, and in it must teach man to love and glorify their Maker."[62] Like many Association members, Wight owned pictures by his colleagues, including works by John Henry Hill and Charles Herbert Moore, as well as some pencil studies by Farrer, his *Jack-in-the-Pulpit* (fig. 21) and his *Orchid Cactus Flower*, the only extant still lifes by Farrer. Such drawings may have inspired the decorations of the Academy building. Following Ruskin's recommendations, Wight attempted to replicate both the methodology and the naturalistic foliate detail of authentic Gothic buildings. For the capitals of interior columns, and the lilies and the bullrushes on the staircase spandrels, Wight trained his workmen to study drawings, probably

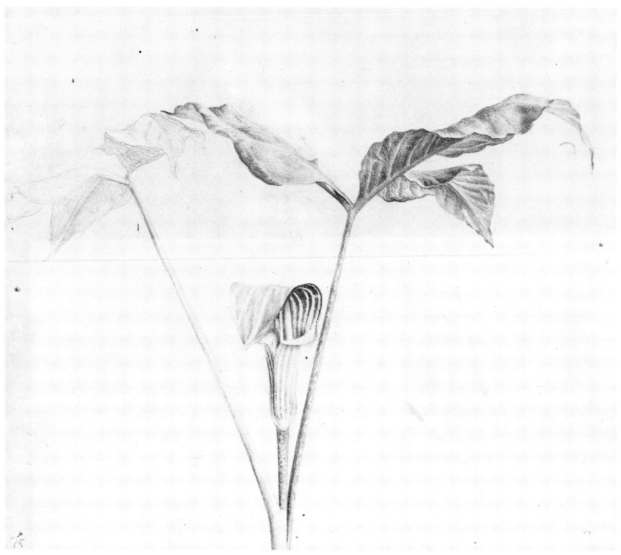

Figure 21
Thomas C. Farrer
Jack-in-the-Pulpit *circa* 1860
Pencil on paper, 8⅝₁₆ × 9½ in. (21.2 × 24.2 cm.)
Collection: The Art Institute of Chicago, Department of Architecture
Cat. no. 6

like Farrer's, photographs, and actual plants, and to make clay models based upon their study in order to emulate the realistic stone carving of Gothic architectural ornamentation. The workmen took pleasure in finding motifs in the field and among garden plants, though some of the Academy's carved work was not considered sufficiently stylized. Wight admitted to variations in the carving because of the inexperience of his workmen; but he was particularly pleased with the capitals and the native water plants adorning the drinking fountain. All of the Academy ornamentation has now disappeared, but the carved foliate decoration of the capitals and bases of the columns of Street Hall at Yale still remains.[63]

The year 1865 was the only one in which Pre-Raphaelite principles held sway in three of the principal critical journals in New York—*The New Path,* the *Tribune,* and the newly founded *Nation.* Thomas Farrer, Moore, and Newman all exhibited still lifes in the National Academy spring exhibition. Newman showed four, including works owned by Russell Sturgis, Charles Eliot Norton, and John E. Lauer, a major Pre-Raphaelite patron who also lent landscapes by Farrer and Moore. Cook's full column on Farrer of June 5 began auspiciously, but ended by ridiculing his attempts at the figure. Characteristically, it ignored Farrer's studies of a dandelion and a pumpkin vine. Cook praised Moore's *Study in Catskill Valley* but made no mention of his *Mandrakes*, owned by Farrer. Sturgis, however, commended Farrer's still-life studies as "work of a class which would have been thought peculiar to Mr. Farrer but that Mr. Moore has one quite similar in this exhibition. The delicate beauty of the drawing of the large leaves on the pumpkin vine is hardly to be surpassed." *The New Path* writer also admired Farrer's two nature studies, but both he and Sturgis agreed with Cook about Farrer's figure paintings.[64]

Perhaps such criticism turned Farrer increasingly to still life. During his summer in Northampton, Massachusetts, in 1865, he painted two of his finest known paintings of the 1860s, the views of Mount Tom and of Northampton. But despite the wealth of attractive scenery, he did not neglect still life, especially fruit subjects. A private showing of his work in October at Colonel J.B. Parsons' on West Street in Northampton was reviewed by the *Northampton Free Press* on October 13: "There was a large number of fruit pieces, presenting an exceedingly attractive appearance. High coloring is a peculiarity of the school of artists to which Mr. Farrer belongs, and these fruit paintings are therefore among the most attractive of his productions."[65] Farrer exhibited with the New York Artists' Fund Society in 1864, and again in 1865 when he was joined by Moore, Robert Pattison, and Fidelia Bridges. The Society had been formed in 1860 to assist indigent artists and their families.

Again, Farrer's work was reviewed at length and faulted. Sturgis, in the *Nation*, criticized his inability to paint middle-distance landscapes convincingly and to combine local with general truths, but he observed that "fruit on a table he has painted admirably; fruit and flowers on the tree he has painted admirably; a bush with large leaves and close at hand he has both drawn and colored admirably ... any near and tolerably simple thing, of which all the details can be thoroughly made out and elaborated, he can almost perfectly render."[66] Farrer seems to have taken a cue from the adverse criticism of his figure and landscape work, along with the growing reception of his still lifes. In December 1865 he held an exhibition of eighteen watercolors at Knoedler's in New York. The majority of these were still lifes—many of them fruit pieces—done the previous summer. The exhibition was reviewed at length in *The Nation*, and among the still lifes one of dead blue jays and some of the fruit paintings were especially admired. For Sturgis the paintings were noble work, but he found Farrer limited to indoor subjects. Considering his Pre-Raphaelite affiliations, the critic made a curious comment when he said Farrer's "backgrounds are happily chosen. The fruit in the drawings of the great master of this kind of subject, William Hunt, is generally laid on the ground, with a bit of moss or grass for background. There is something incongruous in the juxtaposition by bank-side of a pear and a bunch of grapes, or an apple, three plums, and a handful of nuts. But the same group on a plate or table-cloth is comprehensible and looks real."[67]

Cook, in the *Tribune*, both admired and denigrated Farrer's work in the Knoedler show, objecting to the very treatment Sturgis had admired. These "finished studies of fruit and flowers from nature made this past summer," he wrote, are the "most striking and effective work that has been done in watercolor in this country." But "two of these drawings," he continued, "are seriously injured by the introduction of an unendurable queer green, which has given us a headache. Why could he not have put his fruit on the grass or on a lichened rock. Nature seldom makes a table-cloth. She has done it, in times past, but she has of late turned her attention to other things. This of Mr. Farrer's she had, of course, nothing to do with."[68]

None of the major American Pre-Raphaelites exhibited at the National Academy in 1866, because they were increasingly dissatisfied with the installations of their delicate work. Margaret McDonald and Henry Newman each showed several works, Newman a *Study of Fruit*, and Robert J. Pattison exhibited six pictures. Sturgis, in the *Nation*, found Pattison's *The Young Mullein* remarkably successful. The absence of Farrer, Moore, and the Hills was acknowledged universally and generally deplored. The critic for *Harper's New Monthly Magazine*, for instance, recognized the Pre-Raphaelite manner in work by McDonald and Pattison, but noted, "not without regret, that the Pre-Raphaelite brethren are very imperfectly represented." Ever-cantankerous Clarence Cook made a long plea for their participation. "All in all," he concluded, "if they throw the blame upon the Academy, then we charge them with hiding their light under a bushel, and with doing it in pride of heart, and thinking that the people are incapable of understanding their work." In this June 27 review, Cook noted that Farrer again had sent his work to Knoedler's rather than to the Academy.[69]

Pre-Raphaelite dissatisfaction with the National Academy may well have been justified, but the Academy at the time may have reflected the uneasiness of many outsiders. Other major dailies in New York, such as the *Times* and the *Evening Post*, were often far less sympathetic, and even the perceptive writers in the weekly *Round Table* and the *Continental Monthly* found the work too literal, lacking feeling, mystery, and the superstructure of beauty. The *Round Table* critic, reviewing the National Academy show of 1864, said that "they offend not because they are truthful but because they are limited in their truth."[70] These writers recognized the work of both the more conventional painters and that of the new men, but they sought some kind of compromise between the two schools—between the "ideal" and the "real." American art writing of the mid-1860s is filled with the names of hopefuls championed by the critics, artists who were sometimes praised to extremes for a number of years, who continued to exhibit for decades, and who are totally forgotten today. Most of these artists were far more obscure than even the Pre-Raphaelites themselves, and most were landscape specialists, such as Frank Anderson, Henry A. Ferguson, or Stephen J. Shaughnessy.

None of this obscurity is more perplexing than that of the brothers Victor Moreau Griswold and Casimir Clayton Griswold. Casimir Griswold, particularly, seems to have been the great hope of American art in the mid-1860s. His work was first seen at the Academy in 1861, but his *December*, shown in 1864, took the critics by storm. The *Round Table* called him "a painter who has given with truth and simplicity a phase of winter that is new in art," and compared "the unaffected truths of Mr. Griswold's picture with the more pretentious literalness of the landscapes by Mr. J. Henry Hill and Mr. Farrer." Even the Pre-Raphaelite-oriented writers acclaimed Griswold. A suggestion of what Griswold's painting was like at this time is offered by the fictional interests and descriptions that appear in the roman à clef *Hugo Blanc, the Artist*, a novel of contemporary artistic life published in 1867 by Victor Moreau Griswold. In one episode Hugo's sister, Louise, and her companion return from a stroll in the woods, and Louise tells her brother that "we did not pass an old moss-covered log, or gray old rock, or a wild patch of herbage and grass, but she [her companion] would exclaim, 'Oh, what a beautiful study for Hugo!'"[71] The Ruskinian landscape and the Ruskinian ideal thus provided the inspiration for Victor Griswold's tale and perhaps the basis for his brother's art. There is no evidence of intercourse between Casimir Griswold and the American Pre-Raphaelites, although they were obviously very aware of each others' work. But, by 1866, Griswold had become significant enough to join another artist on the movement's periphery, William Hennessy, as a board member of the Artists' Fund Society.

At the Society's December exhibition that year the Pre-Raphaelites enjoyed their greatest triumph and their widest New York exposure. One may assume that the sympathies of their colleagues on the board must have encouraged Farrer and his colleagues, as opposed to the Academy's disdain, and they certainly realized the need for public exposure. Furthermore, artists had been urged to submit to the Society the very kind of painting in which the Pre-Raphaelites specialized. Perhaps what stimulated abundant Pre-Raphaelite representation in the Society's 1866 exhibition was the interest in watercolor. In 1865, and possibly earlier, watercolors were not accepted by the Society. Sturgis that year, in the *Nation*, mentioning both European and American work, commented that the Society "rejects nothing, apparently, except water-color drawings, though why it rejects these so uniformly we have never been informed."[72] This policy was reversed because of the enthusiasm and activity of John M. Falconer, an active promoter of the medium since the days of the earliest watercolor society in New York in the early 1850s. Falconer chose to organize a separate watercolor section for the Society's 1866 show, because exhibitions of oils had been lagging. John F. Kensett, president of the Artists' Fund Society, wrote on the 1866 show in the Society's annual report that year: "Lovers of Art are indebted for the most rare and beautiful collection of water color drawings ever placed before the public in this city, marking an era in that department. . . ."[73]

Falconer and his committee did not choose this course to further the cause of Pre-Raphaelitism, but the Pre-Raphaelites were natural participants. Falconer, like Hennessy and Griswold, certainly knew many of the new group and may have been sympathetic to them and their ideals. Falconer, John William Hill, and even William Stillman, had been members of the early New York Society for the Promotion of Painting in Water Colors, and Falconer was an active participant in the Brooklyn Art Association, which was especially sympathetic to Farrer, the Hills, and other Pre-Raphaelites. Earlier, in 1866, Falconer joined Alfred Cadart's French Etching Club in New York, which also had enlisted John Henry Hill, Charles Herbert Moore, and Henry Roderick Newman.

So unusual and so impressive was the watercolor section that it received a separate review by Stillman Conant in *Galaxy* titled "The Exhibition of Water Colors." Conant observed that "it was the largest collection of the kind ever gathered together in America; and as such, and also as the commencement of an earnest effort to popularize the art of water-color painting in this country, it had an importance quite distinct from the merits of the paintings on exhibition ... the art has been totally neglected in this country; partly because it was popularly regarded as a kind of 'lady's art,' and partly because it is more easy to obtain a commonplace proficiency in oils." After discussing the more traditional Charles Parsons as dean of American watercolorists, Conant spoke at length of the Hills, "some of whose finest work was in the exhibition" and who "belong to an entirely different school of art—a school severe, realistic and limited in range. Neither of them has yet produced a picture, all their works being nothing more than studies or sketches. As such their drawings are deserving of the very highest praise for accuracy of form, beauty and purity of color, and exquisite delicacy of finish. In these qualities they are unrivalled in American art." Conant singled out the still lifes of John William Hill as "perfection of imitation."[74]

All the Pre-Raphaelites were in the exhibition, and Charles Eliot Norton even lent his watercolor of *Dante Meeting Beatrice* by Dante Gabriel Rossetti. Never again were the Americans so well represented at the Artists' Fund Society, and this was the sole time when a substantial number of their still lifes were prominently displayed. Over a dozen Pre-Raphaelite still lifes and nature studies were in the exhibition, as well as some obviously related works, such as John B. Duffey's *Nothing but Leaves*. Yet despite the acclaim, the innovations of 1866 were not continued; watercolor painting did not remain a significant part in the Society's annual shows; and the Pre-Raphaelites ceased to participate in them. Changes on the Society's board may have been responsible in part, for in 1867 Hennessy and Griswold no longer served. More important, dissatisfaction among the watercolorists at the installation and handling of their work by the Society at the National Academy, where the 1866 show was held, led to the exploration of alternative exhibition possibilities. Many of the watercolors had been relegated to the Academy corridor, and some of the frames had been tampered with to make room for more pictures. This occurred with a dead-game still life, the single submission of Gilbert Burling. Burling set out to form a separate watercolor society, with the agreement of Samuel Colman and the assistance of Falconer and others, and they moved swiftly, holding their first meeting in early December. A year later the new Society of American Painters in Water Color held its first exhibition at the National Academy. Among the active members of the new organization were Thomas and Henry Farrer, Henry Roderick Newman, and Charles Herbert Moore, although Moore did not exhibit with the group for a number of years. The other Pre-Raphaelites did, however. John Henry Hill showed almost a dozen works, and many of the younger artists related to the movement, such as Robert Brandegree, Sarah S. Tuthill, Maria Nims, Nina Moore, and Miss E.C. Field, were also included. Of the approximately forty Pre-Raphaelite works in the first Watercolor Society show, almost half were still lifes.

The Pre-Raphaelites, nevertheless, did not particularly shine at the Watercolor Society exhibitions. Perhaps, in part, this was because they were overwhelmed by the profusion and diversity of entries, and perhaps also because the movement was winding down in these last years of the 1860s. The critic for *Putnam's* noted that "their studies of fruits are exquisitely finished," but Thomas Farrer was told to "confine his ambition to subjects within the reach of his powers—peaches, plums, bits of grass, a leaf or two, a single strip of bark with a little moss clinging to it. Such things he can paint with exquisite delicacy of drawing and color. . . ."[75]

In the second Water Color Society Show, in winter 1868–69, the Pre-Raphaelites exhibited just over half the number of pictures shown the previous year, and about half of these again were still lifes. Henry Farrer and Margaret McDonald's work was admired, but the work of the others was either ignored or disparaged. In 1869–70, the group had lost cohesiveness and there were even fewer Pre-Raphaelite-related works. The Hills, Thomas Farrer, and Charles Moore did not exhibit in the third annual, although they returned to Society exhibitions of the 1870s; Henry Roderick Newman carried the movement's principles abroad; but after 1867, Pre-Raphaelitism was no longer in the mainstream of American art.

Yet in 1867 the American Pre-Raphaelites, except for the Hills, returned in force for the last time to the National Academy annual. Thomas Farrer was particularly well represented with eight works, most of them still lifes, from lenders associated with the old Association for the Advancement of Truth in Art; Miss Tuthill loaned *Peaches* and Mary Booth, *Fleur de Lis*. Some major Pre-Raphaelite patrons also lent works, such as John E. Lauer with his *Chinese Cup and Saucer* and William C. Gilman with his *Summer Flowers* and a picture of *Fruit*; only Farrer's *Dandelions* seems to have been for sale. The still lifes were discussed at length by the critics, and some of them, such as *Fleur de Lis* and *Summer Flowers*, were admired. Yet Cook continued to denigrate Farrer's work, especially his landscapes: "While we do not admit that Mr. Farrer's success in painting landscape has been very great thus far, we hope to see him devote himself to it steadily, and give as little time as may be to these studies of fruit and flowers. . . ." And of the entire movement he complained that "the artists do not get the *effect* of nature; they have produced principally studies of fruit, flowers, birds—many of them very precious—but still incapable of making any profound impression of the public."[76]

Cook's attack in the *Tribune* on June 14, however, hit Farrer hardest. Cook charged him with having little sense of beauty, lacking a feeling for color, and rarely treating his subject tastefully. Farrer finally retorted with a letter written on June 19 and published on July 8, in which he briefly reviewed his career, pointing out that only late in 1859 had he begun to paint out-of-doors; that not until 1863 had he completed a finished oil study outdoors; and that from winter 1861 until spring 1865 he had spent four years in a vain attempt to teach. Therefore, only for two years had he been able to study uninterruptedly.[77]

For Cook, Farrer's significance by 1867 seemed to lie in his proselytizing spirit and the inspiration he offered pupils, rather than in his own art. That year some of Farrer's followers were well represented in the Academy annual by still lifes. Charles Herbert Moore had come into contact with Farrer's Pre-Raphaelitism by 1860 and had become an avid convert in that decade, passionately defending it in *The New Path*. He specialized in landscape and painted still lifes only occasionally. In 1867, however, among his four works in the Academy show were two fruit pieces owned by Joseph and Samuel Wilde, two major Pre-Raphaelite patrons. Cook ignored the still lifes to review the two Catskill landscapes; but Sturgis praised Moore's *Apples*, although he objected to its placement in the show.[78]

Samuel Wilde lent Henry Farrer's *Dead Bird* to the Academy show, marking the first appearance of Thomas's brother in the annuals. Henry Farrer arrived in America about 1862 and trained under Thomas. In the late 1860s and early 1870s, he became a leading American watercolorist, specializing in harbor scenes in a late Luminist manner. He also produced a number of soft, delicate studies of a few flowers in neutral settings, lovely pieces that represent his still-life manner (cat. nos. 101 and 102). In the late 1860s, however, he exhibited an equal number of fruit and floral watercolors as well as several dead-bird studies. The fruit paintings were especially well received. *Study of Apples* was in the first Watercolor Society show in December 1867 and was judged by the *New York Herald* critic to be "one of the very best studies in the exhibition . . . No picture better illustrates the unlimited scope of water colors. Such Pre-Raphaelitism as this the most prejudiced must accept." And by 1869, the writer in *Putnam's* found his *Currants* at the Water Color Society "beautifully painted, natural as life, and very tempting." Thomas Farrer must have found it particularly galling to read such commendations while his own picture shown that year, *Atlantic Ocean, 2,000 Miles From Land*, was called a "wretched daub" that should have been rejected.[79] Henry Farrer rose to greatest prominence as a pioneer of the etching revival. He began to work in this medium about 1868, and by 1870 had begun a series of *Scenes of Old New York*. In it a Pre-Raphaelite specificity was still evident, and the Ruskinian fascination with the humble, the old, and the accidental was transfered from transcriptions of nature to a loving description of old, worn brickwork and paving stones, among the relics of the urban past.

Henry Roderick Newman from Easton, New York, also was guided by Thomas Farrer, beginning in 1863. Newman was born the son of a doctor who encouraged him to study medicine. But the boy manifested artistic inclinations early, supported by his mother. After studying from nature around Stockbridge, Massachusetts, Newman exhibited a group of landscapes at the National Academy in 1861. His father's death in 1863 may have confirmed him in the artistic profession, and that summer at Factory Point in the Green Mountains of Vermont, he did fieldwork, made firsthand pencil studies from nature, read *The New Path*, and corresponded with Farrer. He sent a drawing of *Ferns* to Farrer in October, saying that it was full of faults but hoped there was also some truth; and he told Farrer he would turn to color studies the following year. Newman returned to Factory Point in spring 1864, but that May he resumed public exhibition of his work, perhaps encouraged by Farrer. These were still lifes, and while landscapes always remained a staple for him, still-life painting became an equal and significant aspect of his art. That year he exhibited a *Corn and Apples* and a *Study of a Duck* at the spring exhibition of the Brooklyn Art Association. The following year *Corn and Apples* appeared at the National Academy, along with three other still lifes. By this time Newman had picked up some very distinguished patronage: *Study of Pigeons* was owned by Charles Eliot Norton, *Study of a Lemon* belonged to Russell Sturgis, *Milkweed* to John E. Lauer, and *Corn and Apples* to "S. W.", presumably Samuel Wilde.

Newman and the landscape painter Robert J. Pattison were the only leading Pre-Raphaelites to exhibit at the National Academy in 1866. Newman showed a landscape and another fruit picture at the Academy as well as still lifes that year at Brooklyn and at the Artists' Fund Society. In 1867 he again showed two works at the National Academy, a Stockbridge landscape and a *Japanese Still Life*. Both Sturgis and Cook considered the latter at length, and while both seemed somewhat puzzled by the painting, they were extremely impressed by Newman's rich, decorative color scheme of red, black, and gold.[80] Newman came to concentrate more and more on flower pictures but of cultivated varieties such as camellias and geraniums, or often flowers of Oriental derivation—Japan lilies, Japanese anemones.

Another Farrer student at the 1867 Academy exhibition was Frank Lathrop, who exhibited his *Study of a Beech Tree*. Lathrop's early, Pre-Raphaelite works have not been identified, and little is known about his early years. He first exhibited, at the Academy in 1865, a *Study of a Calla Lilly*, and showed two fruit still lifes at the Water Color Society in 1870. In 1867, however, Lathrop had left New York to study at the Royal Academy in Dresden, and from 1870 to 1873 he worked in London in the studio of Ford Madox Brown. Thus Lathrop seems to be the only American artist allied with the movement who actually worked with the English Pre-Raphaelites. In London, Lathrop associated with many artists of the later phase of Pre-Raphaelitism, such as Edward Burne-Jones, William Morris, and Spencer Stanhope, working particularly with stained glass and other decorative work. He returned home in 1873 and continued to work in stained glass and in mosaic; he also established a specialty in mural painting, beginning as an assistant to John La Farge at Trinity Church, Boston, in 1878. One of his first American commissions was to illustrate *House Beautiful*, published in 1878 by Clarence Cook, but Lathrop's well-known Pre-Raphaelite style of the last decades of the century had little to do with his formative years with Farrer.

One other significant Farrer pupil in the Academy show of 1867 was Margaret J. McDonald. Among the most active artists associated with Pre-Raphaelitism, well into the 1870s, McDonald first came to public notice in spring 1866 at the Academy. Clarence Cook championed her watercolor landscapes—having learned of her portrait drawing during a studio visit in April—praising her "study from Nature, and from Nature only." He attributed this devotion to Farrer's inspiration; her teacher was "himself, an unwearied student." By the end of 1866, at the Artist's Fund Society, McDonald had branched out into floral still life, and she ultimately devoted most of her talents to this genre. The *Tribune* reported in 1867 that she sent little to the National Academy show because "she is getting ready to send the best she can do to the Fall Exhibition of the Water Color Society."[81] And beginning in the late 1860s, the Water Color Society and the Brooklyn Art Association consistently included her watercolors, primarily flower still lifes. In the late 1860s she lived in Wappinger's Falls, north of New York, and she taught in Tarrytown in the summers during the 1870s. From 1871 she lived in Manhattan but maintained her Brooklyn ties; she taught at the school of the Brooklyn Art Association in 1874, perhaps because of her friendship with the Gordon Fords. Sometime in the mid-1870s, her work may have taken a more decorative turn, for in 1873 she exhibited a *Flowers on Satin* at the Association, and from 1877 she began to give her address as 4 East 20th Street, the home of the newly founded Society of Decorative Art. The society specialized particularly in embroidery and other needlework by women, as well as in other decorative arts. Its premises were taken over later by the New York Exchange for Women's Work. Little is heard of McDonald after the

1870s, though she exhibited at the Brooklyn Art Association in 1881 and 1884. Margaret McDonald died in 1892, a year after her teacher, Thomas Farrer.

Virtually all members of the Pre-Raphaelite group joined in summer 1867 in a culminating public presentation, an exhibition mounted to inaugurate the new art building at Yale College in New Haven built by the Pre-Raphaelite architect Peter Bonnett Wight. The event was propitious, made to order for celebrating members of the Association for the Advancement of Truth in Art. Sixty-nine oils, watercolors, and drawings—constituting almost twenty-five percent of the exhibition—were by Pre-Raphaelite painters. Of these, about a third were for sale; the rest were lent by about twenty owners, many of whom were either colleagues such as Farrer, Cook, Sturgis, and Wight, or leading collectors of Pre-Raphaelite art, Dr. Lauer, the Wildes, and especially William C. Gilman, the major single lender, with five works by Farrer, two by John William Hill, and one each by Moore and Henry Farrer. Surprisingly, the collector Gordon Ford, and the artist John Henry Hill were not represented. Hill's absence is unexplained, although at just this time he was deeply involved in producing his elaborate book of etchings, *Sketches from Nature.*

Such unprecedented Pre-Raphaelite representation probably had several causes. One was the abundant discussion recently engendered by their work—an art exhibition for a new and "modern" building naturally would include what was then avant-garde. Wight's own Ruskinian affiliations would lead to invitations to his colleagues. And certainly the presence of Daniel C. Gilman, professor of geography at Yale, on the executive committee for the exhibition, would provide a conduit for those artists so heavily patronized by his brother, the collector William Gilman.

While the majority of paintings in the Yale show, like those in the British Exhibition of 1857, were not Pre-Raphaelite, works in the style were hung and catalogued together, and they attracted great attention. The Pre-Raphaelite style, with its specificity and clarity of form, and above all its brilliance of color, compensated for the still limited numbers and small scale of these landscapes, still lifes, and portraits. Indeed, still life constituted an especially large portion—almost thirty—of the Pre-Raphaelite paintings. Thomas Farrer showed more pictures than any other artist, and eight of his twenty examples were still lifes. Over half of Henry Farrer's eleven were still lifes, as were three of Newman's four pictures, and several by John William Hill. Even Charles Herbert Moore showed four fruit and flower pictures, and Robert J. Pattison, almost exclusively a landscape and animal painter, showed a rare picture of a *Dandelion.* Only Margaret McDonald avoided the theme in her six pictures, but all four by the otherwise unknown Maria Nims were still lifes.

Local Connecticut newspapers all singled out the Pre-Raphaelite contingent, even as they stated their reservations. A writer for the *Hartford Daily Courant* noted on July 12 that in the south gallery of the new Street Hall "hang close together the largest collection yet brought together of our American pre-Raphaelites—Farrer, Moore, and Hill. They look at first repulsive, so hard and harsh, and real are their every feature, but after an half an hour's study, . . . I begin to wonder whether, after all, these men and this school have not a future, and whether revolutions in art are not as necessary as revolutions in politics." And the writer in the *New Haven Daily Palladium* emphasized that "perhaps no pictures challenged so much comment as the collection of the Pre-Raphaelite works. They will NOT be passed by. The marvellous finish and the almost painful minuteness of detail can only be appreciated after long and close study. Whether admired or not they must not be lightly condemned because they seem strange. The more they are examined, the less likely will any one be to dismiss them with a shrug of ignorant contempt."[82] Local writers were more appreciative and discerning than the *New York Times* critic whose report on July 19 was published three days later and offered the usual reservations. But such reservations paled beside the enthusiasm of Sturgis and Cook. In the *Nation* of August 8, Sturgis called the Wight building the best picture gallery in the country and devoted most of his column to the Pre-Raphaelite display. He gave special attention to the still-life entries, calling Farrer's *Summer Flowers*, in the National Academy's spring exhibition, a real success and one of the numerous "foreground studies," which also included Farrer's *May* (of dandelions), *June* (of columbines), another of dandelions, and another of columbines. He singled out Farrer's *Trailing Arbutus* as the finest of all, a work not exhibited before except at Knoedler's. He mentioned a group of Moore's still lifes: *Pansies,* a *Study of an Orange,* and especially his three large *Apples* on a Japanese tray, which he called "the most perfect instance yet given of Mr. Moore's way of work." Of John William Hill's *Fruit* he wrote, "The moderation of this work, the noble quietness of it, the absence of any attempt to get projection and 'force' at the expense of color and delicacy, the charm of the suggested detail of its background are all parts of its excellence. It is within its necessary limitations a thoroughly great drawing."[83]

Cook's enthusiasm was more measured. His detailed review in the *Tribune* on August 14 offered more encomiums for some of the still lifes than for the landscapes. He was enthusiastic about Hill's *Fruit*, but even more so about Henry Roderick Newman's *Raspberries and Blackberries*, owned by Samuel Wilde, which Cook referred to as "a beautiful and truthful study likely enough to pass unnoticed from its entire avoidance of the usual extravagances of fruit painters, who seem to deal at shops where fruit is grown in Brobdignag or Utopia. Mr. Newman's berries are such as one finds growing by the roadside, large and small together, homely, but fully ripe." Cook also singled out Maria R. Nims "whose name is new to the public, but who gives good promise." Perceptively, he observed that this exhibition marked an era in the history of the group: "Thus far, they have worked a good deal in common, and with many points of likeness. Now divergence has begun, and a strong individuality is making itself felt."[84]

About 1867 the Pre-Raphaelite movement attracted its last significant adherent, though Robert Brandegee, the Berlin, Connecticut, artist, was not part of the Yale exhibition. He showed his *Lobelia* at the Water Color Society later that year and continued to exhibit watercolor nature studies in New York for several years—*Laurel* at the Academy in 1868 and *Laurel, Morning Glories,* and *Tulips* at the Water Color Society in 1869. His work generally reflects that of his teachers, John Henry Hill and Thomas Farrer. Although Brandegee's *Apple Blossoms* (cat. no. 87) resembles the blossoming fruit tree branches of John William Hill, the round format and the decorative sense in Brandegee's early watercolors suggest the work of the younger Hill. Brandegee, like Farrer, became a teacher, instructing several women in Hartford for two years, before he went to Europe in 1872 on the advice of the Connecticut sculptor Truman Bartlett. Brandegee's painting changed radically with European training, and the rather monumental figure and portrait work that characterizes his maturity relates to the early, pre-Impressionist painting of his longtime friend Julian Alden Weir. Yet Brandegee's reverence for nature retained Ruskinian overtones that derived from his instruction under the Pre-Raphaelites in the 1860s. His book of essays of 1901, *From the Open Book of Nature,* gives clear evidence of this influence.[85]

Despite the appearance of new artists such as Brandegee and Nims in exhibitions of the late 1860s, Cook's suggestion that the Pre-Raphaelite movement be evaluated was well taken. Evident in still-life painting was a greater precision and an interest in botanical and geological accuracy. This materialistic emphasis may account in part for the reaction of contemporaries such as John La Farge, who searched for the soul of the flower at the expense of naturalistic specificity. Certainly, this was the source of the reverential faith in nature that James Jackson Jarves recognized in La Farge's still lifes, and that caused Jarves to part company so drastically with Clarence Cook. And the Pre-Raphaelite movement and Ruskin's writings clearly engendered the new, "natural-setting" still lifes, which vied in popularity with more traditional tabletop compositions in the 1860s and 1870s.

It is interesting to consider the work of an artist as significant as George Inness in evaluating the Pre-Raphaelite influence on American art. Inness spoke of Pre-Raphaelitism often and always with contempt. In 1879 he recalled the movement as "a true outgrowth of the scientific tendency of the new age. It was false as a philosophy, though necessary as a reactionary force. It carried the love of imitation into irrational conditions. Objects were painted without regard to their distances. . . ." Considerably later, Inness's son quoted a letter written by his father that referred to the "puddling twaddle of Preraphaelism."[86] Yet, even Inness, so unmerciful toward the movement, produced in the mid-1860s a few pictures, such as his 1863 *Noon Hill, Medfield* and his 1864 *Harvest Time,* that suggest a concern with closely observed and recorded foreground detail. In *Harvest Time,* particularly, the logs and weeds abutting the picture plane are established with a botanical accuracy worthy of the American Pre-Raphaelites as, indeed, is the subject matter itself. In several of Inness's watercolors, too, of the 1860s—among his rare excursions into this medium—emphasis on the geological structure of prominent rocks and boulders is not unlike that in the rock studies of several artists in the present exhibition.

The innovations of Pre-Raphaelitism may have continued to affect the course of American art, but the movement itself experienced a rapid decline after its stunning visibility in late 1866 and the first part of 1867. A writer in *Frank Leslie's Illustrated Newspaper* in August 1867 could ask the following: "Two questions arising out of one subject, are now much in debate among art critics. The first query is with regard to the so-called Pre-Raphaelite School of Art, and it invites information as to whether that school is dead. The second query turns upon the same school, and expresses a desire to know whether it ever existed." Two years later Sturgis wrote in the *Nation* that "landscape art disappears year by year from our exhibition," and, referring to the artists of the once-innovative movement, he concluded that "it is idle now to discuss them as champions or exemplars of the once famous pre-Raphaelite school. The small group of artists who united in the hearty protest against sham in painting, which gained them the undeserved title of a school, are no longer united even in that protest which has gradually been silenced in the vigor of their devotion to work."[87]

About this time, there was a discussion in the press on the two Hills and the two Farrers. Entitled "Four 'Pre-Raphaelites',", it examined the reason for the movement's decline. The clipping is undated and unidentified, but we may assume a date of 1870, because Clarence Cook was in Paris for the *Tribune* covering the "tipping over of the Napoleonic throne." "What has become of the 'Pre-Raphaelites?'," the writer asked. He concluded that Cook's departure had deprived the traditionalists of a lively, witty opponent and the movement itself of the "indirect provocative," and he added that "the men and women, or woman, who have been christened Pre-Raphaelites, have worked hard at a slight number of pictures, and some of them have withheld their pictures entirely from the walls of the New York Academy, though the owners have, happily, done otherwise in Brooklyn." But the most important reason for the movement's decline was that "there no longer exists between the artists referred to the obvious similarity which enabled the most cursory critic to recognize them as belonging to one school, and which consisted in qualities unmercifully, and not always unjustly, denounced by the older painters, as might naturally have been expected from the central principles of fidelity in study and practice from nature, professed by the Pre-Raphaelites, their work has grown more and more unlike in result, the longer each pursued and adhered to the patient and close use of his own eyes."[88]

Indeed, by 1870 the Pre-Raphaelite *movement* was a thing of the past. Its leader, Thomas Farrer, had returned to Europe, clearly discouraged by negative criticism. Farrer had planned to open a school in New York with Charles Moore in 1868, but there is no evidence that this happened; and in March 1869, Farrer announced a private viewing to sell his remaining pictures before returning to Europe. His later years are obscure; in 1869–70 he travelled in Italy and Switzerland and seems to have continued to copy Turner's work as well as paint watercolor landscapes in the English provinces, which he brought to New York in 1871. In 1884 he had an exhibition of English, Venetian, and Dutch views at Herman Wunderlich's gallery in New York. Although reviews mentioned his early connection with the Pre-Raphaelites, these works seem to have been much more conventional watercolors, as were his few later works known today.

Henry Farrer remained in New York, an active figure in the art community. He adopted some of the strategies of Pre-Raphaelitism but utilized them ultimately in a quite un-Ruskinian manner. Similarly, both William Trost Richards and his pupil, Fidelia Bridges, abandoned a commitment to the Pre-Raphaelite mode, though neither did so completely. Among Farrer's pupils, interest in the Pre-Raphaelite approach was short-lived with Frank Lathrop and Robert Brandegee, and while Margaret McDonald seems to have continued the manner into the 1870s, and perhaps even later, the total disappearance of her work to date prevents any assessment of her continued involvement or significance. William Stillman all but abandoned painting as early as the 1860s, though he continued occasionally to produce critical writings, often directed against his former mentor, Ruskin.

Charles Herbert Moore, primarily a landscapist, was briefly acknowledged as the finest American Pre-Raphaelite in the mid-1860s with a group of Catskill landscapes. Most of these, owned by specialized collectors of this style, have disappeared, while his Pre-Raphaelite White Mountain scenes of the end of the decade, which are known and included in the present exhibition, were painted when the movement had already lost popular interest and thus seem to have attracted little commentary. In 1871, Moore accepted an instructorship at the Lawrence Scientific School and moved to Harvard in 1874 to teach with Charles Eliot Norton. In the 1870s, Moore moved away from a commitment to Pre-Raphaelitism, replacing it with an allegiance to the Venetian Renaissance. As Stillman had done, Moore published his evaluation of Ruskin: he acknowledged the Englishman's greatness in his grasp of the larger values of art, admired his penetrating writing on natural phenomena, and yet recognized his serious defects as a critic.[89]

The continuation of Pre-Raphaelitism among American artists lay principally in the hands of the Hills in this country, and of Henry Roderick Newman abroad. Newman was in Fontainebleau and Chartres late in 1869, and he also studied with Jean-Léon Gérôme in Paris for a few weeks in 1870. With the Franco-Prussian War, he headed for Switzerland and Italy, settling in Florence in September and visiting Venice the following spring. His work was still seen occasionally in American exhibitions: a *Fruit* still life at the Boston Athenaeum in 1873; floral still lifes at the Water Color Society in 1875 and at the Brooklyn Art Association in 1884. Through his colleague Charles Herbert Moore, who went abroad in 1876, Newman met Ruskin. Charles Eliot Norton had introduced Moore to Ruskin, and in 1877 Moore showed Ruskin one of Newman's architectural drawings of S. Maria Novella. This began a correspondence and a friendship between the two men which blossomed further when Newman visited Ruskin in England in summer 1880 on his way to America for a visit.

From the 1870s, Newman specialized in landscapes and architectural studies but also in flower painting, sometimes combining the two themes as in his spectacular *Italy*. In 1878, while some of his work was on view in London at the Grosvenor Gallery, a reviewer for the London *Academy*, visiting Newman's Florentine studio, found his floral watercolors among his most successful efforts. A *Study of Pink and White Oleanders* was admired for its "Japanese effectiveness," and his *Grapes and Olives* (cat. no. 60) drew critical praise for its glittering sea and autumnal effect.[90] In such a work, the Ruskinian principles of the still growing and living still life hold sway, and the colors are rich in Pre-Raphaelite intensity. In a major article for the *Manhattan Magazine* in 1884, H. Buxton Forman spoke of Newman's watercolors that were "minutely finished in the open air, with no sweep or flash, but with that intense earnestness which marked the landscape work of the early days of preraphaelitism in England." Forman also identified the particular floral subject that inspired Newman most, ". . . the anemone pictures in which Mr. Newman not only attains his best results in flower combinations, but also, I think, surpasses all that has been done elsewhere in that department of modern art, there are good examples in England in the hands of Mr. Ruskin. . . ." (fig. 22).[91] Indeed, while Ruskin owned a *Study of Plums* by Newman and a watercolor of *Florentine Roses* was in the Saint George Museum that Ruskin developed to support his artistic theories, he selected a series of anemone watercolors from Newman's portfolio as models of flower drawings. These were painted in the spring of 1881: a watercolor of the entire plant, one of detail studies of five different violet flower heads, another of six separate flowers of various colors, and one of just yellow anemones.

After his marriage in 1883 to Mary Watson Willis, a wealthy Englishwoman, Newman travelled extensively, wintering in Egypt in 1885 and visiting Japan in the late 1890s. Many marvelous watercolors resulted from his travels, but he remained especially identified with flower painting. His Florentine studio in 1891 was described as a room filled with flower-laden landscapes, and the writer asked, "Does the critic complain that this is the work of a botanist? He can not say that he who painted the Florentine hillside, is not as well a poet-lover of flowers, and if he has so shown them that we can call them by name, do we any the less value the bouquet because we may whiff its perfume, and recognize our own favorites from its nearness?"[92] Newman in Italy and the Hills in Nyack carried the Pre-Raphaelite commitment through the end of the nineteenth century and even into the twentieth (John William Hill died in 1879, but his son lived until 1922, and Newman died four years earlier, in 1918).

Too little is known of the major Pre-Raphaelite patrons to judge them a factor in the movement's demise. A number of collectors acquired Pre-Raphaelite work, but their means or their interest may have been limited. Certainly, very few major patrons of more traditional artists or of European art seem to have been much inclined to acquire American Pre-Raphaelite work. Of course, in abandoning Pre-Raphaelitism, American artists had before them the examples of some of their major English colleagues: John Everett Millais achieved tremendous popular success with another kind of art, and even Rossetti's

Figure 22
Henry R. Newman
Anemone 1884
Watercolor and graphite on paper, 15⅛ × 11¹¹/₁₆ in. (38.3 × 28.0 cm.)
Collection: Harvard University Art Museums (Fogg Art Museum), gift of Dr. Denman W. Ross
Cat. no. 59

later work was not consonant with the Pre-Raphaelite ideals that he, Millais, and Holman Hunt had adopted in the late 1840s.

Perhaps, too, both the practical and the formal limitations of the Pre-Raphaelite aesthetic became increasingly recognized by the Americans. The work *was* difficult, time-consuming, and ultimately quite boring. Artists constantly had to be concerned with the exigencies of weather and with change and the aging process in landscape and still-life elements. What they produced was usually quite small and thus not very commanding when hung in large group exhibitions. They may well have concluded that the critics were correct—that they were just making studies and not finished pictures; that they were losing sight of the whole for the parts; and perhaps that they were not revealing the soul of Nature by recording her physical properties; nor were they expressing their own personal emotional reactions or sufficiently indulging their imaginations. Finally, the artists may have concluded that the criticism of the principal of the Woman's Art School of Cooper Union may not have been totally wrong when she declared that Farrer's assignments did not seem very difficult to execute; that such studies were only the first elements of art.

If the Pre-Raphaelite architect Peter Bonnett Wight recalled the movement positively in 1884,[93] Charles Henry Miller, the Barbizon-related landscape painter, writing under the pseudonym of Carl DeMuldor, in *The Philosophy of Art in America* published in 1885, revived the bitter attacks of the 1860s in his section "American Pre-Raphaelitism." He recalled the work

> which, in fact, always appeared not sufficiently pre-Raphaelite . . . No perception or grasp of larger truths, values of tone, controlling harmonious or decorative relations, that go to make an acceptable artistic entirety in any example of the Fine Arts, through the skillful arrangements of the materials employed and the exercise of rare eclectic tastefulness. And where are those morbid curious to be seen to-day? They must have inevitably disappeared, being *sans* soul, *sans* thought, *sans* inspiration and poetry, though produced through rarest ape-like imitation, apparently with eyes able to see a little fly upon a bar door 'a mile and a half off' without including a sight of the barn itself.[94]

In 1887 a brief reference to Pre-Raphaelitism by the very able Charles de Kay appeared in "Moments in American Painting" in the English periodical *Magazine of Art*. And a thoughtful, sympathetic essay was published in *Harpers*, in 1890, by Lucy Cecil Lillie on the art inspired by the Catskill Mountains. It compared the earlier work of Thomas Cole with that of the American Pre-Raphaelites and was illustrated by works of Thomas Farrer and both the Hills. In 1901, Frank Weitenkampf of the *New York Times* had discovered John Henry Hill on the Nyack Turnpike and wrote an affectionate piece on him and his father titled "A Hackensack Ruskin Disciple."[95]

Edward Cary, once editor of the *Brooklyn Daily Union*, and his daughter, the art writer Elisabeth Luther Cary, carried the memories of the movement well into the twentieth century. In 1900, Elisabeth Cary wrote a thoughtful essay on the history of Pre-Raphaelitism in America and included it in her book *The Rossettis*. The Carys still owned Pre-Raphaelite works acquired in the 1860s, and Elisabeth wrote with examples of Thomas Farrer and both of the Hills before her. Six years later, her aged father published his invaluable historic article, "Some American Pre-Raphaelites: A Reminiscence," in the magazine *The Scrip*, edited by his daughter. It was illustrated with their works by Farrer and the Hills.[96]

In 1932, Elisabeth Cary wrote again of the American Pre-Raphaelites in the *New York Times*. Considering the increasing American interest in exhibitions of modern art, she observed that "we have always had a severely critical modern school." She recalled the Association, *The New Path*, and Thomas Farrer, who proselytized "with the ecstasy of a revivalist"; she noted that the Macbeth Gallery was then holding a Hudson River School exhibition, work that Society members had aligned themselves against, a show that would be "received more cordially than would a similar exhibition of the American pre-Raphaelites of the '60s." She went on to encourage what would have been an innovative, although impossible, exhibition: "Why not try both? Why not show all the 'new days' of which dawn has ripened to noon, and sunk to twilight? . . . If we add to the exhibitions mentioned that of the 'Impressionist' of America at the Brooklyn Museum we can link the parts together in a quite illuminating picture of our middle years between Colonial art and that of the present day. But we have left out the agonizingly faithful pre-Raphaelites of the New Path." Over half a century later, Elisabeth Cary's vision has been realized.[97]

1. Henry T. Tuckerman, *Book of the Artists, American Artist Life* (New York, 1867), p. 568; first quoted by me in "The Influence of Ruskin and Pre-Raphaelitism on American Still-Life Painting," *The American Art Journal* 1 (Fall 1969): 80–81.

2. James Jackson Jarves, *Art Studies: The "Old Masters" of Italy; Painting* (New York, 1861), pp. 29–30.

3. Charles Herbert Moore, "Fallacies of the Present School," *The New Path* 1 (October 1963): 61–64.

4. James Jackson Jarves, *The Art-Idea* (New York, 1864; new edition, edited by Benjamin Rowland, Jr., Cambridge, Massachusetts, 1960), pp. 141–143.

5. James Jackson Jarves, *Art Thoughts* (New York, 1869), pp. 294–295.

6. (William James Stillman?), "The Academy Exhibition—No. 1," *The Crayon* 1 (March 28, 1855): 203.

7. Thomas Farrer, "Art as a Record," *The New Path* 1 (August 1863): 42.

8. "Pictures and Studies," *The New Path* 2 (July 1864): 38–42.

9. Daniel Fanshaw, "The Exhibition of the National Academy of Design, 1827," *The United States Review and Literary Gazette* 2 (July 1827): 241–263.

10. John Ruskin, *Modern Painters*, vol. 3 (1856). The edition used throughout this book is the standard *The Works of John Ruskin*, edited by E.T. Cook and Alexander Wedderburn (London 1903–12); in this instance, see vol. 5, p. 50.

11. Ibid., vol. 5, 1860, C&W, vol. 7, p. 52.

12. John Ruskin, *Notes on Some of the Principal Pictures Exhibited in the Rooms of the Royal Academy and the Society of Painters in Water-Colours, Etc.*, no. 3. (1857); C&W, vol. 14, pp. 115–116.

13. John Ruskin, *Notes on Some of The Principal Pictures Exhibited in the Rooms of the Royal Academy, The Old and New Societies of Painters in Water-Colours, The Society of British Artists, and the French Exhibition.* no. 4. (1858); C&W, vol. 14, p. 154.

14. John Ruskin, *Modern Painters*, vol. 2 (1846); "Epilogue," which appeared in the edition of 1883. C&W, vol. 4, p. 344.

15. *The Letters of John Ruskin, 1827–1869*, C&W, vol. 36, letter to his father, August 25, 1847, p. 76.

16. John Ruskin, *The Elements of Drawing* (1857); C&W, vol. 15, p. 97; and *Proserpina* (1878); C&W, vol. 25, p. 230.

17. John Ruskin, *Proserpina* (1878); C&W, vol. 25, p. 239.

18. Ibid., pp. 287, 303.

19. Letter of February 29, 1860, from Hill to Farrer; in Gordon Ford papers, New York Public Library, on microfilm at the Archives of American Art.

20. "Art Instruction for the People. Mr. Ruskin's Evidence before a Parliamentary Committee," *The Working Men's College Magazine* 2 (August 1, 1860): 129.

21. William Cullen Bryant, *Letters of a Traveller; or, Notes of Things Seen in Europe and America* (New York, 1850), pp. 402–403.

22. *The Letters of John Ruskin*, C&W, vol. 36, p. 211.

23. (William James Stillman?), "Dii Majores ac Minores," *The Crayon* 2 (December 26, 1855): 399–400.

24. John Ruskin, *Modern Painters*, vol. 2 (1846); C&W, vol. 4, p. 223.

25. John Ruskin, "The Relation of Art to Use," *Lectures on Art* (1870); C&W, vol. 20, p. 101.

26. William James Stillman, *The Autobiography of a Journalist*, 2 vols. (Boston and New York, 1901), 2, p. 115.

27. Ibid., p. 130.

28. William James Stillman, "Extracts from Letters of a Tourist—No. 7," *The Sabbath Recorder* 7 (October 24, 1850), letter written from London on August 19.

29. Stillman, *Autobiography*, pp. 140–141.

30. Ibid.

31. (William James Stillman), "The Artist as Teacher," *The Crayon* 1 (April 4, 1855): 209.

32. *New-York Daily Tribune*, April 22, 1854, p. 6; *Putnam's Monthly* 3 (May 1854), pp. 567–568.

33. *The Crayon* 1 (March 28, 1855): 202 and 203; and (February 28): 140.

34. *New-York Daily Tribune*, April 12, 1856, p. 4; Tuckerman, *Book of the Artists*, pp. 560–561; "Recent Art Criticism," *The Round Table* 1 (January 2, 1864): 42.

35. *The Crayon* 4 (July 1857), 221.

36. *New-York Daily Tribune*, June 14, 1867, p. 2.

37. Charles Herbert Moore, "An Artist's Memorial," in John Henry Hill, *John William Hill. An Artist's Memorial* (New York, 1888), pp. 7–8.

38. Letters from John Henry Hill and John William Hill to Thomas Farrer, Gordon Ford collection, New York Public Library; on microfilm at the Archives of American Art. The letter from John William Hill is dated August 18, 1860.

39. *New-York Daily Tribune*, June 14, 1867, p. 2; "The Seventh Annual Exhibition of the Artists' Fund Society of New York," *The Nation* (November 29, 1866): 435.

40. The obituary from *The New York Times* is reproduced in John Henry Hill, *John William Hill. An Artist's Memorial*, p. 11.

41. Ford collection, see note 38.

42. John Henry Hill, *Sketches from Nature* (Nyack Turnpike, N.Y., 1867[?]), n.p.

43. See *The Athenaeum* 35 (May 26, 1860): 726; and *The Art Journal* 22 (June 1860): 163.

44. "Art Items," *The New-York Daily Tribune*, March 3, 1862, p. 8.

45. George W. Sheldon, *American Painters* (New York, 1879), p. 62.

46. Tuckerman, *Book of the Artists*, p. 524.

47. For information on The Working Men's College, see, J.P. Emslie, "Art-Teaching in the College in Its Early Days," *The Working Men's College 1854–1904*, edited by J. Llewelyn Davies (London, 1904), pp. 34–53; John Fletcher Clews Harrison, *A History of the Working Men's College 1854–1954* (London, 1954), esp. pp. 31–68; F.J. Furnivall, "History of the London Working Men's College," *The Working Men's College Magazine* 2 (September 1860): 144–148; (November 1860): 165–170; (December 1860): 188–192. For recollections of Ruskin at the College, see J.P. Emslie, "Recollections of Ruskin," *The Working Men's College Journal* 10 (May 1908): 321–346; Thomas Sulman, "A Memorable Art Class," *Good Words* 38 (August 1897): 547–551; and William Gershom Collingwood, *The Life of John Ruskin* (Boston, 1900), pp. 149–155.

48. The Gordon Ford collection, see note 38, is especially rich in correspondence between Farrer and the Fords, both Hills, Samuel Avery, and others of the American Pre-Raphaelite circle; when not otherwise specified, correspondence references are to the Ford collection papers. Frank Lathrop's study with Farrer in 1860 is cited in "Pictorial Decorators," *The Art Interchange* 6 (April 14, 1881): 82, but the early date is almost surely incorrect.

49. Adam Badeau, *The Vagabond* (New York, 1859), with a whole chapter on Pre-Raphaelitism, pp. 235–241; see p. 238 for this quotation.

50. *The Crayon* 6 (June 1859): 191.

51. *The Crayon* 7 (September 1860): 270–271.

52. I am greatly indebted to Virginia Weimer, Archivist, and the staff of the Library of the Cooper Union for the Advancement of Science and Art for allowing me to study the records and monthly reports for the early years of the Woman's School. The reports are usually unsigned and sometimes undated, so that it is often difficult to ascertain if they apply to the period of time when Farrer was teaching there; Thomas Addison Richards was head of the school in 1860–61; Henrietta Field was "Principal" from 1860 to 1863; and Lucy A. Cuddehy from 1863 to 1866. Perhaps one better at handwriting identification than I could determine which reports fell into the period of supervision of the various heads of the school.

53. *The Round Table* 2 (October 14, 1865): 93.

54. See the reminiscence by Ruskin's pupil George Allen in the "Introduction" to volume 3 of *Modern Painters*, C&W edition of Ruskin's collected writings, pp. xxxvi–xxxvii.

55. For Brandegee as a pupil of Farrer and Hill, see Henry W. French, *Art and Artists of Connecticut* (Boston and New York, 1879), p. 158; for the instruction of his aunt Sarah Tuthill, see the New Britain Museum of American Art, *An Exhibition of the Work of Robert Bolling Brandegee, A.N.A. 1849–1922*, essay by Charles B. Ferguson (New Britain, Connecticut, 1971), p. 4. A watercolor of *Peaches* by Thomas Farrer was lent to the inaugural exhibition at Street Hall in Yale University in 1867 by "Tuthill."

56. See the section on the American Pre-Raphaelites by Elisabeth Luther Cary in *The Rossettis, Dante Gabriel and Christina* (New York and London, 1900), pp. 43–52; Edward Cary, "Some American Pre-

Raphaelites: A Reminiscence," *The Scrip* 2 (October 1906): 1-7.

57.   *The New Path* 1 (June 1863): 23-24.

58.   "Art as a Record," *The New Path* 1 (August 1863), p. 42.

59.   *The New Path* 2 (May 1864): 13.

60.   Peter B. Wight, "Reminiscences of Russell Sturgis," *The Architectural Record* 26 (August 1909): 124-125.

61.   *The New-York Daily Tribune* (May 21, 1864), p. 3; June 4, 1864, p. 4; two in a series of reviews of selected pictures in the 1864 annual exhibition of the National Academy of Design.

62.   Letter from Wight to Farrer in the Gordon Ford collection, see note 58, dated August 11, 1863.

63.   For Wight see the essay by Sarah Bradford Landau in the exhibition catalogue, *P.B. Wight: Architect, Contractor, and Critic, 1838-1925* (Chicago: Art Institute of Chicago, 1981); the foliate carving is discussed on pp. 19-20. See also Elisabeth Luther Cary, *The Rossettis*, p. 48; and Wight's own "Reminiscences of the Building of the Academy of Design," *The New York Times*, April 22, 1900, p. 25.

64.   Cook published a series of six articles reviewing the 1865 Academy exhibition between May 13 and July 3; the article on Farrer appeared on June 5, p. 6; that on Moore's work on July 3, p. 6. Sturgis' reviews appeared in the first numbers of the new *Nation* magazine: 1, July 6, 1865, pp. 26-28, and July 13, 1865, pp. 56-59. *The New Path* discussed Farrer's work at the Academy in 2 (June 1865): 93-96.

65.   For Farrer's activities in the Connecticut River valley, see the discussions by Betsy R. Jones in George Walter Vincent, *Arcadian Vales*, exhibition catalogue, pp. 68-69; and Ms. Jones' *Edwin Romanzo Elmer 1850-1923*, Smith College Museum of Art, Smith Art Museum, Springfield, Mass. (1981-1983), p.45.

66.   *The Nation* 1 (November 30, 1865): 692-693.

67.   *The Nation* 1 (December 28, 1865): 819-820.

68.   *The New-York Daily Tribune*, December 16, 1865, p. 4.

69.   *The Nation* 2 (May 25, 1866): 667; *Harper's New Monthly Magazine* 33 (June 1866) 117-118; *New-York Daily Tribune*, June 27, 1866, p. 8.

70.   *Round Table* 1 (April 30, 1864): 312. See also the article "An Hour in the Gallery of the National Academy of Design," *Continental Monthly* 5 (June 1864): 688.

71.   *Round Table* 1 (May 7, 1864): 326. The critic for *The New York Evening Post*, June 7, 1865, p. 1, praised Griswold over the Pre-Raphaelites, referring to him as a "Realist" but not a "Literalist." Victor Griswold, like Ruskin in the first volume of *Modern Painters*, did not acknowledge his authorship of *Hugo Blanc, The Artist, A Tale of Practical and Ideal Life. By an artist* (New York, 1867; set in Connecticut and New York about 1851). See especially pp. 9-11, 127.

72.   *The Nation* 1 (November 16, 1865): 631.

73.   For an early discussion of the origins of the American Water Color Society and the prior role of the Artists' Fund Society, see Francis A. Silva, "Our Art Clubs. II-The American Water Color Society," *The Art Union* 3 (July-September 1885): 51.

74.   Stillman S. Conant, "The Exhibition of Water Colors," *Galaxy* 3 (January 1867): 53-59.

75.   *Putnam's Magazine* 1 (February 1868): 257.

76.   *New-York Daily Tribune*, June 14, 1867, p. 2, from a column totally devoted to Farrer.

77.   "Art Criticism" (letter by Farrer on June 19), *New-York Daily Tribune*, July 8, 1867, pp. 2-3.

78.   *New-York Daily Tribune*, July 3, 1867, p. 2; *The Nation* 4 (May 16, 1867): 399.

79.   *New York Herald*, December 29, 1867, p. 8; *Putnam's Magazine* 3 (March 1869): 378.

80.   *The Nation* 4 (May 16, 1867): 399; *New-York Daily Tribune*, July 3, 1867, p. 2.

81.   *New-York Daily Tribune*, April 27, 1866, p. 4; June 3, 1867, p. 2.

82.   *The Hartford Daily Courant*, July 12, 1867, p. 4; *The New Haven Daily Palladium*, July 1867, p. 2. A review also appeared on July 12 in the *New Haven Daily Morning Journal and Courier*, p.2. I am much indebted to my colleague Dr. Susan Casteras for so thoroughly researching the Connecticut as well as the New York newspapers for reviews of this watershed exhibition.

83.   *The Nation* 5 (August 8, 1867): 115-116.

84.   *New York Daily Tribune*, August 14, 1867, p. 2.

85.   Robert B. Brandegee, *From the Open Book of Nature*, n.p., 1901. Even individual essay titles, such as "New England Ferns" and "The Thrush Family," suggest Brandegee's continuing Ruskinian allegiance. His adulation of the wild anemone reads like a paraphrase of Ruskin himself, p. 4.

86.   "Mr. Inness on Art-Matters," *Art Journal* (New York) 5 (1879): 374-377; George Inness, Jr., *Life, Art, and Letters of George Inness* (New York, 1917), pp. 168-169.

87.   *Frank Leslie's Illustrated Newspaper*, August 24, 1867, p. 355; *The Nation* 8 (April 1869): 340.

88.   This clipping is among the Gordon Ford papers, see note 38. Although efforts to locate its source have so far been unsuccessful, it probably was published in a Brooklyn newspaper, perhaps Ford's own *Brooklyn Daily Union*. The writer's reference to the continued appearance of Pre-Raphaelite work in the exhibitions of the Brooklyn Art Association would seem to confirm this.

89.   In 1875, Moore was involved in a controversy with William Morris Hunt over the respective merits of the Venetian Renaissance Old Masters and the French Barbizon masters Corot and Millet. The controversy was aired publicly in the *Boston Daily Advertiser*, on June 2, p. 2, June 9, p. 2, and June 29, p. 2. Moore remained faithful to this new allegiance: his article "The Modern Art of Painting in France" (*Atlantic Monthly* 68 [December 1891]) criticized the slovenliness and incompleteness of French Impressionism; he saw its derivation from the work of Corot and maintained that "We get the fullest and truest illustration of the fundamental principles of painting yet reached in the art of Venice only," p. 814. His "John Ruskin as an Art Critic" appeared in the same magazine (86 [October 1900]: 438-459).

90.   "American Artists in Florence," *The Art Journal* (New York) 4 (1878): 288.

91.   H. Buxton Forman, "An American Studio in Florence," *Manhattan Magazine* 3 (June 1884): 525-539, esp. pp. 533-534.

92.   "In a Florentine Studio—That of Henry Newman," *The Art Interchange* 27 (August 1891): 46-47.

93.   Peter Bonnett Wight, *The Development of New Phases of the Fine Arts in America* (Chicago, 1884), pp. 13-24. This monograph was composed of two articles by Wight published consecutively in *The Inland Architect and Builder* of November and December 1884.

94.   "Carl DeMuldour," "American PreRaphaelitism," in *The Philosophy of Art in America* (New York, 1885), pp. 49-50.

95.   Charles de Kay, "Moments in American Painting," *Magazine of Art* 10 (February 1887): 37-38; Lucy Cecil White Lillie, "Two Phases of American Art," *Harper's New Monthly Magazine* 80 (January 1890): 206-216; pp. 212-216 are on the American Pre-Raphaelites; Frank Weitenkampf, "A Hackensack Ruskin Disciple," *New York Times*, December 8, 1901, "Supplement," p. 11.

96.   See note 56.

97.   Elisabeth Luther Cary, "Art Trends: the Years Between," *New York Times*, January 31, 1932, sect. 8, p. 13.

Plate 4
John Henry Hill
Fringed Gentians *circa* 1867
Watercolor on paper, 10½ × 7¼ in. (26.7 × 18.4 cm.)
Collection: Mr. and Mrs. Wilbur L. Ross, Jr.
Cat. no. 23

The Pre-Raphaelite Medium: Ruskin, Turner, and American Watercolor

KATHLEEN A. FOSTER

The American Pre-Raphaelites loved watercolor. Their special affection for this medium sets them apart from the English Pre-Raphaelite Brotherhood, whose members only occasionally worked in watercolor; it also distinguishes them from the ranks of the Hudson River School, whose adherents, by 1860, rarely used watercolor at all. In conjunction with a detailed, naturalistic style, a predilection for watercolor marks the truly radical Ruskinian painter in America. Every artist-member of the Pre-Raphaelite Association for the Advancement of Truth in Art produced elaborate, finished watercolors for exhibition. Most of the painters in the larger group known as the American Pre-Raphaelites worked frequently in watercolor, and some never worked in oils at all.[1] Together, their efforts in watercolor made an enduring contribution to American art, for they lent critical support to the first exhibitions of the American Watercolor Society and so laid the foundation of the medium's lasting popularity in the United States.[2]

The continuing devotion to watercolor tells us much about the identity of the American Pre-Raphaelites, both as an unconsciously related and as a self-consciously constructed group. Viewed separately, they appear as an assortment of individuals with similar components in their life histories, such as British birth or parentage, that made watercolor an easy or familiar choice. Many learned to paint in watercolor as children, either at home or in school. But not every painter with this background became "Pre-Raphaelite." As adults, the American Pre-Raphaelites were united by choice, purposely gathering to promote art based on shared principles.

For all of these painters, the figure who stood in both the background and the foreground of their individual and collective histories was John Ruskin. The premises that joined them, and even the personal variations that articulate them, found a common inspiration in Ruskin's teachings. His version of the Pre-Raphaelite story, his sense of the original Pre-Raphaelites' ambitions and goals, his interpretation of their work, and even his roster of their number—all affected American opinion much more than direct experience of Pre-Raphaelite art.

And Ruskin loved watercolor. "There is nothing that obeys the artist's hand so exquisitely," he wrote, "nothing that records the subtlest pleasures of sight so perfectly."

> All the splendours of the prism and the jewel are vulgar and few compared to the subdued blending of infinite opalescence in finely-inlaid water colour; and the repose of light obtainable by its transparent tints, and absolutely right forms to be rendered by practiced use of its opaque ones, are beyond rivalship, even by the most skilful methods of other media.[3]

Other Ruskinian watercolorists appearing in the first several exhibitions also failed to revise older, unfavorable opinions of their work, despite the sympathetic new circumstances. Although the Hills, Moore, and Newman could take heart from a few friendly words from their friend and Association alumnus Clarence Cook, who wrote for the *Tribune*, none of the group continued to earn much praise, or even much attention, from other quarters.[77] By common consent, only their still-life subjects were deemed admirable. Henry Farrer's *Study of Apples*, shown at the Society's first exhibition in '67-68, struck one critic with its "astonishing force in color and photographic fidelity in imitation." "No picture better illustrates the unlimited scope of water colors," claimed the *Herald*. "Such pre-Raphaelitism as this the most prejudiced must accept."[78] Farrer's brother, Thomas, was said to be at his best when painting "peaches, plums, bits of grass, a leaf or two, a single strip of bark with a little moss clinging to it. Such things he can paint with exquisite delicacy of drawing and color," wrote *Putnam's* critic. "But he cannot, as yet, paint a landscape; no not even a single tree."[79] Regardless of the "unlimited scope of water colors," the Ruskinians won few admirers when they expanded their range outside still life. The Hills' landscapes were criticized as either crudely or thinly colored, Moore's work was dismissed as hard and false, and T.C. Farrer's "wretched daub" was judged unfit for public viewing.[80]

In defending Moore, who did not show at the Society for three years following his drubbing from "Paletta," Clarence Cook praised his "patient, affectionate, discerning observation of Nature" and then paused to speculate about the disdain for the work of Moore, Newman, and Farrer felt by "half-educated" visitors to the exhibitions. These artists "make no appeal to anything in the vulgar mind but the sense of wonder and rouse that only feebly, while educated, thoughtful, sensitive people find nothing in their work to stir deep feeling, or excite and elevate the mind." Giving the public its due, Cook admitted that for all the Realists' labor ("for we throw overboard the unmeaning nickname 'Pre-Raphaelite' "), their work lacked "the effect of nature." In pursuit of a "lower and more hidden charm," their paintings missed the "higher more immediate charm" of natural effect and imaginative suggestion. Not all their efforts were to be regretted, of course, for truthful work gained "a right foundation for future excellence." If not poetic themselves, they have "prepared the way for poets." Said Cook, "the realists need to take another and a higher step."[81]

Clarence Cook was among the first of the Association members to stray from the Ruskinian path. His call for a more inspired, poetic naturalism echoed in the ears of the Ruskinian "Realists" for more than a decade, but few of his friends were able to achieve that next, higher step. The fortunes of the school sank in the late '60s as their participation in the Watercolor Society's exhibitions declined. The year 1870 was a low point for them all, when, for various reasons, both Hills, both Farrers, and C.H. Moore all failed to show at the Society, Robert Brandegee and Nina Moore[82] made their final appearances, and H.R. Newman submitted work for the last time before leaving, permanently, for Europe. Within a year, T.C. Farrer departed, too. Although he submitted work from afar in 1873 and 1878, his watercolors received little notice and even less praise.[83] His brother Henry showed five or six items every year without comment from anyone other than the friendly Ruskinian critic of *The Nation*, who praised his "delicacy and careful workmanship" and complained that his pictures were all skied—hung too high for proper appreciation.[84] After 1872, following the "jest" of some member of the Hanging Committee, who (according to *The Nation*) impertinently titled one of his watercolors "A Flying Peach," Farrer never exhibited another still life.[85]

Ruskin's ecstatic opinion must have borne weight, because there were few actual Pre-Raphaelite paintings (either English or Italian) to inspire American students until the British Loan Exhibition of 1857-58—an event for which most observers had been well prepared by Ruskin's writings. Several important figures, such as W.J. Stillman, T.C. Farrer, and John La Farge, had studied or travelled abroad and witnessed the English Pre-Raphaelite phenomenon at close hand, but their disparate experiences hardly explain the level of American interest in watercolor, particularly since the most celebrated works of the English movement were in oils.[4] The enthusiastic turn to watercolor grows even more remarkable in the context of the general disregard for the medium prior to the American Pre-Raphaelite period. The New York Water Color Society rose and then vanished between 1850 and 1855, without establishing lasting support from artists or patrons.[5] But by 1858, the climate had changed. A new generation of painters, a new exhibition of watercolors, and a new book from Ruskin—*Elements of Drawing*—coincided to begin reshaping American opinion.

"Our public know little of the beauty and variety of the Water-colour School of Art," wrote John Durand in *The Crayon*, whose Ruskinian pages promised an attractive and educational introduction to the medium at the British Loan Exhibition of 1857-58.[6] Curiosity also ran high in Boston, according to the *Transcript*:

> But owing to the absence of sufficient examples, and the presence of numerous rumors and reports of very contradictory character about the power and durability of this virtually new medium or vehicle, as compared with the long familiar one of oil color, [Americans] have failed, thus far, to obtain any satisfactory conclusions.

Denied real knowledge, persons "whose inclinations and abilities turn to watercolor" needlessly

Figure 23
Ford Madox Brown
Hampstead—A Sketch from Nature 1857
Watercolor on paper, 5½ × 9 in. (13.9 × 22.8 cm.)
*Collection: Delaware Art Museum, gift of the estate of Samuel and
Mary R. Bancroft*

wasted time on efforts in oil. "Sufficient examples" of British watercolor—particularly work by Turner—could liberate such misguided or hesitant talents.[7]

The British Exhibition provided the teaching survey needed by the American public. Half of the show was devoted to watercolors.[8] A few works came from the circle of the Pre-Raphaelites (Brett, Boyce, Collingwood, W. Hunt, Siddal, Sutcliffe, F.M. Brown's fresh *Hampstead—A Sketch from Nature*, fig. 23, and Ruskin's own study *Fragment of the Alps*, pl. 5), but these examples were far outnumbered by the work of older, more mainstream Victorian watercolorists like Bennett, Callow, Cattermole, Cox, Corbould, Fripp, Harding, Penley, Prout, Roberts, Rowbotham, Stanfield, Warren, and Wehnert. Five examples by Turner were a high point for many New Yorkers. The survey, if not consistently excellent, accurately represented contemporary British work; and overall, the watercolors were judged to be better than the oils in the show.[9] While hardly uncritical, *The Crayon* found the effect "exceedingly interesting and instructive."[10] Certainly watercolor painting received a new level of attention and respect in America as a result of this show. Still, the application of Pre-Raphaelite methods to watercolor would not have been well demonstrated by the exhibition. The broad handling of the older school, led by Turner and Cox, or the (to Ruskin) false finish and conventionalized picturesqueness of the 1840s could be expected from this group, not the disciplined observation and principled content of the work of the Pre-Raphaelite Brotherhood. The handful of watercolors that displayed Pre-Raphaelite qualities must have carried special authority, particularly Ruskin's *Fragment of the Alps*,[11] but the force of the word that preceded these images must be given a credit equal to or even surpassing the eloquence of the pictures themselves. Alone, the exhibition could not be expected to generate a new generation of Pre-Raphaelite watercolorists.

The British Exhibition can be relegated to secondary importance, considering the briefness of the visual experience and the staying power of the printed word in America. The bookishness of American artists followed upon the dearth of visual models, and conditioned their response to those images they did encounter. From the time of West and Copley, American artists learned how to see and how to make art from books, imbibing principles before experience.[12] Learning from a distance, far from the compromises and complexities of Pre-Raphaelite reality, Americans were likely to adhere to the letter of Ruskin's Pre-Raphaelite law. "I have much to thank America for," said Ruskin in 1855, acknowledging a "heartier appreciation and a better understanding of what I am and mean, than I have ever met in England."[13]

Ruskin complimented himself as he thanked his American readership, for his audience in the United States, being dependent on texts, chose its literary and intellectual heroes wisely. The enthusiasm of West and Copley reflects the light of Reynolds' cogent program; the dedication of the American Pre-Raphaelites honors the genius of Ruskin. A man whose energy and eloquence as a writer perfectly matched the intelligence, erudition, and artistic sensibility of his soul, Ruskin deserved all the attention he demanded. He was hard to ignore, easy to criticize, and impossible to read dispassionately; Modern Painters, "one of the sensation books of the time ... fell upon public opinion of the day like a thunderbolt from a clear sky."[14] In the realm of art and ethics, where his opinion held special authority, Ruskin made himself the mentor or nemesis of almost every American artist active between 1845 and 1875; as late as 1900, he held even greater sway over an enormous popular American audience.[15]

Philosophically, the writer and his readers were well matched. Ruskin's linking of art, nature, and morality found a receptive audience in America, where mid-century Transcendentalism encouraged reverence for nature and the conviction that good art revealed both divine order and human ethics.[16] "The duty of the painter is the same as that of a preacher," wrote Ruskin in the first volume of Modern Painters, a work he dedicated in 1843 to the landscape artists of England.[17] Americans, who were used to viewing their own landscape as a fountainhead of national virtue and strength, willingly became students of a painter/preacher who declared, "I would rather teach drawing that my pupils may learn to love nature, than teach the looking at Nature that they may learn to draw."[18]

Ruskin's emphasis on the moral value of studying Nature joined a practical premise that also appealed to Americans: landscape was an easier subject for beginners, particularly those with few opportunities to study either live models or the work of other artists. "I do not think figures, as chief subjects, can be drawn to any good purpose by an amateur," said Ruskin, who therewith excluded all discussion of figure subjects from his manual, Elements of Drawing. "The best drawing-masters are the woods and the hills."[19] Such an opinion suited the tastes as well as the resources of American artists, who took to the woods and hills eagerly, bypassing the complex narrative figure subjects that were popular with the English Brotherhood. With a few exceptions—usually portraits, like C.H. Moore's watercolor of Ruskin himself (Fogg Art Museum, Harvard University)—the American Pre-Raphaelites overwhelmingly favored landscape and still life, proving again that they were more American and Ruskinian than Pre-Raphaelite.

The American tendency to follow Ruskin's teaching rather than Pre-Raphaelite example should lead us to scrutinize his writings on watercolor and to search for heroes who might have inspired the American fondness for the medium. In Ruskin's pantheon, high places were given to John Lewis and William Hunt, two watercolor specialists working in a brilliant, elaborate technique that earned them, in Ruskin's eyes, a place in the "modern Pre-Raphaelite" school regardless of their actual detachment from the Pre-Raphaelite Brotherhood.[20] And, turning from the contemporary scene to consider the great sweep of European landscape art encompassed by Modern Painters, Ruskin found many earlier watercolorists worthy of emulation. In this larger historical context, the Pre-Raphaelites appeared in perspective, as exemplary modern reformers. They demonstrated what disciplined observation, painstaking method, and earnest sentiment could accomplish.

Above the Pre-Raphaelite Brotherhood, and above all others in Ruskin's view, loomed J.M.W.

Turner, who showed what years of Pre-Raphaelite study could achieve with the gift of genius: the highest art, expressed in color, revealing the deepest spiritual truths. Ruskin's abiding passion for Turner saturated the first two volumes of *Modern Painters*, shaping his sense of what was beautiful, powerful, and truthful in landscape art. Likewise, long study of Turner's watercolors helped form Ruskin's belief in the versatility and force of the medium while confirming his opinion of Turner's genius. Through *Modern Painters*, these convictions were pressed upon two generations of American artists, with telling effects on the native watercolor school.

If we must go to Ruskin in order to comprehend the American Pre-Raphaelites, we must seek out Turner in order to understand Ruskin. Conveniently, Turner will spiral us back to the American landscape school, for his influence in the United States both predates Ruskin's advocacy and outlasts the Pre-Raphaelite period, stretching across three-quarters of the nineteenth century. Surely no single artist had a more diverse and enduring impact on American landscape painting between 1820 and 1890.[21] His work was more accessible to the American audience than the P.R.B. because his huge oeuvre was frequently exhibited and engraved. Turner also produced work more useful to both the topographic and the idealistic intentions of the Hudson River School. Over the years, according to their preparation or to the nature of their encounter, different viewers found different Turners exactly suited to their needs. For Thomas Cole, visiting London before Millais and Rossetti were born, Turner confirmed a vision of landscape art that was at once topographical, national, historical, and emotional. Turner's blend of naturalism and idealism, developed from the landscape tradition of eighteenth-century England, helped codify American conventions of the sublime and picturesque view. At mid-century, Ruskin's rapturous prose swayed a new generation, most of whom knew only engravings and *Modern Painters* and who therefore believed in a crisper, more tonal, more "Ruskinian" Turner than actual experience of his work would reveal. Americans of this period, such as Thomas Moran and J.H. Hill, usually disliked the "wild color vagaries" of Turner's late career when they encountered his work at first-hand.[22] Ruskin's Turner could remain the pinnacle of Pre-Raphaelite endeavor only if students remained loyal to the engravings and remembered that the abstract late work belonged to an artist liberated by long study and genius. Ruskin's Turner was also, as *The Crayon* noted, "the originator of the new school of water-color Art in England, if not of the Art itself."[23] Turner's late work earned more reverence as the truth-seeking of the Ruskinians yielded to increasing calls for mystery and poetry in art. After 1870, his moody atmospheric effects, strong color, and suggestive, subjective handling won new attention, sometimes from old admirers. Moran, W.T. Richards, Henry Farrer, and George Inness all learned anew from Turner in the 1870s, years after their first experience of his work through the writings of Ruskin.

As the stylistic pendulum swung from breadth to delicacy and back again, Turner's reputation survived—but the American Pre-Raphaelites' did not. Most of them matured in the second, Ruskinian phase of Turner's popularity and refused to adjust as tastes changed. The older artists, including Moran and Richards, who absorbed a strong dose of the Romantic Turner before turning Pre-Raphaelite, often fared better in later years by recovering a portion of their youthful style.

Moran began his Turner studies in the early '50s, by trading his own watercolors for bound volumes of prints after Turner's work. Copying Turner's watercolors, and learning from local Philadelphia Turnerites like James Hamilton, Moran was an astonishingly adept imitator by the age of nineteen. His large watercolor from 1858, *Ruins on the Nile* (fig. 24), commands Turner's range of technique, from transparent glazes to opaque highlights and from broadly painted areas to zones of hairline (often pen line) detail. Moran's watercolors look tighter, denser, and stronger in value contrast as well as more elaborately finished than Turner's equivalent exhibition pieces, probably demonstrating the effects of copying engravings. Prints may also have taught Moran Turner's ability to manipulate light and to suggest monumentality and space within the smallest vignette. More important, however, than shared technique was a kinship of romantic spirit, which in Moran's fantastic and literary way led him to illustrate a scene from Shelley's poetry set in a landscape visited only by the imagination.[24]

Figure 24
Thomas Moran
Ruins on the Nile 1858
Watercolor on paper, 21½ × 16¾ in. (54.0 × 42.5 cm.)
Philadelphia Museum of Art, The W. P. Wilstach Collection

W.T. Richards evidently studied Turner after the fashion of Moran, consulting prints and texts like *Modern Painters* at a tender age. One of his earliest projects, a portfolio of pencil drawings made in 1854 to illustrate "The Landscape Feeling of American Poets," implies a familiarity with etchings after Turner's work in popular books like Samuel Rogers' *Italy*, a volume Ruskin would recommend to students in *Elements of Drawing* three years later.[25] Anticipating Ruskin's suggestion that students copy such tiny engravings to master the subtleties of black and white, Richards' work, as seen in *Landscape Vignette Illustrating a Passage from Whittier's "Pictures"* (fig. 25), shows all the delicacy of Turner's views, as well as the "landscape feeling" of Rogers' *Italy* and Moran's Egypt, brought to bear upon American scenes and poets. The vignette style of Richards' composition, his sweeping enclosure of space, and his variety of technical effects—from miniaturistic hairline vegetation to misty aerial reaches—shows Richards' acquaintance with the different landscape modes Turner (and his engravers) used for the prints published in gift books, in his own compendium of landscape subjects, the *Liber Studiorum*, and in epic topographical surveys such as *The Rivers of France*.[26] A friend from the '50s, W.H. Willcox, remembered Richards at this moment: "Turner and English art was in the ascendency," he recalled, "and Richards became an imitator of the former with large ambitious canvases of which the chief merit lay in the skillful drawing."[27]

Figure 25
William T. Richards
Landscape Vignette Illustrating a Passage from John Greenleaf Whittier's "Pictures" 1854
Pencil on paper, 11⅝ × 15⅛ in. (29.5 × 38.4 cm.)
Collection: The Brooklyn Museum, gift of Edith Ballinger Price

The transformation of style from adulation of Turner to Ruskinian observation took place gradually for most American painters in the 1850s, as Ruskin's message began to sink in. The later volumes of *Modern Painters*, appearing between 1855 and 1860, and Ruskin's defense of the Pre-Raphaelite Brotherhood, published in 1851, linked Turner and the young Brotherhood in a progressive system of talent and skill. According to Ruskin, the beginning artist or amateur should go to Nature, after the fashion of the modern Pre-Raphaelites, to learn the truths of design within the natural (divine) order while mastering basic descriptive skills. After a long and humble apprenticeship to mundane specifics, one might (according to one's genius) graduate to the inspired generalizations of a mature master such as Turner. Not everyone was destined for such greatness, but even the most modest talents could achieve rewarding results from earnest Pre-Raphaelite study. And, by implication, even the greatest genius would remain unrealized or misspent without the kind of disciplined study that made Turner's transcendent accomplishment possible. Ruskin encouraged the study of engravings after Turner's work for their lessons in composition, gradation, and suggestive handling of detail, but he warned students that premature flights of fantasy and synthesis would lead to falseness and superficiality.[28] Moran paid no attention to Ruskin's advice until the early '60s, but Richards abruptly ceased depicting his imaginary literary landscapes about 1854. "All the previous absurd Turneresque imitating (was) thrown aside," remembered his friend Willcox, as Richards began to paint "directly and most elaborately from nature," spending months on a single production. "It was a complete revolution," said Willcox, "and was the beginning of his future success."[29]

Richards' Ruskinian reformation expressed itself more fervidly after the British Loan Exhibition, when his first truly "Pre-Raphaelite" oils were produced, along with his first important watercolors. Richards' careful pencil sketches, previously relieved only by touches of gouache, were now developed from isolated botanical notations into elaborate watercolor paintings such as *Red Clover, Butter-and-Eggs, and Ground Ivy* (cat. no. 71). Close observation, anonymous handling, an unselective slice-of-nature composition, and an informal worm's-eye vantage point make this watercolor a Ruskinian enterprise from first to last.[30]

The few Pre-Raphaelite watercolors in the British exhibition may have inspired Richards, but they could not have adequately instructed him. A veteran watercolorist, like John W. Hill, could have accomplished such a style change by a study of Pre-Raphaelite work in any medium, but a novice like Richards must have needed additional advice and encouragement. Richards' "revolution" in the face of the Loan show probably coincided with his introduction to *Elements of Drawing*, which proposed a complete course of landscape study without recourse to oils. Published in England the year the exhibition opened, *Elements of Drawing* arrived in the United States in time to reinforce the visual impact of the show and to stand as a clear and emphatic technical handbook—a guide to subsequent work on the new path.

Ruskin's argument for watercolor in *Elements of Drawing* was simple and persuasive: the medium was convenient (especially outdoors)—being clean, "wholesome," and, in practiced hands, swift—and versatile, allowing a wide range of descriptive and artistic effects.[31] Ruskin had seen Turner's oils alter in color within a year of their completion, and so appreciated the purity and permanence of watercolor.[32] Finally, Ruskin found watercolor appropriate and accessible to a variety of talents and uses, from pleasant amateur sketching to the most ambitious artistic expression:

> If you wish to learn drawing that you may be able to set down clearly, and usefully, records of such things as cannot be described in words, either to assist your own memory of them, or to convey distinct ideas of them to other people; if you wish to obtain quicker perceptions of the beauty of the natural world, and to preserve something like a true image of beautiful things that pass away, or which you must yourself leave; if, also, you wish to understand the minds of great painters, and to be able to appreciate their work sincerely, seeing it for yourself and loving it, not merely taking up the thoughts of other people about it; then I *can* help you, or, which is better, show you how to help yourself.[33]

The rewards Ruskin promised at every level of endeavor made *Elements of Drawing* an appealing book for Americans. Both practiced artists like Hill and youthful beginners like Moore and Newman could learn from it, partly because of the breadth of its curriculum and partly because of the plain, schoolmasterly charm of its prose. Holding his poetic and rhetorical impulses in check, Ruskin composed his lessons as three letters to an imaginary student. He assumed that the reader had little or no access to drawing classes or museum collections and must therefore proceed slowly, turning to "the hills and the woods" for guidance and using specific supplementary sources for additional instruction: certain engravings after Turner, J.D. Harding's *Lessons on Trees*, Dürer's woodcuts, Cruikshank's illustrations—all items that Ruskin knew to be in popular circulation. Other models, such as Flaxman's prints, were decisively forbidden.

Such explicit guidelines and step-by-step procedures must have reassured provincial students, exactly as Ruskin hoped they would. When the book appeared in 1857, *The Crayon* recommended it "first, on account of the author's reputation; and secondly, through the intrinsic excellence of the work itself"—its admirable clarity and brevity.[35] J.H. Hill, addressing an American audience in 1867, added a personal and specific endorsement: "The best instruction for beginners in landscape art is to be found in *The Elements of Drawing* and *Modern Painters*, both by John Ruskin, which contain all the information necessary for those who have sufficient industry and love of nature to persevere as artists in the right track."[36]

The basic premise of *Elements of Drawing* reiterated Ruskin's conviction that to draw well one must first see well: "The chief aim and bent of the following system is to obtain, first, a perfectly patient, and, to the utmost of the pupil's power, a delicate method of work, such as may ensure his seeing truly." Excellence in art depended entirely on the artist's "refinement of perception," a quality that united all national schools and individual masters. "The only rule which I have, as yet, found to be without exception respecting art," wrote Ruskin in his preface, "is that all great art is delicate."[37]

Ruskin's one rule carried certain implications for style and handling, particularly for students, but he denied confining his readers within a "system" *per se*. With nature as the best corrective and certain old masters as guides, the personal, expressive choices of the student could unfold freely. *Elements of Drawing* was no Pre-Raphaelite tract. The landscape watercolorists of the 1830s and '40s, such as Prout and Harding, received more discussion and praise than any of the English Pre-Raphaelite Brotherhood. The absence of polemic and the catholic selection of models undoubtedly increased the acceptability and usefulness of the book. Anticipating his critics as well as the needs of students, Ruskin proposed a course of study that could be adapted to many tastes and purposes.

Elements of Drawing opened with pen-and-ink exercises. Immediately, the student had to grapple with nature's infinite shades, armed only with a very fine, very black point. "Till you can draw with that, you can draw with nothing," wrote Ruskin; "when you can draw with that, you can draw with a log of wood charred at the end." At first, crisp contours were avoided as unnatural; instead, networks of tiny lines and dots, conveying evenly gradated values from dark to light, were built up with patient hatching and knife work. After mastering delicate gray tones that signified color and texture as well as value, the student was directed to go outdoors and study tree branches in order to practice steady, accurate outline drawing.[38]

The power of Ruskin's teaching—including his advice to copy prints—made expert pen draftsmen and printmakers out of several American Pre-Raphaelite artists. Because pencil drawing so dominated the sketching practice of contemporary American landscape artists (including the American Pre-Raphaelites), the occasional American pen drawing seems to point directly to the teachings of Ruskin. Some productions, like C.H. Moore's exquisite *Pine Tree* of 1866 (cat. no. 48), obviously betray the senior student of tree contours, Exercise VI, *Elements of Drawing*. Francesca Alexander's delicate floral decoration, *S. Zita* (cat. no. 81), marries Pre-Raphaelite subject and method to fashionable book illustration. More subtle, but equally telling of Ruskinian influence, was the transference of Ruskin's laboriously hatched and stippled pen technique to softer, more flowing media like etching, pencil, and wash. Moore and J.H. Hill, who also worked frequently in pen and ink, carried Ruskin's style (or Turner's) into a series of etchings in the mid-'60s (see cat. nos. 18 and 19).[39] Most illuminating, however, are the figure subjects that, regardless of medium (pen, pencil, wash, gouache, or watercolor) show the same miniaturistic, linear technique: Brandegee's *Writing to Mother* (cat. no. 86), T.C. Farrer's portraits of *John William Hill* (cat. no. 5) and *Clarence Cook* (fig. 3), and, most importantly, R.J. Pattison's *Portrait of John Henry Hill*, (fig. 26), portraying a student of Ruskin who is himself at work with a quill pen.[40]

Having mastered the pen, the student picked up pencil and brush, practicing the same gradated effects in tints as well as in shades. Ruskin insisted that the "only distinctive [principle] in my system, so far as it *is* a system," was "the attaching its full importance, from the first, to local colour."[41] Even his initial pen studies attempted the rendering of color values. The first brush exercises taught the use of overlaid washes to build color from the palest to the most saturated hues. Maintaining that color looked more lovely when applied in fresh, undisturbed strokes, Ruskin advised laying on broad zones that later could be corrected, gradated, or evened out by delicate work with the brush point. The techniques of cross-hatching and of stippling overlaid tints "like chopped straw" had the advantage of letting "one hue be seen in minute portions, gleaming between the touches of another."[42] The painter avoided the risk of muddiness that occurred in overwashing and gained "the nobler translucence which is obtained by breaking various colours amidst each other." For Ruskin, this was "the most important of all processes in good modern oil and water-colour painting."[43]

Figure 26
Attributed to Robert J. Pattison
Portrait of John Henry Hill 1860
Pen and ink on paper, 4 × 3⅛ in. (10.2 × 8.0 cm.)
Collection: Mr. and Mrs. Wilbur L. Ross, Jr.
Cat. no. 65

The American Pre-Raphaelites adopted both watercolor techniques, using washes to define simple shapes, overlaying "chopped straw" in foregrounds or foliage, and combining the two methods to model large color zones. H.R. Newman, in *The Elm* (pl. 14), inflected the sky and clouds with alternately washed and hatched areas. C.H. Moore, in his *Mt. Washington* (cat. no. 51), applied the idea of pure colors broken together. Most of them used these techniques on white paper to produce the luminous, high-valued effect that critics found harsh but that Ruskin recommended to painters as suitably flat and ultimately more natural.[44]

These mixed techniques, in conjunction with gouache, help identify the Ruskinian watercolorist. Some purists disapproved of hatching, claiming that the beauty of the medium resided in simple, unmanipulated tints. Others rejected the use of gouache, insisting that the transparency of watercolor must be maintained in order to appreciate its unique capabilities. Ruskin answered the latter point by noting the range and force to be gained by the restrained use of gouache in tandem with transparent pigments. Certain milky gouache mixtures, said Ruskin, could describe "the bloom and mist of distance," or the solidity of earth and stone with an effectiveness impossible to attain by other means. "Body colour is, in a sketch, infinitely liker nature than transparent colour." Certainly the use of gouache made the medium even faster, easier, and more responsive.[45] And, if such technical advantages failed to convince, Ruskin leapt to a grander level of assertion: long study of Italian fresco painting led him simply to conclude that "the greatest things that are to be done in art must be done in dead colour."[46]

Ruskin's position received its most convincing support, and probably its inspiration, from the example of Turner, who tried every known trick in watercolor, personally invented others, and frequently combined several techniques in a single work, all with undeniable success. The closer an American painter came to Turner, as did Richards, Moran, and Hamilton, the more likely he was to use gouache extensively—especially after 1870, when eccentric tinted papers that demanded the use of body color became popular. Ruskin did not recommend anything but white or gray paper, and the strictest of his followers held to the use of transparent tints with only the most sparing application of gouache. However, all the radical Ruskinians used a full spectrum of tints, thereby distinguishing themselves from the Hudson River School sketchers like Church, Cropsey, or Kensett, who used pencil on lightly tinted (usually gray) paper, with white highlights and a rare, pale wash of ink or watercolor.

The presence of this mixed gouache technique may be one signal of Ruskinian influence, although some practitioners, like James Hamilton, may have learned it directly from Turner without the intervention of Ruskin. The breadth of Hamilton's manner, which earned him the sobriquet "The American Turner," disqualifies him as a true Ruskinian. If one directive can characterize Ruskin's teaching, it is his insistence on careful, delicate handling. Boldness should manifest itself only as dauntlessness; "good and beautiful work is generally done slowly."[47] Whether exquisitely refined or painfully cramped, this slowness and smallness of gesture set apart Pre-Raphaelites like Newman, the Hills, C.H. Moore, and Richards. Telltale shortcuts, generalization, or conventional "recipes" (usually in foliage) reveal the insincere student or the adherent of other popular manuals such as Aaron Penley's *The English School of Painting in Water-Colours* (1861) or Thomas Rowbotham's *The Art of Landscape Painting in Water Colours* (1851). These hallmarks identify the work of more mainstream watercolorists like William R. Miller or A. F. Bellows, whose work derives from sources common to the Ruskinians (the Hudson River School, the English landscape tradition), but identifies itself with popular British adaptations of Pre-Raphaelite effects, as seen in the bright and sentimental landscapes and figures of Birket Foster.[48] The increase in detail that occurred throughout the Victorian mainstream after 1850 (and the appearance, to Ruskin's horror, of a "false" Pre-Raphaelitism, exemplified by Foster's watercolors)[49] makes it difficult to measure the extent of Ruskin's personal influence beyond the circle of his self-declared followers. The gradual constriction in handling that could be seen by 1860 in the work of older watercolorists like F.O.C. Darley and J.M. Falconer could have come indirectly, from the Ruskinian example of younger reformers, or—more likely—from the more diffuse influence of the mainstream, which was surely affected, if not entirely directed, by Ruskin.[50] Of course the decision of working in watercolor at this moment does not necessarily imply the influence of Ruskin, since many artists (such as Miller, Falconer, Darley, and Hill) would have been familiar with the medium already, and the call for more detailed, disciplined rendering could be heard simultaneously from other quarters in Europe. Nevertheless, it is hard to imagine a professional American watercolorist (excluding folk painters) without even indirect experience of Ruskin's writings by 1860, and the popularity of careful finish in America has long been connected to Ruskin's exhortations on the subject. Certainly no other source addressed watercolorists so directly, connecting the medium to the Pre-Raphaelite style with such explicitness.

After technique and style, subject matter confirms the identity of a Ruskinian watercolorist. As W.H. Gerdts has shown, American still-life painters earnestly responded to Ruskin's teaching. Microscopic inspections of nature, seen informally and outdoors, appear as a hybrid landscape-still-life genre in the watercolors of Richards, Hill, Newman, Moore, Bridges and others.[51] Turning to *Elements of Drawing*, we find all these subjects suggested by Ruskin: "Make intimate friends of the brooks in your neighborhood," he counselled. "In woods, one or two trunks, with the flowery ground below, are at once the richest and easiest kind of study: a not very thick trunk ... with ivy running up it sparingly, is an easy and always rewarding subject."[52] Dutifully, the American Pre-Raphaelites avoided Ruskin's "don'ts" (shiny surfaces, neat and trim subjects) and sought the "rough, worn, clumsy, ugly" objects that rewarded study. As a model for students, Ruskin offered William "Bird's Nest" Hunt, "the best painter of still life, I believe, that ever existed."[53] Hunt was also a master watercolorist, whose technique surely inspired much of Ruskin's instruction in *Elements of Drawing*. Assuming John W. Hill's acquaintance with both Hunt's work and Ruskin's text, it is

Top:
Figure 27
Charles Herbert Moore
Rocks by the Water
Watercolor and gouache over graphite on paper
5⁹/₁₆ × 7³/₄ in. (14.1 × 19.7 cm.)
*Collection: Harvard University Art Museums (Fogg Art Museum),
transferred from the Fine Arts Department*
Cat. no. 49

Bottom:
Figure 28
William T. Richards
Study of a Boulder *circa* 1869 (detail)
Watercolor and pencil on gray paper, 10¹/₈ × 14¹/₂ in. (25.6 × 37.3 cm.)
Private collection
Cat. no. 78

hard to separate the sources of his style: both Hunt and Ruskin suggested the same content and the same mixed technique, using hatching, stippling, dry-brush textures, and slight gouache touches on classic white watercolor paper.[54] (Compare cat. nos. 31 and 124.)

The landscape-still life featuring rocks comes closer to the teaching of Ruskin alone. An appreciative student of the wondrous forces and organizing principles of rock formations,[55] Ruskin was quick to praise the accurate geological depictions of the Pre-Raphaelite Brotherhood, and he pressed this skill into the earliest exercises in *Elements of Drawing*. After mastering gradation in pen, pencil, and watercolor drills, the student turned with some relief to "Exercise VIII" and the study of "the first round or oval stone" at hand. "Now if you can draw that stone," said Ruskin, "you can draw anything."[56] The roundness of the stone, its variations of local color, shadow, and reflected light, all presented the most basic problems of visual transcription. Later, Ruskin suggested that first essays in mountain landscape begin with such a rock study, "with its variegated lichens ... getting its complete roundings, and all the patterns of the lichen in true, local color ... when once you have done this, the forms of distant hills will be comparatively easy."[57] Perhaps as a demonstration of this exercise, Ruskin loaned his own watercolor, *Fragment of the Alps* (cat. no. 125), especially for the British Loan Exhibition.[58] Doubting students needed no further proof of the force and delicacy of Ruskin's gouache technique. As Ruskin himself admitted to his friend Charles E. Norton, who received the watercolor as a gift from its author in 1858, "There is no drawing of a stone by my hand so good as your boulder."[59]

Instructed by Ruskin's example, several Americans turned to roadside, lake-shore and streambed geology. In oils, Asher B. Durand had already given special attention to rocky woodland glades and streams (see cat. no. 98); in watercolor, the American Pre-Raphaelites turned to large isolated boulders. C.H. Moore's *Rocks by the Water* (fig. 27) and *Landscape: Rocks and Water* (cat. no. 50) and Richards' tiny *Study of a Boulder* (fig. 28) all follow the model of Norton's gouache; since Moore knew Norton well, he may consciously have emulated Ruskin's work. In October of 1863, H.R. Newman wrote to his colleague T.C. Farrer that he was "trying to get acquainted with a fragment of flint rock (in water color) and I find it very interesting."[60] Forty years later, Newman remained sensitive to rock surfaces, as seen in his delicate renderings of stone architecture and sculpture in Egypt, Greece, and Italy (cat. no. 62). In wider practice, attention to the correct description of geological formations characterizes all Pre-Raphaelite landscape painting, as well as the Ruskinian work of the Hudson River School as seen in oils by Haseltine, Heade (cat. nos. 109 and 110), Shattuck, and others.

Working primarily in watercolor, Newman and Moore evidently learned Exercise VIII by heart, and then some. Of all the American Pre-Raphaelites, their work best demonstrates the patience and humility taught by *Elements of Drawing*. Both were rewarded by the respect and friendship of Ruskin himself. Their dedication to his methods may have been most extreme and long-lived because, as new artists, they encountered the movement at its most intensely rhetorical, organized moment. Both were too young or too preoccupied to be influenced by the British Loan Exhibition or by the initial publication of Ruskin's work. Their art formed in the early '60s, along with the Association for the Advancement of Truth in Art, under the influence of T.C. Farrer. Farrer's reappearance in New York in about 1862 had an important effect on the popularity of watercolor among the Association's membership, for Farrer had been a student under Ruskin and Rossetti at the Working Men's College in London, where the principles of *Elements of Drawing* were given classroom testing. Farrer's extant pencil drawings (cat. nos. 1-7) show him to be a fastidious Ruskinian draftsman. Exhibition records indicate that he worked in pen and watercolor as well.[61]

Together with the first converts of the late '50s—Richards, the Hills, La Farge—the persistent, even zealous recruits of the '60s, including Moore, Newman, and the Farrer brothers, amounted, by the middle of the decade, to a sizeable cadre of accomplished watercolor painters working in New York. Radical Ruskinism, already an aging cause at the time of the Association's birth in 1863, lost organizational support with the disintegration of the group in 1865, but fresh external encouragement soon came from a sudden growth of interest in Ruskin's medium. Eighteen months after the Association's final meeting, the New York Artists' Fund Society opened their annual show, featuring "the most rare and beautiful collection of water color drawings ever placed before the public in this city."[62] Catalyzed by J.M. Falconer, a veteran watercolorist whose work had recently taken a decidedly Ruskinian turn,[63] the Artists' Fund Society show inspired the formation of the American Watercolor Society that winter. The Society's first exhibition a year later, in December of 1867, provided the Ruskinian camp with a showcase for their work that was far more hospitable than the Academy annuals. Along with a few old-time watercolorists working in the English style of the 1830s and some recent converts from the ranks of the Hudson River School, including Samuel Colman and James M. Hart, the Ruskinians drew the spotlight, if only because their experience and style gave their watercolors unusual technical proficiency and intensity. Despite the declining influence of Ruskin and the increasing criticism of their unimaginative, "photographic" manner, the American Pre-Raphaelites found themselves the principals of the native watercolor school. As Henry Tuckerman wrote in 1867, their works offered "instructive exemplars, not without their inspiring as well as controversial influence."[64]

In 1866, as the American watercolor movement began to take shape, the fortunes of the Pre-Raphaelite School rested on the most accomplished practitioner in the group, John W. Hill. After forty years of specializing in watercolor, Hill began to earn a little belated praise after the Artists' Fund Society turned attention to the medium in 1866. As S.S. Conant remarked in 1868, New York had known only "two or three men—the Hills, father and son, and Charles Parsons—who could with justice be called water-colorists," and none of them had received much attention until recently. "In the case of the Hills, this was partly owing to the peculiarities of their style," he wrote, citing "idiosyncrasies" in their work "that offended people."[65]

For the elder Hill, the offensive (Pre-Raphaelite) idiosyncrasies emerged late in his career. After working as a topographical watercolorist in the early Hudson River School style of Wall, Bennett, and his own father, John Hill, John W. Hill was "revolutionized," like Richards, by *Modern Painters*.

About 1855 his work became much more detailed, as conscientious outdoor study, aiming to "paint Nature just as he saw it,"[66] replaced the early nineteenth-century conventions of his first landscapes. The new acuity and freshness in his work can be appreciated by comparing his linear, generalized style from before 1855 with his Ruskinian landscapes after 1856, such as *Esopus Creek* of 1858.[67] His color strengthened—usually emphasizing bright blue or green and gold—and his technique grew more miniaturistic. In place of flat, transparent washes, crisp contours, and simplified modeling, Hill substituted the techniques recommended by *Elements of Drawing*: stippling, hatching, and myriad small blots overlaid with tiny gouache highlights. About 1858, Hill took up still-life painting in the mode of "Bird's Nest" Hunt, and by 1860 he had proved his accomplishment in this genre with a group of watercolors shown at Nichol's Gallery in New York City. By that time he had fallen in with T.C. Farrer, and soon Hill was recognized as "one of the leaders in the so-called Pre-Raphaelite School."[68]

Hill had been exhibiting his watercolors annually at the National Academy of Design, where, in competition with oils, they generally failed to win much comment. Still, his modest reputation made him one of the featured artists at the Artists' Fund Society show, where his work was finally seen to advantage. Hill sent flower and dead-game subjects to this show, and one of his works (*Hollyhocks*) was singled out by the *American Art Journal* as "an excellent example of American watercolor art, being strong and vivid in color, and at the same time broad in handling and execution." The pseudonymous reviewer, "Paletta," found "a feeling of atmosphere and brilliancy about it which is exquisite."[69] The style of Hill and his son, John Henry, was characterized as "conscientious, finished, never bold, never dashy, never hasty, least of all slovenly," and together they were given credit for the best of the Pre-Raphaelite work at the exhibition.[70] In true Ruskinian fashion, their watercolors were seen as a lesson to artists and scientists alike: said an admirer of John W. Hill's *Rocks at Mount Desert* (probably a work resembling Moore's), "Agassiz could lecture to a class with this drawing."[71]

Truthfulness and technical skill were not enough, however, to exempt the Hills from criticism.

Despite their accomplishment, the school they represented was seen, even by the friendliest critics, as "severe, realistic, and limited in range." Although he had achieved "the perfection of imitation," the elder Hill had nonetheless failed to produce a real *picture*, complained S.S. Conant in his *Galaxy* review.[72] Hill's method yielded only "studies and sketches" lacking the imaginative, spiritual, and interpretive elements that Ruskin himself agreed were the highest qualities in art.

But the Hills fared better than the rest of the American Pre-Raphaelites, who made a "sorry show" at the Artists' Fund Society exhibition, according to Conant. "Paletta," who had been so pleased by John W. Hill's work, denounced C.H. Moore's *Pine Tree at Catskill* (perhaps related to cat. no. 48) as "a water color of the extreme, ultra pre-Raphaelite school, hard, crude, colorless and in every way unsatisfactory. Why is it that these artistic bigots will persevere in their efforts to so painfully distort and belie poor Dame Nature?"[73] Identical descriptive terms were applied to the work of another ex-member of the Association, H.R. Newman. According to "Paletta," the "extremely unpleasant" rawness of color in Newman's *Study of Elms* (perhaps *The Elm*, pl. 14) was ameliorated only by occasional passages of good drawing, "which barely save it from utter condemnation." Newman's landscape, laboriously painted in layered hatchings and stippling over a careful pencil drawing, remains a brilliant, necessarily harsh record of strong mid-summer sun and shadow. A painting by Thomas Farrer in the same exhibition, showing a dead bird in the snow, earned little better: newspaper comments on this item ranged from "peculiar" to caricatural and "ghastly."[74]

Such negativity by no means discouraged the American Pre-Raphaelites, who had heard the same (or worse) opinions before, and many of them showed up at the organizational meetings of the Watercolor Society, held from December of 1866 through the spring of 1867. T.C. Farrer was a founding member, and he quickly nominated for membership his brother Henry and C.H. Moore. H.R. Newman was elected to the Society that spring, and the somewhat peripheral Pre-Raphaelite John La Farge joined a year later.[75] Only the Hills remained on the fringe—as they had with the earlier Association, and as they continued to be in respect to the entire New York community— although both father and son sent their work (as well as a Turner *Coast Scene*) to the Society's first exhibition in 1867-68. Their contributions were awaited with hope. "Much was expected of the Hills, who for many years were almost alone in their devotion to water-colors," wrote S.S. Conant in 1868; "but neither father nor son has done himself much credit in his contributions to the present exhibition." John W. Hill sent "his usual branch of cherries, very truthfully and exquisitely painted," showing the "care, skill and fidelity" of "long and conscientious study." Such studies of branches, blossoms, and fruit as *Peach Blossoms* (fig. 29) indeed follow Ruskin's example, as preached in *Elements of Drawing* exercises and practiced in work such as *Twig of Peach Bloom* (fig. 30). Acknowledging their Ruskinian fidelity, Conant nonetheless admitted to being "a little tired of these bits of fruit painting, with their background of blue sky," and he complained that the landscapes of both Hills were unpleasant.[76]

C.H. Moore also quit New York in 1871, moving to Cambridge, Massachusetts, at C.E. Norton's invitation, to become a drawing teacher. His departure nearly "marked the end of his creative period as an artist."[86] Moore's work in oil ceased almost completely after 1871, as did his appearances at the National Academy of Design and the Watercolor Society. His final exhibition entries in 1870-71 came after a hiatus at the end of the 1860s, when a vast etching project displaced his work in all other media, excepting pen-and-wash drawings in preparation for prints. Like John Henry Hill, La Farge, Richards, Moran, and T.C. Farrer, Moore found black-and-white media particularly engrossing in the mid-'60s. Then, suddenly, in 1872, Moore produced two small, intensely worked watercolors: *The Valley of the Catskill from Jefferson Hill* (cat. no. 53) and *Mt. Washington* (cat. no. 51), both culminating a series of oils, drawings, and etchings begun in the mid-'60s.[87] Finely executed in bright, transparent colors on white paper, these watercolors used Ruskin's method to mix tints clearly by crosshatching strokes of pink, blue, yellow, and green. Moore probably copied his own earlier oils and drawings of the White Mountains, "improving" his own art rather than working again from nature, with a resulting stillness and eeriness of light and color.[88] Though not unpleasant, both these watercolors have exactly the unnaturalness of effect criticized in the pre-Raphaelite

Figure 29
John William Hill
Peach Blossoms 1874
Watercolor on paper, 16⅜ × 9⅜ in. (41.6 × 23.8 cm.)
Collection: *The Metropolitan Museum of Art*
Cat. no. 40

Figure 30
John Ruskin
Twig of Peach Bloom *circa* 1874
Watercolor and gouache on paper, 8¼ × 6⅜ in. (21.0 × 17.0 cm.)
Collection: *Harvard University Art Museums (Fogg Art Museum),*
bequest of Mrs. Alfred M. Brooks
Cat. no. 128

Facing page:
Figure 31
Henry R. Newman
Wildflowers 1887
Watercolor on paper, 15 × 10 in. (38.1 × 25.4 cm.)
Collection: *Museum of Fine Arts, Boston, gift of*
Dr. Denman W. Ross
Cat. no. 64

landscapes of the '60s. His friend H.R. Newman, when attempting the same panoramic format in *Mt. Everett from Monument Mountain in April* of 1867 (pl. 8),[89] had used the same hairline hatching and neat topographical minutiae, and arrived at a similar delicacy of detail and color within a static, slightly homely overall effect.

Neither of Moore's landscapes played a part in the watercolor exhibition of 1872; Moore sent only *Dog-Toothed Violet* to the show that January. This picture, now unlocated, served as a public farewell in the Ruskinian style. It no doubt resembled his other landscape-still-life works, like *Mullen and Rocks* of 1883 (cat. no. 55), or his own outdoor work from about this year, such as the fresh and delicate *Rocks by the Water* (fig. 27), which F.J. Mather described as Moore's "valedictory to Pre-Raphaelism."[90]

Moore's valedictory spoke only of his professional career as a painter. As a teacher and amateur, he retained his allegiance to Ruskin, and his interest in watercolor only increased after 1872. Like Ruskin, he used the medium in his teaching, and as late as 1890 he contrived to produce delicate still lifes, possibly for use in classroom copying.[91] Watercolor also became his preferred sketching medium for summer travel. Taking advantage of a leave in 1876-78, Moore sailed to Europe with a letter of introduction to Ruskin from C.E. Norton. Moore's careful watercolor portrait of his slightly demented friend and a series of Alpine landscapes and Italian views testify to the companionable travels of the two artist-professors.[92] These watercolors show that Moore, though "retired" from the art world, kept his minaturistic technique in trim while he developed a more fluid manner for outdoor sketching. His fresh and sunny *Sawmill at West Boxford* (cat. no. 54) borrows the stronger blue-and-gold tonality of the Hills' landscapes, along with a greater variety and confidence of handling expertly employed to capture a sense of shifting clouds and colored shadows.[93] Like most of his American contemporaries, Moore relaxed his style in the mid-'70s, but retained the impress of his Ruskinian teaching.

The same year Moore "retired," H.R. Newman also showed only a single work at the Society's exhibition—his valedictory entry except for a floral subject lent by its owner in 1875. Like Moore, Newman dropped out of the center of the American watercolor scene and left New York. Also like Moore, his departure in 1870 inaugurated a deeper rather than a shallower interest in watercolor, as well as a continuing commitment to Ruskin. Intending to keep the Pre-Raphaelite faith, both sought friendlier climates: Cambridge for Moore and Italy for Newman, who settled into the circle of Ruskin and the Brownings in Florence by 1870. Before long, he was involved in Ruskin's Guild of St. George, a group of artists dedicated to the preservation and documentation of old artworks and buildings, principally through careful record drawings and watercolors that hoped to remedy the limitations of photography. Like Moore, Newman continued to produce elaborate Ruskinian still-life pieces in watercolor, such as *Anemones* and *Wildflowers* (cat. no. 58 and fig. 31), but the bulk of his later work seems to have been done in the service of the Guild, if not actually on commission from Ruskin. Tuscan cathedrals (cat. nos. 61 and 62), Japanese shrines, and Egyptian temples, all rendered in Newman's consistently dainty style, in brilliant colors and on a monumental scale, appear from his hand until at least 1904.[94] Some of this work returned to appreciative owners in the United States, but Newman was dropped from the rolls of the Watercolor Society in 1876 for failing to participate.[95]

In 1872, the year of Newman's final personal submission and Moore's retirement, John W. Hill enjoyed his last, unequivocal success at the Watercolor Society. Hill "has never done better than in two of his landscapes," declared the *Atlantic Monthly*, and *The Nation* ranked Hill's work alongside that of W.T. Richards as the most admirable landscape painting in the show.[96] Lacking the exact items shown in that year, a look at a slightly earlier work like *Catskill Creek* (cat. no. 36) reveals how closely Hill's work sympathized with the compositional formats of the luminist painters of the Hudson River School. As with Richards, Moore, and Newman, Hill's technique relied on hatching and dotting—even in the sky—and a delicate recording of fact, though his work was never as monotonously handled or maniacally detailed as Moore's or Newman's. Brilliantly painted in his familiar sunny blue and gold hues, Hill's landscape also avoids unnatural harshness of color. The gentle variety and subtlety of effect brought him closer to the Victorian mainstream, and it explains why Hill escaped the censure accorded to most of the other Pre-Raphaelite landscape painters. Hill's *Catskill Creek*, though unassuming and not particularly original, helps us imagine the "enduring charm" and "mastery" seen in his watercolors of 1872. "A true reflection of nature never ceases to give pleasure," concluded *The Nation's* critic, who felt Hill's landscape provided a glimpse through a window "of that light that never was on sea and shore, the consecration and the poet's dream."[97] To an artist who found a "deep moral significance" in the act of painting, this praise must have been welcome, indeed.[98] For some, Hill could take that next, higher step.

But Hill's successes of 1872 were never repeated. He was getting older, and tastes were changing quickly. The following year, despite an unusually large selection of six still lifes and Adirondack views, his watercolors received almost no notice. Only the *Tribune* allowed, politely, that Hill's work was not up to its earlier standard. Admitting that his painting in 1872 had been "the finest, by all odds, in the Exhibition," the critic could only say that Hill's recent work, though excellent, fell short of the mark.[99] The following year he sent only one item, and his submissions thereafter remained sparse and erratic until his death in 1879. All these last entries were still lifes, such as *Blackberries* of 1876 (cat. no. 41); evidently Hill ceased landscape painting in 1872, perhaps because of his health. In 1876 he resigned from the Watercolor Society just as Newman was dropped from the rolls. Commentary on his work ceased almost entirely, and aside from the "generous patronage of a few enthusiasts" he sold few paintings.[100] Even a small retrospective of his work at the Society's exhibition in 1880, following his death, failed to generate a response.[101] Only his lone entry the previous year provoked the *Tribune's* critic to reminisce, somewhat inaccurately, that:

> As long ago as the [World's Fair] exhibition [of 1853] there were, it is true, two or three young men who, under the influence of Mr. Ruskin's teaching, as imported by one of his pupils [T.C. Farrer] produced some very delicate miniature work in water colors, and Mr. John W. Hill's "Marigolds" ... carries us back to a long-ago time when we were seeing and enjoying much of this now venerable artist's strong, clear-headed, truthful report of nature. But, Mr. Hill's work, beautiful and cheerful as much of it was, was simply reporting, it was not interpretation, and was quite empty of all poetry.[102]

John Henry Hill, who lent all fourteen of his father's watercolors to the retrospective in 1880, must have been even more unhappy in 1882, when all five of his own entries were rejected by the Watercolor Society's jury. Regardless of the debt owed to both father and son, who had done "more to create a love for water-color in this country than anyone," the Society had no room for the "detailed, conscientious, utterly mistaken and inartistic work that formed the staple of [its] first exhibition."[103]

For Ruskinian watercolorists after 1870, there were three paths to be taken. Moore, Newman, the Hills, and T.C. Farrer disregarded reports that the school was "dead"[104] and adhered to their original course, now doomed to unfashionability. La Farge, Cook (in his writings), and younger artists like Marie Spartali Stillman and E.A. Abbey[105] drew inspiration from the Rossetti-Burne-Jones-Morris Pre-Raphaelitism of the 1860s, with its emphasis on literary themes, illustration, and decorative arts. Others, mostly landscape painters, followed Ruskin's own program, seeking a transcendence of the "plain faithful recording" that perennial students like Moore accepted as a lifetime assignment.[106] This last group hoped that experience, added to talent and ambition, would now allow "another and a higher step" to poetic levels of expression, following the beacon of Turner. All the Pre-Raphaelite landscapists who survived the depression of 1870-71 to find renewed popular acceptance were those who passed over or through Ruskin (as Ruskin himself advised) directly to the work of Turner. The successful transformation of these Ruskinian inchworms into more Turnerian butterflies marks the major moment of transition for the watercolorists in the group and for the American watercolor movement at large.

The salvation of the Ruskinian cause came in 1872 and '73 from the two Philadelphians who had been peripheral to the group in the 1860s, W.T. Richards and Thomas Moran. Richards had been spotted by T.C. Farrer, who introduced him to the Association for the Advancement of Truth in

Art in 1863—only to see the entire Pre-Raphaelite group described within a year as "Mr. Richards and his followers."[107] Richards was, in fact, steering an independent course that kept him away from the watercolor activity in New York around 1866-68. As with C.H. Moore, his interest in the medium picked up after 1870, and he made his first important submissions to the Watercolor Exhibition in 1872.[108] The six small coastline scenes he showed that year thrust him immediately into the vanguard of the American watercolor school. The geometric simplicity, unified tone, and quiet handling of these first shoreline scenes carried the luminist aesthetic into a novel, almost miniaturistic scale, and with a fresh, translucent technique. Miraculously, Richards applied the most refined and artificial Ruskinian techniques to achieve an effect of atmospheric immediacy. The truthfulness of these marines, and their delicate, unlabored surface, delighted all the observers waiting for another, higher step from the Ruskinians. The partisan critic of *The Nation* heralded Richards' watercolors as "the first time that an American artist has treated the seashore with such fidelity and poetry." Uniting Richards' efforts with those of John W. Hill, he declared that "work like this would be impossible to any man who had not served a laborious and earnest apprenticeship to nature."[109]

The "poetry" discovered in Richards' work bespoke his gradual return to the Turnerian mood of his youth. The intensity of his Pre-Raphaelite woodland interiors had relaxed, and he began to work serially on small watercolors, attempting more momentary observations. Simultaneously, he adapted his materials to his atmospheric ends, choosing "a certain sad-colored paper"[110] that established a gray, tan, or blue background tone. This paper, with its soft surface and mottled color (sometimes produced by myriad broken threads), helped unite the tints and promote a gentle atmospheric shimmer to the distances.[111] Such paper demanded the use of gouache for all areas lighter than the paper tone, and therefore accorded with Ruskin's advice, although *Elements of Drawing* (and the Association's inner circle) avoided tinted grounds. Typically, the habit of working on colored paper came from the Turner following established in Philadelphia in the early '50s. Richards could have learned a taste for tinted paper from his neighbors, Hamilton and Moran, or from Turner's own work, seen in London in 1867. His close friend and patron after 1870, the Philadelphia watercolor connoisseur the Rev. Elias Magoon, doubtless shared his collection of "Old Master" watercolors with Richards and encouraged experimentation. A decade later, Magoon felt the connection between Turner and Richards to be profound enough to merit the foundation of a "Richards Gallery" at the new Metropolitan Museum of Art, in emulation of London's Turner Gallery.[112]

Magoon accompanied Richards on a trip to the Adirondacks in 1874, evidently standing at his shoulder while Richards completed his great series of late luminist landscapes, including *Lake Squam from Red Hill* (fig. 32). These views of mountain and lake scenery, composed in an open, panoramic fashion to emphasize space and light as much as topography, also echo the luminist sensibilities of Heade, Kensett, and especially S.R. Gifford. Comparing Newman's and Moore's work from the same period to Richards' Adirondack scenes, the fraternity of method and intention is clear: the same luminist spirit, almost the identical panoramic bowl of space, the same Ruskinian attention to geology and botany. Richards, the older, more experienced, and more talented practitioner, enlivened his view with a more varied, suggestive, and secure technique. He had been painting such subjects in oil for at least fifteen years, but this new series of watercolors arrived at simpler, less cluttered, even more spacious results, despite their smaller scale. Compared to the earlier coastal watercolors, works like *Lake Squam, The Mount Washington Range from Mt. Kearsarge*, and *Sunset on Mt. Chocorua* (Met. Mus. of Art) of 1872-74 were slightly larger and certainly denser and more brilliant in color, in keeping with the change in subject and perhaps indicating Richards' increasing confidence and ambition in watercolor. The contributing strands of Ruskin, Turner, luminism, and the Hudson River School became indistinguishably interwoven in these small landscapes, where close observation joins with spatial breadth and a meditative luminist intimacy combines with the elegiac grandeur of Frederic Church's *Twilight in the Wilderness*.

Richards' mountain studies, seen at the Watercolor Society in 1873, confirmed the promise of his debut.[113] By 1874, his work in this medium earned praise from all quarters, despite the growing distaste for Pre-Raphaelite finish. Overcoming his critics, Richards "at last forced the public to recognize" his "knowledge of nature, the fruit of unwearied study." According to the *Atlantic Monthly*, this expertise was acknowledged "in spite of a prejudice against the extremely delicate execution through which it is revealed, and which does not please greatly outside the circle of women and the lovers of curiosities." "But in the case of Mr. Richards," wrote the reviewer, "the women have taught the connoisseurs, and they must now admit that all the artist's delicacy, finish and tameness, as they called it, are reconcilable with strength, breadth and a masterly understanding of this subject."[114]

The reputation Richards won from the newspaper critics was borne out by the enthusiastic response of collectors and the even more flattering appearance of students and imitators. His friend and student Fidelia Bridges made a name for herself at the watercolor exhibitions beginning in 1872, showing exquisite gouaches of birds and flowers, mostly based on Richards' compositions of the 1860s such as *Some Fell Among Thorns* (fig. 9). As the decade progressed, her work grew larger, more elaborate, and more popular, artfully blending the decorative and sentimental tastes of the period.[115] Other painters, more distant from the Pre-Raphaelite circle, such as Alfred Bricher, F. A. Silva, J.C. Nicoll, and S.R. Triscott, were frequently listed among the "long procession of disciples" of Richards' seacoast watercolors. "Most raise the flowers now, for all have got the seed."[116] Few of these new offshoots showed Richards' delicacy, however; most displayed the impatience with detail and the interest in broader effects typical of this decade.

Richards' influence on younger watercolor painters as he gradually moved from Ruskinian crispness to Turnerian "poetry" was reinforced in 1873 by the sudden stardom of his colleague Thomas Moran. Unlike Richards, Moran followed the course of several other Philadelphia painters working in the older English tradition—James Hamilton, John Sartain, and his own older brother, Edward—and resisted Pre-Raphaelite extremism when it appeared at the British Loan Exhibition, holding fast to Turneresque landscape fantasies well into the 1860s.[117] Moran's Ruskinian phase, which peaked around 1864 in productions like *Under the Trees* (cat. no. 117), was late and brief; the Turnerian mode first established in his youthful watercolors and confirmed in 1861 by study of Turner's work in England reasserted itself quickly. Although Ruskinian habits of observation, including detailed depiction of geological forms and vegetation, continued to stand Moran well after 1871, when he began to document the wonders of the American West, the influence of Turner worked more strongly to guide his sense of composition, color, and technique (fig. 33). And, most important, Moran remembered Turner's generalizing faculty. Calling Turner a "poet," Moran praised his willingness to sacrifice "the literal truth of the parts to the higher truth of the whole." "And he was right," said Moran. "Art is not nature." Such attempts at revising Ruskin's image of Turner accompanied equally un-Ruskinian attitudes in Moran's own work. "I place no value upon literal transcripts of nature," he said. "My general scope is not realistic; all my tendencies are toward idealization."[118]

Moran reiterated these principles in 1879, hoping to overturn the popular perception of his work at the end of the decade. When he had first returned from the West to lay his oils, watercolors, and illustrations before an amazed public, the novel content and masterly technique of his views received an enthusiastic welcome. The first appearance of his Yellowstone material in the spring of 1872, culminating in his debut at the Watercolor Society exhibition in February of 1873, made Moran an artistic celebrity. His publisher, *Scribner's Magazine*, declared with understandable bias that Moran's views were "the most brilliant and poetic pictures that have been done in America thus far," but even less prejudiced viewers agreed that such "striking and masterly works" showed the triumphant coincidence of "the poet and the scientific observer."[119] Evidently, the Ruskinian apotheosis was at hand. However, the emphasis on poetic truth heard in this praise seems to have been in reaction to the typical criticisms of Moran's work: that it was incredible, and therefore false, or that it was *too* scientific, and therefore ugly. If the subjects were proven accurate, then Moran was attacked for choosing to depict "freaks" of nature. Such complaints increased as the

Figure 32
William T. Richards
Lake Squam from Red Hill 1874
Watercolor on paper, 8¾ × 13½ in. (22.2 × 34.3 cm.)
Collection: Metropolitan Museum of Art, gift of the Reverend
Elias L. Magoon

novelty of Moran's subject matter waned; typecast by his material, Moran lost credit for the poetry he intended.[120] Meanwhile, the more subjective, anti-topographical mood of landscape painters like George Inness, who had learned from Turner's more abstract work, gained favor. Moran's popularity, which peaked at the Centennial, abated within a decade of his return from the Yellowsone Territory. Despite his independence from Ruskinian practice, Moran's strong component of naturalism eventually earned him dismissal along with the Pre-Raphaelites.

Moran doubtless found the Pre-Raphaelites odd company in obscurity or disgrace, for he and Richards were largely responsible for redirecting Ruskinian watercolor to its Turnerian sources and opening the medium to artists who were neither watercolor specialists nor stylistic radicals. Richards had shown the potential for delicacy and truth. Moran's exhibition watercolors (fig. 33), with their large scale and brilliant color, proved the forcefulness possible in the medium; his quick, fluid sketches demonstrated its versatility and speed. Convinced, the rank and file of the Hudson River School had picked up watercolor. The exhibitions of the Watercolor Society began to prosper; the membership roll began to expand. The sudden celebrity of Moran and the crowning of Richards both lent energy to the entire movement in 1873. Talented new recruits like Thomas Eakins and Winslow Homer joined the cause, perhaps encouraged by yet another "British Loan Exhibition" of watercolors that filled the galleries of the National Academy of Design that year. As

Figure 33
Thomas Moran
Hot Springs of Gardiners River, Yellowstone National Park,
Wyoming Territory 1872
Watercolor on paper, 20¼ × 28¾ in. (51.4 × 73.0 cm.)
Collection: James Maroney

with the earlier show, the borrowed watercolors emphasized Britain's romantic tradition, but now such examples of broad handling and simplified form found a more appreciative audience.[121] Impatience with the Ruskinian method, or greater confidence and ambition, may have inspired the gradual loosening of style visible throughout the 1870s, but certainly a selection of the "old Masters" could only have accelerated this change of taste in American watercolor. Within a year, New York would begin to react to the flashy and spontaneous work of the Spanish/Italian watercolorists, who set the stage for the return of the "New Men" from Munich, Venice, Holland, and Paris. Very soon, even the most versatile Turnerites would find themselves in the rear guard.

The course of the Turner style after 1872 is clear in the work of the American Pre-Raphaelites who remained active and prosperous in New York: Richards, Moran, and Henry Farrer. Moran, the most faithful and the most obvious adherent, achieved a dexterity that even confused Ruskin, who insisted that some of Moran's watercolors were really by Turner.[122] Moran's style had been encouraged by direct study of Turner's work in London, and a procession of American watercolorists, including Richards, the Hills, Samuel Colman, and Henry Farrer, found the same pilgrimage inspiring. Farrer, after abandoning still-life painting in 1872, turned all his energy to tranquil, luminist seascapes and moody, literary landscapes in watercolor (such as *Sweet is the Hour of Rest!* in 1880) that found more favor with the critics than his earlier Pre-Raphaelite work. Nearly monochromatic and usually a bit melancholy, Farrer's landscapes showed the influence of Richards' luminism, Inness's tonalism and—according to the *Independent*—of "a studied imitation of Turner's manner."[123] Within a decade after the Ruskinian slump of 1870, Farrer was well established at the Watercolor Society, an officer and a popular, if somewhat monotonous, exhibitor. Like Richards, he had found a more "poetic" landscape mode that would serve him for the rest of his career. Richards, who travelled to England in 1878, about the same time Farrer did, likewise increased his references to Turner's work after renewed study of the master's watercolors. Visual homage, as well as written allusion to Turner, recurs in his watercolors with frequency after the mid-'70s: for example, *Fort Dumpling in Imitation of Turner* (Univ. of Kansas) and, especially, the misty *Commercial England, London*, a large view of the Thames intended to celebrate England's modern commercial empire in the style of the greatest painter of that culture.[124] Richards had reason to fear that "the time is past when American people can hunger for my work,"[125] for his late watercolors—like those of Farrer and Moran—were still too literal for avant-garde taste. However, the gentle broadening of style and willing admission of mood in the work of all three painters ensured a steady appreciation from conservative viewers. After all, Ruskin's popular American readership continued to grow, despite the second thoughts shared by most artists, and the affection for Ruskin's medium, seen in the work of the American Pre-Raphaelites, had taken a widespread, permanent hold.

This essay was developed from material presented in my doctoral dissertation, *Makers of the American Watercolor Movement, 1860-1890* (Yale University, 1982), particularly Chapter II: "Ruskin, Turner and the American Pre-Raphaelites." I renew my thanks here to those who assisted me in that study and lent support to the present publication, particularly Susan Casteras, Linda S. Ferber, William H. Gerdts, Frank H. Goodyear, Jr., Jules Prown, Theodore E. Stebbins, Jr., and, as always, Henry H. Glassie.

1. The founding artists of the Association included Thomas C. Farrer, C.H. Moore, and H.R. Newman; Newman produced but a few oils (none extant), and, with just a few exceptions, Moore's oils predate his most Ruskinian period. The architect-members of the group, P.B. Wight and Russell Sturgis, were both proficient in pen and watercolor for professional purposes; Wight's renderings, in particular, deserve Ruskinian accolades. See Sarah B. Landau and John Zukowsky, *P.B. Wight: Architect, Contractor, and Critic* (Chicago: Burnham Library of Architecture, Art Institue of Chicago, 1981). Clarence Cook, the journalist of the group, seems to have created no watercolors, although his enthusiasm for the medium infected his influential art criticism. In the larger Ruskinian circles, both J.W. and J.H. Hill worked mostly in watercolor; Nina Moore, Fidelia Bridges, and Robert Brandegee are known only for watercolor, and W.T. Richards and John La Farge devoted much time to the medium, especially after 1870. W.J. Stillman, the only American Pre-Raphaelite who knew both Ruskin and Turner personally, studied watercolor in England in 1850 and later reviewed English watercolor exhibitions for *The Nation*, but I have discovered no samples of his work. His second wife, Marie Spartali Stillman, was an accomplished watercolorist whose elaborate figure subjects in the manner of Rossetti were popular entries at the American Watercolor Society's exhibitions in the mid-'70s. Other watercolorists affiliated with the Pre-Raphaelite circle whose work is little known today include Francesca Alexander, Margaret G. MacDonald, "Miss Granberry" (probably Virginia Granbery), and "Mr. Bulson" (cf. a list of the "Realist" school given in the N.Y. *Tribune*, July 3, 1867, p. 2). The watercolors of this entire school have been surveyed with intelligence only by Theodore E. Stebbins, Jr., in *American Master Drawings and Watercolors* (New York: Harper and Row, 1976).

2. See my thesis, *Makers of the American Watercolor Movement*, Introduction and Chapter II.

3. Letter to the London *Times*, April 14, 1886; reprinted in J.C. Robinson, J.D. Linton, et al., *Light and Watercolours* (London: G. Parnell, 1887), and John Scott Taylor, *A Descriptive Handbook of Modern Water Colours* (London: Winsor and Newton, 1887), preface.

4. Discounting the watercolorists Ruskin unilaterally annexed to the movement, J.F. Lewis and W. Hunt, who had little to do with the original Pre-Raphaelite Brotherhood, the English group did not share the enthusiasm for watercolor found in America. Holman Hunt used watercolor for travel sketches and small views and maintained that Pre-Raphaelite oil technique was based on Turner's watercolor method (Hunt, *Pre-Raphaelites and the PreRaphaelite Brotherhood*, London: 1904, I, pp. 276-277). However, Hunt's most innovative watercolors did not come until the later '60s, and these were never seen as his most "serious" work. While Allen Staley has argued that Rosetti's "finest achievements as a painter are his quaintly decorative watercolors from the later '50s," these pictures were not well known in America, except perhaps by Charles E. Norton, and their archaizing style had little effect on the landscape school that dominated the American Ruskinians. Only John La Farge responded seriously to this aspect of Pre-Raphelite work in watercolor. See Staley, *The Pre-Raphaelite Landscape* (Oxford: Clarendon Press, 1973), pp. 71-77, 81. About 1880, Millais turned his hand to watercolor, producing exquisite analogues of his oils such as *The Huguenots* and *Springtime* (1880; both Fogg Art Museum). The second generation of the Pre-Raphaelite movement, led by Rossetti and Burne-Jones on the one hand and by popular "hybrids" like Fred Walker, George Pinwell, and J.W. North on the other, had a later impact on American decorators and illustrators in watercolor (La Farge, Abbey), but this influence arrived after the taste for watercolor was well-established in the American landscape school. See my *American Watercolor Movement*, Chapters V and VI, Abbey and La Farge.

5. See my *American Watercolor Movement*, Part II, pp. 22-23 and note 3. Also see *American Art Annual*, I (1898), pp. 242-245; and Clara E. Clement (Waters) and Laurence Hutton, *Artists of the Nineteenth Century and their Works* (Boston and New York: Houghton, Mifflin, 1879 and 1884, 1907), xxx-xxxi.

6. *The Crayon*, IV (Aug. 1857), p. 251; and see Susan Casteras' essay on the British Loan Exhibition, published in this catalogue.

7. The *Transcript's* reviewer felt that the exhibition offered an opportunity to dispel rumors and encourage young artists who were alternately intimidated by fears of "mechanical difficulties" with watercolor and tempted by the medium's "manifestly superior neatness and convenience." Ruskinian readers of this paper might have been further tempted by learning that watercolor came "nearest to nature's own painting process," with the charm of an etheral, "self-abnegating" vehicle. New England's Transcendentalists also must have been drawn to the purity and immateriality attributed to watercolor, which was "pigment transformed to mere hue; or matter changed to spirit." This reviewer failed to mention any of the oils in the exhibition or any of the Pre-Raphaelite contributions. See (April 8, 1858), p. 2; (April 13, 1858), p. 2; and (April 29, 1858), p. 2.

8. The size and contents of the show changed from city to city as items were sold or added. One hundred eighty-eight watercolors appeared in New York, 127 in Philadelphia, and 108 in Boston.

9. "The watercolor department—a branch of art almost entirely neglected in this country—is superb," announced the *New York Herald*. "The Fine Arts in New York," (Oct. 20, 1857), p. 4. The *New York Evening Post* declared that the public has "never seen so fine a display" of watercolors, even in England (Nov. 14, 1857), p. 2. From England, the *Art Journal* noted that "very many of the leading men in both [watercolor] societies" were included in the display ("Minor Topics of the Month," 1857, n.p.), and the *Knickerbocker* confirmed that "the watercolor galleries are by far the most complete in their representative character; but few great names are wanting, and the pictures are good" ("British-French Art in N.Y.," 51, Jan. 1858, 57). In Boston, *Dwight's Journal of Music* agreed that the novelty and quality of the watercolor display formed the most attractive feature of the show. Impressed by both Ruskin's *Gneiss* and Brett's *Swiss Alps*, the reviewer praised the "nearly-perfect examples of completeness," delicacy and detail shown in the watercolor display. 'Mesos,' "Fine Arts ..., " 13 (July 17, 1858), pp. 127-128. Brownlee Brown, in *The Independent* 9 (Oct. 22, 1857), p. 1, was less enthusiastic, finding Ruskin's *Gneiss* "laborious" and lacking in breadth, and few other watercolors better than "interesting." He criticized the Turner watercolors as unrepresentative of the artist's best work. (I am grateful to Susan Casteras for sharing with me several reviews of this exhibition cited above.)

10. *The Crayon* 5 (Jan. 1858), p. 23.

11. *The Crayon* described *Fragment* as "Masterly, ... one of the completest studies he has ever made," and noted that Ruskin had prepared the picture especially for the exhibition. IV (Oct. 1857), p. 314. The Boston *Transcript* claimed that "Like every picture from Mr. Ruskin, whether painted in colors or words, if not extremely natural is, at any rate, exquisitely beautiful" (April 13, 1858), p. 2. For Brownlee Brown's variant opinion, see note 9 above.

12. As W.J. Stillman confessed, Ruskin led him into "the fatal condition of having theories beyond practice." *Autobiography of a Journalist* (Boston and N.Y.: 1902) I, pp. 130-131. On the literary enthusiasm of American artists, see Jules Prown, *John Singleton Copley* (Cambridge: Harvard Univ. Press, for the National Gallery, Washington, D.C., 1966), I, pp. 16-19.

13. *The Crayon* I (May 2, 1855), p. 283. Quoted in David H. Dickason, *The Daring Young Men; The Story of the American Pre-Raphaelites* (Bloomington: Indiana Univ. Press, 1953), p. 60.

14. *Atlantic Monthly* VI (Aug. 1860), p. 239. Quoted in Lillian B. Miller, *Patrons and Patriotism: The Encouragement of the Fine Arts in the United States, 1790-1860* (Chicago: Univ. of Chicago Press, 1966), p. 27.

15. See Roger B. Stein, *Ruskin and Aesthetic Thought in America, 1840-1900* (Cambridge, Mass.: Harvard Univ. Press, 1967).

16. See Stein, *Ruskin*, and Miller, *Patrons and Patriotism*, pp. 27-29, on Ruskin's appeal to Americans.

17. *Modern Painters*, Vol. I, Ch. IV, ¶ 5. In the *Library Edition, The Works of John Ruskin*, ed. E.T. Cook and A. Wedderburn (London: George Allen, 1903-10), Vol. 3, Ch. IV, ¶ 5.

18. *Elements of Drawing* (London: 1857) and *Library Edition ... Ruskin* (London: George Allen, 1903-10), Vol. XV, Preface, p. 8 (hereafter, "*ED*"). Also, Dover editions, reprint, 1971. (My undated 19th-century American edition follows the pagination of the original edition.) As *The Crayon* commented in its review of this book, "Mr. Ruskin has his pupils drawing from nature almost before they are aware of it; and what is more, he has them *loving* Nature before they have time to think about it." IV (1857), p. 288.

19. *ED*, preface, p. 13.

20. *Ibid.*, p. 187. Hunt's influence is discussed briefly below, and at greater length by W. H. Gerdts, in his essay on Pre-Raphaelite still life in this catalogue. As for J. F. Lewis's bright, miniaturistic Oriental genre subjects, I have found little direct influence in America, other than in the technical aspects advocated by Ruskin, discussed below.

21. See Joseph R. Goldyne, "Criticism and Collecting: 19th-Century American Response to Turner's Achievement," in *J. M. W. Turner: Works on Paper in American Collections* (Berkeley, Calif.: Univ. Art Museum, 1975), pp. 19-38, and intro. p. 12.

22. Hill's comment appeared in a letter from London, published in *The New Path* (May 1865), p. 74. Hill copied Turner's drawings and paintings at the South Kensington Museum (the present Victoria and Albert) in the fall of 1864; he preferred Turner's works that were "most natural, and have least of his eccentricities," p. 73. "Much can be learned from Turner, I think, but not for the sake of imitating him. He will teach me, I hope, to watch nature with greater care, and to strive with more earnestness to reach her infinitude of beauty," p. 75. John Durand, anticipating the British Loan Exhibition, remarked in *The Crayon* that the most interesting feature of the show would be a landscape by Turner, whose reputation had "belted the earth," IV (Aug. 1857), p. 251. Not all the promised items appeared, and the five watercolors shown in New York disappointed and confused many viewers. *The Crayon*, for example, expressed its disappointment and described one landscape as a "blotch of color," IV (Nov. 1857), p. 344. Brownlee Brown, in the *Independent*, agreed that the Turners were not of the best quality; see note 9 above. Brown's article, "John Ruskin," in *The Crayon* (IV, 1857, pp. 329-336), showed that even the pages of the most pro-Ruskin journal, during the most Ruskinian period, could carry critical articles on Ruskin's work. Brown, in particular, was alert to the differences between Turner and "Ruskin's Turner" (see pp. 330, 332-333), and criticized the inconsistencies in *Elements of Drawing* (pp. 332-334).

23. John Durand, "Sketchings," IV (Oct. 1857), p. 314.

24. On Moran's Turner prints, and his early Turner copies, see Thurman Wilkins, *Thomas Moran, Artist of the Mountains* (Univ. of Oklahoma Press, 1966), pp. 21, 28. On the influence of Turner's prints on his work, see Thomas S. Fern, *The Drawings and Watercolors of Thomas Moran* (Notre Dame, Indiana: The Art Gallery, Univ. of Notre Dame, 1976), p. 74. More recent studies of Moran's work have remained attentive to Moran's debt to Turner. In particular, see Carol Clark, *Thomas Moran—Watercolors of the American West* (Austin: Univ. of Texas Press, 1980). I have investigated the style and content of *Ruins on the Nile* in respect to Turner's influence, in *Philadelphia: Three Centuries of American Art* (Philadelphia Museum of Art, 1976), pp. 360-362.

25. Charles B. Ferguson has written that Richards learned about Turner's work from Paul Weber in the early '50s. See *"He Knew the Sea": William T. Richards N.A. 1833-1905 ...* (New Britain Museum of American Art, 1973), p. 5. On Richards' illustration project, see Linda S. Ferber, *William Trost Richards (1833-1905) American Landscape and Marine Painter* (Brooklyn Museum, 1973), pp. 16-17 and cat. nos. 4-5. This catalogue and the author's doctoral dissertation by the same title (New York: Garland Publishing, 1980) are the definitive texts on Richards' life and work. Ferber remarks on Richards' debt to

Turner, particularly in the more fantastic illustration of Poe's *Dreamland*, cat. no. 4. Ruskin's suggestion to seek out Rogers' books appears in *Elements of Drawing*, p. 61. Rogers' *Italy*, first published in 1822, went through several editions with the original illustrations; I have discovered English editions of 1842 and 1852 with the original plates. American editions sometimes have other engravings. Rogers' work represents literally hundreds of British and American volumes of poetry and gift books, with small vignette illustrations similar in organization to Turner's, if not as delicate in execution. Ferber mentions some of the more celebrated American books of this type in *Richards*, p. 16.

26.   Turner's *Liber Studiorum*, a set of etching/mezzotint prints after his designs, was issued in fourteen parts between 1809 and 1819. His topographical surveys, beginning with *Picturesque Views of the Southern Coast of England* (publ. 1814-26), culminated in *Picturesque Views of England and Wales* (1826-38). These prints, or subsequent copies (and engravings after Turner's other works) were available in the United States, sometimes bound into elegant volumes, like D. Appleton's *Turner Gallery* (New York: n.d. ca. 1860-1880), which Richards and Moran surely knew. Goldyne has commented that Turner's *Liber Studiorum* was "relatively inexpensive" in this period; *Turner: Works on Paper*, p. 12.

27.   Quoted in Harrison S. Morris, *William Trost Richards, Masterpieces of the Sea* (Philadelphia, 1912), pp. 21-22.

28.   Of Ruskin's many references to Turner's engravings in *Modern Painters* and *Elements of Drawing*, perhaps the most extensive is his analysis of *Bridge at Coblentz*, ED, pp. 142-152, 163-170. A specific list of other engravings to copy is given in ED, pp. 60 and 83-86.

29.   Morris, *Richards*, 21-22. Ferber, *Richards*, 24 and cat. no. 7. She notes a new discipline in his work by 1854. Ferguson states that the Turnerisms were abandoned in 1853. "*He Knew the Sea*," p. 5.

30.   Perhaps because of the change in his style after the Loan Exhibition, writers like George Sheldon dated Richards' "revolution" to 1858. See "American Painters. William T. Richards," *Art Journal* (U.S. ed.) NS III (1877), p. 242. See also Ferber, *Richards*, 26, 40.

31.   Ruskin described watercolor painting as the "same process [as oil], insofar as handling," only without "its uncleanliness, its unwholesomeness, or its inconvenience; for oil will not dry quickly, nor carry safely, nor give the same effects of atmosphere without ten fold labor." *ED*, p. 116.

32.   Ruskin understood the dangers of light damage to watercolor, and kept his own Turner watercolors in portfolios or behind specially constructed curtains. His opinions are expressed in Robinson and Linton, *Light and Watercolors*, preface.

33.   *ED*, p. 15. Ruskin noted that his course of study did not intend to teach either "dextrous sketching" or mechanical drawing for industrial design, the goals of most drawing manuals, pp. 8-10.

34.   A special appendix entitled "Things to be Studied" listed the recommended sources, including poets and novelists worthy of attention, on pp. 185-195. The book by Harding, who was one of Ruskin's own teachers, is discussed on pp. 95-96; judging from its plates, I would guess that many American landscape draftsmen availed themselves of its advice. On the proper Turner engravings, see note 28. Similar lists for study appear in *Modern Painters*.

35.   "The Elements of Drawing," *The Crayon* IV (1857), p. 288.

36.   Introduction, *Sketches from Nature* (Nyack Turnpike, New York, 1867), quoted in Dickason, *Daring Young Men*, p. 265. The remainder of Hill's quotation is a direct paraphrase of *Elements of Drawing*, 11.

37.   *ED*, preface, p. 8. "I am nearly convinced," said Ruskin, "that when once we see keenly enough, there is very little difficulty in drawing what we see."

38.   Ruskin suggested that students should think of contours as "the edge of the shade," not as an outline. Nature "outlines none." The exercises with tree branches, practicing contour drawing, were more for the sake of observation than for technique. These studies were made in pencil, retraced with pen.

See *ED*, pp. 10, 29-31.

39.   Hill spent the fall of 1864 copying Turner's drawings in London; the impact of the *Liber Studiorum* pen and wash drawings, later reproduced as etching/aquatints, appear in his first prints, such as *Moonlight on the Androscoggin* of 1866. See note 22 above for reference to his letters from London. In 1882, C.H. Moore's etchings were described as "a palpable parody of Turner's *Liber Studiorum*." The N.Y. *Tribune* (Feb. 15, 1882), p. 5. The same might have been said of Henry Farrer's etchings, which also became very Turnerish in the 1870s.

40.   Farrer's portrait of Cook, now lost, is described by Dickason as pen and ink (*Daring Young Men*, 87), although Dickason probably knew only the book illustration, not the original, which may have been in pencil. However, Farrer did exhibit pen drawings at the Pennsylvania Academy in 1862, indicating his interest in this technique. See Anna Wells Rutledge, *Cumulative Record of Exhibition Catalogues, The Pennsylvania Academy of the Fine Arts* (Philadelphia: American Philosophical Society, 1955), p. 71.

41.   *ED*, p. 10.

42.   *ED*, p. 50.

43.   *ED*, pp. 129-130. Ruskin's Neo-Impressionist notions about "atoms of color in juxtaposition," each with a tiny bit of white paper left exposed around the touch, would find a different use twenty-five years later. The technique itself, as a "modern" innovation, appeared first in the watercolors of J.F. Lewis, although the strategy of overlaying hatching in alternating tints (pink, blue, and yellow) was a miniature painting technique from the early nineteenth century.

44.   *ED*, p. 53. Ruskin always favored color at the expense of chiaroscuro. Great art was based on color; cheap effects of relief and shadow were to be avoided. See pp. 114-117, and note 46 below. He counselled the sparing use of black, and advocated that all shadows be composed of color; p. 131.

45.   *ED*, pp. 116, 118. While Ruskin cautioned that all watercolor techniques admitted no correction, gouache did allow certain types of overpainting and glazing. A flat application of Chinese white dried to a smooth and reflective surface, ready for over-glazing with transparent tints. Some masters, like William "Bird's Nest" Hunt and his American counterpart, John W. Hill, employed this surface deliberately, to simulate the luminosity of an ivory ground. See *ED*, pp. 119, 130.

46.   *ED*, p. 117. Ruskin's conviction was based, again, on the belief that the rich "glows and glooms" of oil (or of transparent watercolor) were not the "noblest" aim of the painter. Pure color, unsullied by shadow, and flat non-lustrous effects produced a more spiritual, more artistic painting. See note 45 above. The triumph of this technique was described in *The Atlantic Monthly* (Feb. 1874), p. 249, where it was claimed that "Under the influence of those Pre-Raphaelites who believe in correct drawing and strong, harmonious coloring, a school has come into existence which is really a school of tempera-painters, using body color and the white of egg, or other medium, and thus giving to water-color a richness and consistency equal to that of oil, while preserving its own greater natural purity and softness."

47.   "If Nature is not bold at *her* work, do you think you ought to be at yours?" *ED*, p. 26, and similar comments, pp. 38-39, 22.

48.   See my *American Watercolor Movement*, pp. 168-170.

49.   See Staley, *Pre-Raphaelite Landscape*, pp. 61, 176.

50.   As a correspondent to *The Crayon* from London commented in 1860, "On the whole, I should say that pre-Raphaelism *pur et simple* does not play a prominent part this year, but I observe that the old 'Blotesque' style is dying out fast and that a more careful study of detail is becoming the fashion ... high finish is the present demand of the London market." In this review of the "old" Watercolor Society's show, Birket Foster comes under fire, while William Hunt receives praise. VII (Nov. 1860), pp. 321-322. In America, this detailed watercolor style, only indirectly related to the Pre-Raphaelites, lived on until the turn of the century in the work of artists like J.G. Brown, T.W. Wood, E.L. Henry, and E.A. Abbey.

51.   See W.H. Gerdts, "The Influence of Ruskin and the

PreRaphaelites on American Still-Life Painting," *American Art Journal*, I (1969), 80ff. A variant of this essay appears as Ch. 8 in Gerdts and Russell Burke, *American Still Life* (1971). Also, see Gerdt's essay on this subject in this catalogue.

52. *ED*, p. 93. The exact subjects cited above can be recognized in the work of Richards, Hill, Durand, Moran, Moore, Whittredge, C.L. Fussell, and many others.

53. *ED*, p. 187.

54. Overall, Hill's work tended to be sharper in focus and more informally organized, particularly in tabletop subjects. However, the astonishing similarity between the two painters is ultimately more interesting than their differences. Other remarkably similar Hunt/Hill pairings can be made by studying *Bird's Nest and Blossoms* (Fogg) and *Primroses and Bird's Nest* and others by Hunt at the Victoria and Albert Museum. Ruskin specifically recommended Hunt's dry-brush techniques and broken color application. See *ED*, pp. 51, 131.

55. See Ruskin's *Deucalion; Collected Studies of the Lapse of Waves, and Life of Stones* (London, 1879).

56. *ED*, p. 37.

57. *ED*, p.57

58. *The Crayon* declared that Ruskin painted this watercolor especially for the British Loan Exhibition. IV (Nov. 1857), p. 343.

59. *Library Edition ... John Ruskin*, XXXVIII, 563, cited by Margery Cohn, in *Wash and Gouache* (Cambridge: Fogg Art Museum, 1977), pp. 52, 107-108. Ruskin's letter to Norton was dated May 16, 1886.

60. Kent Ahrens, "Pioneer Abroad, Henry R. Newman (1843-1917): Watercolorist and Friend of Ruskin," *American Art Journal* (Nov. 1976), p. 86.

61. Dickason, *Daring Young Men*, 84-85. See also note 40 above and note 74 below. Although little of this work has been located, Farrer exhibited at the American Watercolor Society from 1868-1873 and in 1878, showing flower subjects and landscapes. On the relation of the Working Men's College classes to the development of Ruskin's curriculum, see *ED*, p. 9.

62. John F. Kensett, in the 7th Annual Report of the Artist's Fund Society, quoted by F.A. Silva, "Our Art Clubs," *Art Union* III, no. 3 (July-Sept. 1885) p. 51.

63. After 1862 his style became finer and more detailed, as in *Girl with a Basket* of 1862 (MFA, Boston). Like most Ruskinians, Falconer moved into a looser, more transparent style in the 1870s. On Falconer, see Linda S. Ferber, *Brooklyn Before the Bridge: American Paintings from The Long Island Historical Society* (Brooklyn Museum, 1982), pp. 128-129.

64. Tuckerman, *Book of the Artists*, (New York: Putnams, 1867) p. 568.

65. S.S. Conant, "Fine Arts" *Putnam's Magazine*, I, (Jan. 1868), p. 131. Earlier, the *Tribune* also had commented on the undeserved obscurity of both Hills, even though they were the "only two men in a country like ours who can make a water-color drawing." (May 14, 1864), p. 4.

66. C.H. Moore, in J. Henry Hill, et al., *John W. Hill: An Artist's Memorial* (New York, 1888). Quoted in Dickason, p. 260.

67. Yale University Art Gallery. Examples of Hill's earlier work are plentiful in the New-York Historical Society, the Metropolitan Museum of Art, and the Museum of Fine Arts, Boston. Accounts of Hill's life and work can be found in J.H. Hill's *Memorial*; in Gerdts and Burke, *Still Life*, p. 117; in Dickason, *Daring Young Men*, pp. 259-263; in Stebbins, *Master Drawings*, pp. 154-155; and in an obituary in the N.Y. *Tribune* (Sept. 27, 1879). See also a brochure published in conjunction with an exhibition at the Washburn Gallery, N.Y.C., *John William Hill and John Henry Hill* (1973). These sources claim that Hill's Ruskinian transformation took place in 1855, although his landscapes of 1856 (e.g. *Piermont on the Hudson*, N.Y.H.S.) continue in his earlier style.

68. From Hill's obituary, *Tribune*, 1879. See Stebbins, *Master Drawings*, p. 157; and Gerdts and Burke, pp. 116-117, 120 for a comparative discussion of Hunt and Hill. The juxtaposition of these two artists was implicit in praise given to one of Hill's still

lifes shown at the Nichols Gallery in 1860: it "may be placed by the side of the best producion of the British School, of a similar character, without losing by the comparison." N.Y. *Tribune* (Dec. 29, 1860), p. 4.

69. "Paletta" also described J.H. Hill's *Study from Nature* as "loveable" and "charming," "good in execution ... almost faultless in drawing." She criticized the elder Hill's *Dead Game* as wanting in relief, although Hill could have pointed to Ruskin's advice that the painter keep "a slight tendency toward flatness." *ED*, p. 53 and note above. "Paletta," "Art Matters," VI (Nov. 29, 1866), p. 87. I have not located a copy of the 1866 Artists' Fund Society exhibition catalogue.

70. Conant, *The Galaxy* (1867), pp. 5-7.

71. "Close of the Artists' Fund Exhibition," N.Y. *Tribune* (Dec. 20, 1866), p. 4.

72. Conant (1867), p. 57. Conant gave the Hills "highest praise for accuracy of form, beauty and purity of color, and exquisite delicacy of finish. In these qualities they are unrivalled in American art."

73. *American Art Journal* (1866), p. 87. Examples of Moore's work from the 1860s are rare. Like Richards, he worked at a very slow pace. *Lilies of the Valley* (cat. no. 45), from 1861 or '64, has the bright color and bow-top format of Richards' *Red Clover* (cat. no. 71). *Snow Squall* (Princeton) from ca. 1865 shows Moore bravely attempting an ambitious subject (also tackled by La Farge at this moment) with rather uncomfortable results. Mather calls this "one of the finest aquarelles ever painted" in America. See Frank J. Mather, Jr., *Charles Herbert Moore, Landscape Painter* (Princeton University Press, 1957), p. 25. See also Stebbins, *Master Drawings*, p. 156 and p. 124.

74. Conant, *Galaxy* (1867), p. 5; *Tribune* (Dec. 20, 1866), p. 4. A contemporary example of this kind of work is John W. Hill's *Dead Blue Jay* (N.Y.H.S.) reproduced in Stebbins, *Master Drawings*, p. 155. For T.C. Farrer, whose exhibition of watercolors at Goupil's the previous December was heralded (by his friend Cook) as "the most striking and effective work that has been done in water-colors in this country," such a reception must have been disappointing. Although criticized for his color, Farrer was advised by Cook to concentrate on watercolor studies as well as pen and pencil drawings in lieu of his misdirected attempts at oils. "Fine Arts: Mr. Farrer's Water-Colour Drawings," *Tribune*, Dec. 16, 1865, p. 4.

75. Minutes American Watercolor Society 1866-67; Archives of American Art.

76. Conant, "Fine Arts," *Putnam's* (Feb. 1868), p. 259. Hill showed six works in this exhibition, including no. 496, *The Upper Hudson from Jessup's Landing*, possibly the watercolor by this title now in the Museum of Fine Arts, Boston.

77. See the N.Y. *Tribune* (Dec. 20, 1866), p. 4, and (July 3, 1867), p. 2, for praise of Newman's Japanese still lifes and Moore's landscapes.

78. "Art Notes: Exhibition of Water Colors at the Academy of Design," N.Y. *Herald* (Dec. 29, 1867), p. 8. The following year *Putnam's* complimented Henry's *Currants* as "natural as life, and very tempting. The relief is singularly deceptive." Conant, *Putnam's* (1869), 378.

79. Conant, *Putnam's* (Feb. 1868), pp. 257-259.

80. Conant, *Putnam's* (1869), p. 378, and sources cited above, notes 74-79. The comments were in response to *Atlantic Ocean (2000 Miles from Land)*, otherwise described as "a sad botch." T.C. Farrer's contributions in 1868 and '69 included many flower subjects and a few landscapes. In 1871 and '73 he sent European views.

81. *Tribune* (July 3, 1867), p. 2.

82. Nina Moore exhibited at the Watercolor Society more than anywhere else, although the work she showed between 1868 and 1870 earned no commentary to my knowledge. All of the eleven items shown during these three years were leaf and flower studies.

83. See N.Y. *Tribune* (Feb. 21, 1873), p. 2; (Feb. 5, 1878), p. 5; N.Y. *Times* (Feb. 9, 1873), p. 5

84. *The Nation*, Feb. 22, 1872, p. 126.

85. *The Nation*, p. 126. I suspect this subject (no. 409 in the

catalogue) followed the format of blue sky and branches behind the fruit, practiced too often (according to S.S. Conant) by J.W. Hill (see note 76).

86. Mather, C.H. Moore, p. 44.

87. Moore's first extant watercolors seem to be from about 1864-65. North Conway began with an oil in 1865 (unlocated) and was reworked in a pen drawing of 1869 (Princeton) and a projected etching (also 1869). The final watercolor is in the Museum of Fine Arts, Boston. Mt. Washington first appeared in an ink and wash variant (Fogg), ca. 1869, evidently for an etching planned that year. A lost oil appearing at the National Academy of Design in 1870 seems to have been similar, providing the basis for the watercolor of 1872. See Mather, pp. 37-47.

88. On Moore's "improvements," see Mather, p. 39.

89. Perhaps no. 414 or 544 in the American Watercolor Society catalogue of 1868. See Kent Ahrens, p. 87.

90. Mather, p. 40.

91. The presence in Cambridge of C.E. Norton, another Ruskin enthusiast and Pre-Raphaelite collector, must have been attractive to Moore. His decision to teach engineering students may have been justified by a desire to work, as Ruskin did for the Working Men's Colleges in England, to educate the designers of his age. Mather (pp. 45-46) discusses this possibility, citing Moore's letter of 1873 professing to follow "Mr. Ruskin's teaching so far as I could." Some of his late still lifes are at the Fogg Art Museum.

92. According to J.S. Dearden, Curator, The Ruskin Galleries, Bembridge School, Bembridge, England, Moore based Ruskin's image on a photograph, which is not surprising considering the manner of Moore's execution. Moore's Swiss village scenes and his Venetian Doorway (all Fogg Art Museum) continue to illustrate the recommended subjects and organization of Elements of Drawing. See ED, 93; Mather, pp. 50-51.

93. Also from this period, Schooners, Ironbound Island, Maine (Princeton); see Mather, fig. 27.

94. Many examples of Newman's work in this genre are reproduced in Ahrens, pp. 91-98.

95. Newman's absence in 1873 was regretted by the Tribune's reviewer, who commented that a portfolio of his work from the previous two years in Italy was now in America, but the owner felt "too delighted" with them to lend them to the exhibition (Feb. 21, 1873, p. 2). American collectors gave Newman's work to The Brooklyn Museum, Yale, and the Museum of Fine Arts in Boston at the turn of the century.

96. Atlantic Monthly (March 1872), pp. 376-377; The Nation (Feb. 29, 1872), p. 144. See also Fine Arts (March 1872), p. 7. Titles and descriptions of Hill's work in 1872 make it appear that panoramic, hill-top perspectives (like those in Richards', Newman's, and Moore's work) predominated. See also A Connecticut River Valley (p.c.) of 1859, or View from High Tor of 1866 (cat. no. 34).

97. The Nation (Feb. 29, 1872), p. 144.

98. C.H. Moore, in Hill, An Artist's Memorial, cited by Dickason, p. 262.

99. Tribune (Feb. 21, 1873), p. 2.

100. Moore, in Hill, An Artist's Memorial. Dickason, p. 261. Late in life Hill was reduced to peddling his drawings door to door.

101. His son lent fourteen works to the American Watercolor Society exhibition of 1880, and later published an Artist's Memorial, containing tributes from Moore and others, along with reproductions of his father's work. A rare bit of commentary on Hill's work from the mid-'70s can be found in Appleton's (Feb. 20, 1875), p. 248.

102. Clarence Cook, "The Water Color Society," N.Y. Tribune (Feb. 16, 1879), p. 5. On the "Sunken Sun of Pre-Raphaelitism," see E. C. Bruce, The Century: Its Fruits and its Festival (Philadelphia: Lippincott, 1877), p. 178.

103. "The Water-Color Society Exhibition," N.Y. Tribune (Feb. 15, 1882), p. 5. M.G. van Rensselaer, "The Water-Color Exhibition in New York," American Architect and Building News, VII (Feb. 28, 1880), p. 80. The Tribune remarked on Hill's absence from the otherwise splendid 1882 exhibition: "A curious

illustration of the change of feeling is shown in the simple fact that of the five drawings which Mr. John Henry Hill sent to the exhibition this year, every one was rejected, so that one of the men, who, with his father, the late John W. Hill, did more to create a love for water-color in this country than anyone else who can be named, is absolutely refused a representation on these walls." This writer commented on Ruskin's appreciation for J.H. Hill's work, but noted that no "artist of the new faith" would be influenced by his opinion. Hill's work was simply "out of date and old fashioned." Now, "For the first time in America, within the last few years, our artists are painting artistic pictures; poetry is at least in bud, and the day of scientific draftsmanship and of map-making as substitutes for painting has, let us hope, passed away forever." After an absence of ten years, C.H. Moore also found some of his work rejected in 1882, although three of his watercolors were shown. The rejected work, Venetian Doorway (Fogg) appeared in the rival "Salon des Refusés" staged by the unusually malcontented "rejecteds" of that year. J.H. Hill also exhibited work with this rival show. See Kathleen A. Foster, "The Watercolor Scandal of 1882: An American Salon des Refusés," Archives of American Art Journal, 19, no. 2 (1979), pp. 19-52.

104. American Art Journal (Aug. 24, 1867), p. 247.

105. Marie Spartali Stillman, the wife of W.J. Stillman, exhibited at the A.W.S. in 1875, '77, and '78, with very sympathetic reviews for her archaizing literary subjects (Launcelot and Elaine; Tristan and Isolde), her color sense, and her careful technique. On La Farge and Abbey as watercolorists, see my American Watercolor Movement, Chapters V and VI; and my "The Still Life Paintings of John La Farge," American Art Journal II (July 1979), pp. 4-37.

106. "I think it is worthwhile 'to spend a life' in doing this, especially when popular art is in such condition as at present," wrote Moore to C.E. Norton in 1866. "I often feel deeply, however, the wide difference between this and anything really GREAT. If my work does anything toward promoting a more universal and true love for nature, it will be the most I hope from it." See Mather, pp. 26, 46. Similar sentiments were expressed in Moore's essay, "The Fallacies of the Present School," in The New Path (Oct. 1863).

107. James Jackson Jarves, The Art Idea (N.Y.: Hurd & Houghton, 1864), 214.

108. Richards was elected to membership in 1870, following his inaugural submission, Lake Avernus, which may have been lent by its owner, the Philadelphia physician F.W. Lewis. Richards' renewed interest in watercolor appears first about 1869, in a series of New England coastline sketches. Examples of his watercolors from this period can be found at the Whitney Museum, The High Museum of Art, the Pennsylvania Academy of the Fine Arts, and The Brooklyn Museum. See Ferber, Richards, cat. nos. 50, 56-58.

109. Claiming to have watched Richards from the beginning of his career, this critic recounted the story of his early artistic efforts: "striving for truth" and precision of detail, he had risked losing the "spirit" of the landscape. However, patient study was finally rewarded. "Now we have his latest work, in which we see all the observation, so sharpened by practice, and all the skill gained by the industry of years, brought to the service of a poetic insight that few of our artists have shown." Responding to the Tribune's review, where praise had been tempered with comments describing Richards' work as "rather microscopic" and "lacking in interest," The Nation defended his sincere "individual experience," so opposed to the "recipes and conventions" of the schools. Those who found the work of Richards or John W. Hill monotonous, weak, or uninteresting simply betrayed their ignorance of nature or lack of sensitivity. "Fifth Annual Exhibition of the Water-Color Society," Nation, XIV (Feb. 29, 1872), p. 144; "Fifth Annual Exhibition of the Water Color Society," Tribune (Jan. 26, 1872), p. 5.

110. The Nation (1872), p. 144.

111. See my American Watercolor Movement, p. 124. On the connection between body color and illustration, see chapters on Homer, Abbey, and La Farge.

112. On Magoon, see Ferber, Richards, p. 32 and cat. nos. 54, 55, 59, 60, 70, 76, and 77; also Ferguson, "He Knew the Sea" p.6., where the Metropolitan Museum's catalogue from 1880 is quoted, substantiating Magoon's impact on Richards' decision to produce finished pictures rather than sketches in water-color: "Mr. Richards, while spending the summer of 1870 at Atlantic City, made several watercolor sketches as notes for oil paintings. They were seen by the Rev. Elias Magoon, D.D., who started a collection, to which new paintings were added as fast as the artist's time and the purchaser's resources would permit. The two friends traveled the New England coast and New Hampshire together, choosing favorite subjects. At the first three exhibitions of the Water Color Society in New York the artist reluctantly allowed his friend to exhibit specimens of his work but he has never pushed his own work into prominence. He did not even know of the present donation until after it was made." The Metropolitan sold many of these watercolors in 1929, though a few returned to the collection in 1966. (See Ferber, cat. no. 70.) In 1877 Magoon described his pre-'64 collection as "undoubtedly the finest collection of Water Color Art in America." After selling the bulk of it to Matthew Vassar about 1864, he began to collect again, and by 1877 owned more than 200 items, which he lent to the Pennsylvania Academy the following year. This collection was also open to visitors at his home in Philadelphia. See correspondence (1877), and brochure, "E.L. Magoon's reception" (ca. 1877) in the Pennsylvania Academy of the Fine Arts Archives. Magoon's meeting with Ruskin in 1852 and his early acquisition of Turner watercolors (1855-56) is discussed by Goldyne, Turner: Works on Paper, pp. 30-31. See also A Catalogue of the Art Collection presented by Matthew Vassar, (The Founder), to Vassar College, June 28, 1864. New York, 1869.

113. The Nation praised their "peculiar airy beauty, coupled with anatomical exactness in which [Richards'] landscapes are apt to excell." "International Water-Color Exhibition," The Nation XVI (Feb. 20, 1873), p. 138. This exhibition probably included fig. 32, Lake Squam. The Times described the entire group as "delicate, refined, artistic, pretty" and "harmonious in tone, and wonderfully good in perspective." "The Water-Color Collection" (Feb. 16, 1873), p. 3. In this year, the Aldine described Richards as among "the best known water-color painters of America." VI (April 1873), p. 87.

114. As if to crown this defense of the virility and "true artistic feeling" possible in "elaborately finished" work, the New York Times invoked the name of a popular French painter of manly military subjects, and called Richards the "Détaille" of landscape. "Seventh Annual Exhibition," Atlantic Monthly XXXIII (April 1874), p. 504; "American Society of Painters in Water Colors," Times (Feb. 1, 1874), p. 3.

115. Said The Nation, her composition "at first sight, as purely and elegantly decorative as a good wall paper design or a Japanese fan, is invariably found to contain some sentiment, lesson, or poem." Earl Shinn, "Fine Arts," XX (Feb. 4, 1875), p. 84.

116. The Times confirmed this sentiment more positively: "Though like many successful men, he had many imitators, he certainly has no equals in the peculiar class of subject he chooses" (Feb. 7, 1875), p. 9.

117. On Edward Moran and the Philadelphia watercolor community, see my American Watercolor Movement, pp. 138-139, and note 104.

118. Moran, in George Sheldon, American Painters (1879), pp. 123, 124.

119. "Thomas Moran's Water-Color Drawings," Scribner's Monthly V (Jan. 1873), p. 394.

120. The Penn Monthly thought Moran's work showed only "true scientific pleasure, and perhaps scientific indifference" (April 1873), p. 259. Ten years later, his watercolors were condemned as "ghastly" in their relentless record of nature's gaudiest, most incredible moments, unmitigated by the interference of "the muse." Tribune (Feb. 20, 1882), p. 5; Clarence Cook, Art Amateur (1882), p. 75.

121. On the Blackburn Loan Collection of 1873, see my American Watercolor Movement, pp. 129, 29-30, 54, 206, 272.

122. Ruskin met with Moran in London in 1882. See Wilkins, Moran, pp. 38-39.

123. Farrer made watercolor copies of Turner's paintings for use in Louis Prang's lithographic reproduction process. See K.M. McClinton, The Chromolithographs of Louis Prang (New York: C. N. Potter, 1973), p. 187. After examining "Sweet is the Hour of Rest!" the Independent commented that Mr. Farrer, "whom once we thought to have come back from his foreign studies with nothing gained but a studied imitation of Turner's manner and an intense admiration for Ruskin's theories, shows us in this American Watercolor Society exhibition that our judgment was incorrect ..." In fact, he had learned from both, but only assimilated what was best for him. "He has learned from Turner how to put the sun into his atmosphere, and that light has a luminous quality independent of color. He has learned of Ruskin that pre-Raphaelitish slavery to Nature is not necessary in order to be faithful to Nature." "Fine Arts. American Water-Color Society. 13th Annual Exhibition," 32 (Feb. 19, 1880), pp. 9-10. Opinion divided on Farrer's "semi-pensive, semi-prosaic" work in the 1870s. In 1876 Scribner's wondered how he could "so closely graze the poetic element in landscape without seizing it." "Water Color Society," XI (1876), p. 901. A friendlier critic in Appleton's found in Farrer's landscapes of that year a "charming delicacy of touch and sentiment. Mr. Farrer paints with almost photographic minuteness, and, while this quality makes his pictures sometimes a little hard, their stillness has a poetical character of its own, and their minuteness even gives one a sense that the artist must have cared very much for the impression he wished to portray." "Water-Color Exhibition" (Feb. 19, 1876), p. 251. Still, for every critic who found this minuteness "a poem in aquarelle," another complained that Farrer was—like Moran or Richards—merely scientific and literal, not pictorial; truthful, not artistic. Compare N.Y. Tribune (Feb. 15, 1882), p. 5 and The Art Amateur II (March 1880), pp. 70-71.

124. See my American Watercolor Movement, pp. 101-102, 155-158. See also Ferber, Richards, p. 90, 33, 37; and Ferber, Tokens of a Friendship: Miniature Watercolors by William T. Richards from the Richard and Gloria Manney Collection (Metropolitan Museum of Art, 1982), particularly pp. 43-45 and cat. items 21, 51, and 56.

125. To his patron, George Whitney, in Ferber, Richards, p. 33.

Plate 5
John Ruskin
Fragment of the Alps *circa* 1854–56
Watercolor and gouache over graphite on cream wove paper
13 × 19½ in. (33.0 × 49.5 cm.)
Collection: Harvard University Art Museums (Fogg Art Museum),
gift of Samuel Sachs
Cat. no. 125

The 1857-58 Exhibition of English Art in America and Critical Responses to Pre-Raphaelitism

SUSAN P. CASTERAS

Our means of acquiring even a slight knowledge of [English art] indeed have been so few that, to untravelled persons, the present exhibition must reveal a mine of art, of whose richness, however familiarized it may have become to them by tradition or repute, they knew almost nothing. A stray picture by Landseer or Herring or Maclise has occasionally found its way to our shores, but what do we know of their contemporaries and compeers, whose works crowd every annual exhibition in England? What do we know of the famous water-color school ... or what of the last, and as many contend, the greatest manifestation of modern art—the works of the pre-Raphaelites? Engravings of these works have not been wanting, but the thing itself, as it left the artist's easel, stamped with the impress of his hand and glowing with the illusions of color, we have not yet seen. German, French, Italian paintings, old masters, and copies innumerable have filled our galleries, auction-rooms, and dwellings; the artists of the mother country are alone unknown. It is eminently proper that this ignorance should cease. Church's picture of Niagara has recently elicited warm and even enthusiastic admiration from the first art-critics of England, and in the language of the circular issued by the projectors of the picture exhibition, 'the time is fully arrived when the kindred intellects of the two countries should be interchanged in other forms besides those of literature.'[1]

As this excerpt from an American journal confirms, by 1857 the New York art world was eager to see English paintings exhibited, so that they could exert a direct impact on audiences whose knowledge of British art was secondhand, gleaned mostly through prints. The exhibition of English art that travelled to major Eastern cities in late 1857 and 1858 was a monumental event, both for that simple reason and also because it provided viewers with some examples of modern, especially Pre-Raphaelite, works. A number of newspapers and art periodicals reported on the exhibition in detail. Since then, however, this key event in both American art and the history of Pre-Raphaelitism has been nearly forgotten,[2] and most of the circumstances of the exhibition have been either overlooked or misrepresented.

The first part of this essay aims to remedy this lack of historical data with an account of the complex chronology of the exhibition and sketches of the individuals who had primary roles in its inception and implementation. After the historical aspects have been traced city by city, with brief data on the content of the exhibition in each city, a concluding section will assess the contemporary journalistic reaction to Pre-Raphaelitism, both in general and in terms of specific works of art and artists.[3]

The idea for an exhibition of English art in America seems to have originated with Augustus A. Ruxton, although others, like the well-known London art dealer Ernest Gambart, had considered undertaking such an enterprise. William Michael Rossetti, who was to play a central role in arranging the exhibition, recalled in his memoirs that it was in 1856 that he first met Ruxton, "a more than commonly good-looking man, of polite and elegant address, and of a rather sanguine temperament."[4] Rossetti himself attributed the origin of the project to Ruxton, "an officer who had retired from the army still youthful" and the brother of George F.A. Ruxton, a popular author who wrote *Adventures in Mexico and the Rocky Mountains* in 1847 and *Life in the Far West* in 1849 (the latter was serialized in 1848 for *Blackwood's Magazine*, which presented it to an English audience enthralled by the adventures of Kit Carson and the "mountain men"). Although he was universally described as affable and competent, Ruxton was in most respects a rather naïve newcomer to the arts, and Rossetti's later remarks about him may have been deliberately ironic: "Capt. Ruxton had no sort of connexion with fine art or its professors but he felt a liking for pictures, and, having all his time for himself, and a wish to come forward in any way which might ultimately promote his fortunes, he partially matured this American project in his own mind and then looked for someone to act as secretary and to serve as medium of communication with artists."

Ruxton asked Rossetti to function as intermediary partly because he wanted to secure works of "Pre-Raphaelite quality"; Rossetti, a founding member of the Pre-Raphaelite Brotherhood, knew all the principal figures in that group. Rossetti also had another asset: his "recent connexion with the American art-journal, *The Crayon,*" to which he had contributed monthly columns as a foreign correspondent, beginning with the April 1855 issue and continuing through December of 1856. Rossetti must have gained faith in the newcomer to the arts, for he wrote that after several interviews with Ruxton, he agreed to take on the job, which provided him with a small salary.

It is not clear exactly when in late 1856 or early 1857 the plan was devised, but prior to June of 1857 Rossetti wrote a circular that was sent to artists and art periodicals in order to explain the scheme and solicit their cooperation. In his text, he revealed his understanding of the best means of appealing to artists—anticipating their anxieties about both the display and the insurance of their paintings. He also rather perspicaciously assessed the likely reception by the American public with its growing taste for art:

> There is good reason for believing that such an Exhibition would be welcomed by the Americans. The wealthy classes in New York are well known to be lavishly sumptuous in the arrangement and decoration of their dwellings; and it is confidently anticipated that they would be glad not only to call in the aid of Fine Art for this purpose, but to have its productions brought home to them for that constant contemplation and study which exhibitions and museums of a similar order receive from the cultivated classes. . . . The taste for Art is growing in America, as it inevitably must grow with advancing wealth, population, and resources. Americans are already in Europe keen competitors at any sale of objects of *virtu,* or of antiquarian interest. The success which appears to have attended the Exhibition of Paintings of the Düsseldorf School—now for some years established in New York—may also be deemed an encouraging precedent. It is difficult to imagine that, if the works of this alien school excite the interest of Americans, those of a race to which they are so closely allied in blood, character, and tradition will be otherwise than successful with them. Active measures are already in progress for making the projected Exhibition a fact. Mr. Augustus Ruxton—the original projector—left London for New York at the beginning of May, with the view of communicating with some of the leading men in the States, and of obtaining a gallery. Mr. Ford Madox Brown—the historical painter—has consented to accompany to America the works that may be offered, and to superintend the hanging and all other such preliminaries. Contributors may, therefore, rely upon it that justice will be done to their works. An unexceptionable guarantee-fund will be obtained before the works are removed for exhibition, including ample insurance—to the extent probably of not less than 50,000£. An eligible offer has already been made for this purpose; and one main object of Mr. Ruxton's visit to America is to prosecute further inquiries on the matter. Exhibitors would be relieved from all expenses of transport; but a moderate per-centage to be fixed before final arrangements are made would be charged upon the sale-price of any works disposed of out of the Exhibition. The first Exhibition will, it is hoped, be opened in New York in October next, and remain open for some months; and it would be for the contributing artists to determine whether any of their works which might remain unsold at the close of the term should be returned to them (transport free) or should be left to re-appear in the Exhibition of the succeeding year.[5]

The brochure provoked immediate responses in several art periodicals, most of which endorsed the basic premise but expressed concern about its feasibility. *The Athenaeum* thought artists would "hesitate to send their works to America, except on the very highest guarantees,"[6] while *The Builder* chimed in with a warning note about previous failures of similar exhibitions of foreign art at the Universal Exposition. "If well managed, we should have no doubt whatever of the success of the scheme," *The Builder* remarked, but "we would suggest the desirability of not confining it, even in appearance, to any one school or party."[7] *The Art-Journal*'s assessment was also quite wary, lauding the project as "admirable in theory" but expressing misgivings about the timing and other factors:

> Our doubts arise from our belief that it is next to impossible to collect a sufficient number of high-class pictures to form an exhibition, which exhibition is to open in New York on the first of November; and we strongly advise its postponement for a year. It will be a serious and fatal mistake to imagine that the Americans will be satisfied with mediocrity—they can distinguish excellence quite as well as we can. . . . The experiment will, therefore, be a failure unless a large number of paintings of the highest merit be submitted to them. The project, originally started, we believe, by a few English artists, is now mainly under the direction of Mr. Gambart: he is a gentleman of intelligence and experience, and is, perhaps, the only person in England in whose hands it will be comparatively safe: but even he will find it difficult, if it be possible, to achieve this object worthily. We confess that our fears on this subject are stronger than our hopes.[8]

By the next month *The Art-Journal* sustained its negative response by adding that, as it had hinted in the June issue, "the committee have evidently found it . . . no easy matter to get together any number of works of the best order, and by our best painters." A long list of eminent artists, some of whose works would not appear in the exhibition, was cited; *The Art-Journal* speculated that watercolor artists were better represented in part because "they are more easily collected than large and important works in oil."[9]

Following the sundry columns acknowledging the project—including the one in *The Athenaeum* that misattributed the exhibition to Gambart—a major difficulty developed. Rossetti delicately alluded to the problem as follows: "When Capt. Ruxton's American project had obtained some degree of publicity, it turned out that Mr. Ernest Gambart, then the most prominent and resourceful picture dealer in London, had also been entertaining a plan of like kind. Some uncertainties ensued...."[10] The latter understatement politely minimized the crossfire of correspondence that took place between Rossetti and Gambart, who was greatly irritated that Ruxton's exhibition would preempt a similar plan of his own.[11] Gambart's July 5, 1857, reply to a (lost) letter from Rossetti nonetheless retains a certain cordiality beneath its insistent tone:

> In reply to your esteemed of Saturday I acknowledge having for a long time entertained the notion of an exhibition of British works of art in New York, but it is only since the reduction of the tarif (sic) that I have taken any decided steps in the matter—I have some time ago sent orders to my correspondent in New York to engage rooms & have since then read in the Athenaeum an article aluding (sic) to a similar object & glad to find by your letter that my project had found already advocates—& Now I will at once state that I have in this as in all other Exhibitions of Pictures in which I am already or may hereafter be engaged no expectations nor wish to secure personal direct remuneration—Interested as I am & deriving revenue from my publishing firm, anything that spreads & promotes the interest in the fine arts, promotes at the same time indirectly the interests of my firm— Therefore if this exhibition can be well managed by you and your friends I shall at once give up my own projects as having no speculative end & competition could not be entertained—I propose going to Paris this evening; therefore I could not see you before next week unless you can call here to-day at five o'clock.[12]

However, within a few weeks the tone of correspondence altered radically to one of icy confrontation; in the interim, Rossetti and Gambart had apparently met and agreed that two English exhibitions opening simultaneously would be "foolish" and "detrimental" to both parties. Gambart also suggested that he had no "direct advantages" to make from the venture (although this seems unlikely), yet he implied that Rossetti would have made a personal profit (although the latter's honorarium was probably quite modest). In his July 21 letter, Gambart reported that various artists had pressured him to reconsider his decision and implied that the Pre-Raphaelite content of the show might be too strong and thus unfairly represent modern English art:

> I am so much upbraided for giving up my scheme of a New York English Exhibition by artists who seem to place their confidence in me & denounce your ability of gathering a genuine English Collection as representing the British School that I must in justice to my friends whom I seem to have deserted too easily ask you what prospects you have of success & the names of the artists who have either given you or promised you Pictures, for if, as I am told on every side, you represent only *a very small body* of men & have no support of the academical body & the generality of artists I would be guilty of gross neglect towards my friends if by my withdrawal I lent myself to the furtherance of the interests of a cottery (sic) to the exclusion of the generality— Now, as I told you above my friends complain & deny you any authority to call yourself their representative; they denounce your utter inability in gathering an exhibition of the British School in works of art contributed by artists, they pretend your efforts will remain unsuccessful, & between your pretentions (sic) and my desertion that they will be either in a very unsatisfactory exhibition or no exhibition at all—I send you a rapid exposé of what I understand to be the state of affairs & ask you for a meeting of your supporters or a list of the names that I may have an answer to give to those who thus assail us.[13]

As a result, there were some delays and probable negotations about merging the two efforts; as Rossetti later wrote in his *Reminiscences*, "finally it was arranged that Gambart should combine his scheme with ours—he being far the stronger in water-colours, while the great majority of the oil pictures came through our agency. Gambart sent at the same time a collection of French pictures to America for separate exhibit, Ruxton obtained through me an introduction to Madox Brown; and at one time it was proposed that Brown should accompany the works across the Atlantic, but this came to nothing."[14] Indeed, the circular had mentioned Brown's involvement in overseeing the New York installations, but Gambart seems to have interfered with this—much to Brown's annoyance, as the artist fumed in his January 17, 1858, diary entry: "I was to have gone over to hang the pictures, however, the scoundrel Gambart put a stop to that and all I had was the trouble of going to select the daubs."[15] Brown's comment neverthless reveals that he did at least help to choose the paintings that were included in the exhibition.

In the meantime, during the summer of 1857, Rossetti busied himself with contacting numerous artists about contributing to the show. For example, he wrote to Millais several times, realizing that this artist's works would be much sought after and admired in America; Millais demurred, however, writing on July 29, "I cannot give you an answer in the American Exhibition matter just yet, but I see very little chance of getting anything of mine."[16] Millais complained about having had only one picture in the famed Manchester Exhibition of 1857 and said he was "tired of being refused. You will understand this." The next missive, dated August 13, seemed more optimistic: "I have made an effort to get the Blind Girl for the American Exhibition as I should like it alone to represent me. I have had a letter from Liverpool saying that Mr. Miller promised them the picture and I ... am going to send the Dream of the Past there also."[17] But by the next month, September 3, Millais wrote apologetically to his friend, "I am sorry that I cannot help you," adding that he would have been pleased "if Mr. Windus had sent one or two to America, or Mr. Arden had lent his but they seem to be sick of exhibitions."[18] Apparently Millais had genuinely wanted to participate in the enterprise, for he later wrote in 1859 to an American patron named Charles Warren, "I have often wished to exhibit a picture in America publicly, but I have never had the opportunity, as my works have always been sold in this country to men who have had the greatest objection to parting with them even for engraving. Do you think it is likely there will be another exhibition of English art in New York, in which case I might retain an important work on purpose."[19] And as Rossetti may have intuited, the absence of works by Millais (and Dante Gabriel Rossetti) was later lamented by the critics. While the English journals projected a rather pessimistic outlook on the forthcoming exhibition, *The Crayon* welcomed it warmly and attributed the conception of it to recent successful exhibitions in London of French and German art. The August and September issues offered the editorial opinion (probably that of founder and co-editor William J. Stillman) that "we do not think any other school appeals so strongly to American sympathies" and, moreover, stated that what rendered "the English school specially interesting at the present time is the degree of development of Pre-Raphaelite reform."[20] Canvases that illustrated this reform were eagerly anticipated as "attractive features of the proposed exhibition," with examples by Millais, Hunt, Rossetti, Hughes, and others mentioned and with many names followed by the initials "P.R." to identify their artistic alliance. Rossetti's brochure was quoted to reinforce the idea that "The names of Longfellow, Bryant, and Prescott are as familiar in the old country as those of Tennyson, the Brownings, and Macaulay in the New, and the co-projectors earnestly hope that, if they succeed in rendering well-known to Americans the best names in living British Art, they shall be no less paving the way to the knowledge of American art in England."

While such paeans were being published prior to the October opening, Rossetti approached John Ruskin, whose *Modern Painters* was avidly read in America, about becoming involved in the exhibition.[21] Ruskin had earlier decided not to write a column for *The Crayon* because he felt he did not know America or its artists, and he rejected Rossetti's request on similar grounds, as a September 23 letter indicates: "You must have thought me very hard not to help you with the American Exhibition; but I have no knowledge of America, and do not choose to write one word about things which I know nothing of."[22]

As it turned out, Ruskin's refusal to help and the general sense of English foreboding about the venture underscored the unfortunate chain of events that accompanied the exhibition: above all, the timing coincided with a desperate financial crisis in the stock market—a subject that dominated the daily newspaper columns with headlines like "The Panic of 1857 and Great Monetary Convulsions," along with related topics on massive unemployment, bank frauds, and the notorious Schuyler swindle. Four sites had originally been chosen for the exhibition—New York, Philadelphia, Boston, and Washington, D.C.; but although Rossetti in his reminiscences named Washington as the place where "a sudden and violent storm of rain damaged several of the watercolors, including a work by Madox Brown,"[23] no proof of the capital showing seems to have survived. The other three sites stayed on the itinerary, and, following the tepid reaction of the press in Boston, at the end, the objects were most likely simply returned to England and their owners or creators. Of the initial stopover, Rossetti recalled that:

> The exhibition arrived in New York just in the thick of one of the most calamitous money-crashes which marked the nineteenth century. ... people had very few dollars to spend, and not much heart for thronging to places of amusement. ... Besides, the British artists had not after all come forward with adequate zeal. It was the year of the great Art-Treasures Exhibition in Manchester, and several men had really nothing to contribute; there was no important oil-picture by Turner, no Millais, no Dante Rossetti,—and the American devotees of Ruskin and sympathizers with Preraphaelism had been specially looking out for all these.[24]

Ruxton's correspondence with Rossetti in late September confirmed that dire circumstances had indeed altered initial plans: "Instead of the four sources of returns which the interchange of the exhibitions between Philadelphia and New York would have yielded, we fell back upon the one chance alone; that chance is weakened, unfortunately, by the position of the rooms, and the sudden panic in the money market. ...We could not have undertaken our enterprise at a more unfortunate, I may say disastrous time. ..."[25] The situation was ameliorated to the extent that there were ultimately three locations for the exhibition, and another felicitous development noted by Ruxton was that "the Commissioner of the Customs has not only given authority to pass the frames as well as the pictures free of duty, but allows them to be handed over to my agent from the ship without examination. ..."[26] However, Ruxton also bemoaned the lack of pictures by Rossetti and Millais. Just before the New York opening at the National Academy of Design, he wrote that "Durand, (of *The Crayon*) requests me to apply to your brother for a portfolio of his drawings. I promised to make the request, but I did not answer for its fulfillment. Your brother will not be displeased to hear that great interest is felt here in his works."[27] Ruxton also reported that in Brown's absence he had assistance from both Durand and W.J. Stillman in hanging the exhibition, using this opportunity as well to express hope that "Mr. Miller will allow Turner's WHALERS to come—Mr. Mulready may obtain two of his—and something must come from Millais. ..."[28]

The New York installment of the exhibition opened in the new gallery of the National Academy of Design (at the corner of Tenth Street and Fourth Avenue, near Broadway) on October 20, 1857, and ran until early December. A total of 356 objects were included, 168 of them oils and 188 of them watercolors. In the negotiations for the show and in subsequent arrangements Ruxton ruled with his "plausible manner and excellent address," despite the fact that the vice-president and shrewd money manager of the Academy, Thomas S. Cummings, had, by his own admission, "opposed the whole scheme" even though his colleagues on the committee had been "perfectly charmed" by it.[29] New York's exhibition was favored by the largest number and highest caliber of objects, for there were several works—by Arthur Hughes and William Hunt, as well as all five of the Turner watercolors—that did not appear in any other city. The majority of works were not Pre-Raphaelite—just as Gambart had wished—and this may have mirrored the dealer's influence in selecting objects. (Indeed, Gambart's name appeared, along with those of the playwright Tom Taylor, Madox Brown, and John Miller, as a member of the Selection Committee; the secretary in America was named as B. Frodsham in the catalogue.) Among the oil paintings most often cited for praise were Mark Anthony's *The Monarch Oak*, F.B. Barwell's *The London Gazette, 1854—Bad News from Sebastopol*, John Cross's *The Burial of the Princes in the Tower of London, 1483*, John Linnell's *Abraham Entertaining the Angels*, and Daniel Maclise's *The Installation of Captain Rock*. Reviews from the press were generally favorable, *The Evening Post* hailing the exhibition as "an epitome of all that is distinguished in contemporary British art"[30] and *The New York Herald* commending the watercolors and remarking of the quality of art in general that "not one of all this number is bad, few are indifferent, nearly all are very good, and many superb."[31] *The New York Times* did not like either the installation of pictures or the absence of pictures by Millais and Rossetti, noting of the former problem that "The paintings are disposed after a strange, incoherent fashion, which dazzles the eyes as you enter and leaves the brain bewildered when you go out.— They are hung without respect to Chevreuil (sic), or the laws of color—Pre-Raphaelite intensities killing 'naturalistic' composure, and flagrant oils literally burning the life out of quiet aquarelles."[32]

The Crayon was especially complimentary, reserving its particular approbation for the Pre-Raphaelites while sharing in the complaint about the absence of works by Millais. All of the New York newspapers and journals made pointed remarks about Pre-Raphaelitism, some pejorative and others laudatory; these reactions will be discussed more fully subsequently.

In the middle of the exhibition (November 3), Gambart fired off another missive to Rossetti complaining that he feared "Ruxton loses sight of our premises, which are *to do the thing in the interest of the artists.*"[33] Stating that their artists/clients wanted primarily "the sale of their pictures or their return as early as agreed," he urged a pre-Christmas deadline so that artists could perhaps sell their works and have money to apply towards their holiday bills. His words acquire an accusatory tone in such sentences as "Ruxton seems to think only of receipts at the door. ... In fact what pictures are not sold in New York stand very little chance of being sold in other places." Gambart was so upset by this alleged breach of a pledge to the artists that he seems to have used this development as a reason to withdraw from the enterprise: "... I think it perfectly useless to consult exhibitors unless a schism is contemplated and for myself I feel the weight of my responsibility and the sooner I am clear of it the better and I wish to be released of all anxiety by the end of the year."[34] However, he did not harbor a permanent grudge against Ruxton; Gambart wrote to Rossetti in August of 1858 that he did not want an exhibition he had organized to injure Ruxton's future prospects—"in fact I would not like to take the matter out of his hands. ..."[35] Given the complications that ultimately transpired, perhaps Rossetti's later evaluation of the situation was most apt: "Ruxton was a loser by his spirited speculation—Gambart, I dare say, not a gainer."[36]

In addition to Gambart's criticism were a number of objections registered by W.J. Stillman. Rossetti had been a correspondent for *The Crayon* when Stillman was its editor, but the two had not personally met. Nevertheless, Rossetti remembered that Stillman "exerted himself vigorously in favour of Ruxton's enterprise," which had "tended all the more to promote the best relations between him and me when eventually he came to London" in early 1859.[37] Although the two later became "fast friends," Stillman felt compelled in November of 1857 to write a candid but rather prickly letter about the official reaction of the National Academy of Design to the show it had sponsored:

> The Committee seem to have thought that things which were second-rate at home were fit to represent English art here, while our amateurs are in the main as well acquainted with English art as the English public itself. ... There are many pictures which the public feel were sent here in presumption of ignorance or bad taste on our part, and we are a sensitive people on such points. ... The preraphaelite pictures have saved the Exhibition so far as oil pictures are concerned, but even they should have been culled more carefully. You should have thought that the eccentricities of the school were new to us, and left out such things as Hughes' *Fair Rosamund* and *April Love* ... with Miss Siddal's *Clerk Saunders* ... all of which may have their value to the initiated, but to us generally are childish and trifling. Then you have too much neglected landscape, which to us is far more interesting than your history painting. ... There must be something vital and earnest in a picture to make it interesting to our public,—and any picture which has not that had better stay in England. The P.R.B. pictures have, I venture to say, attracted more admirers than all the others for this reason, and at the same time have been more fully appreciated than they are *at this day* in England.[38]

Perhaps Stillman overstated the degree of American enthusiasm for the Pre-Raphaelite paintings, but he did reveal a sense of national pride in the ability to ascertain quality and not be fooled by anything less than good art. He also maintained that the lack of landscape paintings frustrated American viewers—a point of greater importance for subsequent advocates of American Ruskinianism.

Rossetti probably intuited the considerable truth of Stillman's complaints even before they were proffered, as evidenced by a handwritten list given by him to an unknown recipient, which chronicled his own feelings about many of the objects in the New York exhibition. While he lauded numerous works, noting whether Ruskin also approved of them (or their makers), he admitted that not all the pictures were of high caliber. For example, some of the Turner watercolors he deplored as "child's work"; W.C. Ross's miniatures of Queen Victoria and Prince Albert were "not firstrate specimens," and other works were slight. In the oil medium, he deemed P.F. Poole's *The Wreath* to be "very faulty in execution," described Sophie Anderson's *Lending a Deaf Ear* as "secondrate Pre-Raphaelitism—somewhat overdone," and reserved for William Huggins the dubious distinction of being called an artist who "ranks perhaps supreme for poultry."[39]

While the exhibition was still in New York, Ruxton proposed a new plan to manage future U.S. exhibitions of European and British artists (seemingly without Rossetti's or Gambart's help), adding to them works of art by American painters. Council minutes of the National Academy of Design from January of 1858 recorded this proposal, along with an accounting (and probably heated discussions) of the unpaid and late rent Ruxton owed on the galleries, which later was undoubtedly one of the reasons Cummings was skeptical about Ruxton's plans.[40] The proposed future enterprise would also have involved the Pennsylvania Academy of the Fine Arts and the Boston Athenaeum, with all three museums sharing the costs (not to exceed $1,666.66) of procuring, insuring, and transporting objects. Ruxton was to be paid for his administrative labors, and any profits from the exhibition were to be used and controlled solely by each participating institution to buy works of art from the show for its own collection.[41]

Meanwhile, the exhibition, with sundry replacements or omissions, moved on to Philadelphia for the period from February 3 to March 20, 1858, the tally now substantially reduced to 232 items—105 oils and 127 watercolors. In early January, Ruxton had contacted the Pennsylvania Academy of the Fine Arts requesting a maximum sum of $1,200 to transport the pictures from New York and to cover some of the freight and insurance fees to England, stipulating as well that any forthcoming profits were to be applied (as agreed) to the purchase of pictures from the exhibition.[42] Initially, the Academy agreed with the terms and with the pending proposal to join the National Academy of Design and the Boston Athenaeum (and also, possibly, the Art Association of Washington or another gallery) in sponsoring subsequent exhibitions of European art. However, the Academy later withdrew from the agreement, probably due to low attendance and receipts from the display of English art. In fact, by February 22 a vote was taken in the Committee on Exhibitions, and chairman J.R. Lambdin "ordered the North and Northeast Galleries to be closed at night for a week in consequence of the small attendance of visitors, to reduce the consumption of gas."[43] Although expectations had been high, the Academy ended by paying only $500 for its share of the exhibition, and there were no profits for acquiring pictures for the permanent collection.[44]

In contrast to these disappointments, several Philadelphia newspapers praised the venture, including *The Public Ledger, The Morning Pennsylvanian,* and *The Pennsylvania Inquirer,* the latter stating that "the surpassing excellence of many of the specimens . . . so far exceeded our anticipation that they excited surprise as well as intense admiration. . . ."[45] *The North American and United States Gazette* maintained that there were no poor or even mediocre works included, while *The Press* lauded the Academy for bravely risking a winter exhibition "brought here to test the probable success of a design entertained on both sides of the Atlantic regarding the need for European art in America."[46] *The Inquirer, The Press,* and *The Sunday Dispatch* all asserted that the watercolors were the principal gems to see, and most of the critics also singled out Pre-Raphaelite canvases as dazzling experiments not to be missed by spectators. *The Sunday Dispatch,* however, hated the Pre-Raphaelite efforts, which were deemed too rigid, false, and even too medieval and "Catholic." Moreover, Ruskin himself was criticized for his part in having "done much to introduce this method of barbaric painting into the English school, and in such proportion has he marred its taste."[47] The author of that review also could not reconcile Ruskin's equal endorsement of both Holman Hunt and Turner, since the latter was capable of producing "wonderful effects by a single stroke of the brush, which neither Hunt, Millais, nor any other Pre-Raphaelite could produce if they lived until dooms-day."

In Boston the total number of objects rose to 321, including 104 oils and 214 watercolors, plus three bronze medallions by Pre-Raphaelite member Thomas Woolner that had not been exhibited elsewhere. The show opened to the public on April 5 of 1858 and closed on June 19. Ruxton was assisted at the Boston Athenaeum by Dr. Robert W. Hooper, E.C. Cabot, and C.R. Codman, all members of the Committee on Fine Arts, and by Superintendent A. Ordway; however, no correspondence among these individuals survives in the archives.[48] As at the other institutions, the plan to have acquisitions made from the exhibition by the participating museums went unrealized. As a writer on *The Crayon* pointed out in its May 1858 issue, "Although the exhibition is a decided success, I do not think that Bostonians take very kindly as yet to the works of the Pre-Raphaelite school," an allusion to the Brahmin-versus-British aesthetic conflict that evolved on this subject.[49] In general, Boston newspapers preferred the watercolor pictures to those in oil, and *The Boston Post* even jingoistically suggested that American works should have been displayed alongside their counterparts in order to prove American superiority, "for in fact there is not a landscape in this whole collection that will come up to our artist, Mr. Church's magnificent picture, exhibited here a year or two since."[50] *The Boston Daily Advertiser* asserted that there was not enough quality art selected and that "many of the most distinguished British artists of the present day are not represented here at all."[51] *Dwight's Journal of Music* (whose critic provided the most lengthy of all analyses of the show) regretted "the losses which the collection has suffered since its arrival in this country, losses for which the recent importations offer us inadequate compensation."[52] Once again, it was the Pre-Raphaelite works that drew the most spirited response—in this city, a testy one, from the critics of *The Christian Register, The Boston Daily Courier,* and *Dwight's Journal of Music,* for example. A public lecture that Stillman gave in early May was derided by one writer precisely because it bestowed "the laurel to the pretentious egotists of the so-called Pre-Raphaelites for turning from the puerile pursuit of beauty to the search for truth, be it ever so hideous or disgusting."[53] While some accused Stillman of espousing this radical new art in America, others blamed Ruskin directly, one author claiming that Ruskin had insisted "art was only rightly to be seen from a nutshell. He accordingly procured one of ample dimensions, fitted up its interior to suit his convention, mounting therein a powerful periscopic lens, and commencing his explorations."[54] Ruskin's remarks in *Modern Painters* were labeled false and dangerous, the source of the Pre-Raphaelite propensity for "prevailing dryness [and] unhealthy coldness" of approach, especially in terms of color.[55] As a result of Ruskin's theories, Pre-Raphaelitism had become a "strong grasping at the actual, striving without the cheering light of internal truth … the intention is all that is expressed, while in the representation of the subtle qualities of nature, their faith seems soulless, and all their labour vain. … Devotees in the new faith seem to be … bending themselves to the fruitless labour of making microscopic, geological, or botanical studies, simply because the voice that calls them speaks in the name of truth."[56]

The analysis of unfolding events that culminated in the 1857-58 exhibition can now be shifted to focus on individual works of art that were displayed. In addition to those artists already named as contributors to the New York portion of the show, there were numerous other painters whose works appeared in all three cities. Among the oil canvases most frequently mentioned were John Calcott Horsley's *Prince Henry Assuming his Father's Crown* and Edward M. Ward's *Izaak Walton Fishing in the Colne*; works by Richard Redgrave, James Collinson, Charles Lucy, and Edward Lear also received attention. Among the modern-life subjects singled out were F.B. Barwell's *The London Gazette, 1854: Bad News from Sebastopol* and Anna Blunden's *The Song of the Shirt* (fig. 34). The latter was a popular sentimental theme inspired by Thomas Hood's poem of the same title, and both Blunden's and Barwell's contributions were described by *The Boston Daily Advertiser* as part of the "groups and studies of the present times."[57] While the Pre-Raphaelite pictures generally stole the headlines (as will be shown), they were definitely outnumbered by more traditional pictures with more conventional stylistic handling. In this less radical category was Frederick Leighton's *The Reconciliation of the Montagues and the Capulets* (fig. 35), which had been included in the great Parisian exhibition of 1855. *The Crayon* alone proffered a positive reading, for in spite of defects of drawing, the work was deemed brilliant: "It is Art which sweeps one away, overcoming every thought of criticism."[58] In contrast, *The New York Times* scorned the picture, and said that the composition consisted of "frantic and cadaverous 'disfigurement' of 'Romeo and Juliet,'" as well as "false sentiment and odious coloring."[59] *The Pennsylvania Inquirer* similarly branded it an "appalling scene … the mournful end … regarded as that great man's masterpiece. To obtain a

Left:
Figure 34
Anna Blunden
The Song of the Shirt 1854
Oil on canvas, 18½ × 15 in . (47.0 × 38.1 cm.)
Collection: Christopher Wood

Bottom:
Figure 35
Frederick Leighton
The Reconciliation of the Montagues and the Capulets
circa 1853-55
Oil on canvas, 70 × 90 in. (117.8 × 231.1 cm.)
Collection: Agnes Scott College

Left:
Figure 36
William L. Windus
The Surgeon's Daughter: Middlemas' Interview with his Unknown Parents
Oil on canvas, 17½ × 13½ in. (44.5 × 34.3 cm.)
Collection: Walker Art Gallery

Bottom:
Figure 37
Ford Madox Brown
King Lear and Cordelia 1848–49, 1853–54
Oil on canvas, 28 × 29 in. (71.0 × 99.0 cm.)
Collection: The Tate Gallery

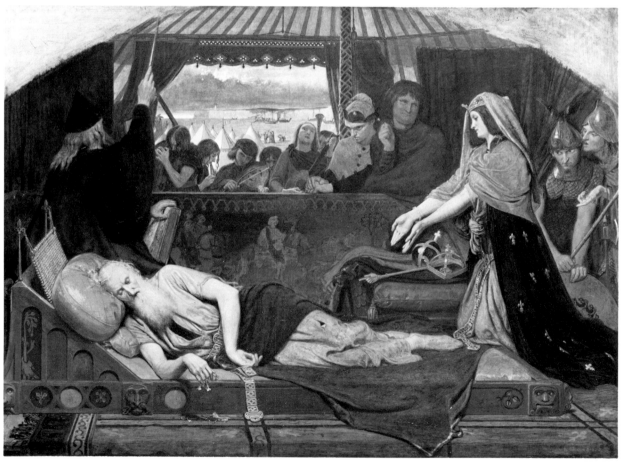

proper concept he induced Fanny Kemble to read the passage to him from the immortal bard. ...."[60] Notwithstanding such attacks, the work was bought by a Philadelphia collector directly from the exhibition. A more serious problem that Leighton faced was censorship, for his (lost) works entitled *Pan* and *Venus and Cupid* were removed from the exhibition early in its itinerary and without Rossetti's knowledge.[61] As Leighton wrote to his mother about this predicament,

> From America I have good and bad news. The bad is that my 'Pan' and 'Venus' are NOT BEING EXHIBITED AT ALL on account of their nudity, and are stowed away in a cupboard where F. Kemble with the most friendly and untiring perseverance contrived to discover them. This is a great nuisance. I have sent for them back at once; they know best whether or not it is advisable to exhibit such pictures in America, but they certainly should have let me know. I have written to Rossetti about it today, expressing my regret and desires. ... Meanwhile I am neglecting the opportunity of showing and disposing of them in England, a possibility I might willingly forego for the sake of supporting an enterprise in which I am interested, but not to adorn a hidden closet in the United States.[62]

Sometimes a painting was approved of partially because it did *not* possess Pre-Raphaelite characteristics. Such was the case with William Windus, whose style is now often associated with the Pre-Raphaelite circle but whose painting in the American exhibition was exempted from most of the criticism heaped on his cohorts. *The Crayon*, for example, generally liked his literary illustration entitled *The Surgeon's Daughter: Middlemas' Interview with his Unknown Parents* (fig. 36), while *The New York Times* pronounced it a "capital" work largely because of its non-Pre-Raphaelite qualities: "Mr. Windus' picture is positively painted with so little Pre-Raphaelite earnestness that he has neglected to deprive Middlemas of his midriff, and has pandered to the popular eye by obeying the laws of perspective."[63] The canvas was also admired in Boston, although the subject, from a Walter Scott novel, seemed to one reviewer to be an "unpromising theme of a vividly drawn picture."[64]

Perhaps the single most frequently mentioned painting was Madox Brown's *King Lear and Cordelia* (fig. 37), which was simultaneously hailed and censured, often in the same review. *The Crayon* called it a work with "superb drawing, powerful color, and originality of composition" that was "one of those vigorous artistic creations that carries away all prejudice."[65] But although *The Crayon* found the other figures in the painting impressive-looking, it excoriated the head of Cordelia for betraying a feebleness of character—a point echoed by the critics for *The Knickerbocker, or New York Monthly Magazine*; Cordelia was, it said, almost comically "a Billingsgate fish-wife gone into high tragedy on the boards of a provincial theatre."[66] *The New York Times* deemed the perspective to be atrocious (contradicting *The Atlantic Monthly*'s praise of the excellent drawing), and agreed that Cordelia was a coarse specimen of femininity.[67] In Philadelphia, *The Sunday Dispatch* preferred more conservative paintings by Cross, Horsley, and Redgrave to Brown's "melodrama" with its ugly Cordelia.[68] Bostonians, however, waxed enthusiastic about the canvas, *The Boston Daily Courier* applauding the "true grandeur of conception, in every respect" and the "penetrating and profound" tragic gloom of the prostrate monarch. "The character of magnificence natural to the subject is strongly though subtly expressed in the royal design of all the costumes and properties of the scene. There is an all-pervading air of romantic regality in it."[69] However, another contribution by the same artist, a watercolor version of *Jesus Washing Peter's Feet* (see oil version, fig. 38) that was displayed only in Boston, had considerable invective heaped upon it. *Dwight's Journal of Music* felt the work embodied "palpable and puerile affectation" and had a muddied background, and a correspondent reporting on Stillman's lecture on English art in conjunction with the Athenaeum show upbraided Stillman for his worship of "ugliness and deformity" in his "eulogy of Pre-Raphaelitism" as well as in his accolades for Brown's "idiotic scribblings ... in *Christ Washing the Feet of Peter*."[71]

In every city, nearly all the periodicals—including the well-informed and articulate *The Crayon*—focused on Pre-Raphaelitism as the most significant revelation of the exhibition, and they attributed its development almost totally to Ruskin's influence. Most of the critics had difficulty understanding the tenets of Pre-Raphaelitism beyond a mere fidelity to nature, and their comments

Figure 38
Ford Madox Brown
Jesus Washing Peter's Feet 1851–56
Oil on canvas, 46 × 52¼ in. (117.0 × 133.5 cm.)
Collection: The Tate Gallery

thus reflect their confused and, at times, contradictory reactions.[72] Even *The Crayon*, a fervent advocate of the Pre-Raphaelites, had some problems in explicating the subject to its readers, although Stillman's earlier articles on "The Two Pre-Raphaelitisms" were in many respects quite lucid and insightful analyses of this revolution in painting.[73] An examination of some of the general interpretations of the movement underscores the blend of positive and negative, simplistic and sophisticated response that was typical in reviews. *The Knickerbocker, or New-York Monthly Magazine*, for example, wrote in early 1858 that "Our unaccustomed eyes are first attracted to strange, bright-colored pictures, vividly distinct in all their details. ... The all-pervading spirit which gives it life are those elements of ideal beauty which Ruskin has, with quaint force, named the Lamp of Truth and the Lamp of Religion ... Much maudlin talk there has been of Earnestness and Earnest Men, but there is behind ... all this ... a genuine love, inborn ... that craves for the truth."[74] Other publications emphasized the rebelliousness of the young band of artists who made up the movement; the author of an *Atlantic Monthly* piece wrote in 1858 that Pre-Raphaelitism was "an abso-

Figure 39
Arthur Hughes
Home from the Sea: A Mother's Grave
Oil on panel, 20 × 25⅝ in. (50.8 × 65.1 cm.)
Collection: Ashmolean Museum

lutely revolutionary movement, and must, therefore, be rejected by the English mind when seen as such,—and all this the more certainly and speedily because Ruskin with his imaginative enthusiasm has raised it to a higher position than it really deserves at present. ... He has merely misunderstood and misstated Pre-Raphaelitism, which will thus one day be the weaker for his support." After attacking Ruskin as a supporter of the group, the author went on to draw the predictable contrast between two kinds of art endorsed by Ruskin, speculating that "Turner would put a rainbow by the side of the sun, if he wanted one there; a Pre-Raphaelite would paint with a stop-watch, to get the rainbow in the right place."[75]

One of the works labelled as Pre-Raphaelite that was frequently cited—and in fact universally condemned—was Arthur Hughes' *Home from the Sea: A Mother's Grave* (fig. 39), a work repainted after the exhibition with the figure of the girl added. *The Crayon's* reaction was the mildest, calling it "a painter's puzzle. Ruskin has said that the checkered sunlight was the finest thing of the kind he ever saw. For ourselves, we are indifferent to the technical problems involved in an analysis of its merits. ... "[76] According to *The Evening Post*, the work was "absurdly drawn and bad in color with the foreground grass more like cut paper than the sod of nature."[77] *The Knickerbocker* chided *The Crayon* for even tentatively endorsing the picture, which it deemed to have an awkward composition and a very ungainly pose for the boy, whom they considered "to have lain so long upon his mother's grave that his ... trousers have become mildewed."[78] *The New York Times* fulminated that the painting was mere "puerile cant," a "miracle of misery and of white mushrooms, while a little lamb skips along, a neat pathetic symbol of orphanage, through the air or rather through the space that should be air, and at some considerable distance above the pea-green turf."[79] When the canvas arrived in Boston, the reviews remained just as pejorative, *The Christian Register* characterizing the alleged stony coldness of the figure as "a piece of malachite."[80] Other entries by Hughes were also lampooned. His *Fair Rosamund* (fig. 40) was described as "childish" by *The Evening Post* and as a "fearsome maiden" with wild tresses by other New York periodicals.[81] A lost work entitled *Two and a Half Years Old* was denounced as badly drawn and a pictorial joke or "abortion," as *The Philadelphia Sunday Dispatch* penned with ironic disgust.[82] *Ophelia* (fig. 41) was similarly attacked as "a powerful representation of a maniac, but not of *our* Ophelia."[83] One of the few works to escape complete scorn was a version of *April Love*, which appeared only in New York. *The Crayon* called this painting "perfectly fascinating; this picture did not please us at first sight, but the more we look upon it, the more we become absorbed in its simple embodiment of deep, pure intense feeling."[84]

Like several of Hughes' canvases, Elizabeth Siddal's drawing of *Clerk Saunders* (fig. 42) was seen only in New York, and was the recipient of kindred criticism about its "childish vagaries" and defective draughtsmanship.[85] William Michael Rossetti had noted in his handwritten memorandum that Ruskin admired Siddal's "power greatly, thinking her ... possessed of more natural genius for art than any other woman."[86] However, *The New York Times* concurred with another periodical's assessment of the picture as "Pre-Raphaelism run mad," deploring *Clerk Saunders* and two works by Hughes as the nadir of quality in the exhibition.[87]

The single Pre-Raphaelite picture that received the most attention was Holman Hunt's *The Light of the World* (fig. 43), which Rossetti himself had characterized in his notes as follows: "the picture of which this is a duplicate is considered by many Hunt's masterpiece and the loftiest effort of Preraffaelitism. ... I have sent Ruxton an enthusiastic letter which Ruskin published in The Times." Both W.J. Stillman and *The Knickerbocker* magazine were aware of this encomium about the picture, the latter reprinting most of Ruskin's letter in its review of the exhibition as a means of explicating the work to an American audience. Among metropolitan critics, *The New York Times*, for example, abhorred all the other Pre-Raphaelite canvases but adored *The Light of the World* for its tender sentiment and splendid tones, "... which would have moved the heart of Albrecht Dürer. ... This is one of the few Pre-Raphaelite pictures in which the artist and his 'elevated motives' do not immediately obtrude themselves between the spectator and the canvas; it is, of course, a piece of mere mystical symbolism, but it has the interest of true power."[88] In Philadelphia, the reaction was more divided. While *The North American and United States Gazette* appreciated the ethereal beauty of the picture, which they felt was "sufficient to immortalize its author,"[89] *The Philadelphia Sunday Dispatch* hated it and wrote scathingly of its faulty drawing, "hard and unnatural color," Christ's "stiff and inactive" pose, and the general tone of "moral blasphemy." Of Ruskin's long exegesis, the reviewer commented, "We could not conceive of any intellect so diabolically humorized as to write five volumes octavo, besides a whole farrago of nonsense in numberless pamphlets, if we did not know of the existence of John Ruskin."[90] Bostonians seemed to agree with this negative evaluation of Ruskin's writings about the picture, stating moreover, that "this enthusiast does not prepare his rhetoric in accord with Pre-Raphaelite rules."[91] Of *The Light of the World* as a visual phenomenon, *The Christian Register* continued, "In vain we turn our eyes from point to point. Everywhere some haunting vision is looking up, or looking down, or across at us; making us shrink and shudder with its strange, spiritless, galvanic life."[92]

Madox Brown and Hunt were the most touted of the artists; Hunt was also represented by a

Figure 40
Arthur Hughes
Fair Rosamund 1854
Oil on academy board, 15¾ × 11¾ in. (39.5 × 30.5 cm.)
Collection: National Gallery of Victoria

Top:
Figure 41
Arthur Hughes
Ophelia 1852
Oil on canvas, 27 × 48¾ in. (68.6 × 123.8 cm.)
Collection: City Art Gallery, Manchester

Left:
Figure 42
Elizabeth Siddal
Clerk Saunders 1857
Watercolor on paper, 11 × 7¾ in. (27.9 × 14.6 cm.)
Collection: Fitzwilliam Museum

Facing page:
Figure 43
William Holman Hunt
The Light of the World
Oil on canvas, 19⅝ × 10⁵⁄₁₆ in. (50.0 × 26.1 cm.)
Collection: City Art Gallery, Manchester

Figure 44
William Holman Hunt
The Flight of Madeline and Porphyro during the Drunkeners
Attending the Revelry (The Eve of Saint Agnes) 1848
Oil on canvas, 30½ × 44½ in. (77.5 × 113.0 cm.)
Collection: The Guildhall Art Gallery

reduced replica of *The Eve of St. Agnes* (fig. 44), which, Rossetti thought, with its new background figures, was "of course, better than the original." However, New York critics largely ignored it. *The Sunday Dispatch* in the next city found it badly drawn, "notorious and wretched," and unattractive, while the neighboring *North American and United States Gazette* claimed it was superb. In Boston the mixture of reactions was complemented by *The Boston Daily Courier*, which maintained that *The Eve of St. Agnes* had much less grandeur than Brown's *King Lear*, "though hardly less unity or intensity; and though it possesses more of the animation of exciting or interesting action, it wants the potential charm of pathos."[93]

A latent aspect of the criticism concerned the American viewer's desire to see the Pre-Raphaelite style translated in terms of landscape, a point Stillman had made to Rossetti when he wrote from New York that the selection of entries "too much neglected landscape, which to us is far more interesting than your history paintings."[94] Several reviewers discussed the technique or approach of the Pre-Raphaelites as it lent itself to the representation of still-life details in the landscape. *The Atlantic Monthly* critic, for example, wrote, "the pre-Raphaelites look at Nature as full of beautiful facts, and, like children amid the flowers, they gather their hands full ... crowd their laps and bosoms, and even drop some already picked, to make room for others which beckon from their stems—insatiable with beauty."[95] Similarly, in Philadelphia *The North American and United States Gazette* commented, "Whatever else we may say of them, there are no daubs bearing their names. ... Their leaves, ferns, grass, stones are all vividly drawn and colored. Those who would see what

Pre-Raphaelitism can accomplish should visit this exhibition."[96] *The Christian Register* of Boston even went so far as to assert that "there is something very touching in the patience with which strong men have painted the details of grass blade and dandelion-down, and the furze on the inner petals of the violet, because they would not slight what God had made!"[97]

As an extension of this idea, in evaluating specific objects, some of the most revealing criticism was dedicated to landscape elements, or, more exactly, to closeup views of a rock or weedy nooks burgeoning with foliage. For example, Mark Anthony's *The Monarch Oak* (now lost) was much praised and even called a facsimile of a tree. Rossetti described this as an effort in which the artist tried to combine "his own color and handling" with "Preraffaelite fulness and precision of detail." *The Crayon* also hailed the Pre-Raphaelite tendencies of lesser-known artists such as William Davis of Liverpool and Thomas Sutcliffe. Of Davis's *Evening* and *An Old Hedge*, Stillman commented that "they are unpretending transcripts of Nature, evincing true feeling and adequate power" and wrote that Sutcliffe's watercolors like *The Banks of Wharfe-Bolton Abbey* mingled the artist's "fine taste" with the "prescribed study of detail."[98] *The Evening Post* also cited William Webbe's *Twilight* and *An English Pastoral* as embodying the new style, a point echoed in Rossetti's remark that Webbe produced "good typical specimens of that class of Pre-raphaelism which confines itself to representation without invention of subject." In a similar vein, brief mention was made elsewhere of W.T. Bolton's watercolor with a quotation from Tennyson—"The rusted nails fell from the knots/ That held the peach to the garden wall"; of W.S. Rose's *A Weedy Nook on the Thames*; and of P.J. Naftel's *One Of Nature's Ferneries*, the latter being hailed as a delectable "place to extract from a July noontide sensations sweet and meditations divine."[99] The very titles of many of these works reinforced the preference for microscopic detail and closeup or "accidental" formats that irked the critic for *The New York Times*, who rather satirically wrote, "Conceived by men of genius the Pre-Raphaelite theory has been adopted by weaker brethren, who are pertinaciously painting up all the weeds, dandelions, bits of straw, old glass, fence-rails, and pokers that can be found in Great Britain, in an orgasm of mingled tenderness for the 'neglected truths of Nature' and contempt for sentimental fellows like Claude Lorrain. ..."[100]

Of the more renowned practitioners of landscape in the Pre-Raphaelite mode was Madox Brown, who was primarily represented in the exhibition by figural compositions in both oil and watercolor (and also in non-Pre-Raphaelite style). In Boston only his *An English Autumn Afternoon—London Outskirts* (fig. 45) was on display and garnered as many accolades as works by Brett and Inchbold. The obvious tendency of these three artists to intensify details and to aim at a kind of topographical objectivity "raises one of the most vexed and difficult problems of the age, namely: whether the utmost practicable exactness to truth may consist with the unity and harmony of art. ... ," as one reviewer observed.[101] The "seeming veracity" of the magnificent suburb of Brown's painting, "relieved from the fire and smoke of the day's battle of life," impressed *The Boston Daily Courier*, as did the vivid power of "the ruling sentiment of emerald freshness, of breadth and richness of shade and cool quietness of light" and the "air of tangibility [that] gives us the body as well as the soul of 'an English Autumn Afternoon.'"[102] Similarly, although *Dwight's Journal of Music* faulted the aerial perspective, it too remarked on the "feeling of drowsy autumnal quiet" that the work exuded.[103]

John W. Inchbold, who was described by Rossetti as "perhaps the highest of the strictly Pre-Raphaelite landscape painters—much praised by Ruskin," contributed a work with the accompanying lines, "When the Primrose flowers/Peeping forth to give an earnest of the Spring," and this picture was intermittently discussed. *The Boston Daily Courier* saw it as a primary example of the Pre-Raphaelite trait of intense sincerity and "nature worship, involving a ritual or aesthetic method of almost sublime faithfulness and simplicity. ..."[104] His colleague John Brett, whose *Glacier at Rosenlaui* (fig. 46) is now considered a stellar exemplar of Pre-Raphaelite landscape, was mentioned only occasionally by the critics; Rossetti remarked his work was "much admired by Ruskin (tho' he has not written about it)." Brett's *The Bank Whereon the Wild Thyme Grows* was hailed by *The Philadelphia Press* because it was "so perfect in coloring, and so elaborate in execution, that one wonders alike at the skill, taste, and patience of the artist—you might blow the dandelion blossom

Figure 45
Ford Madox Brown
An English Autumn Afternoon—London Outskirts
1852–53, 1855
Oil on canvas, 28¼ × 53 in. (71.7 × 134.6 cm.)
Collection: Birmingham Museum and Art Gallery

from its stem."[105] However, more attention was given to the glacier picture, which to *Dwight's Journal of Music* also posed quintessential questions about whether art could serve science as well as its own goals and whether particular truths of verisimilitude are "realized at the expense of the higher, general truths."[106] To this reviewer, the result was a mere portrait of a rock, "an abnegation of *all artistic* truth." In spite of the degree of indefatigable accuracy, Brett had "made no visible record of those bodiless immaterial qualities common to all Nature, without which a picture can have no verity either of representative or imitative art." The same issue was raised by *The Boston Daily Courier*, which also believed that the full expression of detail risked soullessness and failed to convey the awful grandeur of the real scene. Brett's picture served as the vehicle for a provocative digression by the critic, who hypothesized that "it certainly appears that there are effects of details and conditions, especially in the distances of landscape views, really appreciable to our perceptions through the feelings, but wholly intangible to our senses; and therefore, it must be impossible that by the mere faithful imitation of what is only definite and tangible, the sight, effect, or impression of such subjects can be rendered."[107] But both Inchbold's primrose picture and Brett's *Glacier at Rosenlaui* provided almost the ideal fulfillment of "definite drawing to a definite end. In the first, the intense expression of natural color, of rich though saddened tones, confers upon a commonplace subject an impressive character of blended beauty and pathos; and in the second, the pale icefields, the high and purple precipice, and the rock-strewn foreground are realized seemingly to the last line and speck—till, if we only knew the language in which time and the elements write, we could surely find here not only 'sermons in stones' but whole antediluvian histories, maybe, in the cerulean cells of the glacier and upon the cold and expressive faces of its adamantine walls."[108]

Given all these factors as well as Ruskin's general notoriety, it is no surprise that his *Study of a Block of Gneiss* watercolor (pl. 5) triggered myriad responses. Rossetti had commented that this was "one of the completest studies he has yet done," adding, however, that Ruskin was to have sent

Figure 46
John Brett
The Glacier at Rosenlaui 1856
Oil on canvas, 17½ × 16½ in. (44.5 × 41.9 cm.)
Collection: *The Tate Gallery*

"something more important from Scotland but it has not been done in time." Although it was exhibited in all three cities, New York critics referred to it very little, while the writer for *The Philadelphia Sunday Dispatch* found it false to nature and stylistically trivial as well as worthy of being the butt of a joke:

> And how the ladies go into extacies (sic) about this ...! Oh! look what Ruskin has done! Is not this fine in effects! ... We have seen gneiss, but never such a piece as this of Ruskin's; it looks like an unfortunate elephant's back that has been subject to the whip, full of niches elaborately worked out. A friend at our right says it looks like a bundle of oyster-shells tumbled out of a hot kiln. But such a sky! really, Mr. Ruskin, you must have had the *blues* when you painted it. You must have been on a month's spree. It is really incorrigible—nay, contemptible.[109]

And perhaps in keeping with one Boston newspaper's mistitling Ruskin's watercolor as a "block of genius,"[110] *Dwight's Journal of Music* gave it a rather harsh reading: "The opalescent hues of this wonderful block test an artist's power of color much less than the simple grey tones of our mountain boulders; and that, in his rendering of the more quiet tints of sky, mountain distance, and foreground trees, there is a lifeless condition that ill accords with the impressions of natural beauty which we derive from his grandly wrought descriptions. ..."[111] Thus, Ruskin was as much the target of censure as his fellow artists in this genre.

Critical response is one index of success or failure, but so, too, is commercial appeal. Incomplete and scant records survive overall about the sales of works of art from the 1857-58 exhibition, but those details that are extant provide another perspective on the enterprise. As early as February of 1858, Ruxton wrote to Rossetti that he had "accepted an offer, conditional upon Mr. Hunt's approval of £300 for *The Light of the World*. It is from a gentleman, Mr. Wolf, who has the finest collection of pictures in New York and who apologizes for making an offer below the sum named, but pleads the pressure of the times, and inability to pay more just now."[112] *The Crayon* clearly identified the buyer as John Wolfe of New York, one of the most important mid-century collectors in America.[113] For reasons that remain largely inexplicable, as Cummings of the National Academy of Design later wrote, Philadelphia proved "much more favored than in New-York" for the sale of works of art.[114] Ruxton reported that he sold Leighton's *Reconciliation of the Montagues and the Capulets* for £400 sterling to a Philadelphia client named Harrison along with Charles Lucy's *Lord and Lady William Russell* for the same amount.[115] *The Crayon* added that in addition to these works, several watercolor drawings had "passed into the hands of Mr. J. Harrison,"[116] undoubtedly Joseph Harrison, who like Wolfe was one of the most prestigious collectors with money and taste for fine art. The correspondent in *The Crayon* noted that many pictures were disposed of to other "amateurs of that city...Mr. S.B. Fales' collection is enriched by several pictures, embracing specimens of Sutcliffe, Hulme, Collingwood, Hough, and Ferguson. 'The Prussian Fair,' by E. Corbould, has become the property of Mr. W.T. Stewart. Wehnert's 'Ragged School' is disposed of, and other pictures (twenty-eight in all) to parties whose names are unknown to us."[117] In urging Rossetti to arrange for good replacements for the Boston Athenaeum, Ruxton alluded to "talk of a subscription to buy Horsley's *Prince Harry* for the large saloon of the Philadelphian Opera House." Similarly, two landscapes by J.W. Oakes were "reserved for the Academy if there are funds to buy them. ..."[118] Neither hope for a Philadelphia purchaser was realized, however, and efforts to find a patron for Brown's *King Lear* also proved unsuccessful. In Boston, few sales records survive, but "the first picture sold was a landscape, by Miss Fanny Steers, which was purchased by Professor Longfellow, of Cambridge."[119] Although Henry Wadsworth Longfellow bought Steers' *The Reeks*, there were apparently few other buyers, perhaps due to high prices.[120] Many of the asking prices seem rather high, with Horsley's history picture set at $2,500, Maclise's canvas at $2,250, Redgrave's *Mid-Wood Shade* at $1,300, and most of Brown's works (notably *King Lear* and *An English Autumn Afternoon*) listed at $1,000.[121] However, there was no huge commercial success in the venture—partly due to the catastrophic tenor of business at the time—and Ruxton consoled Rossetti that in general "you must consider what has been already done a great success, considering all things."[122]

Ultimately, of course, the exhibition of English art cannot be measured either in terms of journalistic reviews or actual sales, but, rather, by the influence it exerted on contemporary artists. Although the exhibition was besieged with woes and was constantly under attack, American painters forged their own opinions and pictorial interpretations of Pre-Raphaelitism. They clearly chose to pursue the landscape rather than the figure type of the Pre-Raphaelite style, thus heeding the advice given by *The New York Herald* reviewer that "there are some studies of flowers and foliage from which our artists may take a lesson to their profit."[123] The current exhibition begins to examine the somewhat rocky and rather short path of American artists assimilating and re-creating Pre-Raphaelitism on their own, and it is therefore appropriate to end with some pertinent insights from *The Atlantic Monthly* in 1858:

> Pre-Raphaelitism must take its position in the world as the beginning of a new Art—new in motive, new in methods, and new in the forms it puts on. To like or dislike it is a matter of mental constitution. ... In all its characteristics it is childish,—in its intensity, its humility, its untutored expressiveness, its marvellous instincts of truth, and its very profuseness of giving—filling its caskets with an unchoosing lavishness of pearl and pebble, rose and may-weed, all treasures alike to the newly opened eyes, all so beautiful that there can scarcely be choice among them.[124]

Whether in great naiveté or wisdom, the Pre-Raphaelites were seen in the 1857-58 exhibition to be pointing the way toward a divergent but important means of seeking truth in art, and it was this course that their American counterparts followed in their own fidelity to nature and the native landscape.

1. "The American Exhibition of British Art," *The Evening Post* (Oct. 20, 1857), p.2.
2. The sole mention of the exhibition that goes beyond a few paragraphs appears in David H. Dickason, *The Daring Young Men: The Story of the American Pre-Raphaelites* (Bloomington: Indiana University Press, 1953), pp. 65-70.
3. This research was assisted by a grant from the American Council of Learned Societies under a program funded by the National Endowment for the Humanities.
4. William Michael Rossetti, *Some Reminiscences* (New York: Scribner's Sons, 1906), Vol. 1, p. 264.
5. As quoted in "Fine Art Gossip," *The Athenaeum*, 30 (June 20, 1857), p. 796.
6. *Idem.*
7. "Proposed New York Exhibition of British Art," *The Builder*, 15 (July 27, 1857), p. 362.
8. "Minor Topics of the Month," *The Art Journal*, 19 (June 1857), p. 294.
9. "Minor Topics of the Month," *The Art Journal*, 19 (July 1857), p. 326.
10. Rossetti, *Some Reminiscences*, p. 265.
11. The best source on the Belgian-born Gambart is Jeremy Maas, *Gambart, Prince of the Victorian Art World* (London: Barne & Jenkins, 1975). I am also grateful to Mr. Maas for his generosity in sharing information on this subject with me.
12. July 5, 1857, letter from Gambart to William Michael Rossetti, Special Collections Division of the University of British Columbia.
13. July 21, 1857, letter from Gambart to W.M. Rossetti, Special Collections Division of the University of British Columbia.
14. Rossetti, *Some Reminiscences*, p. 265.
15. Virginia Surtees, *The Diary of Ford Madox Brown* (New Haven and London: Yale University Press, 1981), p. 199.
16. July 29, 1857, letter from John Everett Millais to W.M. Rossetti, Special Collections Division of the University of British Columbia.
17. August 13, 1857, letter from John Everett Millais to W.M. Rossetti, Special Collections Division of the University of British Columbia.
18. Sept. 3, 1857, letter from John Everett Millais to W.M. Rossetti, Special Collections Division of the University of British Columbia.
19. June 22, 1859, letter from John Everett Millais to Charles Warren, Special Collections Division of the University of British Columbia.
20. "Sketchings. An Exhibition of English Art," *The Crayon*, 4 (August 1857), p. 251.
21. On the general subject of Ruskin as he was perceived in America, see Roger B. Stein, *John Ruskin and Aesthetic Thought in America, 1840-1900* (Cambridge, Mass.: Harvard University Press, 1967).
22. Sept. 23, 1857, letter from John Ruskin to W.M. Rossetti, as quoted in W.M. Rossetti, ed., *Ruskin: Rossetti: Pre-Raphaelitism. Papers 1854 to 1862* (London: George Allen, 1899), pp. 178-179. Ruskin's letter to Stillman turning down the offer to write for *The Crayon* was written on March 28, 1855, and is quoted in E.T. Cook and Alexander Wedderburn, eds., *The Works of John Ruskin*, 13 (London: George Allen, 1905), pp. 194-195.
23. Rossetti, *Some Reminiscences*, p. 266.
24. *Idem.*
25. Sept. 29, 1857, letter from Augustus A. Ruxton to W.M. Rossetti, as quoted in Rossetti, *Ruskin: Rossetti: Pre-Raphaelitism*, p. 180.
26. *Idem.*
27. Oct. 10, 1857, letter from A.A. Ruxton to W.M. Rossetti, as quoted in *Ibid.*, pp. 181-182.
28. Oct. 20, 1857, letter from A.A. Ruxton to W.M. Rossetti, as quoted in *Idem.*, pp. 185-186. Turner's *Whalers* is now in the collection of the Metropolitan Museum of Art.
29. Thomas S. Cummings, *Historic Annals of the National Academy of Design Drawing Association, Etc. with Occasional Dottings by the Way-Side, from 1825 to the Present Times* (Philadelphia, 1865), p. 267.
30. "The American Exhibition of British Art," *The Evening Post* (Oct. 20, 1857), p. 2.
31. "The Fine Arts in New York," *The New York Herald* (Oct. 20, 1857), p. 4.

32. "Foreign Art: The Exhibition of the British and French Paintings in New-York," *The New York Times* (Nov. 7, 1857), p. 2.

33. Nov. 3, 1857, letter from Gambart to W.M. Rossetti, Special Collections Division of the University of British Columbia.

34. *Idem.*

35. Aug. 15, 1857, letter from Gambart to W.M. Rossetti, Special Collections Division of the University of British Columbia.

36. Rossetti, *Some Reminiscences*, p. 266.

37. *Idem.*

38. Nov. 15, 1857, letter from William J. Stillman to W.M. Rossetti as quoted in Rossetti, *Ruskin: Rossetti: Pre-Raphaelitism*, pp. 187-188.

39. Holograph abstract of a memorandum (untitled) by William Michael Rossetti, Beinecke Rare Book and Manuscript Library, Yale University.

40. Jan. 11, 1858, Council Minutes, National Academy of Design 1848-1862 archives.

41. Jan. 25, 1858, Council Minutes, National Academy of Design archives.

42. Jan. 11, 1858, Minutes of the Board of Directors, Pennsylvania Academy of the Fine Arts archives.

43. Feb. 22, 1858, Minutes of the Board of Directors, Pennsylvania Academy of the Fine Arts archives.

44. Mar. 24, 1858, Minutes of the Board of Directors, Pennsylvania Academy of the Fine Arts archives.

45. "Amusements," *The Pennsylvania Inquirer* (Feb. 3, 1858), p. 2.

46. "British Pictures on Exhibition at the Academy of Fine Arts," *The Press* (Feb. 5, 1858), p. 1.

48. I am grateful to Jonathan Harding of the Library of the Boston Athenaeum for his assistance in researching the trustees' records on this matter.

49. "Sketchings," *The Crayon*, 5 (May 1858), pp. 148-149.

50. "Athenaeum Gallery," *The Boston Post* (April 14, 1858), p. 1.

51. "Gallery of British Art," *The Boston Daily Advertiser* (Apr. 28, 1858), p. 2.

52. "Fine Arts; The Athenaeum Exhibition, I," *Dwight's Journal of Music*, 13 (April 14, 1858), p. 26.

53. May 7, 1858, letter from "T.T.S." to the Editor, *The Boston Daily Evening Transcript* (May 11, 1858), p. 4.

54. "Fine Arts: The Athenaeum Exhibition, I," *Dwight's Journal of Music*, 13 (April 14, 1858), p. 26.

55. *Idem.*

56. "Fine Arts. The Athenaeum Exhibition, IX. Water Colors," *Dwight's Journal of Music*, 13 (July 13, 1858), p. 128.

57. "Gallery of British Art," *The Boston Daily Advertiser* (April 28, 1858), p. 2.

58. "Sketchings. American Exhibition of British Art," *The Crayon*, 4 (Nov. 1857), p. 343.

59. "Foreign Art: The Exhibition of the British and French Paintings in New-York," *The New York Times* (Nov. 7, 1857), p. 1.

60. "Amusements," *The Pennsylvania Inquirer* (Feb. 3, 1858), p. 2.

61. According to a letter Leighton wrote to his mother, Rossetti was unaware of this censorship: "Rossetti answers me (as indeed I did not doubt) that he had not the remotest notion of the fate of 'Pan' and 'Venus.' He has written on my request to beg they may be sent back at once to Europe." As quoted in Mrs. Russell Barrington, *Life, Letters & Work of Frederic Leighton* (London: George Allen, 1906), Vol. 2, p. 46.

62. Letter dated only "Friday, 26th" and quoted in *Ibid.*, p. 45.

63. "Foreign Art: The Exhibition of the British and French Paintings in New-York," *The New York Times* (Nov. 7, 1857), p. 1.

64. "Fine Arts: The Athenaeum Exhibition, VII," *Dwight's Journal of Music*, 13 (June 19, 1858), p. 92.

65. "Sketchings. American Exhibition of British Art," *The Crayon*, 4 (Nov. 1857), p. 343.

66. "British and French Art in New-York," *The Knickerbocker, or New-York Monthly Magazine*, 51 (Jan. 1858), p. 57.

67. "Foreign Art: The Exhibition of the British and French Paintings in New-York," *The New York Times* (Nov. 7, 1857), p. 1.

68. "English Pictures at the Academy of Fine Art," *The Philadelphia Sunday Dispatch* (Feb. 14, 1858), p. 1.

69. "Exhibition of British Art," *The Boston Daily Courier* (May 15, 1858), p. 2.

70. "Fine Arts: The Athenaeum Exhibition, IX," *Dwight's Journal of Music*, 13 (July 13, 1858), p. 127.

71. May 7, 1858, letter from "T.T.S." to the Editor, *The Boston Daily Evening Transcript* (May 11, 1858), p. 4.

72. "Fine Arts. The Athenaeum Exhibition, II," *Dwight's Journal of Music*, 13 (May 8, 1858), p. 46, for example, likens the Pre-Raphaelite style to the strange tattooing customs of Fiji inhabitants: "In the Feejee (sic) Islands tattooing is an expression of the highest Art instinct. What to us seems barbarous and ugly, to the *native*, is beautiful and true art; and but for the exceptions noted, I should incline to consider whatever in the colors of this exhibition seems harsh and discordant to us, is peculiar to the English ideal of excellence and only properly to be judged by it."

73. Stillman's three-part article appeared in *The Crayon* in the fall of 1856; the focus among the modern Pre-Raphaelites was on Millais, Rossetti, and Hunt, with considerable explication given of the latter's *Light of the World* and its pendant, *The Awakening Conscience*.

74. "British and French Art in New-York," *The Knickerbocker, or New-York Monthly Magazine*, 51 (Jan. 1858), p. 53.

75. "Art. The British Gallery in New York," *The Atlantic Monthly*, 1 (Feb. 1858), p. 503.

76. "Sketchings. American Exhibition of British Art," *The Crayon*, 4 (Nov. 1857), p. 343.

77. "The English and French Exhibitions," *The Evening Post* (Nov. 14, 1857), p. 2.

78. "British and French Art in New-York," *The Knickerbocker, or New-York Monthly Magazine*, 51 (Jan. 1858), p. 54.

79. "Foreign Art: The Exhibition of the British and French Paintings in New-York," *The New York Times* (Nov. 7, 1857), p. 1.

80. "The British Gallery," *The Christian Register*, 4 (April 17, 1858), p. 3.

81. "British and French Art in New-York," *The Knickerbocker, or New-York Monthly Magazine*, 51 (Jan. 1858), p. 54.

82. "English Pictures at the Academy of Fine Art," *The Philadelphia Sunday Dispatch* (Feb. 14, 1858), p. 1.

83. "Sketchings, American Exhibition of British Art," *The Crayon*, 4 (Nov. 1857), p. 343.

84. *Idem.*

85. "The English and French Exhibitions," *The Evening Post* (Nov. 14, 1857), p. 2.

86. This and all forthcoming references are to Rossetti's abstract/notes in the Beinecke Rare Book and Manuscript Library, Yale University.

87. "Foreign Art: The Exhibitions of the British and French Paintings in New-York," *The New York Times* (Nov. 7, 1857), p. 2.

88. *Idem.*

89. "British Art," *The North American and United States Gazette* (Feb. 3, 1858), p. 2.

90. "English Pictures at the Academy of Fine Art," *The Philadelphia Sunday Dispatch* (Feb. 14, 1858), p. 1.

91. "The British Gallery," *The Christian Register* (Apr. 17, 1858), p. 3.

92. It is interesting to note that *The Light of the World* was apparently extremely popular among the working class. Ruxton wrote to W.M. Rossetti on Oct. 10, 1857, that he should report to Hunt "That a man said, 'Never mind the gas, the picture will light us up.' ... PR.Bism takes with the working men— they look, and they look, and they look, and they say something that the author of the picture would be pleased to hear. *The Sailor Boy, Try and Remember, King Lear,—*above all, *The*

Light of the World ... are immensely popular among my *hangers*." As quoted in Rossetti, *Ruskin: Rossetti: PreRaphaelitism*, p. 182. On this painting by Hunt see also Jeremy Maas, *Holman Hunt and The Light of the World* (London: Scolar Press, 1984), especially pp. 70-72 about the American exhibition. Apparently Hunt would have preferred to sell the replica to an English buyer, but, as he wrote to Thomas Combe (a friend and patron), "I had no opportunity of selling my sketch of the 'Light' ere its departure. I designed a frame for it which turned out most lovely when completed and made the picture look quite precious" (p. 71).

93. "Exhibition of British Art," *The Boston Daily Courier* (May 15, 1858), p. 2.

94. Nov. 15, 1857, letter from W.J. Stillman to W.M. Rossetti, as quoted in Rossetti, *Ruskin: Rossetti: PreRaphaelitism*, p. 188.

95. "Art. The British Gallery in New York," *The Atlantic Monthly*, 1 (Feb. 1858), p. 503.

96. "British Art," *The North American and United States Gazette* (Feb. 3, 1858), p. 2.

97. "The British Gallery," *The Christian Register* (Apr. 17, 1858), p. 3.

98. "Sketchings. American Exhibition of British Art," *The Crayon*, 4 (Nov. 1857), p. 343.

99. "Exhibition of British Art," *The Boston Daily Courier* (May 15, 1858), p. 2.

100. "Foreign Art: The Exhibition of the British and French Paintings in New-York," *The New York Times* (Nov. 7, 1857), p. 2.

101. "Exhibition of British Art," *The Boston Daily Courier* (May 15, 1858), p. 2.

102. *Idem.*

103. "Fine Art. The Athenaeum Exhibition, VII. Oil Pictures," *Dwight's Journal of Music*, 13 (June 19, 1858), p. 93.

104. "Exhibition of British Art," *The Boston Daily Courier*, (May 15, 1858), p. 2.

105. "British Pictures on Exhibition at the Academy of the Fine Arts," *The Philadelphia Press* (Feb. 5, 1858), p. 1.

106. "Fine Art. The Athenaeum Exhibition, VII," *Dwight's Journal of Music*, 13 (June 19, 1858), p. 93.

107. "Exhibition of British Art," *The Boston Daily Courier* (May 15, 1858), p. 2.

108. *Idem.*

109. "English Pictures at the Academy of the Fine Arts," *The Philadelphia Sunday Dispatch* (Feb. 14, 1858), p. 1.

110. "Exhibition of British Art," *The Boston Daily Evening Transcript* (Apr. 13, 1858), p. 2.

111. "Fine Art. The Athenaeum Exhibition, IX," *Dwight's Journal of Music*," 13 (July 17, 1858), p. 128.

112. Feb. 11, 1858, letter from A.A. Ruxton to W.M. Rossetti as quoted in Rossetti, *Ruskin: Rossetti: PreRaphaelitism*, p. 195.

113. "Sketchings," *The Crayon*, 5 (March 1858), p. 89.

114. Cummings, *Historic Annals*, p. 267.

115. Feb. 11, 1858, letter from A.A. Ruxton to W.M. Rossetti as quoted in Rossetti, *Ruskin: Rossetti: PreRaphaelitism*, p. 195.

116. "Sketchings," *The Crayon*, 5 (March 1858), p. 89.

117. *Idem. The Crayon* also remarked in a footnote in this piece that Fales had "lately acquired one of Turner's finest drawings ... , a landscape gem, and probably the most satisfactory expression of the artist's genius in the country."

118. Feb. 11, 1858, letter from A.A. Ruxton to W.M. Rossetti as quoted in Rossetti, *Ruskin: Rossetti: PreRaphaelitism*, pp. 195-196.

119. "Sketchings," *The Crayon*, 5 (May 1858), p. 148.

120. Stillman had written in a Nov. 1857 piece for *The Crayon* (p. 344) that the previous year William Thackeray had also purchased one of Steers' watercolor landscapes.

121. Mabel Munson Swan, *The Athenaeum Gallery 1827-1893. The Boston Athenaeum as an Early Patron of Art* (Boston: The Boston Athenaeum, 1940), p. 104.

122. Feb. 11, 1858, letter from A.A. Ruxton to W.M. Rossetti as quoted in Rossetti, *Ruskin: Rossetti: PreRaphaelitism*, p. 195.

123. "The Fine Arts in New York," *The New York Herald* (Oct. 20, 1857), p. 4.

124. "Art. The British Gallery in New York," *The Atlantic Monthly*, 1 (Feb. 1858), pp. 505-506.

Plate 7
Henry Farrer
Coastal Highlands 1875
Watercolor on paper, 12 × 18½ in. (30.5 × 46.9 cm.)
Collection: Mr. and Mrs. Wilbur L. Ross, Jr.
Cat. no. 106

Facing page:
Plate 6
Thomas C. Farrer
Gone! Gone! 1860
Oil on canvas, 20 × 14 in. (50.8 × 33.0 cm.)
Private collection
Cat. no. 8

Plate 8
Henry Roderick Newman
Mt. Everett from Monument Mountain in April 1867
Watercolor on paper, 10⅜ × 13¾ in. (26.3 × 35.0 cm.)
Collection: Museum of Fine Arts, Boston, gift of
Mrs. Harriet Ropes Cabot
Cat. no. 57

Plate 9
John William Hill
Hunter and Dog *circa* 1867
Oil on canvas mounted on board, 10 × 16 in. (25.4 × 40.6 cm.)
Collection: Mr. and Mrs. Wilbur L. Ross, Jr.
Cat. no. 35

Plate 10
Charles Herbert Moore
Landscape: Rocks and Water *circa* 1860s
Watercolor and gouache on paper, 7⅜ × 10⅝ in. (49.2 × 26.9 cm.)
Collection: Harvard University Art Museums (Fogg Art Museum),
transferred from the Fine Arts Department
Cat. no. 50

Plate 11
Martin Johnson Heade
Lake George 1862
Oil on canvas, 25 × 49¾ in. (66.0 × 126.3 cm.)
Collection: Museum of Fine Arts, Boston, bequest of Maxim Karolik
Cat. no. 110

Plate 12
David Johnson
The Natural Bridge, Virginia 1860
Oil on canvas, 24 × 20 in. (60.9 × 50.8 cm.)
Collection: Jo Ann and Julian Ganz, Jr.
Cat. no. 113

Plate 13
Thomas Moran
Under the Trees 1865
Oil on canvas, 40 × 35 in. (101.6 × 88.9 cm.)
Private collection
Cat. no. 117

Plate 14
Henry Roderick Newman
The Elm 1866
Watercolor on paper, 16¾ × 19⅛ in. (42.5 × 48.5 cm.)
Collection: Museum of Fine Arts, Boston, bequest of Maxim Karolik
Cat. no. 56

Plate 15
Thomas C. Farrer
View of Northampton from the Dome of the Hospital 1865
Oil on canvas, 28½ × 36 in. (73.9 × 91.5 cm.)
Collection: Smith College Museum of Art
Cat. no. 12

Plate 16
John William Hill
View from High Tor, Haverstraw, New York *circa* 1866
Watercolor on paper, 11¾ × 18 in. (29.9 × 45.8 cm.)
Collection: The New-York Historical Society
Cat. no. 34

Plate 17
John William Hill
Hanging Trophies–Snipe and Woodcock in a Landscape 1867
Watercolor on paper, 20 × 16 in. (50.8 × 40.6 cm.)
Private collection
Cat. no. 33

Facing page:
Plate 18
Aaron Draper Shattuck
Leaf Study with Yellow Swallow Tail *circa* 1859
Oil on canvas, 18 × 13 in. (45.7 × 33.0 cm.), arched top
Collection: Jo Ann and Julian Ganz, Jr.
Cat. no. 118

Plate 19
William T. Richards
The Conservatory 1860
Oil on panel, 10⅞ × 8⁹⁄₁₆ in. (27.7 × 21.7 cm.)
Private collection
Cat. no. 70

Plate 20
William Mason Brown
Raspberries
Oil on canvas, 20 × 16 in. (50.8 × 40.6 cm.)
Collection: *The J.B. Speed Art Museum*
Cat. no. 92

Plate 21
John William Hill
Apples and Plums 1874
Watercolor on paper, 7⅞ × 11⅜ in. (20.0 × 28.9 cm.)
Anonymous loan
Cat. no. 38

Catalogue

This catalogue is arranged by artist in the following order:

MEMBERS OF THE ASSOCIATION FOR THE ADVANCEMENT OF TRUTH IN ART
Thomas Charles Farrer
John Henry Hill
John William Hill
Charles Herbert Moore
Henry Roderick Newman
Robert J. Pattison
William Trost Richards

OTHER AMERICAN ARTISTS
Francesca Alexander
Albert Bierstadt
Robert Bolling Brandegee
Fidelia Bridges
John George Brown
William Mason Brown
Frederic Edwin Church
John B. Duffey
Robert Spear Dunning
Asher Brown Durand
Henry Farrer
George Henry Hall
William Stanley Haseltine
Martin Johnson Heade
William John Hennessy
David Johnson
George Cochran Lambdin
Nina Moore
Thomas Moran
Aaron Draper Shattuck
William James Stillman
(Thomas) Worthington Whittredge
George Bacon Wood, Jr.

ENGLISH ARTISTS
William Henry Hunt
John Ruskin

The works by each artist are in approximate chronological order, with undated material last. Dimensions are in inches (centimeters in parentheses); height precedes width. The collection is given in italics. Under "Provenance" brackets indicate a dealer or gallery.

All of the artists' biographies were written by Annette Blaugrund, Assistant Curator of American Paintings and Sculpture, The Brooklyn Museum. The authors of the catalogue entries are indicated by the following initials:

AB   Annette Blaugrund
HPC Holly Pyne Connor
MC   Margaret Conrads
LSF Linda S. Ferber
BDG Barbara Dayer Gallati
MBH May Brawley Hill
KM   Katherine Manthorne

Bibliography abbreviations are listed below.

SELECTED BIBLIOGRAPHY

AA-U — Cowdrey, Bartlett (ed.). *American Academy of Fine Arts and American Art-Union*. 2 vols. New York: The New-York Historical Society, 1953.

Ahrens — Ahrens, Kent. "Pioneer Abroad, Henry R. Newman (1843-1917): Watercolorist and Friend of Ruskin." *The American Art Journal* (November 1976), pp. 85-98.

Alexander 1883 — Alexander, Francesca. *The Story of Ida: Epitaph on an Etruscan Tomb*. Edited by John Ruskin. New York: John Lovell, 1883.

Alexander 1884 — Alexander, Francesca. *Roadside Songs of Tuscany*. Edited by John Ruskin. New York: John Wiley & Sons, 1884.

Alexander 1897 — Alexander, Francesca. *Tuscan Songs*. Boston: Houghton, Mifflin and Co., 1897.

BA — Swan, Mabel Munson. *The Athenaeum Gallery, 1827-1873; The Boston Athenaeum as an Early Patron of Art*. Boston: The Boston Athenaeum, 1940.

BAA — Marlor, Clark S. *A History of The Brooklyn Art Association with an Index of Exhibitions*. New York: James F. Carr, 1970.

Benezit — Benezit, Emmanuel. *Dictionnaire Critique et Documentaire des Peintres, Sculpteurs, Dessinateurs et Graveurs*. 10 vols. Paris: Librairie Gründ, 1976.

Blaugrund — Blaugrund, Annette. *The Brooklyn Museum American Watercolors, Pastels, Collages*. New York: The Brooklyn Museum, 1984.

BMFA 1921 — *Catalogue of Paintings*. Boston: Museum of Fine Arts, 1921.

Bowness — Bowness, Alan. *The Pre-Raphaelites*. Exhibition catalogue. London: The Tate Gallery, 1984.

Carmer — Carmer, Carl. "Three Centuries of Niagara Falls: Oils, Watercolors, Drawings, Prints." *Albright-Knox Art Gallery*. Buffalo, 1964.

Cary — Cary, Edward. "Some American Pre-Raphaelites: A Reminiscence." *The Scrip* 2 (October 1906), pp. 1-7.

Clement — Clement, Clara E. and Laurence Hutton. *Artists of the Nineteenth Century and Their Works*. 2 vols. Boston: Houghton, Mifflin and Company, 1880.

Cohn — Cohn, Marjorie. *Wash and Gouache*. Exhibition catalogue. Cambridge: Fogg Art Museum, 1977.

Cummings, Rosenblum & Staley — Cummings, Frederick, Robert Rosenblum, and Alan Staley. *Romantic Art in Britain: Paintings and Drawings 1760-1860*. Philadelphia: Museum of Art, 1968.

DAB — *Dictionary of American Biography*. 22 vols. Edited by Dumas Malone. New York: Charles Scribner's Sons, 1946.

Dickason 1942 — Dickason, David H. "American Pre-Raphaelites." *Art in America* 30 (July 1942), pp. 157-165.

Dickason 1953 — Dickason, David H. *The Daring Young Men: The Story of the American Pre-Raphaelites*. Bloomington: Indiana University Press, 1953.

FA — *Francesca Alexander 1837-1917*. New York: Jeffrey Alan Gallery, 1983.

Fabri — Fabri, Ralph. *History of the American Water Color Society: The First Hundred Years*. New York: American Water-Color Society, 1969.

Farrer — Farrer, T.C. "A Few Questions Answered." *The New Path* (June 1863), pp. 13-18.

Ferber & Blaugrund — Ferber, Linda S. and Annette Blaugrund, "American Watercolors and Pastels at the Brooklyn Museum." *The Magazine Antiques* (August 1984), pp. 313-323.

Ferber 1973 — Ferber, Linda S. *William Trost Richards: American Landscape & Marine Painter 1833-1905*. Exhibition catalogue. New York: The Brooklyn Museum, 1973.

Ferber 1980 (a) — Ferber, Linda S. "Ripe for Revival: Forgotten American Artists." *Art News* 79, no. 10 (December 1980), pp. 71-73.

Ferber 1980 (b) — Ferber, Linda S. *William Trost Richards (1833-1905)*. New York and London: Garland Publishing, Inc., 1980.

Fielding — Fielding, Mantle. *Dictionary of American Painters, Sculptors and Engravers*. New York, 1965.

Forman — Forman, H. Buxton. "An American Studio in Florence." *The Manhattan* 3 (June 1884), pp. 525-539.

Foshay — Foshay, Ella M. *Reflections of Nature: Flowers in American Art*. New York: Alfred A. Knopf, 1984.

Foster — Foster, Kathleen Adair. "Makers of the American Watercolor Movement, 1860-1890." Ph.D. dissertation. Yale University, 1982.

French — French, H.W. *Art and Artists in Connecticut*. Boston: Lee and Shepard. New York: Charles T. Dillingham, 1879.

Gerdts & Burke — Gerdts, William H. and Russell Burke. *American Still Life Painting*. New York: Praeger, 1971.

Gerdts 1964 — Gerdts, William H. *Painting and Sculpture in New Jersey*. Princeton: D. Van Nostrand Company, Inc., 1964.

Gerdts 1969 — Gerdts, William H. "The Influence of Ruskin and Pre-Raphaelitism on American Still-Life Painting." *American Art Journal* 1 (Fall 1969), pp. 80-97.

Gerdts 1974 — Gerdts, William H. *Revealed Masters, 19th Century American Art*. Exhibition catalogue. New York: The American Federation of Arts, 1974.

Gerdts 1981 — Gerdts, William H. *Painters of the Humble Truth: Masterpieces of American Still-Life 1801-1939*. Exhibition catalogue. Columbia, Missouri: University of Missouri Press, 1981.

Gerdts 1983 — Gerdts, William H. *Down Garden Paths*. Exhibition catalogue. New Jersey: Associated University Presses, Inc., 1983.

Goldyne — Goldyne, Joseph R. *Francesca Alexander (1837-1917): Drawings for "Roadside Songs of Tuscany."* Woodside, California: Sven H.A. Bruntjen Fine Arts, 1981.

Groce & Wallace — Groce, George C. and David Wallace. *The New-York Historical Society's Dictionary of Artists in America: 1564-1860*. New Haven: Yale University Press, 1957.

Hill 1867 — Hill, John Henry. *Sketches From Nature*. New York: Nyack Turnpike, 1867.

Hill 1888 — Hill, John Henry. *John William Hill: An Artist's Memorial*. New York, 1888.

Jarves 1861 — Jarves, James Jackson. *Art Studies: The 'Old Masters' of Italy; Painting*. New York, 1861.

Jarves 1864 — Jarves, James Jackson. *The Art Idea* (1864), ed. Benjamin Rowland, Jr. Cambridge, Massachusetts: Belknap Press, 1960.

Jarves 1869 — Jarves, James Jackson. *Art Thoughts*. New York, 1869.

Jones — Jones, Betsy B. *Edwin Romanzo Elmer 1850-1923*. Northampton, Massachusetts: Smith College Museum of Art, 1983.

Karolik — *M. and M. Karolik Collection of American Water Colors and Drawings*. 2 vols. Boston: Museum of Fine Arts, 1962.

Kennedy — *American Drawings, Pastels and Watercolors: Part Two: The Nineteenth Century; 1825-1890*. Exhibition catalogue. New York: Kennedy Galleries, 1968.

Koke — Koke, Richard. *American Landscape and Genre Painting in The New-York Historical Society*. Boston: G.K. Hall & Co., 1982.

Landau — Landau, Sarah Bradford. *P.B. Wight: Architect, Contractor, and Critic, 1838-1925*. Exhibition catalogue. The Art Institute of Chicago, 1981.

Lawall — Lawall, David B. *Asher Brown Durand: His Art and Art Theory in Relation to His Times*. New York: Garland Publishing, Inc., 1977.

Letters — *Letters of John Ruskin to Charles Eliot Norton*. 2 vols. Boston, 1904.

Lillie — Lillie, Lucy Cecil White. "Two Phases of American Art." *Harper's New Monthly Magazine* 80 (January 1890), pp. 206-216, passim.

Mather — Mather, Frank Jewett, Jr. *Charles Herbert Moore: Landscape Painter*. Princeton: Princeton University Press, 1957.

Morris — Morris, Harrison S. *Masterpieces of the Sea: William T. Richards, A Brief Outline of his Life and Art*. Philadelphia: J.P. Lippincott Co., 1912.

NAD — Cowdrey, Bartlett (ed.). *National Academy of Design Exhibition Record 1826-1860*. 2 vols. New York: Little & Ives Co., 1943. Naylor, Maria (ed.). *National Academy of Design Exhibition Record 1860-1900*. 2 vols. New York: Kennedy Galleries, 1973.

Novak — Novak, Barbara. *Nature and Culture*. New York: Oxford University Press, 1980.

PAFA — Rutledge, Anna Wells. *Cumulative Record of Exhibition Catalogues: The Pennsylvania Academy of Fine Arts, 1807-1870; The Society of Artists 1800-1814; The Artists' Fund Society, 1835-1845*. Philadelphia: American Philosophical Society, 1955.

Princeton — *Record of the Art Museum, Princeton University*. Volume 13.

RA — Graves, Algernon. *The Royal Academy of Arts: A Complete Dictionary of Contributors and their Work from its Foundation in 1769 to 1904*. London: H. Graves and G. Bell, 1905.

Ruskin — Ruskin, John. *The Works of John Ruskin*. 39 vols. Edited by E.T. Cook and Alexander Wedderburn. London: George Allen, 1903-12.

Sheldon — Sheldon, George William. *American Painters*. New York: D. Appleton, 1879.

Simoni — Simoni, John Peter. "Art Critics and Criticism in Nineteenth Century America." Ph.D. dissertation. Ohio State University, 1952.

Staley — Staley, Allen. *The Pre-Raphaelite Landscape*. Oxford: Clarendon Press, 1973.

Stebbins — Stebbins, Theodore E., Jr. *American Master Drawings and Watercolors: A History of Works on Paper from Colonial Times to the Present*. New York: Harper & Row, 1976.

Stein — Stein, Roger B. *John Ruskin and Aesthetic Thought in America, 1840-1900*. Cambridge, Massachusetts: Harvard University Press, 1967.

Stillman — Stillman, William James. *The Autobiography of a Journalist*. 2 vols. Boston: Houghton Mifflin, 1901.

Taylor 1976 — Taylor, Joshua C. *America as Art*. Exhibition catalogue. Washington, D.C.: Smithsonian Institution Press, 1976.

Taylor 1979 — Taylor, Joshua C. *The Fine Arts in America*. Chicago and London: The University of Chicago Press, 1979.

TB — Thieme, Dr. Ulrich and Dr. Felix Becker. *Allgemeines Lexikon der Bildenden Kunstler von der Antike bis zur Gegenwart*. 37 vols. Leipzig: Verlag von Wilhelm Engelmann, 1907.

Troyen — Troyen, Carol. *A Private Eye: Fifty Nineteenth-Century American Paintings, Drawings and Water-*

	colors from the Stebbins Collection. Exhibition catalogue. Huntington, New York: The Heckscher Museum, 1977.
Trump	Trump, Richard S. "Life and Works of Albert Bierstadt." Ph.D. dissertation. Ohio State University, 1963.
Tuckerman	Tuckerman, Henry T. *Book of the Artists.* New York: G.P. Putnam and Son, 1967.
Whittredge	Whittredge, Worthington. "The Autobiography of Worthington Whittredge, 1820-1910." Edited by John I.H. Baur. *Brooklyn Museum Journal* (1942), pp. 7-66.
Wight	Wight, Peter Bonnett, "The Development of New Phases of the Fine Arts in America." Chicago: Privately printed, 1884 from *The Inland Architect and Builder,* November/December 1884.
Wilmerding, Ayres & Powell	Wilmerding, John, Linda Ayres, and Earl A. Powell. *An American Perspective: Nineteenth-Century Art from the Collection of Jo Ann and Julian Ganz, Jr.* Exhibition catalogue. Washington, D.C.: National Gallery of Art, 1981.

EXHIBITIONS

AFA 1976	American Federation of Arts, New York. *American Master Drawings and Watercolors: A History of Works on Paper from Colonial Times to the Present.* Minneapolis Institute of Arts, Minnesota, September 1-October 26, 1976; Whitney Museum of American Art, New York, November 23, 1976-January 23, 1977; The Fine Arts Museum of San Francisco, California Palace of the Legion of Honor, February 19-April 17, 1977.
Brooklyn 1973	The Brooklyn Museum, New York. *William Trost Richards: American Landscape & Marine Painter 1833-1905.* June 20-July 29, 1973; Pennsylvania Academy of the Fine Arts, Philadelphia, September 13-October 21, 1973.
Heckscher 1977	The Heckscher Museum, Huntington, New York. *A Private Eye: Fifty Nineteenth-Century American Paintings, Drawings & Watercolors from the Stebbins Collection.* September 30-November 6, 1977; The George Walter Vincent Smith Art Museum, Springfield, Massachusetts, November 22, 1977-January 8, 1978.
Montclair 1971	Montclair Art Museum, New Jersey. *A.B. Durand 1796-1886.* October 24-November 28, 1971.
Montclair 1983	Montclair Art Museum, New Jersey. *Down Garden Paths: The Floral Environment in American Art.* October 2-November 30, 1983; Terra Museum of American Art, Evanston, Illinois; Henry Art Gallery, University of Washington, Seattle.
National Gallery of Art 1981	National Gallery of Art, Washington, D.C. *An American Perspective: Nineteenth Century Art from the Collection of Jo Ann and Julian Ganz, Jr.* October 4, 1981-January 31, 1982; Amon Carter Museum, Fort Worth, Texas, March 19-May 23, 1982; Los Angeles County Museum, California, July 5-September 26, 1982.
Newark 1974	The Newark Museum, New Jersey. *Revealed Masters, 19th Century American Art.* September 28-November 17, 1974; Mobile Art Gallery, Alabama, February 2-March 9, 1975; Georgia Museum of Art, University of Georgia, Athens, March 30-May 4, 1975.
Philbrook 1981	Philbrook Art Center, Tulsa, Oklahoma. *Painters of the Humble Truth: Masterpieces of American Still Life 1801-1939.* September 27-November 1, 1981; Oakland Museum, California, December 8, 1981-January 24, 1982; Baltimore Museum of Art, Maryland, March 2-April 25, 1982; National Academy of Design, New York, May 18-July 4, 1982.
Whitney 1984	Whitney Museum, New York. *Reflections of Nature: Flowers in American Art.* March 1-May 20, 1984.

MANUSCRIPT SOURCES

AAA	Archives of American Art, New York.
GLF/NYPL	The Gordon Lester Ford Collection, Rare Books and Manuscripts Division, The New York Public Library, Astor, Lenox, and Tilden Foundations.
HL/Moore Papers	Charles Herbert Moore Papers by Permission of the Houghton Library, Harvard University.
Minutes	Minutes of The Association for the Advancement of Truth in Art, Ryerson Library, The Art Institute of Chicago.

Thomas Charles Farrer 1839-1891

Thomas Charles Farrer, older brother of watercolorist Henry Farrer, was born in London on September 16, 1839. He was trained in London at the Working Men's College, where from 1854 to 1858 John Ruskin (q.v.) taught elementary classes and landscape paintings and Dante Gabriel Rossetti (1828–1882) taught the figure class. He totally embraced Ruskin's aesthetic dogma and upon his arrival in New York in the late 1850s (possibly 1857) championed Ruskinian principles, thus providing a direct link between Ruskin and the American Pre-Raphaelites. (Edward Cary in *The Scrip*, vol. 2, October 1906, gives Farrer's arrival date as 1857. A letter from Farrer in the Gordon L. Ford Collection at the New York Public Library seems to be dated 1856, but as no other evidence for such an early date exists, the question of Farrer's arrival in New York remains unresolved.)
Farrer returned to England during the summer of 1860, made some copies there of Turner's paintings, and upon his return to New York began exhibiting at the National Academy of Design. In November 1861 he began teaching the women's drawing class at The Cooper Union, a position he held through 1865. As an instructor, he championed the techniques and ideas set forth by Ruskin, using fruit, leaves, and other natural objects instead of prints and plaster casts to teach drawing.

Motivated by strong antislavery sentiments, Farrer joined the Union Army and served for several months during the spring and summer of 1862, the same year he began to exhibit at the Brooklyn Art Association. The following January he was instrumental in founding the Association for the Advancement of Truth in Art and in 1864 he married Annie R. McLane, a fellow member of the Association. Drawn by his friendship with Charles Eliot

Norton, who summered at Ashfield, Massachusetts, he spent the summer of 1865 in Northampton and the winter of 1865 and the spring of 1866 in Ashfield, teaching at the Ashfield Academy and exhibiting several paintings.

Farrer had a one-man exhibition at the Knoedler Galleries in New York in 1865 and continued to exhibit landscapes and still lifes at both the Academy and the Brooklyn Art Association throughout the sixties and seventies and once in 1884. He also exhibited with the American Society of Painters in Water Colors, to which he was elected in January 1867. In November 1868 he and Charles Herbert Moore (q.v.) sent out notices that they were giving drawing and painting lessons. He went abroad in April 1869 and returned to New York by 1871 with more copies of Turner's work.

In 1872, the year Farrer probably permanently settled in England, he exhibited at both the National Academy in New York and the Royal Academy in London. Active as a printmaker and a watercolorist, he continued to exhibit at the Royal Academy every few years until 1887. The possibility exists that he returned to New York in 1884, perhaps to visit his brother, since his pictures, which no longer demonstrated the Ruskinian aesthetic, appeared that year in three places in the New York area—the Academy, the Brooklyn Art Association, and a private gallery. He died in London on June 16, 1891.

REFERENCES
I am grateful to William H. Gerdts for providing the dates of Farrer's teaching position at The Cooper Union.

BAA; Kennedy; GLF/NYPL; Cary; William H. Gerdts Art Reference Library and Archive, City University of New York Graduate Center; Jones; RA; NAD.

1

Self-portrait Sketching *circa* 1859

Pencil with Chinese white on paper prepared with cream ground
10½ × 7⅝ (26.7 × 19.4)
Inscribed on reverse: "T.C. Farrer in Meek home at 52nd Street/drawn by T.C. Farrer"
Private collection
PROVENANCE
[Kennedy Galleries, New York]; private collection.
EXHIBITED
Kennedy Galleries, 1968.
REFERENCES
Maria Naylor, *American Drawings, Pastels and Water Colors . . .* (exhibition catalogue, Kennedy Galleries, New York, April 16-May 6, 1968), pp. 42-43, illus.

1

2
Woman Sewing 1859

Pencil with Chinese white on paper prepared with cream
ground
11⅞ × 9¼ (30.3 × 23.5)
Inscribed lower left (initials in monogram in circle): "TCF/
1859"
The Art Museum, Princeton University
PROVENANCE
Charles Ryskamp, 1969; The Art Museum, Princeton University.

2

3
Practicing her Lesson 1859

Pencil with Chinese white on paper prepared with cream
ground
11⅞ × 9¼ (30.3 × 23.5)
Inscribed lower left: "TC Farrer/1859"
Inscribed on reverse: "Sketched by T.C. Farrer/Practicing
Her Lesson"
The Pierpont Morgan Library, New York
PROVENANCE
Charles Ryskamp, 1970; The Pierpont Morgan Library.

Thomas Charles Farrer was the only member of the
Association for the Advancement of Truth in Art who
consistently drew from the figure. His portrait and
figure drawings, dating from early in his career, are
among the most impressive products of the Ruskinian
exactitude demanded by *The New Path* and are of
great interest not only for their astonishing technical
accomplishment but also for the insight they offer into
Farrer's intentions for figure paintings such as *Gone!
Gone!* (cat. no. 8) and *Home Scenes—Morning* (unlocated).
They incidentally serve as extremely accurate documents
of specific domestic interiors.

3

The three pencil drawings illustrated here—*Self-portrait Sketching*, *Woman Sewing*, and *Practicing her Lesson*—are related not only in date but also in the location depicted. They were drawn when Farrer lived in the New York home of Edward Meek, an English-born cabinetmaker whose business and residence were located on West 52nd Street near Eleventh Avenue. The neighborhood was then rather thinly settled, with the private houses and shops of merchants and craftsmen mixed with tenements housing Irish and German immigrants. Meek, who had emigrated with his father from England about 1843, supported a large household that included two grown daughters and a number of younger children. Although Farrer listed himself as living at Meek's address in the 1861 National Academy exhibition catalogue, by the spring of that year he had apparently worn out his welcome. On March 28, 1861, Charles Herbert Moore (q.v.) wrote him, "Can't you remain at Meek's for the present . . . tell him how you are situated and if he has any heart at all I am sure he will have compassion enough to let you remain there at present" (GLF/NYPL).

In *Self-portrait Sketching*, Farrer shows himself in shirt sleeves comfortably settled in the Meek parlor on a stool belonging to the piano seen in *Practicing her Lesson*. He depicts the details of the interior with as much accuracy and attention as he gives his own finely drawn features, sketching the floral decoration of the ornate barometer (its face completely legible even though seen in reverse), the grain of the furniture, and the patterns of the carpets with the finest possible pencil point. There is no editing of appearances. The carelessly knotted handkerchief that serves as his cravat, the missing button on his shirt, the torn horsehair seat on which he rests his foot, and the shoes under the bed in the background are all carefully noted.

This sort of scrupulous realism, which continued unabated in Farrer's larger figure paintings, was difficult for even the most sympathetic critics to appreciate. In a review of the 1865 National Academy exhibition, Clarence Cook castigated Farrer's *Home Scenes—Morning* for a "want of taste" that he found inadmissable even on the grounds of accuracy. "It is no excuse," he wrote, "when the arrangement of the furniture in a room . . . is found fault with, to say that it was so in reality, and had always been so. The artist should have arranged it properly" (*New York Daily Tribune*, June 23, 1865, p. 6).

Farrer did in fact arrange objects, not in order to make a room appear "proper" but to reinforce the meaning of a subject. He was the only member of the Association who would have had an opportunity to see the paintings of the English Pre-Raphaelite Brotherhood on their first appearance, and he followed the lead of John Everett Millais (1829-1896), Dante Gabriel Rossetti (1828-1882), and William Holman Hunt (1827-1910) in their desire to paint modern moral subjects. In his portrait and figure drawings he employed a pervasive symbolism, and the mundane objects he so lovingly rendered represent not only facts but also ideas.

In *Woman Sewing*, the setting is the bedroom glimpsed in the background of *Self-portrait Sketching*. The window with its painted shade, the Empire side chair, the floral carpet, and the draped bed are the same, but a print of Raphael's *Madonna of the Chair* has been substituted for the Landseer dogs seen in the self-portrait, its arched top echoing that of the drawing itself. The vine outside the window now bears grapes, and there is an infant geranium in a pot on the table beside a nosegay of wild flowers. The young woman wears a wedding band; she may be pregnant, but such a loose blouse was the current fashion. She is not, however, sewing baby clothes, but mending her own blouse. The figure is set within a box-like space formed by the upward tilting floor plane, the draped bed, and the table, and daylight from the window forms an aureole around her face. These features, together with the crisp, angular folds of drapery and the quiet concentration of the figure suggest a conscious emulation of the Flemish fifteenth-century paintings admired by the English Pre-Raphaelites. Farrer could have seen some of these works—for example, Jan van Eyck's (1385-1441) *Arnolfini Wedding*—in the National Gallery in London.

The sitter for *Woman Sewing* was probably one of Meek's daughters, either Maria, whose features are known from a profile pencil portrait by Farrer (unlocated), or her older sister Amelia. The drawing is signed with Farrer's distinctive monogram.

Maria Meek was almost certainly the model for *Practicing her Lesson*. She is shown from the back playing an arrangement of Vicenzo Bellini's romantic opera *Norma*, a dramatization of the conflict between carnal love and religious vocation. The girl wears virginal white, but there are a top hat, scarf, and gloves on the piano, placed there by an unseen listener. The elegance of the figure's dress and the splendor of the rosewood piano are somewhat compromised by the large mended tear in the carpet. A glimpse of the contents of the room, as well as the girl's face, is afforded by an elaborate mirror wrapped in netting that during the summer would protect the gilded frame from insect stains. An Argand lamp stands next to a clock under a glass bell on the marble mantelpiece. To the left is a stereoscope on an inlaid console table; the guitar leaning against it seems to imply a duet to come. The prints on the walls serve emblematic as well as decorative functions. One of birds hangs above the table, and a smaller print (of Cupid?) above the lamp. The mirror itself is flanked by two Landseer stags, *At Bay* on the right and *The Sanctuary* on the left.

Although the subject of this drawing, conventional courtship, is of a very different nature from that of Holman Hunt's 1853 painting of illicit love, *The Awakening Conscience* (Tate Gallery, London), there are similarities between the two, not least in the emotional potency that infuses ordinary objects, although Farrer's are less highly charged. A rosewood piano and a white petticoat trimmed with eyelet lace worked in a heart-shaped pattern appear in both paintings. The use of the mirror was probably suggested to Farrer by Hunt's painting, but its ultimate source is Jan van Eyck's *Arnolfini Wedding*.

The technical accomplishment of these three drawings, done with the finest point on paper prepared with a cream-colored ground, is quite extraordinary. In the unfinished *Self-portrait Sketching* Farrer's procedure can be followed. First the composition was roughly sketched in, then individual areas were prepared with an opaque paint. Each detail was carefully transcribed in pencil strokes that seem to become the object they depict, and the highlights were added with Chinese white. Incredibly, the closer one looks, even with a magnifying glass, the tighter the drawing appears. All three drawings exhibit the slight distortions of figure proportions and three-dimensional space that result from the careful transcription of exactly what the eye sees, item by item, rather than from following perspectival or anatomical schema.   MBH

4
The Fiddler 1859

Pencil and Chinese white on paper
9⅞ × 7¾ (25.1 × 19.7)
Inscribed lower right (initials in monogram in circle):
"TCF/1859"
Hirschl & Adler Galleries, Inc.

PROVENANCE
Charles Ryscamp, 1969; Benjamin Sonnenberg, 1979; [Sotheby's sale
4260, June 5–9, 1979, no. 662 as *Self-portrait with Violin*; [Hirschl &
Adler Galleries, Inc.].

5
Portrait of John William Hill

circa 1859

Pencil and Chinese white on paper
4¾ × 4½ (12.1 × 11.4)
Inscribed lower right: "A Lover of Ruskin/Drawn by
Ruskins pupil/TC Farrer"
The New-York Historical Society

PROVENANCE
Samuel Verplanck Hoffman, 1927; The New-York Historical Society.

4

The Fiddler relates to the three drawings by Farrer discussed above (cat. nos. 1–3) not only in date and technique but also in its placement of a figure engaged in some significant activity within a carefully defined interior. The setting is an artist's studio in which the walls are hung with small matted watercolors and a few framed paintings lean on an easel. An oil lamp that provides the only illumination stands on a table covered with etching tools, a copper plate, and an open sketch book. The etcher, who has just put down his work and picked up a fiddle, is probably John Henry Hill (q.v.), and the studio is most likely the one in West Nyack, New York, that he shared with his father. Hill mentioned this studio in a letter to Farrer of November 20, 1860, in speaking of his father's return from a visit to New York: "We talked over the city news in our good old studio by the good old stove that keeps us warm these cold days." He mentioned the drawing in a letter to Farrer of December 6, 1859, reporting that he had been to visit Samuel P. Avery and that Avery "seemed rather determined to find fault with your drawings; thought the fiddler looked as though he would slide out the picture cushion and all . . ." (Letters GLF/NYPL). Indeed, the drawing is unsettling, due not only to the awkward placement of the figure but also to the looming shadow of the violin cast by the oil lamp.

The Fiddler may be a picture of Hill that Farrer included in the 1860 National Academy exhibition and that Hill discussed in an undated letter to Farrer. "I wish," Hill wrote, "I was an outsider—then I would say the best things in the exhibition were those by the three P.R.G.'s [sic], but as I am not, I may say and I do say that your pencil drawing of myself has a finer and more subtle reaching of expression than will be found in any other figure drawing in the exhibition" (GLF/NYPL). Another (unlocated) Farrer drawing of Hill, inscribed "A Lover of Ruskin/Sketched by Ruskins pupil/TC Farrer 1859," shows the etcher at work with a mirror, leaning forward above his table.

Farrer's sketch of John William Hill (q.v.) seen here is similarly inscribed, and was probably executed in 1859 as well. In the autumn of that year Farrer spent a good deal of time with the Hills in West Nyack, attempting his first outdoor landscape studies. His drawing of "Poppy" Hill, an affectionate characterization of the older man, manages to suggest not only the strength and quirkiness of John William's personality but also his dry humor.

There are several watercolors on the wall behind John William, and the only one given some definition can also be seen to the right of John Henry's head in *The Fiddler*. Its prominent position in both drawings suggests that it was a highly valued work, perhaps the Turner coastal scene John William is known to have owned. Farrer may have meant it to suggest the admiration both Hills had for Turner. Such use of paintings or prints as emblems of vocation or belief occurs in other known portraits by Farrer, including his unlocated drawing of Clarence Cook (fig. 3).   MBH

5

6

Jack-in-the-Pulpit   *circa* 1860

Pencil on paper
8⁵⁄₁₆ × 9½ (21.2 × 24.2)
Unsigned
Department of Architecture, The Art Institute of Chicago

PROVENANCE
Peter B. Wight, *circa* 1918; The Burnham Library of Architecture,
The Art Institute of Chicago.
EXHIBITED
The Art Institute of Chicago, *P.B. Wight: Architect, Contractor, and
Critic, 1838–1925*, January 22–July 31, 1981; NAD, September 29–
December 7, 1981; PAFA, December 22–February 7, 1982; The American
Institute of Architects Foundation, Washington, D.C., March 1–May 2,
1982, no. 3.
REFERENCES
Landau, p. 86, no. 3.

6

7
Jack-in-the-Pulpit *circa* 1860

Pencil on paper
11 11/16 × 9¼ (29.7 × 23.4)
Unsigned
Department of Architecture, The Art Institute of Chicago
PROVENANCE
Peter B. Wight, *circa* 1918; The Burnham Library of Architecture,
The Art Institute of Chicago.
REFERENCES
Landau, p. 87, no. 9.

These two pencil drawings represent the sort of careful studies from details of nature recommended by *The New Path*. In an article titled "Pictures and Studies," the magazine advised students to pursue such work for at least five years before attempting a finished picture (July 1864, p. 38). As *The Round Table* reported in 1865, Farrer himself employed this sort of study in his drawing classes at the Cooper Institute School of Design for Women:

> Single leaves, small twigs and boughs, a lichened branch or stone, small stuffed birds (employed as studies in color), an apple, or a pear, a pine-cone or a cluster of acorns—were placed before the pupils, and they were set at copying them with all the accuracy possible to their unaccustomed hands. Mr. Farrer diligently taught them how to observe, how to study . . . he instilled into their minds the doctrine that the power of drawing correctly is not to be looked upon as an ornamental accomplishment, but only as an aid in studying nature—as a means of recording what we have learned of her; and that, to this end, we cannot be too rigorous in our devotion to truth ("The Cooper Institute School of Design for Women," *The Round Table*, October 14, 1864, p. 93).

For Farrer, such meticulous drawing was neither tedious nor burdensome. As he wrote in his essay "A Few Questions Answered," "The right practice of Art, and the study of it, is essentially a work of love. In the artist, it is the love of beautiful forms, and lively colors, and the overbearing desire which he feels to give it expression, that first sends him out into the fields to work; this work being the greatest enjoyment he finds in life" (*The New Path*, vol. I, no. 2, June 1863, p. 13).   MBH

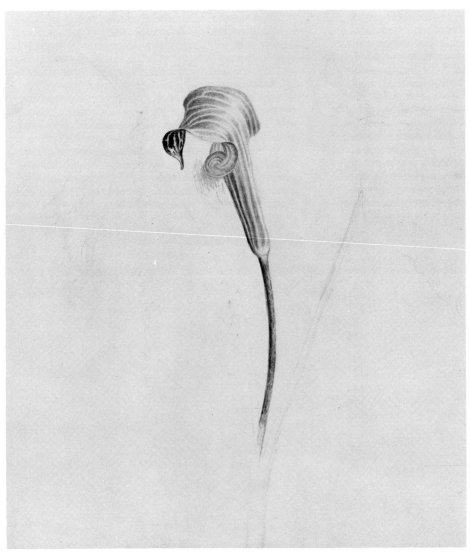

7

8

Gone! Gone! 1860

Oil on canvas
20 × 14 (50.8 × 33.0)
Inscribed lower right (initials in monogram): "TCF"
Inscribed on frame: "Come unto me, all ye that labor and
are heavy laden, and I will give you rest. Take my yoke upon
you and learn of me; for I am meek and lowly in heart: and
ye shall find rest unto your souls."
Private collection
PROVENANCE
Samuel Putnam Avery by 1862; private collection.
EXHIBITED
NAD 1861; PAFA 1862; Fermoy Art Gallery, King's Lynn, England, *The
Pre-Raphaelites as Painters and Draughtsmen*, July 24–August 8, 1971.
REFERENCES
Graham Reynolds, "The Pre-Raphaelites and Their Circle," *Apollo* 93
(June 1971), p. 501 illus.

Farrer exhibited *Gone! Gone!* at the National Academy of
Design in 1861 together with another painting of an interior, *Evening Thoughts*; a landscape, *At the Foot of the
Delectable Mountains*; and two figure drawings (all unlocated). Unfortunately, the works were not much noticed.
The Civil War had just begun, and the National Academy
exhibition closed after a few weeks because no one was
interested in looking at pictures. *The Crayon*, however, did
note *Gone! Gone!* and *Evening Thoughts* as "curiosities" in
which Farrer "presents Pre-Raphaelitism according to
systematic conditions" ("Sketchings," *The Crayon*, 8, April
1861, p. 94). For Clarence Cook, looking back three years
later, Farrer's *Gone! Gone!* marked a milestone in the progress of painting in America: "Since his first picture was
exhibited—the *Gone! Gone!*—there has been more discussion as to the principles of art, more excitement of the
whole subject, more interest felt in it, than ever at any time
before in our history" ("National Academy of Design,"
New York Daily Tribune, May 21, 1864, p. 3).

Gone! Gone!, a modern moral figure subject such as the
English Pre-Raphaelite Brotherhood advocated, belongs
in the lineage of paintings of star-crossed lovers that begins
with John Everett Millais' 1852 work *A Huguenot, on St.
Bartholomew's Day, Refusing to Shield Himself from Danger
by Wearing the Roman Catholic Badge* (fig. 4). Indeed, an
engraving of Millais' painting hangs on the wall behind the
grieving young woman. In composition, however, *Gone!
Gone!* is much closer to a painting by the English artist
John Roddam Spencer Stanhope (1829–1907), *Thoughts of
the Past*, exhibited at the Royal Academy in 1859, which
shows a young woman standing beside a window in a
reverie of regret, looking out onto the Thames. Because
Stanhope's studio was near Dante Gabriel Rossetti's,
Farrer may have seen this painting while in London in
the spring of 1860. Included in the 1860 Royal Academy
exhibition that Farrer did see was Millais' *The Black
Brunswicker*, in which the sweetheart of a soldier tries to
restrain him from going off to war.

The cause of the lovers' separation in *Gone! Gone!* is
unspecified. Had it been painted later, a reference to the
Civil War would be implied, as in Farrer's 1865 *April 1861*
(unlocated). As it is, a more general interpretation is called
for. All the elements in the painting contribute to the
theme of separation or perhaps death. The window itself
becomes an emblem, framing a twilight sky with threaten-
ing clouds, autumn foliage, and a view of the Hudson River
and the New Jersey Palisades. The last of the cold daylight
illuminates the woman's hands, while the dark green
curtain and blouse cast a green shadow on her face. The

Biblical quotation inscribed on the frame, taken from
Matthew, Chapter 11, offers some consolation for the
bereft. *The New Path*, in a discussion of "Pictures and
Studies," of which *Gone! Gone!* was seen to be both,
emphasized that "As it is made to call for sympathy with
the desolate, and to bid the desolate look for the best
sympathy to their Savior, it becomes, therefore, a picture of
worthy aim and noble subject" (*The New Path*, vol. II, no. 3,
July 1864, p. 47).   MBH

8

9

A Buckwheat Field on Thomas Cole's Farm   1863

Formerly *Mt. Hope Bay, Rhode Island*

Oil on canvas
11¾ × 25 (29.8 × 64.0)
Inscribed lower right (initials in monogram): "TCF 63"
Museum of Fine Arts, Boston

PROVENANCE
[Charles D. Childs, 1955]; Maxim Karolik, 1962; Museum of Fine Arts, Boston.
EXHIBITED
NAD 1864; Parrish Art Museum, Southampton, New York, *American Painting from 1851 to 1865*, 1961.
REFERENCES
American Painting from 1851 to 1865 (exhibition catalogue, Parrish Art Museum, Southampton, New York, 1961), no. 36 illus.; *American Paintings in the Museum of Fine Arts, Boston* (Boston: Museum of Fine Arts, 1969), vol. 1, p. 107, and vol. 2, p. 189 illus.

This painting had previously been identified as *Mt. Hope Bay, Rhode Island*, because of an inscription on the stretcher. It is, however, a view looking northeast up the Hudson River from a field in Catskill, New York, beside the present Rip Van Winkle Bridge. The field was formerly part of Thomas Cole's farm, which extended down to the river. Farrer spent much of the summer of 1863 with Charles Herbert Moore (q.v.) in Catskill, and he exhibited two landscapes painted there, the present painting and *The Catskills from the Village* (unlocated), at the National Academy of Design the following spring. These were among his earliest finished landscapes. As he wrote to the editor of the *New York Daily Tribune* in 1867, "ten years ago I could not paint or draw a single tree, bird, stone or flower accurately, and had not even made an attempt to paint from nature. Late in the season of 1859 I made my first effort to paint out of doors. Even as late as the Summer of 1862 (only five years ago) I had made but one finished oil study from nature . . ." ("To the Editor," July 8, 1867, p. 2, transcript courtesy William H. Gerdts).

The appearance of these landscapes aroused a good deal of attention. The critic of the *Continental Monthly* found them "bald, hard, cold and unnatural," lacking "abstract truth" and a "sense for beauty" ("An Hour at the National Academy of Design," *Continental Monthly*, 5, June 1864, p. 688). While the reviewer of *The Round Table* damned them in similar terms, calling them "crude and rank in color, devoid of feeling, bald, literal, unpleasing," he held out some hope. "Farrer's pictures offend not because they are truthful," he wrote, "but because they are limited in their truth. Yet there is growth possible for Farrer" ("Art," *The Round Table*, 1, May 1864, p. 312).

Clarence Cook, on the other hand, writing in the *New York Daily Tribune*, hailed the landscapes for what he felt was their importance to the future development of American art. "These two pictures," he wrote, "are made forever precious and valuable by the faithful record of the truth of Nature that is in every square inch of them." But even he concluded that "there is scarcely anything in them which rises to the rank of art; and that, while there is abundant reason for the interest they excite, and large promise for the future in them, yet there is also very good cause for the dislike which many persons have for them" ("National Academy of Design," May 21, 1864, p. 3).

It was left to *The New Path* to give unstinting praise, with a detailed description of *A Buckwheat Field*. In the middle distance, the magazine wrote, appeared "the broad blue lake-like expanse of the Hudson, *veined* as it were with cloudy white, where the summer wind goes by, and dotted with snowy sails. . . ." On the far shore, it noted, the town of Hudson was visible, and in the foreground the buckwheat field was enlivened with purple shadows cast by the conical cedar trees, creating "so lovely a chord of color it is not often our good fortune to see." The sharp definition of forms and lack of atmospheric softening found objectionable by most critics was interpreted by *The New Path* as "delicate and careful" drawing, and it concluded, "all of this beauty comes of following Nature" ("Exhibition of the National Academy of Design," *The New Path*, vol. II, no. 1, May 1864, p. 12).   MBH

9

10
Twilight *circa* 1864

Oil on academy board
8 × 4⅞ (20.3 × 12.4), arched top
Inscribed lower right (initials in monogram): "TCF"
Inscribed on label on back: "Twilight by TC Farrer/46
Stuyvesant Street City"
Mr. and Mrs. Wilbur L. Ross, Jr.
PROVENANCE
[Hirschl & Adler Galleries, Inc., 1984]; Mr. and Mrs. Wilbur L. Ross, Jr.
EXHIBITED
Artists' Fund Society, 1864.
REFERENCES
Gerdts 1969, p. 89.

This painting can be dated by the address given on the
back. Farrer moved into 46 Stuyvesant Street in New York
after his marriage to Annie McLane and his trip to the
White Mountains in the summer of 1864 and remained
there less than a year. The painting may be the *Twilight* by
Farrer included in the Metropolitan Fair exhibition in aid
of the United States Sanitary Commission in the spring
of 1864, and it is almost certainly the *Twilight* given to the
Artists' Fund Society for sale in December of that year.
Most of the items in the Society's auction were small, as
indeed were many of the pictures in its exhibition, since
most artists reserved their important pictures for the
National Academy. It is likely that William C. Gilman

bought the painting because a *Twilight* by Farrer was lent
by him to the First Annual Exhibition of the Yale School
of Fine Arts in 1867 (catalogue courtesy of William H.
Gerdts).

As in Farrer's *Gone! Gone!* (cat. no. 8), the sunset here
seems to suggest an ending, although the new moon in a
clear sky, with its reflection visible in the still water, adds
a more hopeful note for the embracing couple. The critic
of the *New York Times*, in a review of the Artists' Fund
exhibition, perhaps had this work in mind when noting
"some marvelous imitations of the so-called English
school of Pre-Raphaelitism. . . . One of these specimens
ostentatiously displays the paradoxical wonder of far-
distant mountains, successfully competing for prominence
with foreground figures" ("Art Notes," November 24,
1864, p. 5). The painting is unusual in its simplification of
the forms of both the mountain and the figures, but each
of the foreground rocks is defined and the pine trees are
given specific outlines. The paint is thickly applied, and
the colors vivid; the dark blue of the mountain and the
black of the trees are thrown into relief by the clear blue of
the sky, and the lovers are silhouetted against the glassy
water. MBH

11
Mount Tom 1865

Oil on canvas
16 × 24½ (40.6 × 62.2)
Inscribed lower right (initials in monogram): "TCF"
Mr. and Mrs Wilbur L. Ross, Jr.
PROVENANCE
William C. Gilman by 1867; [Christie's, New York, November 24, 1979,
lot 37]; [Berry-Hill Galleries, New York, 1979]; Mr. and Mrs. Wilbur L.
Ross, Jr.
EXHIBITED
Northampton, Massachusetts, 1865; BAA, March 1867; The Vatican
Museum, Vatican City, *A Mirror of Creation, 150 Years of American
Nature Painting*, 1980; George Walter Vincent Smith Art Museum,
Springfield, Massachusetts, *Arcadian Vales: Views of the Connecticut
River Valley*, 1981.
REFERENCES
John I.H. Baur, *A Mirror of Creation* (exhibition catalogue, The Vatican
Museum, December 17, 1980–January 31, 1981), no. 21 illus.; John I.H.
Baur, "God, Man and Nature," *Museum Magazine* 1 (September 1980),
p. 80 illus.; *Arcadian Vales* (exhibition catalogue, Smith Art Museum,
November 22, 1981–February 7, 1982), pp. 68–69 and p. 44 illus.; Joseph
S. Czestochowski, *100 American Landscapes* (New York: E.P. Dutton,
1981), p. 99 illus.; Ferber 1980 (a), p. 70 illus.

10

11

Farrer and his wife spent the summer of 1865 in Northampton, Massachusetts, boarding with a Colonel J.B. Parsons. At the end of August a local paper reported that he had completed two landscapes, one of Mount Tom and the other of Northampton from the dome of the lunatic asylum (cat. no. 12). The Mount Tom painting was mentioned again in the same paper on the occasion of a private viewing of his work at Colonel Parson's. "A view of Mt. Tom from the north is also very fine," the paper wrote, "and this piece was the favorite with many of the visitors" (*Northampton Free Press*, August 29 and October 13, 1865; references courtesy of Betsy B. Jones).

William C. Gilman loaned a Farrer painting titled *Mount Tom* to the Brooklyn Art Association in March 1867, and an old label with Gilman's name and address on the back of the painting seen here identifies it as that work. In July 1867, Farrer sent a painting titled *Mount Tom in October* to the First Annual Exhibition of the Yale School of Fine Arts (catalogue courtesy of William H. Gerdts). But although William Gilman was listed in the catalogue as the owner of several of Farrer's works included in the exhibition, his name did not appear with the *Mount Tom in October*. Since the *Mount Tom* seen here is thought to be the painting Farrer completed at the end of August 1865, the October view is probably another painting.

When shown in Brooklyn, *Mount Tom* received mixed reviews. The critic of the *New York Times* admitted that "it was painted with great care, and with the most painstaking attention to minute details," but felt that it was "not an artistic realization of the scene." This reviewer found the smallness of touch and definiteness of form particularly objectionable:

> The almost numberless small touches on the mountain, intended for tree-shadows, are perceived to be all alike, even after conveying the impression of limitless monotony and not that of infinite variety. The reflections on the lake are not natural, and the leaves of the near trees stand hard and black against the sky, as if cut out of sheet iron ("Art Matters," April 3, 1867, p. 8).

In contrast, the critic of the *Brooklyn Daily Union*, a newspaper consistently sympathetic to the aims of the Association for the Advancement of Truth in Art, felt that the painting was "full of the tender light and genial influences of actual nature," adding, "The mountain lifts itself from the water's edge with that supreme buoyancy that is the test of mountain drawing, and the forest veil wanders over the sides with the charm of infinite detail harmonized, not blurred" ("The Art Exhibition," March 28, 1867, p. 1).

Indeed, the mountain and its reflection do have a presence that dominates the painting, lending it a monumentality that has nothing to do with actual size, and a sense of heightened reality is sustained throughout.   MBH

12

View of Northampton from the Dome of the Hospital   1865

Oil on canvas
28½ × 36 (73.9 × 91.5)
Inscribed lower right (initials in monogram): "TCF 65"
Smith College Museum of Art, Northampton, Massachusetts

PROVENANCE
Porter Fitch, 1865; [Avis and Rockwell Gardner, Stamford, Connecticut, 1953]; Smith College Museum of Art.
EXHIBITED
Artists' Fund Society of New York, 1865; Connecticut Valley Historical Museum, Springfield, Massachusetts, *Paintings of the Connecticut Valley*, 1955; Smith College Museum of Art, *Five Anonymous American Paintings in the Smith College Museum of Art Collection*, 1975; Old Sturbridge Village, Massachusetts, *The Landscape of Change: Views of Rural New England 1790-1865*, 1976, and *The Exhibition of the Century: 100 Years of Collecting at the Smith College Museum of Art, 1879-1979*, 1979; George Walter Vincent Smith Museum of Art, Springfield, Massachusetts, *Arcadian Vales: Views of the Connecticut River Valley*, 1982; New Orleans Museum of Art, Louisiana, *The Waters of America: 19th-Century American Paintings of Rivers, Streams, Lakes, and Waterfalls*, 1984.
REFERENCES
Paintings of the Connecticut Valley (exhibition catalogue, Connecticut Valley Historical Museum, Springfield, Massachusetts, April 29-June 10, 1955), cover illus.; *Five Anonymous American Paintings* (exhibition catalogue, Smith College Museum of Art, Northampton, Massachusetts, March 6-April 20, 1975), pp. 4-6, and 7 illus.; Jay Cantor, "The Landscape of Change," *Antiques* 109 (April 1976), p. 774 illus.; Robert Bishop and Patricia Coblentz, *The World of Antiques, Art and Architecture in Victorian America* (New York, 1979), color plate 35; *Arcadian Vales* (exhibition catalogue, G.W.V. Smith Art Museum, Springfield, Massachusetts, November 22, 1981-February 7, 1982), pp. 68-69, and p. 44 illus.; Joseph S. Czestochowski, *American Landscape Tradition: a Study and Gallery of Paintings* (New York: E.P. Dutton, Inc., 1982), color plate 100; *The Waters of America* (exhibition catalogue, New Orleans Museum of Art, May 6-November 18, 1984), p. 32 illus.

This panoramic view of Northampton, Massachusetts, which includes not only the town but also the Mill River in the foreground and the Connecticut River and Mount Holyoke in the distance, was Farrer's principal work during the summer he spent in Northampton in 1865 (see also cat. no. 11).

The previous year, the architect P.B. Wight (1838-1925) had urged Farrer to paint on a larger scale in order to compete with the landscapes of John Henry Hill (q.v.) and William Trost Richards (q.v.). In a letter of August 19, 1863, Wight had written, "I insisted upon your covering three feet of canvas. I think I can see the way to make your

12

work appreciated better than you can." But when Farrer attempted to enlarge one of his summer landscape studies that winter he met with a notable lack of success. After seeing the painting, Charles Herbert Moore (q.v.) wrote him on April 25, 1864, "It is not at all worthy of you. . . . I always thought you might have added much more truth to your *study* even . . . but this picture, tho' so greatly enlarged, has not *half* the amount of truth which is in that" (both letters GLF/NYPL).

Farrer took no chances with his second attempt at a three-foot picture, painting his *View of Northampton* directly on the spot from the top of the local lunatic hospital, not in a studio. At its first public exhibition in Northampton, a writer for the *Free Press* praised the work as remarkably true to nature:

> The large picture of *Northampton from the Dome of the Hospital* on which we believe Mr. Farrar (sic) was engaged for months, has an accuracy of detail, and a natural coloring, rarely seen. The fog resting on the eastern hills is beautifully portrayed, while the mountains near and far, the wide-spread meadows and the spires and dwellings of our own town and of those beyond the river, are true to their originals (October 13, 1865, transcript courtesy of Betsy B. Jones).

When the painting was exhibited at the Artists' Fund Society in New York, it received mixed reviews. Most critics admired Farrer's treatment of the distant mountains and the sky but objected to the brilliance of color and definiteness of forms in the middle distance. Clarence Cook, writing in the *New York Tribune*, granted the painting's truth of detail but grumbled, "We are annoyed . . . by the crudeness of the color, and the hardness with which everything is made out" (December 27, 1865, p. 5). In contrast, Russell Sturgis praised the clarity of objects, writing, "It is very pleasant to see every house and every tree in this picture carefully painted, as if it alone were the thing under observation, with its own peculiar and measurable shadow, and it is very new and delightful to see all these shadows with sharp edges. . . ." Sturgis, however, faulted the strong contrasts of light and shade and the painting's "force rather than refinement, ponderousness rather than delicacy, and violent contrast rather than subtle gradation" ("Fine Arts," *The Nation*, 1, November 30, 1865, pp. 692–693).

Farrer's evident difficulty in fitting a curving view of more than ninety degrees onto a flat canvas caused some of the distortions noticed by the critics. Cook, for example, complained that the water was not all on the same level. The strong focus on the middle distance seems to have resulted in an optical blurring of the foreground trees which the critics unanimously found to be "woolly" and conventional. *The New Path*, in its review, termed the painting "rather a disappointment than a delight," principally because of faults in the foreground ("The Artists' Fund Society," vol. II, no. 12, December 1865, p. 193). All agreed that Farrer's failure to unify detail and general effect, apparent in previous landscapes, was exaggerated in this one by the immensity of the subject depicted.

The painting is perhaps most successful in suggesting the languid stillness of a lush summer landscape. The intensity of focus on individual objects seems to recreate the artist's sensation of looking with an almost hallucinatory concentration.   MBH

John Henry Hill   1839–1922

John Henry Hill, grandson of the English engraver John Hill and son of the artist John William Hill (q.v.), was born in West Nyack, New York, on April 28, 1839. He studied painting with his father, who by 1855 had become a devotee of the Ruskinian aesthetic, and first exhibited at the National Academy of Design in 1856. Elected an Associate Academician two years later, he contributed watercolors, aquatints, and etchings there on and off through 1891, while also exhibiting fairly regularly at the Brooklyn Art Association from 1865 to 1885. Both he and his father were founding members of the Association for the Advancement of Truth in Art, and their work was praised in *The New Path*.

During 1864–65 Hill spent about eight months in England studying the work of Turner. Upon his return, he went to Ashfield, Massachusetts, to join the Ruskinian band congregated there and soon after executed twenty-four etchings meant to exemplify his theories about the proper way to draw from nature, publishing them in 1867 as *Sketches from Nature*. The following year, and again in 1870, he travelled to the Far West as a staff artist for a government surveying expedition headed by his friend and fellow Association member, geologist Clarence King. In 1878 and 1879 he visited England and the Continent, at one point following an itinerary proposed by John Ruskin (q.v.) in a letter of March 26, 1879.

The death of his father in September 1879 brought Hill back to West Nyack, where he continued to paint watercolors in a studio built by his father. In addition to publishing *An Artist's Memorial* honoring his father in 1888, he promoted his father's works by reproducing some as etchings and donating others to The Metropolitan Museum of Art. His own works were praised by Ruskin, who told him in a letter of 1881 that he had a "very great art gift." He died on December 18, 1922.

REFERENCES
Letter from John Ruskin to John Henry Hill, August 23, 1881, and other letters from John Henry Hill to Metropolitan Museum of Art, Archives of The Metropolitan Museum of Art; Koke; *Northampton Free Press*, August 29, 1865; DAB; BAA; NAD.

13

13
Dandelions 1858

Watercolor on paper
6 diameter (15.2)
Inscribed lower left: "J. Henry Hill/ 1858"
Inscribed lower right: "Dandelions"
Lent anonymously
PROVENANCE
Estate of the artist; Christian Olsen, *circa* 1922; Dorothy Olsen Davis;
[Washburn Gallery, New York]; private collection.
EXHIBITED
Washburn Gallery, New York, *John William Hill, John Henry Hill*, 1973.
REFERENCES
Martica Sawin, *John William Hill, John Henry Hill* (exhibition catalogue,
Washburn Gallery, New York, June–July 1973), illus.; Stebbins, p. 155.

Following the lead of his father, John Henry Hill embarked
on a series of close studies from nature in the mid 1850s.
In this Ruskinian watercolor of a humble weed, the weed's
carefully drawn flowers emerge from a dense mat of
background foliage. The close focus is emphasized by the
circular format.   MBH

14
Sunnyside *circa* 1860

Pencil with Chinese white on brown paper
12 3/8 × 18 7/8 (31.4 × 48.0)
Unsigned
Peter A. Feld
PROVENANCE
Estate of the artist; Christian Olsen, *circa* 1922; Dorothy Olsen Davis;
[Washburn Gallery, New York, 1975]; John Wilmerding, 1980; [Hirschl
& Adler Galleries, Inc., New York, 1981]; Peter A. Feld.

This meticulous rendering of Washington Irving's home
at Sunnyside probably preceded the 1860 watercolor by
Hill (cat. no. 15), which concentrates on the house, elimi-
nating the enframing trees seen here. Only one of the
foreground figures in the watercolor appears in this
drawing, lightly sketched on the far right. In July 1860,
Hill wrote to Thomas Farrer (q.v.) that he had made "some
pencil drawings lately for Putnam to illustrate Irvings
works," and this sketch may have been one of that group
(GLF/NYPL).

Hill continued to produce drawings of Sunnyside, as it
proved a popular subject. In a letter to Farrer of August 18,
1860, he wrote, "I got a letter today from Mr. Goodman.
He had been after my Sunnyside but was too late so he
wants me to duplicate it" (GLF/NYPL). Two of his pen
drawings of Sunnyside in the 1860 exhibition at the
National Academy were noted in the May 1860 *Crayon*
as "remarkable for conscientious study" (p. 139), and one
of his pen-and-ink Sunnysides also appeared in the
1861 exhibition of the Troy, New York, Young Men's
Association (catalogue courtesy of William H. Gerdts).
MBH

14

15
Sunnyside in 1860, Tarrytown, New York   1860

Watercolor on paper
10 × 13 %/16 (25.4 × 35.4)
Inscribed lower right: "J. Henry Hill/1860"
Museum of Fine Arts, Boston
PROVENANCE
Maxim Karolik, 1960; Museum of Fine Arts, Boston.
EXHIBITED
AFA 1976.
REFERENCES
Karolik, vol. 2, p. 189 illus.; Stebbins, pp. 155–156 illus.

Views of Sunnyside, the home of the literary idol
Washington Irving (1783–1859), seem to have been as
popular in mid-century as images of Irving himself. Irving's
picturesque house on the Hudson near Tarrytown, New
York, appeared in paintings by artists like George Inness
(1825–1894) as well as in more popular media.

John Henry Hill made an etching of Sunnyside in 1857,
the same year his father did a sketch of it (Ernest Knaufft,
American Etchings, Part XII, New York, 1882). He
included another etching of it as plate sixteen in his 1867
book *Sketches from Nature*, writing in his introduction that
the house was "one of the prettiest cottages on the Hudson
and of more interest still from its having been the residence
of the late Washington Irving." Finally, in 1884 he did yet a
third etching of the home from a drawing by his father for
inclusion in *An Artist's Memorial*.

Both the 1867 and the 1884 etching repeat the point of
view and arrangment of the house and figures found in the
work seen here and in a small watercolor sketch of the
same date (private collection). Here, the architectural
details of the house, half hidden behind a luxuriant growth
of wisteria, are given careful attention. The blue shadows
Hill used in later landscapes do not appear here, for the
grass and trees are uniformly green. The two figures in the
foreground may be the unmarried nieces of Irving, who,
with their father, inherited the house on Irving's death.
MBH

15

16
Sunnyside with Picknickers 1878

Watercolor on paper
19½ × 29 (49.5 × 73.7)
Inscribed lower right: "J. Henry Hill 1878"
Sleepy Hollow Restorations, Tarrytown, New York
PROVENANCE
[Downtown Gallery, New York, by 1948]; Mrs. John D. Rockefeller, Jr.,
1979; Sleepy Hollow Restorations.
EXHIBITED
The Brooklyn Museum, *Drawings of the Hudson River School*, 1970;
Hudson River Museum, Yonkers, New York, *Time, Man and the River*,
1970, and *The Gilded Age in Westchester*, 1978; New York Public Library,
*Diedrich Knickerbocker, Geoffrey Crayon, Washington Irving: The Lives of
an American Writer in the 19th Century*, 1980.
REFERENCES
Terry B. Morton, "What Good is a Poet's House?" *Historic Preservation*
12 (1960), cover illus.; Jo Miller, *Drawings of the Hudson River School*
(exhibition catalogue, The Brooklyn Museum, New York, November 25,
1969-February 22, 1970), illus.; Joseph T. Butler, *Washington Irving's
Sunnyside* (Tarrytown, New York: Sleepy Hollow Restorations, 1974), fig.
28; Joseph T. Butler, *Sleepy Hollow Restorations* (Tarrytown, New York:
Sleepy Hollow Press, 1983), p. 221, illus.

This watercolor shows the southeast side of Washington
Irving's house from a slightly different angle than Hill's
1860 view (cat. no 15) and goes far beyond the earlier effort
in conveying the brilliance of color and clarity of forms
seen in full sunlight. The stuccoed walls of the house are
exploited as a reflective surface for the glare of the sun, and
even the vivid green lawn seems to reflect the light. The
figures on the right are flattened into colored planes, and
their sharp shadows, together with the shadows cast by the
trees on the left, emphasize the effect of the blazing sun.

Hill's continuing interest in Sunnyside (there is an
undated watercolor study for this painting in the Amon
Carter Museum in Fort Worth, Texas) may reflect the
importance given such vernacular architecture by the
Association for the Advancement of Truth in Art. In the
September 1863 issue of *The New Path*, architect P.B.
Wight praised Dutch farmhouses as the "first step in
sensible construction and picturesque arrangement" in
American domestic architecture, citing Irving's Tarrytown
estate as a fine example of the conscious adaptation of
these admirable elements. "You perhaps have seen pictures
of 'Sunny Side,'" he wrote, "where our historian has
perpetuated the architecture of our ancestors in
substantial brick and mortar, as faithfully as his pen has
recorded their heroic deeds" ("What Has Been Done and
What Can Be Done," *The New Path*, vol. I, no. 5,
September 1863, p. 54).   MBH

16

17

A Study of Trap Rock
(Buttermilk Falls)   1863

Oil on canvas
20 × 24 (50.8 × 61.0)
Inscribed lower left: "J.H. Hill 1863"
The Metropolitan Museum of Art, New York
PROVENANCE
John Henry Hill; The Metropolitan Museum of Art, 1882.
EXHIBITED
Rockland Center for the Arts, West Nyack, New York, *In Touch with Our Past*, 1974.
REFERENCES
Natalie Spassky, et al., *American Paintings in The Metropolitan Museum of Art*, vol. 2 (New York: The Metropolitan Museum, 1985).

John Henry Hill wrote of this painting in two letters now in The Metropolitan Museum of Art archives. On May 8, 1882, he offered to the museum, along with two watercolors by his father, "a study from nature of my own called *A Study of Trap Rock*." In a letter of May 14, 1911, he wrote, "I hope you have taken a look at the most elaborately literal study from nature I ever made. It was done in July and occupied me nearly every afternoon in the month . . ." The "trap rock" of the title refers to the geological origin of the stone outcropping, which was formed by the cooling of molten rock forced upward through rifts in the Triassic sandstone underlying the Hackensack, New Jersey, meadows.

This fully realized Ruskinian study is remarkable not only for the geological and botanical accuracy of each rock and tree but also for the suggestion of the actual presence of the scene depicted. The viewer seems to join the artist, half hidden in the lower right, in a sun-dappled forest interior. Tumbled boulders and fallen tree trunks draw the eye back along ordered diagonals to a shady hollow where a stream splashes down to a rocky bed framed by trees and flowering plants.

The painting was exhibited in the 1882 National Academy annual and praised by Charles Herbert Moore (q.v.) in a *New York Evening Post* review of April 27, 1882. "*Study of Trap Rock* by J. Henry Hill," Moore wrote, "contains more good painting than any other picture in the galleries . . . . Everything in it is perfectly and felicitously characterized, yet it is broad and true in total effect."

Hill made an etching of *Trap Rock*, a reverse view of the lower two-thirds of this painting, for *Sketches from Nature*, describing it as "a scene in a pleasant rocky dell, in the rear of the Palisades at Nyack." He also did a large replica called *Buttermilk Falls of West Nyack* for the Nyack Free Library in 1905 (*Nyack Evening Star*, March 23, 1905). He may have first painted the subject in 1862, for on August 23 of that year his father wrote to Thomas Charles Farrer (q.v.) that "John has done some nice things—he is now painting a large study of the Falls . . . thinks he will be able to finish it this week if he has fair weather"
(GLF/NYPL).   MBH

17

18 not illustrated
Sketches from Nature   1867

Twenty-five etchings
16 × 12¼ × ¾ (40.7 × 31.2 × 2.0)
Unsigned
*The New York Public Library, Astor, Lenox, and Tilden
Foundations, Print Collection*

REFERENCES
"Fine Arts," *The Nation* 4 (April 1867), p. 319; S.R. Koehler, "The Works
of the American Etchers XII, J. Henry Hill," *American Art Review* 1
(1880), pp. 429–430; Gerdts 1969, p. 93.

Even though John Henry Hill viewed etching as a pleasant
diversion and not a full-time pursuit (the etchings he
published in *Sketches from Nature*, he wrote, were "drawn
upon the copper at intervals between more persistent and
serious work"), he etched more than seventy plates during
his lifetime. The twenty-five in *Sketches from Nature* were
described by S.R. Koehler in an *American Art Review*
article of 1880 (p. 430) as having been "worked with
painstaking minuteness, and often with the finest possible
point—and printed *dry*, i.e. clean wiped, in cold black ink,
on white plate paper. . . . In their artistic character these
plates must be accepted for what they are meant to be, the
honest endeavor to carry out a preconceived artistic
theory." Russell Sturgis, writing in *The Nation*, not only
praised the etchings but also recommended Hill's
introduction: "It will be useful to any student of drawing to
read these two pages carefully and repeatedly."

All of the etchings in *Sketches from Nature* were made
in 1866 except plate one, dated 1859, and plate five, dated
1860. Many of the plates are unfinished in the corners,
some have a tondo or arched-top format, and others are
vignetted. Plate ten is quite literally "vignetted"—a view
of Mount Washington framed by a wild raspberry vine
arching across the top. There are a few close foreground
studies, the most striking of which is plate eleven, titled
Burdocks. This print, Hill wrote in the introduction, "was
commenced with the intention of drawing three times the
number of leaves seen here. . . ."   MBH

19
Black Capped Titmouse   *circa* 1866
Plate no. 7: *Sketches from Nature*

Etching on white paper
4¾ × 7½ (12.0 × 19.0), plate
2½ × 5¾ (6.1 × 14.5), image
Inscribed lower right on plate: "Chicadee-dee"
*The New York Public Library, Astor, Lenox, and Tilden
Foundations, Print Collection*

PROVENANCE
Samuel P. Avery, 1900; The New York Public Library.
REFERENCES
Gerdts 1969, p. 88, fig. 3 and p. 93.

This etching was included as plate seven in John Henry
Hill's *Sketches from Nature*, published at the beginning of
1867. Most of the etchings for the book were made the
previous year, but this particular one is not dated. In his
introduction, Hill apologized for plate seven, writing, "It
has lost some of the firmness or decision of the original
pen drawing from which it was copied." To the aspiring
student, he pointed out, "Dead birds make excellent
studies; many of [William Henry] Hunt's most beautiful
water-color drawings are of dead game; do not waste time
on stuffed specimens if you can get the real." John William
Hill (q.v.) also treated the subject of a dead bird (cat. no.
30), as did Thomas Charles Farrer (q.v.), and Robert
Brandegee (q.v.) may well have used the example of Hill's
etching as a model for his own study *Dead Bird* (cat. no.
85).   MBH

19

20

Thrush's Nest   1866

Pen and ink on paper
16 × 12½ (40.7 × 31.2)
Inscribed lower left: "J. Henry Hill 66"
Mr. and Mrs. Leonard L. Milberg
PROVENANCE
[The Old Print Shop, New York]; Mr. and Mrs. Leonard L. Milberg.
REFERENCES
Gerdts 1969, p. 88, fig. 7, and p. 93.

This drawing was the model for plate three in *Sketches from Nature*. In his introduction to the etchings, Hill pointed out that "the shadows on the right side of the eggs are cast by fibers around the edge of the nest."

Charles Eliot Norton, an early supporter of the Pre-Raphaelite circle, owned a similar drawing by Hill signed and dated 1866 and inscribed "Nest of the Brown Thrush/ Turdidus Rubus" (illustrated in *Harper's New Monthly Magazine*, 80, January 1890, p. 216). Gordon L. Ford loaned a Hill *Bird's Nest* to the 1871 exhibition of the Brooklyn Art Association, and a *Partridge Nest* by Hill was included in the 1875 exhibition of the American Society of Painters in Water Colors.   MBH

20

21
Six Plant Studies

Buttercups 3⅜ × 3¼ (8.6 × 9.1)
Star of Bethlehem 5⅞ × 5 (14.9 × 12.7)
Hellebore 3¾ × 4⅜ (9.5 × 11.0)
Yellow Water Lily 4 × 5¼ (10.3 × 13.4)
Lark's Nest 6⅞ × 5⅝ (17.6 × 14.3)
Skunk Cabbages 4⅜ × 4½ (11.1 × 11.4)

Pen and ink on paper
Inscribed on *Star of Bethlehem*, top center: "Star of
Bethlehem J. Henry Hill"
Inscribed on *Lark's Nest*, bottom center: "Lark's Nest"
*Harvard University Art Museums (Fogg Art Museum),
transferred from the Fine Arts Department*

These six plant studies are matted together in the following
order, from the upper left: *Buttercups, Star of Bethlehem,
Hellebore, Yellow Water Lily, Lark's Nest,* and *Skunk
Cabbages.* John Henry Hill drew several of the plates in
his 1867 book *Sketches from Nature* from this sort of close
study. The yellow water lily, for example, appears in the
foregrounds of plates one, nine, twelve, and twenty-one.

In his introduction to the book, Hill recommended
work in black and white as "very essentially instructive,
even to an artist who has an eye for and who takes most
delight in the representation of nature with color." He
preferred pen and ink to pencil because he felt that with
the former "a more powerful transcript is made."

In these pen-and-ink studies, the concentration on a
central image results in a more or less circular composition,
most obvious in *Lark's Nest* but also evident in *Star of
Bethlehem.* The arrangement of blossoms in the latter
resembles that in plate nineteen of *Sketches from Nature*; in

21

both, the flowers form a white circle against a dense mat of dark leaves. In his introduction to *Sketches from Nature*, Hill advised the student on drawing such a flower:

> In drawing this subject from nature with pen and ink, first sketch the position of the flowers and their petals slightly with pencil, then strike a firm black line around each petal, looking carefully at the inner edge so as to secure the correct form and proportion. Multiplied lines make the local color of the green leaves, and thicker lines, gradually closing up, make the deeper shades. For the more delicate shades cast upon the flowers the ink should be thinner, and the lines finer and closer together, and so placed as to indicate the direction of growth or undulation of surface.

Gordon L. Ford loaned some Hill works also titled *Sketches from Nature*, perhaps a group of drawings much like these, to the March 1868 exhibition of the Brooklyn Art Association. The group of drawings seen here, originally in the Fine Arts Department of Harvard University, was perhaps used by Charles Herbert Moore (q.v.) in his lectures there.   MBH

22
Shoshone Falls   1868

Watercolor on paper
12 × 17 (30.5 × 43.2)
Inscribed lower left: "J.H.H. 1869 Study from Nature"
Private collection
PROVENANCE
Estate of the artist; Christian Olsen, *circa* 1922; Dorothy Olsen Davis; [Washburn Gallery, New York]; private collection.

In the summer of 1868, John Henry Hill joined the United States Geological Survey exploration of the fortieth parallel led by Clarence King, a fellow member of the Association for the Advancement of Truth in Art. In September the party reached the basin of the Snake River in Idaho and spent ten days camped above the Shoshone Falls. King's description of the falls published in his 1871 *Mountaineering in the Sierra Nevada* provides a verbal equivalent to Hill's on-the-spot depiction:

> We looked down into a broad, circular excavation, three quarters of a mile in diameter, and nearly seven hundred feet deep. East and north, over the edges of the cañon, we looked across miles and miles of the Snake plain, far on to the boundary mountains. The wall of the gorge opposite us, like the cliff at our feet, sank in perpendicular bluffs nearly to the level of the river. . . . We saw a horizon as level as the sea; a circling wall, whose sharp edges were here and there battlemented in huge, fortress-like masses; a broad

21

river, smooth and unruffled, flowing quietly into the middle of the scene, and then plunging into a labyrinth of rocks, tumbling over a precipice two hundred feet high, and moving westward in a still, deep current, to disappear behind a black promontory. It was a strange, savage scene: a monotony of pale blue sky, olive and gray stretches of desert, frowning walls of jetty lava, deep beryl-green of river stretches, reflecting, here and there, the intense solemnity of the cliffs, and in the center a dazzling sheet of foam (pp. 233–234, 1905 edition).

In Hill's panoramic watercolor, painted from high on the rim of the canyon, the inclusion of the tiny figure in the distant foreground intensifies the drama of the river's vertiginous plunge toward the vortex in the center of the drawing. The use of washes rather than minute stippling here is appropriate to the scale of the subject and probably reflects Hill's study of Turner watercolors during his trip to England in 1864–65.

This plein-air painting of the falls served Hill as the model for several other versions in watercolor or oil. In a diary preserved in the Adirondack Museum at Blue Mountain Lake, New York (transcript courtesy of Roger Stein), he noted on January 23, 1871, that he had "nearly finished [a] drawing of Shoshone Falls 12 × 18 on grey tinted paper for King." A few weeks before, on January 8, 1871, he had written that he had "sketched out subject Shoshone Falls 3 ft. × 4." This ambitious painting (private collection) was not finished until 1880. A smaller oil dated 1870 (private collection) received a rather mixed review when exhibited in the 1871 National Academy exhibition. In his diary on March 14, 1871, Hill responded to a critic who had found the falls too opaque in appearance with a defense of the painting's truth to nature:

What struck me about the falling water was its opacity compared with the transparent green water above . . . but the long and short of it is they would have had me put plenty of yellow ochre into the white and tone it down, and make it indistinct and harmonious. . . . A friend to whom I showed the study made on the spot from which the picture is painted and a photograph taken from nature said I am astonished, they are identical.   MBH

22

23
Fringed Gentians *circa* 1867

Watercolor on paper
10½ × 7¼ (26.7 × 18.4)
Inscribed lower right: "J.H. Hill"
Mr. and Mrs. Wilbur L. Ross, Jr.
PROVENANCE
William C. Gilman (?); [Christie's New York March 27, 1981, lot 520];
Mr. and Mrs. Wilbur L. Ross, Jr.

This may be the watercolor of fringed gentians by John Henry Hill that William C. Gilman loaned to the first exhibition of the American Society of Painters in Water Colors in 1866–67. This uncultivated plant was not a frequent subject, although Thomas Farrer is also known to have drawn it (see "Fine Arts," *The Nation*, 3, May 1867, p. 399). Hill has contrasted its slender shape and azure coloration with the brilliant red leaves of Virginia creeper beside it and has set both plants against a background of dry brown grass. Clarence Cook's sonnet "To The Fringed Gentian," published in the October 1865 issue of *The New Path* (p. 165), celebrated the "azure flowers" and "cloistered life" of this uncommon wildflower.   MBH

23

24
Evening on Lake George   1869

Watercolor on paper
12 × 18 (30.5 × 45.8)
Inscribed lower left: "J. Henry Hill/Oct 1869"
Inscribed reverse: "Evening on Lake George"
Mr. and Mrs. Wilbur L. Ross, Jr.
PROVENANCE
[Berry-Hill Galleries, New York, 1984]; Mr. and Mrs. Wilbur L. Ross, Jr.

This is one of many Lake George subjects exhibited by
John Henry Hill in the late 1860s and '70s. Hill first visited
Lake George in August 1867 in company with his brother
George, a well-known mathematician, and an unidentified
newspaper clipping records that he stayed on an island in
the lake in 1869 after camping in the Adirondacks (see
letter of John William to Emma Hill, August 25, 1867, and
also clipping in GLF/NYPL). He liked the area so much
that he built a cabin on an island near Bolton's Landing,
where he spent part of the winters as well as the summers
in the early 1870s. A visit that his brother paid him
sometime in 1871 is documented by an illustrated etched
map of *The Narrows Lake George* inscribed, "surveyed by
George W. Hill 1871." One of the miniature views of the
lake that frame the map is identical to that in the present
watercolor, and the same view appears in another Hill

etching of 1871 titled *The Island Pines, Lake George.*
  Lake George was a popular sketching ground for other
painters at this time. J.F. Kensett's (1816–1872) large oil
Lake George of 1869 (The Metropolitan Museum of Art)
shows a similar view looking north toward several
pine-covered islands, and Charles H. Moore's undated
watercolor *Landscape: Rocks and Water* (cat. no. 50)
depicts the lake and its islands with an incredibly detailed
rocky foreground.
  While carefully delineated rocks occupy a prominent
place in the foreground of Hill's watercolor, they are not
given the obsessive attention of Moore's work. Rather, the
focus here is on the feathery forms of the pines on the
small island and their reflection in the glassy surface of the
lake. The composition emphasizes a circular space, leading
the eye from the deep shadow of the foreground rocks to
the encircling hills on the left, to the white sail of the small
boat, to the island, where the reflection of the pines
completes the circle to the foreground. The pervasive
golden glow of sunset illuminates the flanks of the western
hills, which cast violet shadows on the lake. The subtle
modulations of hue seen in this watercolor and others of
the same period support Russell Sturgis's opinion that
John Henry Hill was "on the whole the greatest colorist
among our painters" ("Fine Arts," *The Nation,* 2, May
1866, p. 666).   MBH

24

25

Lake George   1873

Watercolor on paper
6¾ × 9¾ (17.2 × 24.8)
Inscribed lower left: "Lake George"
Inscribed lower right: "Oct. 15, 73"
Inscribed bottom right margin by John Ruskin (q.v.):
"excellent only sky careless and stones unfinished JR"
Washburn Gallery, New York

PROVENANCE
Estate of Christian Olsen, *circa* 1922; Dorothy Olsen Davis; [Washburn Gallery].
EXHIBITED
Washburn Gallery, New York, *John William Hill and John Henry Hill*, October 10–November 3, 1979.

John Henry Hill's work was brought to John Ruskin's (q.v.) attention as early as 1860. On March 4 of that year Charles Henry Moore (q.v.) wrote to Thomas Farrer (q.v.), "I am glad to learn that Ruskin speaks well of John's drawings" (GLF/NYPL). Hill corresponded sporadically with Ruskin through the early 1880s, and extant letters from Ruskin to Hill contain such comments as, "Finish every drawing from corner to corner—don't go blotting or scrawling. . ." (letter of March 26, 1879, reprinted in *American Etchings*, XII, 1882). In another letter Ruskin admonished Hill, "You must draw *trees* with great pains—Mountain *outline* also—the mountain and cloud in the Turner vignettes are quite weak in outline." But in conclusion he conceded, "You have a very fine eye for color" (undated letter, The Metropolitan Museum of Art Archives). It is tempting to attribute the latter comment to this watercolor, which so brilliantly depicts golden autumn foliage and its reflection in the lake.

The work was probably executed at Hill's island retreat on Lake George, where he lived in the early 1870s. That Hill viewed his time there as a self-imposed exile is evidenced by an entry in his diary for this period (preserved in the Adirondack Museum, Blue Mountain Lake, New York). He wrote that he was visited at his cabin on March 24, 1872, by an acquaintance who "wanted to know what he was to say about this establishment. Said there was a great deal of curiosity manifested and many enquiries made about it." His response was characteristic:

Yes, thinks I, I have had a studio in Broadway and have exhibited pictures on the academy walls for a number of years and have received high recommendation from most of the New York artists and from Rossetti and Ruskin and thousands of people have seen my works and precious few enquiries made about them, and now when I choose to take them at their word and cut clear of their unconcern and tend to my own business these numbskulls are wide awake with astonishment, asking, "I don't see how he lives, I should think he would be awful lonesome."

This watercolor is one of a group of works by both Hill and his father that was rescued in the 1920s from a bonfire of the contents of Hill's last studio by a neighbor named Christian Olsen. Sadly, most of the unsold paintings of both Hill and his father were destroyed as one after another of the family houses was sold (see John Scott, "The Hill Family of Clarksville," *South of the Mountain*, 19, January–March 1975, pp. 5–18). That this amounted to a considerable number of completed watercolors is evidenced by a letter of Hill to Mrs. Gordon L. Ford after his father's death. "I have been getting together," he wrote, "the finished drawings of father's—they count up over 300. I hope some day the best of his work will be brought together and exhibited to the public" (letter of November 6, 1879, GLF/NYPL).   MBH

25

26

Natural Bridge, Virginia 1876

Watercolor on paper
21¼ × 14⅛ (40.0 × 35.9)
Inscribed lower right: "J. Henry Hill 1876"
The Brooklyn Museum, gift of Mr. and Mrs. Leonard L. Milberg
PROVENANCE
[The Old Print Shop, New York]; The Brooklyn Museum.

The best-known precedent for this subject is David Johnson's close view of the Natural Bridge painted in 1860 (cat. no. 113). Another version of the subject by Johnson (q.v.) was owned by Samuel P. Avery and engraved by Samuel Valentine Hunt (1803–1893) as the frontispiece for the August 1865 *Ladies Repository*. The composition of the engraving differs in many details from that of the 1860 painting but is very similar to that of a small oval oil on paper by Johnson (private collection) that may be a replica of, or a study for, the painting owned by Avery.

John Henry Hill would certainly have seen the Johnson view in Avery's collection. In addition, he was personally acquainted with Johnson and recorded a visit from Mr. and Mrs. Johnson in his diary on June 12, 1871. Thus it is not surprising that Hill's *Natural Bridge* is quite close in composition to Johnson's version seen in the etching. The viewpoint is nearly identical, with the void under the arch occupying a central position and the stream issuing from it running directly down toward the viewer. In Hill's painting the lack of foliage on the trees reveals the rocky formation of the arch and its gaping aperture. However, Hill's interest by this date was not so much in the Ruskinian delineation of rocks as in the drama of opposing lights and shadows around the central void, most evident on viewing the painting from a distance. Close examination reveals the subtle blending of colors in the rocks and water and the brilliance of the blue sky, as well as the small figure almost hidden in the shadowed right foreground.   MBH

26

John William Hill 1812–1879

John William Hill was born in London on January 13, 1812, the son of engraver John Hill. His family followed his father to Philadelphia in 1819 and then moved four years later to New York, where he was apprenticed to his father for the next seven years. During this period he worked on the aquatint plates for William Guy Wall's *Hudson River Portfolio* (1820–25), and his early work resembles Wall's. He exhibited at the National Academy of Design as early as 1828, was elected an Associate in 1833 (the same year he visited London to see old master paintings and to study), and contributed to the annual exhibitions regularly until 1873.

Hill served as a topographical artist for the New York State Geological Survey from 1836 to 1841 and provided illustrations for two natural history publications from 1842 on. After joining the Smith Brothers publishing firm in the late forties, he travelled extensively in New England and upstate New York preparing watercolor views of major cities in North America. On one of these trips, about 1855, he read John Ruskin's *Modern Painters.*

Ruskin's ideas significantly changed Hill's direction and style. Henceforth he devoted himself to painting directly from nature, depicting flowers, plants, fruit, and birds in natural backgrounds. By adopting the stipple technique, he was able to achieve brilliant color and a high degree of exactitude. In 1850 Hill helped found the short-lived New York Water Color Society, a group which exhibited only once, at the Crystal Palace in 1853. By 1860 he had become close friends with T.C. Farrer (q.v.), and in February 1863 he was elected President of the Association for the Advancement of Truth in Art. Since he never attended many Association meetings, the position must have been an honorary one in recognition of his dedication to Ruskinian principles.

The artist's later watercolors increasingly focused on subjects around his home in West Nyack, New York, where he settled with his father in 1838 and where he died on September 24, 1879. His son John Henry carried on his work and continually sought to keep his name in the public eye.

REFERENCES
Hill 1888; Koke, pp. 134–135; NAD.

27

27
Valley of the Androscoggin at Burbanks Ferry, New Hampshire 1859

Oil on panel
9 × 13¾ (22.8 × 35.0)
Inscribed lower right: "J.W. Hill 1859"
Sheldon Memorial Art Gallery, University of Nebraska, Lincoln
PROVENANCE
Estate of John Henry Hill; Christian Olsen, *circa* 1922; Dorothy Olsen Davis; [Washburn Gallery, New York]; Sheldon Memorial Art Gallery.

According to Charles Herbert Moore (q.v), writing in *An Artist's Memorial*, John William Hill first painted in the White Mountains in the summer of 1857. He showed two views of the Androscoggin valley in Maine in the 1858 annual of the National Academy of Design and executed this small oil study of the New Hampshire portion of the valley the following year. In Moore's words, this work demonstrates how he tried to "match in some more adequate measure, the golden green of sun-lighted foliage, and the blues and purples of distant hills" (p. 6).

Contemporary travel books such as Seth Eastman's *White Mountain Guide* and Thomas Starr King's *The White Hills*, both published in 1859, recommended the Androscoggin valley as a perfect site for "landscape beauty," because in the meadows along the Androscoggin River one is far enough from the mountains to fully appreciate their sublimity (*The White Hills*, Boston: Crosby and Ainsworth, 1859, pp. 5–6). In this study, Hill gives the meadow flowers in the foreground as much attention as the distant hills. A small undated watercolor by Hill in the same collection shows the same view under a cloudy sky.   MBH

28
Plums, Pears, Peaches, and a Grape 1864

Watercolor on paper
8⅝ × 13 (22.0 × 33.0)
Inscribed lower right: "J.W. Hill, 1864"
Private collection
PROVENANCE
Private collection.

John William Hill frequently exhibited still lifes of fruit after 1860. As evidenced by a letter of his to Thomas Charles Farrer (q.v.) dated August 18, 1860, they served not only as a staple of winter work but also as an alternative to outdoor work in the summer. "I shall go into plums on Monday in the house," he wrote, "and a water color drawing out of doors in the afternoon . . ." (GLF/NYPL).

Although this formal arrangement of fruit on a platter rather than on a bough is hardly Ruskinian, Ruskin would have applauded the meticulous stipple technique for the glowing color and palpable physical reality it gives each object. Indeed, it was probably Ruskin's instruction in *Elements of Drawing*, first published in 1857, that introduced Hill to this method. Charles Herbert Moore (q.v.) wrote in *An Artist's Memorial* (p. 6) of Hill's attempt in that year to "attain more brilliancy and luminousness," and Hill would have read with great interest Ruskin's advice to "practice the production of mixed tints by interlaced touches of the pure colors out of which they are formed, and use the process at the parts of your sketches where you wish to get rich and luscious effects. Study the

28

works of William Hunt, of the Old Water-Colour Society, in this respect . . ." (Ruskin, vol. XV, pp. 152–153).

In this watercolor the fruit is painted with unmixed colors applied in tiny strokes over a wash of another color. The smoky surface of the plums is formed by light blue and purple stippled over darker purple; the color of the peaches by pure red and orange applied over yellow, their fuzzy texture conveyed by variations in the stippling. The shadowed edges of the central pear contain strokes of both red and green.

Although this formal still-life arrangement on a tabletop is unusual in Hill's oeuvre, it is not unique. One other, even more elaborate watercolor of this type is known (private collection), and there may be others, given the frequency with which Hill seems to have painted fruit.   MBH

29

Pineapples   *circa 1864*

Watercolor on paper
10½ × 15⅛ (26.6 × 38.4)
Inscribed lower right: "J.W. Hill"
The Brooklyn Museum, purchased with funds given by
Mr. and Mrs. Leonard L. Milberg
PROVENANCE
[Village Green Antiques, Brattleboro, Vermont]; [Post Road Antiques, Larchmont, New York]; Jo Ann and Julian Ganz, Jr., 1984; The Brooklyn Museum.
EXHIBITED
National Gallery of Art 1981.
REFERENCES
Wilmerding, Ayres & Powell, pp. 99, 142, fig. 88.

In the manner of William Henry Hunt (q.v.), John William Hill has here placed two rather exotic pineapples in a natural bower of mosses, ferns, and grasses. Tiny, stippled brushstrokes, often in unmixed colors, meticulously define each object. The moss is composed of both purple and green strokes, the pineapples of vivid red in the shadows, and the grasses and ferns of a variety of greens. The dry, ripe, rotund pineapples seem to be deliberately contrasted with the soft, living greens of their surroundings, as though Hill were having a private joke about outlanders in the forest.

The subject of pineapples is mentioned only once by Hill, in an undated letter to Gordon L. Ford. "I sold my pineapple drawing to Mrs. Parker this morning," he wrote, while also mentioning a visit to "Miss McLane" (GLF/NYPL). If the pineapple drawing referred to is this one, it would then date to the early 1860s, before Annie McLane's marriage to Thomas Charles Farrer (q.v.).   MBH

29

30
Dead Blue Jay *circa* 1865

Watercolor on paper
5¾ × 12 (14.6 × 30.5)
Inscribed lower left: "J.W. Hill"
The New-York Historical Society
PROVENANCE
Mrs. Charlan Whitley Plummer Gellatly, by 1957; The New-York
Historical Society.
REFERENCES
Stebbins, p. 155, illus.; Gerdts 1969, pp. 88–89, fig. 6; Koke, vol. 2, p. 143,
illus.

This meticulous life-size drawing of a dead blue jay resting
on a table goes beyond the naturalist's enumeration of
anatomy and coloration in its poignant commentary on the
fragility and impermanence of life. The rigidity of the bird
is keenly felt in contrast with the still-brilliant color of its
wings and the softness of its breast feathers, while its
lifelessness is emphasized by the open window that frames
a tree, the bird's natural habitat, just above its head. The
cumulative, patient, and loving labor given this drawing
adds weight to the moral implications of the subject.

Dead songbirds were not an unusual subject for the
Pre-Raphaelites, as can be seen in John Henry Hill's
etching and advice to the student in his *Sketches from
Nature* (cat. no. 18). Thomas Farrer (q.v.) showed several
watercolors of dead blue jays in his exhibition of still lifes
at Knoedler's in 1865.   MBH

31
Bird's Nest and Dogroses   1867

Watercolor on paper
10¾ × 13⅞ (27.3 × 35.2)
Inscribed lower right: "J.W. Hill/1867"
The New-York Historical Society
PROVENANCE
Gordon Lester Ford, Brooklyn, New York, before 1879; Mrs. Roswell
Skeel, Jr., by 1947; The New-York Historical Society.
EXHIBITED
Whitney 1984.
REFERENCES:
Gerdts & Burke, p. 117 and plate XV; Koke, vol. 2, pp. 140 and 142,
illus.; Jones, p. 53, illus.; Foshay, pp. 45–46, fig.33.

This type of informal still life combining sprigs of flowers
and birds' nests in a natural setting was a specialty of
English watercolorist William Henry Hunt (see cat. no.
124). That both John William and John Henry Hill (q.v.)
were aware of Hunt's work by the late 1850s is evident in
their correspondence with Thomas Farrer. John William
Hill may have seen Hunt's paintings at the Old Water-
Colour Society exhibitions during his trip to London
about 1833. In any case, by the 1850s Hunt's still lifes were
widely reproduced in lithographs and chromolithographs.

The stipple technique Hill used in this and other still
lifes is similar to Hunt's, though hardly identical. Hunt
often used a ground of Chinese white over which he glazed
transparent color, while Hill used the white of the paper
for luminosity and often left areas bare to serve as
highlights. Both, however, used stippled brushstrokes of
unmixed hues interlaced to achieve the greatest possible
brilliance and accuracy of color.

Hill showed a *Bird's Nest* in the March 1869 exhibition
of the Brooklyn Art Association, and *A Fruit and Bird's
Nest* owned by Alexander Forman was included in his
1879 memorial exhibition along with this work, which was
then owned by Gordon L. Ford. John Henry Hill (q.v.)
included a *Thrush's Nest* in his *Sketches From Nature*
the same year that his father painted this work
(cat. nos. 20 and 18).   MBH

30

31

32
Hanging Game—Ducks 1867

Watercolor on paper
19¼ × 13¼ (48.9 × 33.6)
Inscribed lower center: "J.W. Hill/1867"
Private collection

PROVENANCE
[Parke-Bernet sale 2492, 1966, lot 82]; [Kennedy Galleries, New York];
[Hirschl & Adler Galleries Inc., New York]; private collection.
EXHIBITED
Kennedy Galleries, New York, *American Drawings, Pastels and
Watercolors, 1825–1890*, 1968; Hirschl & Adler Galleries Inc., New York,
American Drawings and Watercolors, 1979.
REFERENCES
Kennedy, p. 38, illus.; Katherine E. Manthorne, "American Drawings and
Watercolors," *Arts Magazine* (January 1980), p. 9.

33
Hanging Trophies—
Snipe and Woodcock in a Landscape
1867

Watercolor on paper
20 × 16 (50.8 × 40.6)
Inscribed lower right: "J.W. Hill/1867"
Private collection

PROVENANCE
[Parke-Bernet sale 2492, 1966, lot 82]; [Kennedy Galleries, New York];
private collection.
EXHIBITED
Kennedy Galleries, New York, *American Drawings, Pastels and
Watercolors, 1825–1890*, 1968; Kennedy Galleries, New York, *Wildlife
and Sporting Paintings*, 1979; The Art Museum, Princeton University,
Princeton Alumni Collections—Works on Paper, 1981.
REFERENCES
Kennedy, p. 38, illus.; *Princeton Alumni Collections* (exhibition
catalogue, The Art Museum, Princeton University, Princeton, New
Jersey, 1981), p. 95 illus.

John William Hill is known to have painted at least eight
game still lifes, six or seven exhibited during his lifetime
and two included in the Hill sale at S. Field's Art Gallery in
Brooklyn in 1888. Four have been located, three in private
collections and one in the Yale University Art Gallery.
Only one is a tabletop still life. The others combine hanging game in the foreground with distant landscape or sky,
an arrangement Hill used frequently with flower subjects
as well. According to Russell Sturgis, writing in *The
Nation*, these works represented "a class of pictures which
is almost peculiar to this artist, of which he has painted
many, though only a few have been exhibited. They
contain a singularly successful combining of foreground
detail and distant landscape" ("Fine Arts," *The Nation*,
3, November 1866, p. 435).

32

33

The brilliance of color and the astonishing clarity of objects in both of the watercolors illustrated here are achieved through the use of unmixed colors and minuteness of touch that successfully suggests the infinite detail of nature. Each object is drawn with great specificity, if not with as much detail as the foreground group of birds. In the watercolor with landscape the distant leafless trees are as identifiable by their characteristic outlines as the winterberry bush on the right is by the arrangement of its scarlet berries. The transition from foreground to distance is expertly handled, with the point of view placed low behind a small rise so that most of the middle distance is eliminated. The painting of the game birds themselves is a *tour de force*, if a technique so self-effacing can be so described.

Sturgis, writing of similar works in the article cited above, felt that "it is probable that there is no man now alive, as there is certainly none in this country, who could surpass these drawings in the simplicity of means and admirable completeness of results . . . We have spoken of these drawings in words that might apply to William Hunt's work, and with reason . . . it is doubtful if even he could have better expressed the character of those feathers, or have done the work more naturally and simply." John Ruskin himself (q.v.) executed several watercolors of dead-game subjects in the mid-1860s. His interest, however, was primarily in the meticulous definition of the birds' plumage rather than in their placement in a landscape setting.   MBH

34
View from High Tor, Haverstraw, New York   *circa* 1866

Watercolor on paper
11¾ × 18 (29.9 × 45.8)
Inscribed lower left: "J.W. Hill"
The New-York Historical Society
PROVENANCE
[The Old Print Shop, New York, 1958]; The New-York Historical Society.
REFERENCES
Koke, vol. 2, pp. 139 and 140, illus.

High Tor, a point of land rising more than eight hundred feet above the west bank of the Hudson River, provided the vantage point for this minutely detailed panorama. In fact, it is this massive curving ridge, which marks the

northern end of the Hudson Palisades, rather than the river itself that is the focus here.

John William Hill was undoubtedly aware of the geological formation of this immense sill of molten rock—of how it was shaped first by contraction in cooling and then by glacial abrasion. In this watercolor, the precise outline of each furrow and depression in the underlying rock is indicated, even though covered in glowing autumn foliage. Moreover, geographical as well as geological specificity is achieved. Croton Point and Ossining, New York, are visible far across the river, a road and tilled fields occupy the near side of the ridge, and in the right distance Rockland Lake and Hook Mountain can be discerned.

Hill's meticulous watercolor technique contributes to the tremendous visual impact made by this small landscape. The brushstrokes are inseparable from the objects they construct, sometimes forming a shadowed edge or even the complete form of a leaf or a blade of grass. The tiny trees on the farthest hills are formed by separate strokes, while the foreground rocks are painted so carefully that the touches of the brush are almost imperceptible. The color is carefully modulated from the golden foliage and blue shadows on the ridge to the blue green of the distant hills.

Hill painted innumerable views along the Hudson, though apparently no others of High Tor. His *View on the Hudson*, for example, was included in the March 1868 exhibition of the Brooklyn Art Association. A date of about 1866 was given *View from High Tor* on the basis of a similarly dated view by John Henry Hill (q.v.) (Koke, p. 140).   MBH

35
Hunter and Dog   *circa* 1867

Oil on canvas mounted on board
10 × 16 (25.4 × 40.6)
Inscribed lower left: "J.W. Hill"
Mr. and Mrs. Wilbur L. Ross, Jr.
PROVENANCE
[Kennedy Galleries, New York, 1980]; Mr. and Mrs. Wilbur L. Ross, Jr.
EXHIBITED
Rockland Center for the Arts, West Nyack, New York, *In Touch with Our Past*, 1974.

This small oil shows a rocky stream bed with distant mountains like that in Hill's 1867 watercolor *View on Catskill Creek* (cat. no. 36). The sky here is a deep limpid

34

35

blue with a few white clouds. The approach of autumn is evident in the yellowish brown of the foliage, which is painted in feathery brushstrokes.

Hill seems to have preferred to work in watercolor, but a number of his oil paintings are known, some much larger than this and executed in a looser manner. *Hunter and Dog* demonstrates how ably he could translate the precise brushwork and vivid palette of his watercolors into the oil medium.   MBH

36
View on Catskill Creek   1867

Watercolor on paper
9½ × 14¾ (24.1 × 37.5)
Inscribed lower left: "J.W. Hill/1867"
The Metropolitan Museum of Art, gift of the artist, 1882
PROVENANCE
John Henry Hill, 1882; The Metropolitan Museum of Art, New York.

Charles Herbert Moore (q.v.), in *An Artist's Memorial*, wrote of John William Hill's studies made in the Catskills during the autumn of 1856, mentioning "mountain streams with the finely grouped and delicately colored stones peculiar to that delightful region" (p. 5). This view, along with *Hunter and Dog* and *Fawn's Leap* (cat. nos. 35 and 37), evidences Hill's continuing fascination with the subject.

The particular combination of water, rocks, foliage, and distant hills in the Catskills appealed to other members of the Association for the Advancement of Truth in Art as well. Mrs. L.C. Lillie, in an 1890 article on "Two Phases of American Art," pointed out that "singularly enough the same region which had encouraged and inspired the first landscape school in America attracted the pre-Raphaelites; there the best work of Farrer, Moore and the two Hills, father and son was executed" (*Harper's New Monthly Magazine*, 80, January 1890, p. 215). Moore, who had settled in the village of Catskill, New York, as early as 1861, wrote to Thomas Charles Farrer (q.v.) on October 25, 1863, that he was making a study of a stream bed with a ledge of rocks (GLF/NYPL), and his fascination with rocks was even more intense than Hill's, judging by such studies as *Landscape: Rocks and Water* and *Rocks by the Water* (cat. nos. 50 and 49).

In this watercolor, Hill devotes as much attention to the trees on the hills, which appear golden in the sunlight and blue in the shadows, as to the foreground rocks. Indeed, the rocks are painted with washes of color, while the feathery stippling is reserved for the foliage. A related watercolor *Landscape* of 1863 (New-York Historical Society) shows a similar rocky stream with two figures.   MBH

36

37

Fawn's Leap, Catskill, New York   1868

Watercolor on paper
13¾ × 17¾ (34.9 × 45.1)
Inscribed lower left: "J.W. Hill/1868"
Lent anonymously

There are several known versions of this subject. The
one seen here may be the *Fawn's Leap, Catskill Mountains*
that was owned by William C. Gilman and included in
the March 1868 Brooklyn Art Association exhibition.
Another version, a large oil painting dated 1868, is perhaps
the *Fawn's Leap, Catskill Mountains* that Hill showed in
the 1872 annual exhibition at the National Academy. Yet
a third, an unfinished, more broadly handled oil of *Fawn's
Leap* in the Washburn Gallery, is probably by John Henry
Hill (q.v.) rather than John William Hill, as it is one of the
works rescued from the bonfire of the contents of John
Henry's studio and seems closer in style to his work than
to his father's. Thomas Farrer (q.v.) also painted a view of
Fawn's Leap that was included in the 1867 First Annual
Exhibition at the Yale School of Fine Arts (catalogue
courtesy of William H. Gerdts).

Judging from a somewhat later stereoscopic view of the
falls taken from the same viewpoint, John William's
depiction of the falls and their rocky surroundings here
was extremely accurate. The only license he seems to have
taken with observed fact was in making his figures
somewhat smaller than they would have appeared in order
to emphasize the grandeur of the falls.   MBH

37

38

Apples and Plums   1874

Watercolor on paper
7⅞ × 11⅜ (20.0 × 28.9)
Inscribed lower left: "1874 J.W. Hill"
Lent anonymously

PROVENANCE
[Post Road Antiques, Larchmont, New York, 1974]; private collection.
EXHIBITED
Heckscher 1977; AFA, no. 85; Philbrook 1981.
REFERENCES
Stebbins, pp. 155–158, illus.; Troyen, pp. 64–65, illus.; Gerdts 1981, pp. 98–99, illus.

There was some disagreement within the Association for the Advancement of Truth in Art as to the legitimacy of this sort of still life, which was pioneered in England by William Henry Hunt (q.v.) and adopted in America by John William Hill. Russell Sturgis wrote critically of a similar painting exhibited in 1866:

A cut off branch of fruit thrown upon the ground is not dignified. It is a good study but poor picture making. Even the great and authorative example of William Hunt proves only that a picture may be made admirable in spite of a poor subject; for a poor subject cut flowers and plucked fruit must always remain ("Fine Arts," *The Nation*, 3, November 1866, p. 435).

Sturgis's main objection seems to have been to the artificial arrangement involved—natural objects out of context, although out-of-doors. His orthodox Ruskinianism would have preferred the branch of plums to be seen against the sky (as in cat. nos. 39, 40, and 128) and the leaf-strewn patch of earth to serve as a setting for a growing plant. Hill, however, seems to have been undaunted by such criticism. A notice in the *Brooklyn Union* emphasized his distinctiveness even among the artists of the Association, pointing out that he "stands aloof from any school of artists feeling that there is a higher or at least more delicate and spiritual conception of art than finds expression in the columns of *The New Path*" ("Art in Brooklyn," vol. II, no. 1, May 14, 1864, p. 4).

Hill's long career as a painter and his experience in the use of watercolor made him conscious of such formal elements as color and compositional unity. While the apples and plums seen here are painted meticulously and lovingly for their own sake, they also exist as colored objects carefully placed for maximum impact: the yellow and red of the apples, for instance, contrasts with the blue plums and the brilliant accent of the blackberries. A similar watercolor of two apples and two branches of plums, dated 1870, is in The Metropolitan Museum of Art.   MBH

38

39
Apple Blossoms   *circa* 1874

Watercolor on paper
15⅞ × 8⅞ (39.0 × 22.3)
Unsigned
The Brooklyn Museum
PROVENANCE
Estate of John Henry Hill; Christian Olsen, *circa* 1922; Dorothy Olsen Davis; [Washburn Gallery, New York, 1974]; The Brooklyn Museum.
EXHIBITED
Washburn Gallery, New York, *Works on Paper*, 1976; Hunt Institute for Botanical Documentation, Pittsburgh, *American Cornucopia*, April 5–July 30, 1976; The Brooklyn Museum, *American Watercolors and Pastels from the Museum Collection*, 1976.
REFERENCES
American Cornucopia (exhibition catalogue, Hunt Institute for Botanical Documentation, April 5–July 30, 1976), p. 17; Blaugrund 1984, p. 38, illus.; Ferber and Blaugrund, p. 314, illus.

As early as 1860, John William Hill painted flowering branches seen close up against a background of blue sky. In a letter of July 1860, John Henry Hill (q.v.) wrote Thomas Farrer (q.v.), "Father has been hard at work as usual . . . he has repeated moss rose with blue sky background which I know you would like" (GLF/NYPL). The tangled profusion of branches seen here is painted in full sunlight against the distant sky. Hill showed an *Apple Blossoms* in the November 1874 Brooklyn Art Association exhibition, and two paintings of that subject—one owned by Alexander Forman and the other by Edward Cary—were included in his memorial exhibition at the Brooklyn Art Association.   MBH

40
Peach Blossoms   1874

Watercolor on paper
16⅜ × 9⅜ (41.6 × 23.8)
Inscribed lower left: "J.W. Hill 1874"
The Metropolitan Museum of Art, New York
PROVENANCE
John Henry Hill, 1882; The Metropolitan Museum of Art.

Like the undated *Apple Blossoms* (cat. no. 39) this vertical watercolor depicts a flowering branch seen close up in full sun against a blue sky. The more rigid arrangement of twigs and blossoms here, however, suggests botanical illustration rather than transcription from nature. Even so, the meticulous painting of the blossoms and sky, the brilliant pinks and lavenders of the petals, and the bright green of the leaves gives the branch a plein-air immediacy and corporeality lacking in a botanist's drawing. The resemblance of this watercolor to Ruskin's own *Twig of Peach Bloom* (cat. no. 128) is striking.   MBH

39

40

41

Blackberries 1876

Watercolor on paper
9⅝ × 13⅜ (24.5 × 34.0)
Inscribed lower left: "1876 J.W. Hill"
Stephen Rubin
PROVENANCE
Stephen Rubin.

This is one of the most beautiful of Hill's paintings of fruit or flowers against the sky. The shiny black of the ripe berries and the luscious red of the unripe ones are thrown into relief by the spacious sky with its white clouds.

Hill was well known for these subjects, which were not, however, always well received. An unidentified reviewer of the first exhibition of the American Society of Painters in Water Colors in the winter of 1867–68 noted that "much was expected of the Hills, who, for many years were almost alone in this country in their devotion to water colors; but neither father nor son has done himself much credit. . . . John W. Hill sends his usual branch of cherries, very truthfully and exquisitely painted . . . but we are a little tired of these bits of fruit-painting with their background of blue sky, always of the same tint, lightened with suggestions of white cloud" (GLF/NYPL).

Nevertheless, as the dates of other examples demonstrate (cat. nos. 39 and 40), he was not discouraged and continued to paint fruit and flowers in this distinctive manner. A *Black-Berry* by him was included in the 1875 exhibition of the American Society of Painters in Water Colors, and a watercolor *Blackberries* in the Philadelphia Centennial exhibition the following year was probably his, although it was listed in the catalogue as being simply by "Hill."   MBH

41

42
Still Life: Fruit
Watercolor on paper
7 × 10 (17.8 × 25.4)
Unsigned
The New-York Historical Society
PROVENANCE
Gordon Lester Ford, by 1879; Mrs. Roswell Skeel, Jr., 1947;
The New-York Historical Society.
EXHIBITED
BAA, December 1879.
REFERENCES
Koke, vol. 2, p. 143; Gerdts 1969, pp. 88–89, fig. 5.

This casual grouping of an apricot, a peach, three
strawberries, and a fig on an indeterminate surface, neither
tabletop nor forest floor, is painted with a more relaxed,
hatched brushstroke than the 1864 still life *Plums, Pears,
Peaches, and a Grape* (cat. no. 28). Strokes of pure color are
most obvious in the large peach, whose shadowed edge is
defined by purple and violet, with blue and green mingled
in the highlights. This is probably the fruit watercolor
owned by Gordon L. Ford that was included in Hill's
memorial exhibition at the Brooklyn Art Association in
December 1879.   MBH

42

43

Afterglow mid-1870s

Watercolor on paper
4¾ × 8¼ (12.1 × 20.9)
Inscribed lower left: "J.W. Hill"
Lent anonymously
PROVENANCE
[Adam A. Weschler and Son, Washington, D.C., sale February 13–16, 1975, as *Sunset on the Hudson*]; private collection; [Jeffrey R. Brown, Fine Arts, Amherst, Massachusetts]; private collection.

John William Hill rarely painted twilights. He preferred the mid-afternoon or even the mid-morning light because it more fully reveals the details of nature. This was in contrast to his son John Henry Hill (q.v.), who was more interested in portraying ephemeral light effects. In a letter to Thomas Farrer (q.v.) in July 1860, the younger Hill mentioned seeing Frederic Edwin Church's (q.v.) great *Twilight in the Wilderness*, certainly the ultimate twilight landscape of the time. And in 1866, John Henry showed a painting of 1856 entitled *Sunset off Boston* in the Artists'

Fund Society exhibition (see "Fine Arts," *The Nation*, 3, November 1866, p. 435).

By 1870, however, even the elder Hill seems to have been affected by the taste for atmospheric effects. He showed a *Moonlight, Lake George* at the 1873 exhibition of the American Society of Painters in Water Colors and a *Sunset on Lake George* at the Louisville Industrial Exposition of 1878 (reference courtesy of William H. Gerdts), and *Sunset on the Androscoggin* was included in the 1888 Hill sale at S. Field's Art Gallery. Charles H. Moore (q.v.) in *An Artist's Memorial* (p. 7) wrote that John William Hill "sometimes preferred the more transient effects of opening or closing day, when the shadows are lengthened, and the air is filled with a pervading warmth of hue." Even so, the simplification of shapes and the extraordinary colors in this painting are unusual in Hill's oeuvre. The sky is yellow and dotted with orange clouds that reflect the light of the sun, which has already set beyond the line of black hills. The foreground water is a deep purple and forms a horizontal band that echoes that of the sky.   MBH

43

Charles Herbert Moore 1840-1930

Charles Herbert Moore was born in New York City on April 10, 1840, and was educated in the city's public school system. He never attended college but went on to become an accomplished artist, writer, and teacher of fine arts who was awarded an honorary A.M. degree from Harvard in 1890. Around the age of thirteen he studied drawing with Benjamin Coe (1779-after 1883) and within a short time began to sell his work to two New York art dealers. Although his family moved to a farm in Connecticut in 1856, he remained in New York, joining forces with his former teacher and with Elmer Parmelee to form an art school in a studio in the University Building.

In 1859 Moore rented space in the prestigious Tenth Street Studio Building, where such neighbors as the Hills (q.v.) probably stimulated his interest in the writings of John Ruskin (q.v.). With his enthusiasm further encouraged by T.C. Farrer (q.v.), whom he met around 1860, he helped found the Association for the Advancement of Truth in Art in 1863 and wrote several articles for *The New Path*. Early in 1861 he moved to Catskill, New York, and in 1865 he married and had a daughter. That summer he visited with the author and educator Charles Eliot Norton, another great admirer of Ruskin, in Ashfield, Massachusetts. During the period between 1858 and 1870 he contributed paintings regularly to exhibitions at both the National Academy of Design and the Brooklyn Art Association, and in 1861 he exhibited a work at the Boston Athenaeum.

The year 1871 marked the end of Moore's professional painting career and the beginning of his career as a teacher. At Norton's request he began teaching drawing and water-color at Harvard's Lawrence Scientific College. Three years later Norton appointed him a lecturer to Harvard undergraduates, and his course on the principles of design, painting, sculpture, and architecture helped establish the fine arts as a subject worthy of inclusion in a liberal arts education. In the fall of 1876, with a letter of introduction from Norton to Ruskin, he went abroad and subsequently worked and travelled with the English critic in Italy.

Upon his return Moore devoted more and more time to the study of the structure of medieval architecture. He visited Europe again in 1885 to further his architectural knowledge and in 1890 published his pioneering book *Development and Characteristics of Gothic Architecture*. Harvard appointed him an assistant professor of design in 1891, and in 1896 he was elevated to full professor and made the director of the university's newly built Fogg Art Museum. His next book, *Characteristics of Renaissance Architecture*, was published in 1905. Four years later he retired and emigrated to Hartfield, England, where he continued to write, publishing *The Medieval Church Architecture of England* in 1912 and *Swedenborg: Servant of God* in 1918. He lived there with his second wife and his daughter and died on February 15, 1930.

REFERENCES
BAA; DAB; Koke; Mather; NAD.

44

44
The Catskills in Spring   1861

Oil on canvas
12⅛ × 20⅜ (30.9 × 51.7)
Inscribed lower right: "C.H. Moore/1861"
Vassar College Art Gallery, Gift of Matthew Vassar
PROVENANCE
The artist; Elias Lyman Magoon, 1864; Matthew Vassar, Vassar Female
College Art Gallery.
EXHIBITED
Vassar College Art Gallery, Poughkeepsie, New York, *All Seasons and
Every Light: Nineteenth Century American Landscapes from the
Collection of Elias Lyman Magoon,* October 14–December 16, 1983,
no. 52.
REFERENCES
Ella M. Foshay and Sally Mills, *All Seasons and Every Light: Nineteenth
Century American Landscapes from the Collection of Elias Lyman
Magoon* (exhibition catalogue, Vassar College Art Gallery, Poughkeepsie,
New York, 1983), color illus. frontispiece, pp. 23, 77; Mather, p. 13, fig. 9.

This early work by Moore, painted when he was just
twenty-one, was one of four oils purchased in the early
1860s by the Baptist preacher Elias Lyman Magoon, a
collector of American art who sold his collection to
Matthew Vassar for the Art Gallery of Vassar Female
College in 1864 (Foshay and Mills, p. 7).

Moore suggests the regeneration and hope of spring by
contrasting bright new growth against dull winter brown.
In a letter to Magoon of May 26, 1861, he describes a
similar scene: "I went to the place where we walked in the
evening, this evening, and oh! if you could only see it
under such a sky, I never saw anything more *glorious.* The
mountains were of the pure blue that you love so dearly,
with rays of rosy light bursting through the cloves and
kindling the highest points into living light" (quoted in
Foshay and Mills, p. 23). Here, the demarcations
delineating the topographical landmarks draw the eye
diagonally back to the distant mountains, which, although
crisply outlined, are not as microscopically detailed as
Moore was wont to make them in later works depicting the
same valley and range (see cat. no. 53). Still, the evening
cloud formations demonstrate Moore's acute observation
of natural details, for he carefully differentiates high
cirrostratus fibratus clouds from lower cumulous ones
with the kind of accuracy stressed by John Ruskin (q.v.).
The sense of light and immediacy he achieves further
testifies to his working outdoors.

A transitional work lacking the meticulous details of
later pieces, *The Catskills in Spring* is perhaps
representative of Moore's "success as a popular artist,"
which he gave up "with the patience and modesty of a
beginner, to open a new career as a painter of the truth,"
probably under the influence of T.C. Farrer (q.v.), whom
he met about this time (*The Round Table,* vol. I, no.7,
January 30, 1864, p. 108).   AB

45
Lilies of the Valley   *circa* 1861

Watercolor on paper
8⅛ × 4⅜ (20.7 × 11.1)
Inscribed lower right (in monogram): "CHM"
*The Art Museum, Princeton University, gift of
Frank Jewett Mather, Jr.*
PROVENANCE
Mrs. Florence Vincent; Frank J. Mather, Jr., 1950; The Art Museum,
Princeton University.
REFERENCES
Record of The Art Museum, Princeton University, vol. 9, no. 2, 1950, p. 15.

46
Woodbine   1873

Watercolor over graphite on paper
7⅜ × 8¾ (18.8 × 22.2), sight
Inscribed lower right: "CHM Oct. 1873"
*Harvard University Art Museums (Fogg Art Museum),
gift of Dr. Denman W. Ross*
PROVENANCE
Fogg Art Museum.

45

"Studies . . . must be made in earnest," *The New Path* wrote in 1864. "Their record must be true record; they must be made for a purpose, each one must be of something not yet thoroughly known or fit; each one must add something to the previous stock of recorded observation" (vol. II, no. 3, July 1864, p. 38). Like other American Pre-Raphaelites and such contemporaneous American landscape painters as Frederic Edwin Church (see cat. no. 94), Moore often made intense small-scale studies of individual botanical specimens or of small segments of earth covered with plants growing *in situ*.

The artist painted *Lilies of the Valley* in 1861, soon after the commencement of his friendship with Thomas Charles Farrer (q.v.) and after his move to Catskill, New York, to a house located just half a mile from the studio and home of Thomas Cole (1801–1848). Moore became fast friends with Thomas Cole, Jr., and their relationship, which flourished during the time *The New Path* was directing criticism at the senior Cole's landscapes, is evidenced in part by Moore's paintings of Cole's house, his studio, and his dog Ponto (Information supplied by William B. Rhoads; letter from Moore to T.C. Farrer, November 15, 1863, GLF/NYPL). This picture was in the Cole collection, for it was given to F.J. Mather, Jr., by Mrs. Florence Vincent, Thomas Cole, Jr.'s daughter.

In its brilliant stippled blue ground, which reflects John Ruskin's call for natural settings, *Lilies of the Valley* resembles John William Hill's *Apple Blossoms* (cat. no. 39) and *Peach Blossoms* (cat. no. 40), both of which are set against a clear blue sky. In its arched top, it is reminiscent of William T. Richards' *Red Clover, Butter-and-Eggs, and Ground Ivy* (cat. no. 71), and many other small Pre-Raphaelite pictures utilizing the same format. Centrally placed in the picture space, these sprigs of lilies devoid of leaves are as decorative as Richards' more elaborate composition and as much a close-up magnification of nature as the boughs of Hill's trees.

Woodbine is a much later but equally precise study with a different purpose. Not really a finished composition, it is rather more like a botanical illustration, a single branch minutely observed, frayed leaves and all. It was probably made to gain greater knowledge "of something not yet thoroughly known" and was possibly incorporated into a more finished work. As a reviewer wrote about Moore's painting of *Mandrakes* in the *New York Tribune* on July 3, 1866, it consists of "the patient study of nature for the sake of understanding her . . ." and shows "refinement of feeling, sympathy with nature and love of God's handiwork" (p. 6). Although by the eighties Moore's intense dedication to Ruskinian ideals had lessened, this study demonstrates that there were certain aspects of these ideals that he retained.   AB

47
Winter Landscape, Valley of the Catskills 1866

Oil on canvas
7 × 10 (17.8 × 25.4)
Inscribed lower left (in monogram): "CHM 1866"
The Art Museum, Princeton University, gift of Frank Jewett Mather, Jr.
PROVENANCE
Frank J. Mather, Jr., 1953; The Art Museum, Princeton University.
EXHIBITED
Possibly Artists' Fund Society, 1865, no. 192.
REFERENCES
Mather, 1957, pp. 24-27, fig. 11; *Record of the Art Museum, Princeton University,* 1954, vol. 13, no. 1, illus. p. 17, no. 2, p. 62.

Moore painted several winter landscapes. In a letter to Thomas Charles Farrer (q.v.) dated December 11, 1864, he mentions a snowstorm that he hoped would give him "a chance to complete my snow mountains—commenced last winter," evidence of his working on paintings over several years. Four months later, in a letter dated April 26, 1865, he speaks of a snow picture for sale (GLF/NYPL). A painting of his called *Winter Study in the Catskills* was exhibited at the Artists' Fund Society in November 1865, and a detailed description of this "very little picture of a great deal of country" was given in *The Nation* of November 16, 1865 (I, no. 20, p. 664). From that review it would seem that this topographically accurate landscape dated 1866 may be the same painting. Only one other winter scene is mentioned in the subsequent literature, a watercolor entitled *October Snow Squall* exhibited in 1867 and 1868 (NAD 1867, no. 7; BAA, March 1868, no. 58).

Since Moore worked on paintings more than one season, it is very possible that he continued to work on this one after exhibiting it, which would account for the date. "My principle [sic] winter work is a view of the mountains and the valley in snow. . . . ," he reported to Charles Eliot Norton in February 1866, and two months later he noted in another letter that he had "just finished my little winter study . . ." (quoted in Mather, p. 24).

The same valley and mountains are seen in *The Catskills in Spring* (cat. no. 44), painted four years earlier, in the pen-and-ink drawing *The Valley of the Catskills from Jefferson Hill,* done in 1869 (The Art Museum, Princeton), and in a subsequent watercolor of 1872 (Museum of Fine Arts, Boston). "The peculiar structure of these hills is very marked in Winter, & their sculpture brought out in most ineffably subtle light and shade . . .," Moore wrote to Norton (quoted in Mather, p. 24). Underscoring the importance of attempting to approach subjects without selection, he referred to the "ugly white houses" he included here in the middle ground, concluding that they are not "altogether ugly associated as they are with the rest of the subject and drawn in various perspectives and light and shade—It is quite wonderful how the 'play of light of heaven' makes many ugly things interesting" (quoted in Mather, p. 24). Emphasizing the accuracy achieved by his slow and painstaking technique, he noted of this painting, "I could not make it larger without risk of being unable to finish it while the snow lasts."

A review in *The Round Table* of the sixth Artists' Fund Society exhibition deemed this painting one of the few works "worthy of notice" (November 25, 1865, p. 185), and in December 1865 *The New Path* described it as being "even more truthful and more carefully painted" than previous works by Moore, adding, "The drawing seems faultless . . . there is truth of strength as well as truth of delicacy" (p. 192). *The Nation* commented that "Mr. Moore shows a power of steady growth and apparently illimitable aspiration. He now uses oil color with singular mastery. He draws trees better than any artist who exhibits in American galleries. . . . His color, though [is] still too pale for the highest truth . . . not allowing him to render the full force of effect that art can produce . . ." (vol. 1, no. 20, November 16, 1865, p. 664). As if in answer to this criticism, Moore commented to Norton, "The color of the shaded parts in clear mornings is purest blue . . ." (quoted in Mather, p. 24). Thus, true to Ruskinian tenets, he tried to simulate what he saw even if it was not dramatic in color or composition, making his "evident purpose . . . to get perfect truth" (*The Nation*, vol. 1, no. 2, July 13, 1865, p. 57).   AB

47

48

Pine Tree 1868

Pen and ink and pencil on tan paper
25¹¹/₁₆ × 20 (65.3 × 50.8)
Inscribed lower right: "Catskill/1868"
*The Art Museum, Princeton University, gift of
Elizabeth Huntington Moore*
PROVENANCE
The artist; Miss Elizabeth H. Moore, 1951; The Art Museum, Princeton
University.
EXHIBITED
Exhibition unknown, Boston, 1868.
REFERENCES
Mather, p. 31, fig. 16; Taylor 1976, illus. p. 124; Barbara T. Ross, *American Drawings in The Art Museum* (Princeton University, 1976, no. 97, illus.); Stebbins 1976, p. 124; Daniel Marcus Medlowitz, *Guide to Drawing* (New York: Holt, Rinehart and Winston, 1981), illus. p. 194.

Perhaps when Moore sat down to draw this pine tree he recalled Ruskin's advice in *The Elements of Drawing* to the effect that "most people in drawing pines seem to fancy . . . that the boughs come out only on two sides of the trunk, instead of all round it: always, therefore, take more pains in trying to draw the boughs of trees that grow *towards* you than those that go off to the sides; anyone can draw the latter, but the foreshortened ones are not easy" (Ruskin, vol. XV, p. 93). Here, Moore takes care to include both the lateral and the foreshortened branches.

This was not the first time that Moore had attempted the subject. In a letter to Thomas Charles Farrer (q.v.) dated November 30, 1863, he wrote that he was "making some pen drawings—with the utmost care of tree anatomy." The following July his *Cedar Tree*, which was probably similar to *Pine Tree*, was described in *The New Path* as "portraiture more accurate than that of the photograph, which never perfectly renders tree forms and foliage . . ." and became part of the series of paintings issued in photograph form by the Association for the Advancement of Truth in Art as prime examples of American Pre-Raphaelitism (vol. II, no. 3, p. 45). Writing to Farrer again on April 26, 1865, Moore mentioned that "The Pine Tree is nearly done and I shall send it as soon as possible to Russell Sturgis" (GLF/NYPL). This drawing dated 1868 is a later refinement of the subject, since it was given to Princeton University by the Moore family and not by Sturgis.

Not everyone was impressed by this incomplete "specimen of Pre-Raphaelitism." It was no surprise to a Boston reviewer that ". . . a man who sat down before a large pine tree and began to draw its 'countless myriads' of leaves one by one did not get through with it. [The work,] which is certainly excellent, being unfinished . . . seems principally a question of mechanical skill and endurance" (I am grateful to Katherine Manthorne for supplying an unidentified newspaper clipping reviewing an exhibition including Moore's work, Boston, 1868; AAA, J. Eastman Chase papers, Roll 996).

Emphasis upon technical facility rather than imagination was a topic Moore addressed in "The Office of the Imagination," published in *The New Path* of November 1863. "The office of the imagination," he wrote, "is not to distort the 'Creator's work,' . . . but by its deep perception and reverence, to give us the highest truths in their noblest association. . . . It is simply and strictly illumination, and it is sometimes 'near akin to inspiration'" (vol. I, no. 7, p. 77). By adhering closely to the facts of nature and recording them accurately, an artist, according to Moore, could arrive at something higher than mere illustration.   AB

48

49

Rocks by the Water

Watercolor and gouache over graphite on paper
5⁹/₁₆ × 7¾ (14.1 × 19.7)
Unsigned
*Harvard University Art Museums (Fogg Art Museum),
transferred from the Fine Arts Department*
PROVENANCE
The artist; Fogg Art Museum.
EXHIBITED
Fogg Art Museum, Cambridge, Massachusetts, *Wash and Gouache: A
Study of the Development of the Materials of Watercolor*, May 12–June 22,
1977, no. 42.
REFERENCES
Mather, p. 40, fig. 25; Cohn, no. 42, pp. 9, 103, 105.

50

Landscape: Rocks and Water   *circa* 1860s

Watercolor and gouache on paper
7⅜ × 10⅝ (49.2 × 26.9)
Unsigned
*Harvard University Art Museums (Fogg Art Museum),
transferred from the Fine Arts Department*
PROVENANCE
Fogg Art Museum.
EXHIBITED
AFA 1976, no. 86.
REFERENCES
Mather, p. 40, fig. 24; Stebbins 1976, p. 156, fig. 124.

"How wonderful is this rock on which I am lying; a little
world of varied beauty and interest, changing with every
new inch of surface. Look down closely upon it, so as
to shut out the surrounding world, and concentrate
the attention upon the minutest details," a writer in *The
New Path* of December 1865 advised (vol. II, no. 12,
p. 199). In *Rocks By the Water* Moore has done just that,
concentrating on every fissure and crevice of a massive
boulder so that his narrow focus obscures most of the
"surrounding world."

In *Modern Painters*, John Ruskin (q.v.) spent much time
expounding the importance of rock study. "Every class of
rock, earth and cloud, must be known by the painter, with
geologic and meteorologic accuracy," he wrote . . . "Every
geological formation has features entirely peculiar to itself;
definite lines of fracture, giving rise to fixed resultant
forms of rocks and earth . . . among which farther
distinctions are wrought out by variations of climate and
elevation" (Preface to the Second Edition, Ruskin, vol. III,
p. 38). In *The Elements of Drawing* he advocated picking up
"the first round or oval stone you can find," adding, "if you
can draw that stone, you can draw anything . . ." (Ruskin,
vol. XV, pp. 48–49).

Moore's intensity of focus in *Rocks by the Water* may
have also been inspired by Ruskin's *Study of a Block of
Gneiss, Valley of Chamouni, Switzerland, 1856* (cat.
no. 125), which was exhibited in the 1857–58 American
Exhibition of British Art. After the exhibition, Ruskin's
work came into the collection of Charles Eliot Norton,
at whose home Moore would have had an opportunity
to see it.

Landscape: Rocks and Water is less closely focused but
more meticulous in its handling. The hyper-real clarity of
the foreground rock formation and the airlessness of the
picture space, even though half of it is devoted to sky and
water, creates a hermetic timelessness. Moore plays crisp
linear outlines against delicate transparent colors, using
this technique to underscore not only the microscopic
details of the surface of the rocks but also their intrinsic
geometric forms.

The anonymity of stroke, virtual airlessness, and equal
attention to foreground and background details that
characterize this landscape are qualities shared by
nineteenth-century Luminist painters, as exemplified in
Martin Johnson Heade's *Lake George* (cat. no. 110), and
by later Surrealists. Geologic subjects also interested
American artists outside the Pre-Raphaelite circle. Asher
B. Durand (q.v.), in *Landscape: Creek and Rocks* (cat. no.
98), and William S. Haseltine (q.v.), in *Rocks at Nahant*
(cat. no. 109), reveal a similar preoccupation, though their
treatment is more painterly.   AB

49

50

51
Mount Washington 1872

Watercolor on paper
6¼ × 9 (15.9 × 22.9)
Inscribed on rock lower left (in monogram): "CHM '72"
The Art Museum, Princeton University, presented by Mrs.
Frank Jewett Mather, Jr., as a gift of Elizabeth Huntington
Moore
PROVENANCE
The artist; Miss Elizabeth H. Moore, 1955; The Art Museum, Princeton
University.
REFERENCES
Mather, p. 39, fig. 23; *Record of the Art Museum, Princeton University,*
vol. 15, no. 1, 1956, p. 27.

52
Mount Kearsarge 1872

Oil on canvas
11⅞ × 17 (30.2 × 43.2)
Inscribed lower right (in monogram): "CHM 1872"
The Art Museum, Princeton University, gift of
Frank Jewett Mather, Jr.
PROVENANCE
The artist; Dr. Clark; Miss Rosamund Clark; Frank J. Mather, Jr., 1946;
The Art Museum, Princeton University.
REFERENCES
Mather, pp. 40–41, fig. 26.

New Hampshire's White Mountains, popular among nineteenth-century artists, supplied picturesque subject matter for such diverse men as Winslow Homer (1836–1910), John F. Kensett (1816–1872), and Aaron Draper Shattuck (q.v.), all of whom painted Mount Washington several times. Moore's painting is the most topographically precise of them all, providing not only a crisp outline of the Presidential range and its foothills but also a meticulous description of foreground detail with a focus on the anatomy of the terrain inclusive of rocks and fences.

Moore spent the summers of 1869 and 1870 at North Conway, New Hampshire, as did Homer, but while Homer depicted vacationers and artists scaling the mountain (see, for example, *Mount Washington*, 1869, The Art Institute of Chicago), Moore avoided humanizing his landscapes and focused on "plain faithful recording" (Letter to Charles Eliot Norton, April 8, 1866, quoted in Mather, p. 26).

Moore's earliest known attempt to capture Mount Washington is a pencil drawing dated 1869 (Collection of Mrs. Theodore Krueger, Connecticut); the second is another pencil sketch titled *White Mountain Country* (Fogg Art Museum, Cambridge). These two may have been studies for a lost oil exhibited as *White Mountains, Autumn* at the National Academy of Design in 1870 (NAD, no. 405; Mather, p. 39). A third pencil drawing, titled *White Mountains* (Fogg Art Museum, Cambridge), is a

51

study for this watercolor painted in 1872. Another water-color, *circa* 1870, in the collection of The Art Museum, Princeton University, was previously thought to be Mount Washington but has been reidentified as Moat Mountain (Donald Keyes, Catherine H. Campbell, et al., *The White Mountains*, Durham, New Hampshire: University of New Hampshire, 1981, pp. 106–107).

In all of these studies, Moore's focus on the mountain peak is progressively intensified by a sharp outline, but in the watercolor the contours of the mountain recede while the foreground details seem more magnified. This view of the White Mountains' highest peak (6,288 feet) shows none of the "scarred, weather-beaten … grandly impressive" features described by Benjamin Champney (1817–1907), who specialized in White Mountain scenery (Benjamin Champney, *Sixty Years' Memories of Art and Artists*, Woburn, Mass.: Wallace & Andrews, 1900, rept., Garland Publishing Inc., 1977). Moore was perhaps following his own dictates that artists should "paint the great mountain in its strength, but not despise the little flower at its foot for fear of its attracting too much attention" ("Fallacies of the Present School," *The New Path*, vol. I, no. 6, October 1863, p. 63).

The same year he painted Mount Washington, Moore also painted another New Hampshire mountain, Mount Kearsarge. "Kearsarge, too, is a noble peak," Champney wrote, "more isolated than any of the near mountains, and possessing many elements of grandeur. It is especially a fine peak to look from, and really the view from it is more satisfactory than from Mount Washington" (Champney, p. 156).

Although the mountain, isolated against the sky, is emphasized in Moore's picture, the subject of the work is as much the log dam in the foreground as it is the imposing peak. This combination of logging facilities and mountain scenery is reminiscent of the juxtaposition of Swiss architecture and the Alps in John Ruskin's *circa* 1844 drawing *The Glacier des Bossons, Chamonix* (Ashmolean Museum, Oxford). Moore and Ruskin (q.v.) did not meet until 1876, but their shared interests in geology and architecture are clearly expressed in these works.

In contrast to *Mount Washington*, *Mount Kearsarge* has a more atmospheric perspective and a somewhat diminished focus on background detail. Instead of placing equal emphasis on all parts, Moore balances the accumulation of foreground details with the grandeur and mass of the centrally placed mountain. Although still very precise, this work appears to be more painterly than *Mount Washington*. The use of oil may account for the slightly broader handling, but Moore was at this time moving away from the tight painting technique seen in earlier watercolors.   AB

52

53

The Valley of the Catskill from Jefferson Hill 1872

Formerly *North Conway, New Hampshire*

Watercolor on paper
5⁷⁄₁₆ × 8¹⁵⁄₁₆ (13.8 × 22.7)
Inscribed lower left (in monogram): "CHM 72"
M. and M. Karolik Collection, Museum of Fine Arts, Boston
PROVENANCE
Mr. Williams (?); Mr. Childs; Maxim Karolik, 1956; Museum of Fine Arts, Boston.

Previously thought to be a scene in North Conway, New Hampshire, this work, dated 1872, without doubt derives from the minutely detailed 1869 pen-and-ink study *The Valley of the Catskill from Jefferson Hill* (The Art Museum, Princeton University). Indeed, it is also the same valley and point of view, the same stream and farmhouse, seen in *The Catskills in Spring* (cat. no. 44), and is as well a more distant vista of *Winter Landscape, Valley of the Catskills* (cat. no. 47).

That Moore returned to this view repeatedly over a period of eleven years reveals not only his interest and affection for this region but also a persistence in exploring the same subject in different mediums—first oil, then pen and ink for an unrealized etching, and finally watercolor.

Moore devoted himself to etching in 1869 after noting on the back of the pen drawing mentioned above his desire to make a series of etchings illustrating the Hudson River from its source to the sea (Mather, p. 34). This interest in etching was shared by such colleagues from the Association for the Advancement of Truth in Art as the two Hills and the Farrer brothers. Its motivation may be attributable to both English Pre-Raphaelite illustrations and to the renascence of the so-called minor arts, including watercolor, in America at this time.

Except for two small figures in the lower right corner of the elaborate pen drawing, the watercolor is identical, leading to the conclusion that Moore did not work on this from nature. In fact, some of the freshness and crispness of his earlier plein-air watercolors is lacking. The patterned brush strokes, somewhat like enlarged stipple, are used primarily in areas of vegetation and give the painting a mannered effect; this trait may stem from Moore's attempt to translate the innumerable fine lines of the drawing. He strives for a looser, more atmospheric appearance in the sky and clouds. In combining calligraphic detail with broader atmospheric features, Moore demonstrates a new and different style, a departure not only from his earlier plein-air accuracy but also from his meticulous finish.   AB

53

54
Sawmill at West Boxford   *circa* 1874

Watercolor on paper
11⅞ × 18 (30.2 × 45.7)
Unsigned
The Art Museum, Princeton University, presented by
Mrs. Frank Jewett Mather, Jr., as the gift of Elizabeth Moore
PROVENANCE
The artist; Miss Elizabeth H. Moore; Frank J. Mather, Jr., 1955;
The Art Museum, Princeton University.
REFERENCES
Mather 1957, p. 46, fig. 28; *Record of the Art Museum, Princeton University*, vol. 15, no. 1, 1956, p. 27; Barbara T. Ross, *American Drawings in The Art Museum, Princeton University* (The Art Museum, Princeton University, 1976, no. 100, illustrated).

After he began teaching, Moore had little time for painting, and in the summers he devoted himself to small watercolors and drawings. He maintained a summer house in West Boxford, Massachusetts, from 1874 to 1909, and it was there that he painted this highly finished watercolor—a personal favorite that he took with him when he moved to England in 1909 (Ross, p. 101).

Although it is precisely painted and quite detailed, this painting, because it does not depict a panoramic view, seems less topographical than earlier works by Moore. Attention to light and shadow allows for more dramatic contrast and gives the piece a picturesque

quality often lacking in such topographically exact pictures as *Winter Landscape* (cat. no. 47). The closed composition framed by trees, the sun-filled center opening into the distance, and the patterned calligraphic stroke approximate such contemporaneous works as William R. Miller's (1818–1893) *A Woodland Glade, Manhattanville, New York* (1869, The Brooklyn Museum).

Although Moore is listed as a member of the American Society of Painters in Watercolor from 1867 to 1871, he never contributed works for exhibition, as did many of his fellow members of the Association for the Advancement of Truth in Art, perhaps because of his teaching obligations at Harvard from 1874 on (Fabri). His lectures to his students during the last quarter of the century disclose that although he continued to admire Pre-Raphaelite impulses "to correct the artificial conventions of modern painting," he concluded that the Pre-Raphaelites had gone too far in ignoring such formal elements as composition and idealization for the sake of selecting nothing (HL/Moore, Pre-Raphaelitism, p. 1). Their "indiscriminate zeal for uncompromising truth to reality" he felt, had made them lose track of the "elements of beauty suitable for pictorial treatment" (HL/Moore, Pre-Raphaelitism, pp. 6 and 11). In this watercolor, Moore demonstrates a successful compromise between absolute fidelity and artistic arrangement.   AB

54

55
Mullen and Rocks 1883

Watercolor and gouache over graphite on paper
7⅛ × 10⅝ (18.1 × 26.9)
Inscribed lower right: "CHM 1883"
Harvard University Art Museums (Fogg Art Museum),
transferred from the Fine Arts Department
PROVENANCE
The artist; Fogg Art Museum.

By 1883 Moore had met and spent extended time with
John Ruskin (q.v.), with whom he shared not only art-
historical but also architectural interests. He continued to
paint landscapes and seemingly uncomposed studies from
nature such as this, although he later admitted that
unselectiveness could lead to "insensitiveness to beauty of
form and composition" and that there was "no need for the
artist to depict what is awkward, or ugly" (HL/Moore, Pre-

Raphaelitism, p. 5). There is a difference, however,
between this and earlier works. Although here the mullen
and the lichen on the rocks are careful likenesses, the close
focus and meticulous technique of earlier studies are
diminished. The immediate foreground lacks specificity
and is broadly painted. Softening of light and shadow make
for less-defined outlines and more-subdued colors.

In his lecture on Pre-Raphaelitism at Harvard, Moore
declared, "In their implicit reliance on fact the Pre-
Raphaelites failed to perceive that the manifold aspects
under which every fact of nature may be regarded are not
of equal value" (p. 6). By softening his color and loosening
his technique, he made adjustments in his own work while
persisting in earlier ideals about natural, unarranged,
growing still lifes. As most other artists of the group
discovered, it was too difficult to sustain the time-
consuming intensity of detail over a long period of time; so
he reverted to more conventional modes of
representation.   AB

55

Henry Roderick Newman   1843–1917

Henry Roderick Newman, a watercolor painter who specialized in architectural subjects and flower pieces, was born March 1843 in Easton, New York, and moved to New York City with his family about 1845. Although he acceded to the wishes of his father, a physician, and began studying medicine, he abandoned his studies in 1861 when his father died. Given one year to prove himself as an artist by his mother, he then secluded himself in Stockbridge, Massachusetts, for six months and produced several highly finished nature studies, three of which he exhibited at the National Academy of Design at the end of that year.

Between 1861 and 1870 Newman became an active member of the American art community, exhibiting almost every year at the Academy and at the Brooklyn Art Association. Encouraged by his friend Thomas Charles Farrer (q.v.), he developed his interest in accurately portraying nature and was elected a member of the Association for the Advancement of Truth in Art on March 29, 1864. Farrer also helped him gain a teaching position at the Free School of Art for Women at The Cooper Union, where he taught from 1865 to 1866. Always of delicate health, Newman moved to Florida for the climate after the death of his mother in 1868. Although by the following year he was back north living in Sing Sing, New York, his health continued to decline, and he decided to seek more beneficial climes in Europe in 1870.

At first, Newman enrolled in the atelier of Jean-Léon Gérôme (1824–1904) at the Ecole des Beaux-Arts in Paris, but his studies were curtailed within three weeks by the Franco-Prussian War, and he soon moved to Italy, first to Florence in September 1870 and then to Venice in the spring of 1871. His meticulous brushwork and vivid colors, which he had developed on his own under the influence of American Pre-Raphaelites, remained unchanged in Paris. But in Venice, according to a contemporary, his technique became looser, losing its dry, brittle quality.

Newman first met Ruskin in 1879. The critic, who had been introduced to Newman's work by Charles H. Moore (q.v.) in 1877, purchased several of Newman's watercolors and supposedly travelled with him to Italian cities in search of illustrations for his books, both sharing a common interest in architectural subjects.

After his marriage to Mary Watson Willis, an Englishwoman, in June 1883, Newman settled permanently in Florence, where his home and studio became a meeting place for such luminaries as the Brownings, the De Morgans, Henry James, and Nathaniel Hawthorne. Perhaps as early as 1885, but regularly from 1888 to 1891 and again in 1894, he wintered in Egypt, where the architecture provided new subjects for his paintings. In the late nineties he also visited Japan. He died in Florence in December 1917.

REFERENCES
Ahrens, pp. 85–98; BAA; DAB; Forman, pp. 525–539; NAD.

56
The Elm   1866

Watercolor on paper
16¾ × 19⅛ (42.5 × 48.5)
Inscribed lower right: "H.R. Newman/66"
Museum of Fine Arts, Boston, bequest of Maxim Karolik
PROVENANCE
Maxim Karolik, 1973; Museum of Fine Arts, Boston.
EXHIBITED
Montgomery Museum of Fine Arts, Alabama, *The American Scene: Watercolors from the M. and M. Karolik Collection*, April 8–May 6, 1979, cat. no. 31; Museum of Fine Arts of St. Petersburg, Florida, May 15–July 5, 1979.
REFERENCES
Paletta, "Art Matters," *American Art Journal*, 6 (1866), p. 87; Foster, pp. 114, 115, 423, 424, 560, fig. (R-10).

In the summer of 1863, Newman began making small-scale pencil drawings outdoors. On October 22 of that year he wrote to his good friend Thomas Charles Farrer (q.v.) that this had been the first summer that "I ever tried close study & the first pencil study of any amount" (GLF/NYPL). Three years later, as evidenced in *The Elm*, he was capable of painting competently on a much larger scale in watercolors.

Newman's plein-air working method, his use of brilliant colors, and his meticulous stipple technique in this, his earliest known work, clearly derive from Ruskin's writings. As described by his contemporary biographer, his approach involved direct study of nature: "Here were reminiscences of American sketching days—drawings minutely finished in the open air with no sweep or flash, but with that intense earnestness which marked the landscape work of the early days of preraphaelitism in England" (Forman, p. 525).

Thomas C. Farrer's essay "A Few Questions Answered" in the June 1863 issue of *The New Path* may have been on Newman's mind when he painted *The Elm*. "When they see artists . . . drawing leaves on trees in such a fanatical manner," Farrer wrote, "that you can really tell, by looking at their pictures, whether it is an Oak, an Elm or a Pine . . . 'What!' say the discerning public 'are painters to become

56

botanists and geologists!' . . . The public, instead of opening their hearts and receiving these signs of vitality and life with joy and gladness receive them with a howl of scorn and disdain" (vol. I, no. 2, p.13). In fact, *The Elm* would be severely criticized when it was exhibited.   HPC

57

Mt. Everett from Monument Mt. in April   1867

Formerly *Hilly Landscape with Factories on a River Bend*

Watercolor on paper
10⅜ × 13¾ (26.3 × 35.0)
Inscribed lower left center: "H R Newman 67"
Museum of Fine Arts, Boston, gift of
Mrs. Harriet Ropes Cabot

PROVENANCE
Mrs. Samuel Hooper, Boston; Ann Hooper Lothrop; Mrs. Algernon Coolidge; Mrs. Harriet Ropes Cabot, Boston, 1950; Museum of Fine Arts, Boston.
EXHIBITED
(Possibly) NAD, *First Winter Exhibition Including the First Annual Collection of the American Society of Painters in Water Colors*, 1867-68, cat. no. 326.
REFERENCES
Ahrens, pp. 86, 87, fig. 1.

In 1867, Mrs. Samuel Hooper of Boston lent a Henry Newman watercolor titled *Mt. Everett from Monument Mt. in April* to the National Academy of Design's *First Winter Exhibition Including the First Annual Collection of the American Society of Painters in Water Colors*. The water-

color seen here, previously known as *Hilly Landscape with Factories on a River Bend*, is probably that picture, since its provenance can be traced to Mrs. Hooper and it has now been positively identified as a view of Mount Everett, the second highest peak in Massachusetts. (My thanks to Mrs. Harriet Ropes Cabot for providing the provenance and to William H. Tague of Lanesboro, Massachusetts, and Bartlett Hendricks of The Berkshire Museum, Pittsfield, Massachusetts, for identifying the mountain.) Newman, who was living in Stockbridge in 1867, would have had easy access to this peak, which is less than fifteen miles to the southwest.

In its emphasis on distinct geological features, crystalline atmosphere, and a detailed stipple technique, this view of Mount Everett with the Green River in the foreground clearly illustrates Newman's absorption of Ruskinian principles. As early as 1863, the artist was conscientiously following John Ruskin's instructions in *The Elements of Drawing* to first sketch individual rock studies before attempting mountain landscapes. "I am trying to get acquainted w/a fragment of flint rock (in water color)," he wrote to his good friend Thomas Charles Farrer (q.v.), "& find it very interesting" (October 22, 1863, GLF/NYPL).

Another, more immediate influence on this watercolor may have been the landscapes of Charles H. Moore (q.v.), particularly *Winter Landscape, Valley of the Catskills* (cat. no. 47), painted the previous year. Newman and Moore were both active members of the Association for the Advancement of Truth in Art. It is, therefore, possible that Newman was aware of Moore's painting since both works have similar formats—panoramic views of peaceful valleys enclosed by distant mountain ranges.   HPC

57

58

Anemones 1876

Watercolor on paper
18 × 11¾ (45.7 × 29.8)
Inscribed lower right: "H.R. Newman/1876"
Jeffrey R. Brown Fine Arts, Inc., Boston
PROVENANCE
Mrs. Donald Lewis, Sr., Norfolk, Virginia; private collection,
1982; [Jeffrey R. Brown Fine Arts, Inc., Boston].
EXHIBITED
Montclair 1983; Whitney 1984.
REFERENCES
Gerdts 1983, pp. 15, 16, 86, 137; Foshay, p. 141, fig. 112.

59

Anemone 1884

Watercolor and graphite on paper
15⅛ × 11 1/16 (38.3 × 28.0)
Inscribed lower right: "H R Newman/Florence 1884."
Harvard University Art Museums (Fogg Art Museum),
gift of Dr. Denman W. Ross
PROVENANCE
Dr. Denman W. Ross, 1923; Harvard University Art Museums
(Fogg Art Museum).
REFERENCES
Ahrens, pp. 92, 94, fig. 8.

Although Newman exhibited a number of flower subjects while living in America, it was apparently only after he settled in Florence that he made this genre and architectural views his two main specialties. He painted his favorite flower, the Florentine anemone, either alone as a single blossom (cat. no. 59) or as part of an outdoor grouping (cat. no. 58). As his friend and biographer Henry Buxton Forman wrote, "it is from the wild *Anemone coronaro* that he obtains the most poetic combinations." Through the use of precise preparatory studies and a meticulous stipple technique, he was able to incorporate a wealth of clearly rendered botanical details into watercolors like these and *Wildflowers* (cat. no. 64). His painstaking working method, clearly illustrated in *Anemone*, was to make "an individual portrait of every flower he introduces into his picture" because "no two blossoms of the same species, are in fact, precisely alike" (Forman, pp. 533, 534, 533).

Newman's approach had great appeal for John Ruskin (q.v.), who in the spring of 1881 bought four watercolors of Florentine anemones from the artist's portfolio. These were to serve as models of flower painting in Ruskin's St. George's Museum, a portion of which is now housed in the Sheffield City Art Museums. They are close in subject and interpretation to these two watercolors: one depicts the flowers growing in their natural setting, while the other three are accurate individual floral studies (see Ruskin, *First Catalogue of the St. George's Museum*, vol. 30, pp. 240, 241). HPC

58

59

60
Grapes and Olives 1878

Watercolor on paper
26 × 17 (66.0 × 43.2)
Inscribed lower left: "H.R. Newman/1878"
Mr. and Mrs. Wilbur L. Ross, Jr.
PROVENANCE
[Jeffrey R. Brown Fine Arts, Inc., Boston, 1980]; Mr. and Mrs.
Wilbur L. Ross, Jr.
EXHIBITED
Philbrook 1981.
REFERENCES
Clement and Hutton, vol. 2, p. 147, states that *Grapes and Olives* was
exhibited in Florence in 1878; Gerdts 1981, pp. 6, 98, pl. 6.

Newman's dramatic and highly personal formula for
integrating a closely observed foreground still life with a
distant landscape vignette is clearly illustrated in this
watercolor and in *Italy* (cat. no. 63). Although five years
separate the two works, their style and format are very
similar, and in each the Gulf of La Spezia, a favorite subject
of Newman's, occupies the middle distance. Like *Italy*,
Grapes and Olives would have been executed from detailed
studies made outdoors, probably near San Terenzio, a small

fishing village that Newman's close friend H. Buxton
Forman characterized as "the loveliest spot in the whole
Riviera del Levante" (Forman, p. 536). If this is the case,
the two islands depicted on the horizon are Palmaria and
Tino, while the promontory in the foreground may be
Portovenere Point.

Newman would return to this area again in the summer
of 1883, when he painted *Italy* and the now unlocated
The Priest's Garden, a work that, judging from Forman's
description, is almost identical to *Grapes and Olives*. The
overt religious content of *The Priest's Garden* raises the
question of whether or not there is also religious symbolism in this earlier watercolor. Indeed, Newman may have
had in mind the well-known passage from Matthew
26:29–30 in which Christ addresses his apostles at the Last
Supper: "'But I say unto you, I will not drink henceforth of
this fruit of the vine, until the day when I drink it new with
you in my Father's kingdom.' And when they had sung a
hymn, they went out into the Mount of Olives." Newman's
watercolor seems to allude to these verses in its unusual
juxtaposition of grapes and olives framing a serene landscape in which the distant island rises from the Gulf like
a mountain.   HPC

60

61

View of Santa Maria Novella 1879

Watercolor on paper
18¼ × 22¼ (46.3 × 56.5)
Inscribed lower left: "H. Roderick Newman, 1879"
*Maier Museum of Art, Randolph-Macon Woman's College,
Lynchburg, Virginia, Louis Jordan Smith Fund*
PROVENANCE
[Angelo Valenti, Boston, 1974]; [Childs Gallery, Boston, 1976]; Maier
Museum of Art, Randolph-Macon Woman's College.

In 1877, Charles H. Moore (q.v.) showed John Ruskin (q.v.)
a watercolor drawing by Newman of the piazza and facade
of the church of Santa Maria Novella in Florence. Ruskin
was to express his enthusiasm in a letter to Newman dated
June 9, 1877: "I cannot tell you . . . how much your
drawing of Sta. M. Novella has delighted me. I have not
for many and many a day seen the sense of tenderness
and depth of color so united—still less so much fidelity
and affection joined with a power of design which seems
to me, though latent, very great."

Ruskin's admiration for that now unlocated record
of the famous fifteenth-century facade may logically be
extended to this version, painted two years later. A *tour
de force* in its minute transcription of Leon Battista
Alberti's (1404?–1472) intricate Renaissance facade with its
geometric designs of brilliantly colored marble inlays,
this view of Santa Maria Novella clearly illustrates why
Ruskin later wrote that Newman's drawings of Florence
were "quite the most valuable records yet existing of the
old city" (Introduction to vol. XXX, pp. ixxiii, ixxiv).

In this first of many letters to Newman, Ruskin went on
to suggest that the artist paint "those three old arches, seen
right in front on the left of the steps going up to Sta. M.
Novella. If they are still uninjured and wear their weeds,
there's nothing lovelier in Florence" (Introduction to vol.
XXX, p. ixxiii). Newman, whose early artistic life had been
guided by Ruskin's writings, willingly obliged this request,
painting the arches on at least two separate occasions.
(An 1884 version is currently in the collection of the Fogg
Art Museum of Harvard University in Cambridge,
Massachusetts.) Ruskin must have been particularly
attracted to this subject because the arches were Gothic,
a style he had extolled at great length in both *The Stones
of Venice* and *The Seven Lamps of Architecture.*   HPC

61

62
Study of a Tuscan Cathedral

Watercolor and graphite on paper
13¹³⁄₁₆ × 11⅜ (35.0 × 28.9)
Inscribed lower left: "H R Newman"
Harvard University Art Museums (Fogg Art Museum), gift of Dr. Denman W. Ross
PROVENANCE
Dr. Denman W. Ross, 1917; Harvard University Art Museums (Fogg Art Museum).

Newman's abiding fascination with architecture seems to have first manifested itself in the mid-1860s while he was living in Manhattan. "My earliest work was careful studies of the old buildings of New York City with their tiled roofs," he is quoted as saying. "Every one of these houses is now gone, but they helped me to understand European architecture. My first introduction to that was at Chartres. From here I went to Italy" (Helen Zimmern, "An American Watercolorist," *The Sun*, August 20, *circa* 1890, undated clipping).

After settling in Florence in 1870, Newman specialized primarily in architectural subjects, painting important historic buildings (cat. no. 61), picturesque street views, and meticulously rendered studies such as this one of the facade of a Tuscan church. His special sensitivity to worn building surfaces and detail is clearly illustrated in this watercolor, bringing to mind the statement of William White, the second curator of Ruskin's St. George's Museum, that "each particular item is copied with such precision and exactitude as if every block and every subject was to be taken singly as a separate archaeological study and no such work as these drawings by Mr. Newman had ever before been accomplished so effectively" (Ruskin, *First Catalogue of the St. George's Museum*, vol. XXX, p. 211).

For many years, Newman was involved with the Guild of St. George, a group of artists committed to making careful drawing and watercolor records of ancient art works threatened with destruction or insensitive restoration. Ruskin, who organized and financed the guild, purchased a number of Newman's elaborate architectural subjects for St. George's Museum; three of these works are now part of the Ruskin Collection in the Sheffield City Art Museums. HPC

62

63

Italy 1883

Formerly *Grape Vines and Roses: An Italian View*

Watercolor on paper
39½ × 26⅜ (100.3 × 66.9), sight
Inscribed lower right: "Henry Roderick Newman/1883"
Mr. and Mrs. Leonard L. Milberg

PROVENANCE
Mrs. John J. Donaldson, New York, *circa* 1883; [Virgil L. Holmes, Parsippany, New Jersey, 1973]; Jo Ann and Julian Ganz, Jr., 1984; Mr. and Mrs. Leonard L. Milberg.
EXHIBITED
Los Angeles County Museum of Art, California, *Pertaining to the Sea*, March 23–May 2, 1976, no. 36 as *Grape Vines and Roses: An Italian View*; AFA 1976 as *Grape Vines and Roses: An Italian View*; National Gallery of Art 1981.
REFERENCES
Forman, p. 536; Stebbins 1976, pp. 172, 173, 436, fig. 137; Wilmerding, Ayres & Powell, pp. 99, 154, fig. 90; Gerdts 1981, p. 98.

In the autumn of 1883, Newman began this *tour de force* on commission from Mrs. John J. Donaldson of New York. The Donaldsons were patrons of Newman, having previously purchased *The South Door of The Duomo, Florence* (unlocated), a replica of which Newman painted for Ruskin (Ruskin Collection, The Sheffield City Art Museums).

In 1884, Newman's good friend Henry Buxton Forman would describe and analyze *Italy* at great length: "This piece . . . is, to a certain extent, an ideal composition, though in all essential particulars realistic. It was executed from faithful studies made at San Terenzio in the Gulf of [La] Specia . . . famous for its connection with the wanderings of the mighty and sombre Dante and the tragic fate of another antipodal poet and exile, Percy Bysshe Shelley. . . . The castle of Lerici forms a picturesque central object, to the right stand the ruins of the convent at which Dante left the manuscript of the 'Inferno' when he fled into France; and between the convent and the horizon line is the point at which Shelley's Torbay-rigged Don Juan was last seen before the sudden squall came up on that fatal 8th of July, 1822, and overwhelmed the frail bark with her precious freight of potential poetry" (Forman, p. 536).

Newman was intimately familiar with the area around the Gulf of La Spezia, having previously painted there *Grapes and Olives* (cat. no. 60) in 1878 and *Casa Magni, San Terenzio* in 1879. The latter was commissioned by Forman to serve as the frontispiece for Volume 4 of *The Prose Works of Percy Bysshe Shelley*, which Forman edited (London: Reeves & Turner, 1880). In commissioning *Italy*, Mrs. Donaldson was probably aware of *Casa Magni* (Wilmerding, Ayres & Powell, p. 154). Newman's special talent at painting large-scale watercolors in a meticulous stipple technique without resorting to the use of wash is clearly demonstrated in *Italy*.   HPC

63

64
Wildflowers 1887

Watercolor on paper
15 × 10 (38.1 × 25.4)
Inscribed lower left: "H.R. Newman/1887"
Museum of Fine Arts, Boston, gift of Dr. Denman W. Ross
PROVENANCE
Dr. Denman W. Ross, 1917; Museum of Fine Arts, Boston.
REFERENCES
BMFA, p. 222, cat. no. 746; Ahrens, pp. 92, 94, fig. 9; Foshay, pp. 45–47, fig. 34.

Newman is one of the few American Pre-Raphaelites who remained committed to Ruskinian technique and subject matter into the late 1880s. "He said that he considers his leading characteristic is his perfect consistency from the first start," a New York newspaper reported around 1890. "He has never changed his art views, his manners or methods." Perhaps Newman's personal contact with the famous English art critic, beginning in 1877, strengthened the ideas that he first developed around 1861 under the influence of *Modern Painters*. Newman shared Ruskin's reverence toward the vocation of the artist, saying, "Art

which is the most sacred thing in the world, should not be pursued as an amusement, but should be held by a man as the most holy thing like a religion" (Helen Zimmern, "An American Watercolorist," *The Sun*, August 20, *circa* 1890, undated clipping).

Newman's sustained interest in the intense focus of Ruskin's approach is clearly illustrated by a comparison of this 1887 watercolor with the 1876 watercolor *Anemones* (cat. no. 58). The two works are remarkably similar in style, subject, viewpoint, and even coloration, with the red and purple tints of the blossoms shown against what Henry Buxton Forman described as "a background of that light green peculiar to the springtide grass of Tuscany." Both works demonstrate Forman's observation that "Mr. Newman selects foregrounds full of flowers and paints these foregrounds at the shortest possible range" (Forman, pp. 534, 533). In the later watercolor, however, there is an even more subtle transition from the worm's-eye view of the foreground to the limited distance. Newman's interpretation, which parallels that of other American Ruskinians, fused the traditional categories of flower painting and landscape (see cat. nos. 90 and 96).   HPC

64

Robert J. Pattison 1838-1903

Robert J. Pattison was born in New York City in 1838 and was educated at the University of the City of New York. He became active as a painter in 1858, exhibiting one picture, *View Near Flushing, Long Island,* at the National Academy of Design, while listing his address as 306 Second Avenue. In 1861 he moved to 839 Broadway for two years and registered his occupation in the New York Directory as a landscape painter. Until 1866 his entries at the Academy were fairly regular. Some titles—such as *Study from Nature* (1861), *Young Mullen* (1866), and *Study of Leaves and Grasses* (1866)—reveal his partiality to landscape painting and indicate that he looked at nature with a magnifying glass similar to that of the American Pre-Raphaelites, while the places named in other titles—Long Island, New Jersey, and New York—suggest that he never wandered far from home.

Pattison seems to have been acquainted with the work of T.C. Farrer (q.v.) by 1860. His name appears as a member in the minutes of the Association for the Advancement of Truth in Art for February 18, 1863, and he attended most meetings that year. In April 1864 he was listed as one of ten artists whose work was to be photographed for *The New Path* as a paradigm of Pre-Raphaelite ideals, and he is also mentioned in letters between members. In 1864, however, he was not listed among the subscribers to the second volume of *The New Path.*

Along with other American Pre-Raphaelite work, three of Pattison's pictures were sent to the inaugural exhibition of the new art building at Yale in 1867. The artist also exhibited at the Boston Atheneum and the Brooklyn Art Association from 1873 to 1891, at the Artists' Fund Society during the first half of the sixties, and at the American Society of Painters in Watercolor in 1874–75. He made his last contribution to the National Academy in 1886. This painting, *Niagara Falls,* was criticized in a contemporary periodical for "too much conscientious study and careful execution," indicating that he had persisted in his meticulous style.

Pattison gave his address as Elizabeth, New Jersey, in 1878, and judging by the titles of his landscapes he probably lived there at least from the mid-seventies until 1880, when at the age of forty-two he went to France. According to the directory of New York's Tenth Street Studio Building, he rented space there from 1885 to 1888, a period during which he spent part of his time working as a mural decorator with the artist Vincent G. Stiepevich (1841- after 1910). Around 1890, he moved to Brooklyn, where he was a professor of drawing at Boy's High School, listed himself variously as an artist or teacher in the Brooklyn Directory, and sent two landscapes to the Brooklyn Art Club in 1898. He died in Brooklyn on September 3, 1903, survived by his wife and two sons

REFERENCES
I am indebted to Doreen Burke for connecting Pattison with Vincent Stiepevich.

American Art Annual I; William H. Gerdts Art Reference Library and Archive, City University Graduate Center; BA; BAA; *The Critic* 1886, no. 120, p. 196; *New York Times* Obituary, September 15, 1903, 9:6; NAD; New York City Directories.

65
Portrait of John Henry Hill 1860
Attributed to Robert J. Pattison

Pen and ink on paper
4 × 3⅛ (10.2 × 8.0)
Inscribed lower right (initials in monogram): "R J P/1860"
Mr. and Mrs. Wilbur L. Ross, Jr.

PROVENANCE
[Kennedy Galleries, New York, 1960s–1981]; Mr. and Mrs. Wilbur L. Ross, Jr.

Although Robert J. Pattison exhibited a good number of paintings between 1858 and 1898, this pen-and-ink drawing is his only known surviving work. The attribution to Pattison has been made on the basis of the monogram in the lower right corner, which seems to combine the letters "R," "J," and "P" in a decorative monogram similar to those used by the members of the English Pre-Raphaelite Brotherhood and by Thomas Charles Farrer (q.v.), who was probably Pattison's mentor. Compositional similarities between this work and Farrer's unlocated portraits of Samuel P. Avery (1860) and John Henry Hill (1859), both of whom are shown engraving and set in an arched format, suggest that by 1860, the date of this drawing, Pattison was acquainted with Farrer's art. Pattison also exhibited his first Ruskinian subject, *Study from Nature,* at the National Academy of Design in 1860.

The sitter, formerly identified as Farrer, is now thought to be John Henry Hill because of the facial resemblance and similarity in attire to Farrer's drawing of Hill, which, although unlocated, is known through a reproduction in the New York Public Library inscribed in pencil by an unknown hand, "John Henry Hill." Another Farrer drawing, called *The Fiddler* (1859), seems also to be a likeness of the bearded Hill. The only known self-portrait by Farrer (cat. no. 1) shows an unbearded, youthful man quite different from the one in the Pattison drawing.

Pattison portrays Hill engrossed in the task of drawing with a quill, setting him in a shallow space relieved only by the illusion of a window above. He reverses Farrer's figure, showing the right side of Hill's face and the unparted side of his hair; otherwise the work is very close to its assumed model, but for the missing background details of the engraving table and the paintings on the studio walls, and the lack of flawless precision seen in Farrer's pencil drawings. A variety of techniques, such as stipple in the face and hatching in the jacket and ground, are seen; the changes in intensity of stroke contrast the figure with the unadorned wall behind. Simplification and perspective inconsistencies reveal some naiveté on the part of an artist who, at twenty-two, was just commencing his career.

This sketch may have been a private endeavor meant as the souvenir of an ardent Ruskinian, or, more likely, a practice piece. Although Ruskin's *Elements of Drawing,* published just three years earlier, excluded any discussion of figural drawing, it did advise artists to copy prints and use pen and ink.

Perhaps this is one of two works Pattison exhibited some years later at the Brooklyn Art Association—the portrait he submitted in 1873 or the pen-and-ink sketch he exhibited in May 1875. At any rate, he rarely did such pieces, for he was predominantly dedicated to landscape subjects. AB

65

William Trost Richards 1833-1905

The landscape and marine painter William Trost Richards was born in Philadelphia on November 14, 1833. He attended the city's Central High School in 1846 and '47 but then dropped out to help support his family. While working full-time as a designer and illustrator of ornamental metal work from 1850 to 1853 and part-time until 1858, he, along with William Stanley Haseltine (q.v.), studied draftsmanship and painting with the German artist Paul Weber (1823-1916).

Richards first exhibited at the Pennsylvania Academy of the Fine Arts in 1852 and was elected an Academician the following year. From 1855 to 1856 he toured Europe with Haseltine and Alexander Lawrie (1828-1917), an artist with whom he shared a studio, spending several months in Düsseldorf. Upon his return he settled in the Germantown section of Philadelphia and married Anna Matlock in June 1856.

By this time Richards had most likely read Ruskin's *Modern Painters*, for he had begun to show an interest in geological subjects, spending his summers sketching in the Catskills, the Adirondacks, and the mountains of Pennsylvania. After attending the American Exhibition of British Art at the Pennsylvania Academy in February 1858, he began to paint outdoors, striving for exacting fidelity to nature. Henry T. Tuckerman's *Book of the Artists*, published in 1867, mentions his work as a model of Pre-Raphaelite literalness.

Richards was made an honorary member of the National Academy of Design in 1862 and a full Academician in 1871. He was nominated to membership in the Association for the Advancement of Truth in Art in March 1863 by its founder T.C. Farrer (q.v.) and unanimously elected.

While summering on the East Coast with his family from 1868 to 1874, Richards developed a preference for coastal scenes. At first he treated these as meticulously as his woodland views, but as time went on his technique became broader. In the seventies watercolor became an important part of his vocabulary, and in 1874 he joined the American Water Color Society. From 1875 to 1884 he sent approximately one hundred eighty-five watercolors to the Philadelphia collector George Whitney, his friend as well as one of his major patrons.

In 1879 and 1880 Richards wintered in London and summered on the Continent. When he returned to America in 1881 he spent a year designing and building a summer house in Newport, Rhode Island, that he called Graycliff. In 1884 he exchanged his Germantown house for a farm in Oldmixon, Pennsylvania. He travelled to Europe almost every year until his death in Newport on November 8, 1905.

REFERENCES
Linda S. Ferber, *William Trost Richards, American Landscape and Marine Painter, 1833-1905* (exhibition catalogue, The Brooklyn Museum, New York, June 20-July 29, 1973); Ferber 1980 (b); Linda S. Ferber, *Tokens of a Friendship* (exhibition catalogue, Metropolitan Museum of Art, New York, November 4, 1982-January 16, 1983).

66
Blackberry Bush 1858

Oil on canvas
14¾ × 12½ (37.5 × 31.8)
Inscribed lower right: "W.T. Richards/1858"
Private collection
PROVENANCE
E. L. Magoon, 1864; the artist; private collection.
EXHIBITED
NAD, 1859, no. 410; RA, 1860, no. 75; Sanitary Fair, Albany, 1864, no. 56, as *The Blackberry* by T.W. (sic) Richards (courtesy of William H. Gerdts); Harvard University Art Museums (Fogg Art Museum), 1962.
REFERENCES
Morris, pp. 10, 11, 31, 33 (where he dates the painting 1860); Ferber 1973, p. 26; Ferber 1980(b), pp. 137, 141, 148, 150, fig. 122.

In his chapter on Richards in *American Painters* (1879), G.W. Sheldon recorded 1858 as the year in which Richards began "his pre-Raphaelite . . . studies proper" (Sheldon, p. 60). This date is confirmed by Richards' earliest known all-foreground plant studies in oil, such as this work.

While *Blackberry Bush* is the best documented of Richards' early efforts at Ruskinian or Pre-Raphaelite plein-air study, it was apparently not the first. According to the memoir of his friend William H. Willcox, it was preceded by a work in which "he had painted his subject directly and most elaborately from nature, spending months in its production" (Morris, p. 22). Perhaps this was the study *Out of Doors* exhibited along with *Blackberry Bush* at the Royal Academy in London in 1860. "It was a complete revolution," wrote Willcox, "and was the beginning of his future success. . . . Soon after he painted a blackberry bush in the open air. . . . Mr. J.R. Lambdin made a sketch at the same time not far from where Richards was working. A boy looking at Mr. Lambdin's picture said, 'Mister how long did it take you to make that.'

66

Mr. L. mentioned a few days, when the boy said, 'Good for you, that fellow up there has been all summer over his'" (Morris, p. 11).

Both of these arduous plein-air studies may well have been inspired by Pre-Raphaelite paintings in the Exhibition of English Art shown at the Pennsylvania Academy early in 1858. They parallel the lengthy outdoor labor undertaken by William J. Stillman (q.v.) and John William Hill (q.v.) under Ruskinian inspiration. Richards was also aware of Aaron Draper Shattuck's contemporaneous plant studies (cat. no. 118).

Blackberry Bush made a "marked impression in art circles," selling for six hundred dollars, apparently to E.L. Magoon, who would later be an important watercolor patron. When Magoon became financially embarrassed, the artist bought it back at the same price (Morris, p. 11).

Thomas C. Farrer's (q.v.) comments from London about Richards' work drew an excited response. "You can't imagine," John Henry Hill (q.v.) wrote, "how interested we were in every word of [your letter] particularly that about Richards' studies. I almost think I can see them there in the R.A. looking as though they were painted in black and white with a little color" (John Henry Hill to Thomas C. Farrer, Nyack, New York, July, 1860, GLF/NYPL). The painting, one of the few in which the artist used

bituminous pigments, had already deteriorated by the time Willcox wrote his memoir in about 1912. But today, more than a century and a quarter after Richards painted it, it still confirms Hill's comment about a subdued palette, suggesting that Richards was more interested in correct botanical record than in heightened plein-air color at the moment he first began treating Pre-Raphaelite subjects.   LSF

67
Tulip Trees   1859

Oil on canvas
13¼ × 17¹⁄₁₆ (33.7 × 43.3)
Inscribed lower left: "William T. Richards./ Phil. 1859."
The Brooklyn Museum, gift of Mrs. Arthur Graham Carey

PROVENANCE
William T. Walters, Baltimore, until 1861(?); [Samuel P. Avery, 1862]; the artist; Eleanor Richards Price; Edith Ballinger Price; Nancy Carey, 1981; The Brooklyn Museum.
EXHIBITED
PAFA 1862, S. P. Avery (?) (not recorded but mentioned in letters—see below); Goupil & Co., 1862 (?).
REFERENCES
G. W. Sheldon, "American Painters—William T. Richards," *The Art Journal* ns 3 (1877), p. 242; Sheldon, p. 60; Morris, p. 31, dated 1858; Gerdts 1969, p. 93, dated 1858; Gerdts 1971, p. 120, dated 1858; Ferber 1973, p. 26; Ferber 1980 (b), pp. 150-152, fig. 116.

67

It seems ironic to find examples of Richards' experiments in the use of bitumen, a pigment that darkens with age, in two of his earliest essays in the Pre-Raphaelite approach to landscape, since one of the hallmarks of both the English and American movements was the abandonment of the tonal concerns of conventional painting for an insistence upon vivid color and limited shadow. And yet that, sadly, is the case, for *Tulip Trees*, a small landscape of a grove of trees in full summer leaf that followed *Blackberry Bush* (cat. no. 66) as Richards' second major Pre-Raphaelite effort, is, like that work, painted in bitumen, and has suffered similar, though less extreme, darkening and disfigurement.

Despite its darkened state, however, *Tulip Trees* does record the dappled play of sunlight over tree and ground foliage as well as on the meticulously detailed trunk at the left. The effectively realized glimpses of sunlit distance and vivid blue sky that establish a limited recession look forward to more sophisticated and decorative works such as *In The Woods* of 1860 (cat. no. 73). Harrison Morris wrote that Richards' first full-scale Pre-Raphaelite landscape (which he dated incorrectly to 1858) was the sole occupation of an entire summer (Morris, p. 31). The slightly awkward all-over emphasis upon a laboriously accumulated foreground screen of tree and ground foliage calls to mind the handling of trees and bushes in Ford Madox Brown's watercolor in the 1857–58 American Exhibition of English Art, *Hampstead—A Sketch from Nature* (fig. 23), which was purchased in 1858 by the Philadelphia collector Ellis Yarnall.

According to G. W. Sheldon, *Tulip Trees* was painted for Baltimore collector William T. Walters, who also owned cat. no. 71 in addition to Richards' carefully detailed sepia study of 1859, *Woodland Plants*, and one of his sepia landscape drawings, all now in the Walters Art Gallery. Upon his departure for Europe in 1861, Walters may have left the painting with Samuel Avery for disposal, since the latter mentioned, apparently with ironic intent, that "*my* picture the 'Tulip Trees' will be in catalogue 'for Sale'" in a letter to Thomas C. Farrer (q.v.) discussing the 1862 Pennsylvania Academy exhibition where Farrer's own *Gone! Gone!* (cat. no. 8), which also belonged to Avery, was to be shown (Samuel P. Avery to Thomas C. Farrer, 48 Beekman Place, New York, datable to March/April, 1862; GLF/NYPL). *Tulip Trees* was not among the paintings Walters sold at auction in 1864, a sale which included Richards' *Morning Glories* (no. 20), *Glimpse of Summer* (no. 21, $35), and *The Neglected Garden* (no. 115, $220, sold to a a collector named Burrel), all now unlocated (*Catalogue of a most valuable collection of pictures of the American, French and German Schools . . .* , auction catalogue, New York: Henry H. Leeds and Co., February 12, 13, 1864).

In a letter of April 6, 1862, Richards complained to Avery about the impending Philadelphia exhibition ("I shall have nothing beside the Tulip Trees on my own account.") and closed with a wish ("I am looking forward to the time when I can exchange the Tulip Trees."), suggesting that Walters may have returned the painting directly to the artist and that it was Richards who placed it with the New York dealer (William T. Richards to Samuel P. Avery, Germantown, Pennsylvania, April 6, 1862, Avery Autograph Collection, Art Reference Library, Metropolitan Museum of Art). While Richards seemed qualified in his enthusiasm for the 1859 landscape, no doubt disappointed at its return, the work was apparently admired by Farrer, whose own painting by Richards, *Scene*

from Nature (unlocated), was also exhibited at the Pennsylvania Academy in 1862. In a letter written early in 1862, Avery asked that Farrer "send round to Mr. Knoedler's the little 'Spring' [Richards' *The Spring*, now unlocated, which belonged to Avery when exhibited at the National Academy of Design in 1860 as no. 312] which I left for you . . . the other day—I will bring over 'Tulip Trees' so that Mr. K. can have a Richards show—After which you can have the *Tulips* for your pupils use" (Samuel P. Avery to Thomas C. Farrer, 48 Beekman Place, New York; GLF/NYPL). This suggests that Farrer was employing Richards' paintings as models of Pre-Raphaelite practice for his students at Cooper Union. A second Avery letter indicated that Farrer had drawings by Richards as well, these apparently on loan from the artist: "Richards writes that he shall want to use the pencil drawings very shortly, will you please get them to my place and I will send them" (Samuel P. Avery to Thomas C. Farrer, 48 Beekman Place, New York; GLF/NYPL; all three of these letters were brought to my attention by Madeleine F. Beaufort). By 1888, when he prepared a questionnaire for *Appleton's Cyclopaedia of American Biography*, Richards considered *Tulip Trees* one of his ten "most notable" oil paintings (Frank Weitenkampf Papers, New York Public Library). LSF

68

Ferns in a Glade   1859

Oil on panel
7¼ × 6 (18.4 × 15.3)
Inscribed lower left: "W.T. Richards/1859"
Lent anonymously

PROVENANCE
[Hirschl & Adler Gallery, Inc., New York].
EXHIBITED
Heckscher 1977, no. 43.
REFERENCES
Gerdts 1969, p. 96, dated 1860, fig. 11; Gerdts 1971, p. 120, dated 1860, fig. 8–7; Ferber 1973, p. 24, fig. 5, pp. 25, 63; Troyen, p. 94, illus.; Ferber 1980 (b), p. 142, pp. 154–156, 161, fig. 123.

69
Study for the Conservatory   1860
Pencil and brown wash on paper
10 × 7⅞ (25.4 × 20.0)
Inscribed lower left: "Jan 1860."
The Brooklyn Museum, gift of Edith Ballinger Price
PROVENANCE
Eleanor Richards Price; Edith Ballinger Price, 1972; The Brooklyn
Museum.
EXHIBITED
Brooklyn 1973, no. 29.
REFERENCES
Ferber 1973, pp. 60–63, fig. 29; Ferber 1980 (b), pp. 142, 148, 149,
155, fig. 125.

69

70
The Conservatory   1860

Oil on panel
10⅞ × 8⁹⁄₁₆ (27.7 × 21.7)
Inscribed lower left: "Wm. T. Richards 1860."
Private collection
EXHIBITED
Brooklyn 1973, no. 28; Whitney 1984, no. 93.
REFERENCES
Ferber 1973, pp. 60–63, fig. 28; Ferber 1980 (b), pp. 148, 149, 155–156,
fig. 124; Foshay, pp. 109, 199, fig. 93, detail p. 109.

70

71
Red Clover, Butter-And-Eggs, and Ground Ivy 1860

Watercolor on paper
6⅞ × 5⅜ (17.5 × 13.7)
Inscribed lower right: "Wm. T. Richards. 60."
The Walters Art Gallery

PROVENANCE
William T. Walters; The Walters Art Gallery, Baltimore.
EXHIBITED
Brooklyn 1973, no. 27.
REFERENCES
Edward S. King and Marvin C. Ross, *Catalogue of the American Works of Art Including French Medals Made for America* (Baltimore: The Walters Art Gallery, 1956), no. 99, p. 26; Ferber 1973, p. 60, fig. 27; Ferber 1980 (b), pp. 142, 146, 157, fig. 126.

Richards' interest in the Ruskinian still-life subject is indicated by the series of subjects he treated in the years immediately following *Blackberry Bush* in which he mastered the close views of growing plant life identified with the Pre-Raphaelite movement. While only a few such works are now known, the exhibition records reveal that between 1859 and 1865, the years of his most intense Pre-Raphaelite preoccupation, such subjects formed a kind of sub-specialty, the only period when such motifs were a part of his oeuvre.

The artist's rapid gain in confidence in handling multiplicity of detail is immediately evident in *Ferns in a Glade* and *Conservatory*, a pair of works close enough in date, subject, format, and size to suggest that they may have been intended as seasonal pendants; the former depicts woodland plants in the filtered sunlight of a forest floor, while the latter portrays potted plants growing indoors. Both present a foreground screened off by plant life but for a small opening that permits a glimpse into the distance. The cascade of leafage curves down from left to right in *Ferns* and, balancing this, from right to left in *Conservatory*. The central vertical element of the tree trunk in the former is echoed by the door jamb in the latter. The background elements are rather uncomfortably crowded into an upper corner in *Ferns in a Glade* and the tiny figure appears oddly Lilliputian rather than convincingly distant in space, a problem shared by *Tulip Trees* (cat. no. 67). Such problems of recession are more easily resolved in the indoor space of *Conservatory*, where space is logically defined by architectural elements.

Red Clover, Butter-And-Eggs, and Ground Ivy of 1860 demonstrates Richards' technical capacity to handle the watercolor medium with the control and precision seen in the contemporaneous watercolor work of other members of the Pre-Raphaelite circle, even though he did not begin to specialize in the medium until a decade later. The point of view in this little work is at even closer range than in cat. nos. 68 and 70, suggesting that it was these paintings that prompted Tuckerman's observation that in viewing Richards' work "we seem not to be looking at a distant prospect but lying on the ground with herbage and blossoms directly under our eyes" (p. 524).

71

Study for the Conservatory, which is about the same size as the painting for which it was made, is dated January 1860, further evidence that *The Conservatory* was intended as a winter contrast to *Ferns in a Glade*. The darkened verso of the drawing and the incised lines on its surface indicate that parts were transferred directly onto the panel. A significant alteration is the change from a square to an arched doorway in order to better harmonize the view with the arched format of the painting. This format, which is a characteristic of all three of the finished works here, parallels similar compositions of the period by Aaron Draper Shattuck (cat. no. 118) and Fidelia Bridges (cat. no. 88) and emphasizes the intimate and decorative elements shared by these myopic glimpses into the private life of the plant kingdom.

In *Conservatory*, which is more particularized and vividly colored than *Ferns in a Glade*, each species is rendered with linear precision: a prayer plant, a dracena, a poinsettia, a caladium, and several types of potted ferns are easily distinguishable. Similarly, the brightly hued flora of *Red Clover, Butter-And-Eggs, and Ground Ivy* are all duly catalogued in the botanical specifics of the title. Works like these had an obvious influence on Richards' pupil of the early 1860s Fidelia Bridges (cat. no. 88) and also may have moved the Philadelphia painter George B. Wood, Jr., to undertake *Leaf and Berry Study* (cat. no. 122) in 1864.   LSF

72
Landscape   1860

Oil on canvas
17 × 23¼ (43.2 × 59.0)
Inscribed lower left: "Wm T. Richards. 1860."
Yale University Art Gallery, gift of
Mrs. Nigel Cholmeley-Jones

PROVENANCE
H.G. Sharpless, Philadelphia, 1864; E. Sharpless (sequence uncertain).
EXHIBITED
The Great Central Fair for the Benefit of the U.S. Sanitary Commission, Philadelphia, 1864, no. 396, H.G. Sharpless; New Britain Museum of American Art, New Britain, Connecticut, *He Knew the Sea: William Trost Richards, N.A. (1833–1905) Anna Richards Brewster (1870–1952),* April 11–May 20, 1973, no. 1; Brooklyn 1973, no. 23.
REFERENCES
Charles B. Ferguson, *He Knew the Sea: William Trost Richards, N.A. (1833–1905) Anna Richards Brewster (1870–1952)* (exhibition catalogue, The New Britain Museum of American Art, New Britain, Connecticut, April 11–May 20, 1973), p. 7, fig. 1, p. 8; Ferber 1973, pp. 26, 56, 60, illus. no. 23, p. 59; Ferber 1980 (b), pp. 151–152, fig. 74, p. 473.

72

73
In the Woods   1860

Oil on canvas
15⅝ × 20 (39.7 × 50.8)
Inscribed lower right: "Wm. T. Richards/1860"
Bowdoin College Museum of Art, Brunswick, Maine
PROVENANCE
Misses Mary T. and Jane Mason, Germantown, Pennsylvania, 1955;
Bowdoin College Museum of Art.
EXHIBITED
Meredith Long Gallery, Houston, Texas, *Tradition and Innovation—
American Paintings of the 1860s,* January 10–24, 1974, no. 28; Williams
College Museum of Art, Williamstown, Massachusetts, *The New
England Eye: Masterpieces of American Art from New England College
and University Collections,* September 11–November 6, 1983, no. 21.
REFERENCES
Larry Curry, *Tradition and Innovation—American Paintings of the 1860s*
(exhibition catalogue, Meredith Long Gallery, Houston, Texas, January
10–24, 1974), p. 24, fig. 21; S. Lane Faison, Jr., *The New England Eye:
Masterpieces of American Art from New England College and University
Collections* (exhibition catalogue, Williams College Museum of Art,
Williamstown, Massachusetts, September 11–November 6, 1983), p. 24,
no. 21, fig. 21; Ferber 1980 (b), pp. 148, 152, fig. 117; Bowdoin College
Museum of Art, *Handbook of the Collections* (Brunswick, Maine, 1981),
p. 112; Matthew Baigell, *A Concise History of American Painting and
Sculpture* (New York: Harper and Row, Inc., 1982).

74
Woodland Interior   1861

Oil on canvas
28 × 23 (71.1 × 58.4)
Inscribed lower right: "Wm. T. Richards/1861"
Private collection
PROVENANCE
Hugh Davids, Philadelphia, 1864 (?); private collection.
EXHIBITED
PAFA, 1862, no. 146, *Path in the Wood,* Hugh Davids (?); The Great
Central Fair for the Benefit of the U.S. Sanitary Commission,
Philadelphia, 1864, no. 357, *Path in the Woods,* Hugh Davids (?).
REFERENCES
G.W. Sheldon, "American Painters—William T. Richards," *The Art
Journal* ns 3 (1877), p. 242 (?); Sheldon, p. 60 (?).

Richards spent the summer of 1860 in Bethlehem,
Pennsylvania, where his student Fidelia Bridges recalled
that he "was painting out-of-doors the largest canvas he
had ever painted directly from nature and struggling with
the difficult problems of it" (Morris, p. 32). *Landscape*
seems a logical candidate for the painting Bridges referred
to, although *In The Woods*—only slightly smaller—is also
in high Pre-Raphaelite style.

The Round Table, in citing Richards as one of the early
American adherents of Pre-Raphaelitism, noted that,

73

74

"being more tenacious," he "persisted, and carried imitation in art further" than the other pioneers ("Recent Art Criticism: The New Path," *The Round Table*, vol. I, no. 3, January 2, 1864, p. 42). This observation is borne out by both *Landscape* and *In the Woods*, which demonstrate the artist's complete mastery by 1860 of full-scale landscape in the American Pre-Raphaelite manner—a remarkable advance from the awkwardness of *Tulip Trees*. Not only are these paintings far more sophisticated in composition than the little work painted only a year earlier but they also demonstrate a brilliance of local color and a sensitive handling of violet and blue shadows.

These vivid works also indicate, however, the "difficult problems" of Pre-Raphaelite vision hinted at by Bridges—that is, the difficulty of integrating precise detail with atmospheric perspective. Richards insisted in these works upon a highly detailed foreground while also recording the effects of strong sunlight in the distance. Both paintings, therefore, divide in two; *Landscape* at the rail fence in the middle ground and *In The Woods* in the foreground, where a framing "tunnel" of profuse botanical detail opens abruptly onto a more broadly rendered distance. In both paintings we plunge into a sunlit distance—a surprisingly proto-impressionist vision with broadly brushed greens, violets, and blues—and the union between foreground and distance remains visually unresolved.

These were the paintings that established Richards early, for better or worse, as the best-known figure among the American Pre-Raphaelites. They won Henry T. Tuckerman's admiration for their "perfection of minutiae" but were deplored by the same critic for their "literalness." "Marvellous in accurate imitation are the separate objects in the foreground of these pictures," Tuckerman wrote, "but the relative finish of the foreground, centre, and background is not always harmonious; there is little perspective illusion; what is gained in accuracy of details seems lost in aerial gradation and distances" (Tuckerman, p. 524).

Woodland Interior may be the *Wood-Scene* of 1861 that G.W. Sheldon reported was painted for Philadelphia collector Hugh Davids. It was probably exhibited, as William H. Gerdts has suggested, as *Path in the Woods* at the Pennsylvania Academy in 1862 and again at the Philadelphia Sanitary Fair in 1864. It may depict the vicinity of Bethlehem, Pennsylvania, where Richards spent the summer and fall of 1861. While its local color is as vivid and its detail as fully particularized as the landscapes of 1860, Richards has curtailed recession effectively by treating the closed space of a forest glade. In an upright format reminiscent of that used by Asher B. Durand (q.v.), with the tree tops disappearing beyond the picture edge, a footpath carries the eye into the limited distance in easy stages marked by pools of sunlight relieving forest shade. There are parallels in William J. Stillman's earlier *Saranac Lake* (cat. no. 120), where the detailed delineation of the tree bark is similar to that in this work, and in Thomas Moran's later *Under The Trees* (cat. no. 117), a spectacular Pre-Raphaelite exercise that may well have been inspired by Richards. In 1864, Richards was to utilize this upright forest format for another of his self-described "most notable" oil paintings, *June Woods* (The New-York Historical Society), which was sold by Michael Knoedler to New York collector Robert L. Stuart for one thousand dollars (Ferber 1980 [b], p. 181).

These are the works that demonstrated for *The Round Table* "that Mr. Richards is remarkable for two things—

a slow, keen vision, and a slow, sure hand." Admiring Richards' "capacity for labor," the reviewer qualified his praise, concluding, "He forgot that seeing nature as a botanist is not seeing nature as a poet. . . . Of spiritual or poetic insight we see no sign. . . . For the rare and remarkable work which Mr. Richards has given us we are grateful, but must conclude that he is not destined to give us great creative art" ("Art: Three Pictures by W.T. Richards," *The Round Table*, vol. I, no. 10, February 20, 1864, p. 153).   LSF

75

Sunset on the Meadow   *circa* 1861

Oil on canvas
13 × 19½ (33.0 × 49.5)
Inscribed lower left: "Wm T. Richards/186(1)"
Mr. and Mrs. Wilbur L. Ross, Jr.

PROVENANCE
[Sotheby Parke Bernet Inc., New York, October 22, 1981];
Mr. and Mrs. Wilbur L. Ross, Jr.
REFERENCES
*American 18th-Century, 19th-Century & Western Paintings, Drawings
and Sculpture* (auction catalogue, Sotheby Parke Bernet, New York,
October 22, 1981), illus. no. 46.

In this painting, one of Richards' most successful attempts
to wed Pre-Raphaelite foreground detail with the spatial
requirements of a full-scale landscape, the rolling
topography and low point of view minimize the middle
distance, suggested here primarily by trees silhouetted
against background hills and sky. The delicacy with which
the pale blues of an early twilight sky and the lavender
clouds and haze on the distant hills are realized suggests a
more satisfying resolution, too, of atmospheric perspective
than the brilliant midday sunshine of *Landscape* (cat. no.
72) and *In The Woods* (cat. no. 73), which remain enframed
by and separate from brilliantly colored but comparatively
static foregrounds.

While the goldenrod in the immediate foreground of
Sunset on the Meadow (probably not the original title)
might suggest a link to the work of that name exhibited at
the Pennsylvania Academy in 1861 (no. 84), such a title
could refer as easily to a still-life subject more like cat. nos.
68 and 71. We may also speculate that this work might be
the *Midsummer* painted soon after Richards' *Wood-Scene*
of 1861 (cat. no. 74), for William T. Blodgett of New York
(Sheldon, pp. 60-61). The choice of an evening subject may
well have been inspired by the fame of Frederic Edwin
Church's (q.v.) *Twilight in the Wilderness* of 1860
(Cleveland Museum of Art), a work that stimulated what
James Jackson Jarves termed in 1864, "a virulent epidemic
of sunsets" (p. 190). A small painting of 1864, *Corn Shocks
and Pumpkins* (private collection), demonstrates Richards'
interest in the more dramatic effects Jarves alluded to. The
subtlety of *Sunset on the Meadow*, however, offers more
intriguing parallels to the pale lemon and lavender hues of
the twilight view of the Palisades in Thomas C. Farrer's
Gone! Gone! (cat. no. 8), which was exhibited at the
National Academy of Design in 1860 and the Philadelphia
Academy of Fine Arts in 1862 and was most certainly
known to Richards.   LSF

75

76
Corner of the Woods 1864

Pencil on buff paper
23¼ × 17½ (59.0 × 44.5)
Inscribed lower right: "W.T.R. 1864."
M. & M. Karolik Collection, Museum of Fine Arts, Boston
PROVENANCE
Eleanor Richards Price; Edith Ballinger Price, 1961;
Museum of Fine Arts.
EXHIBITED
Brooklyn 1973, no. 35.
REFERENCES
Karolik, vol. 1, p. 265, no. 620; Ferber 1973, p. 64, no. 36; Ferber 1980
(b), p. 148, fig. 115.

Paralleling Richards' Pre-Raphaelite paintings are pencil
drawings of an equally detailed nature, many, like cat.
no. 69, serving as studies for works in oil or as botanical
references for details of such works. Between 1864 and
1867, Richards also produced large, highly finished
drawings like this one, in which both the subjects and the
precision of the oils and watercolors are translated into the
graphic medium. The application of an almost miniaturist
technique on such a large format makes such work unique
in Richards' oeuvre and, as the dates suggest, was confined
to his years of Pre-Raphaelite enthusiasm.

Charles Herbert Moore (q.v.) also produced minutely
realized black-and-white work on a large scale, such as his
remarkable pen study *Pine Tree* of 1868 (cat. no. 48). That
both were members of the Pre-Raphaelite circle is more
than a coincidence, for the Association for the
Advancement of Truth in Art placed special value and
emphasis upon draftsmanship, as is also demonstrated on a
smaller scale by the black-and-white work of Thomas C.
Farrer (cat. nos. 1-7), Henry Farrer (cat. nos. 103-105), and
John Henry Hill (cat. nos. 20 and 21). The manifesto of the
Association included this passage: "It is moreover [the
young artist's] duty to strive for the greatest attainable
power of drawing, in view of the vast amount of good
talent, of wit, knowledge and pleasant fancy, that is lost and
wasted around us every day, from mere want of ability to
give it due expression " ("Association for the Advancement
of Truth in Art," *The New Path*, vol. I, no. 1, May 1863, p.
11). Already a disciplined and technically polished
draftsman by the late 1850s, Richards was moved under
Pre-Raphaelite inspiration to even more accomplished
graphic work on a grand scale, such as *Corner of the
Woods*. LSF

76

77
Rocks at Nantasket 1869

Watercolor and pencil on buff paper
6¾ × 12 (17.2 × 30.5)
Inscribed lower right: "Nantasket/July 25. 69."
Private collection
EXHIBITED
Brooklyn 1973, no. 47.
REFERENCES
Ferber 1973, p. 72; Ferber 1980 (b), pp. 267-270, fig. 210.

78
Study of a Boulder *circa* 1869

Watercolor and pencil on gray paper
10⅛ × 14½ (25.6 × 37.3)
Unsigned
Private collection
REFERENCES
Ferber 1980 (b), pp. 267-270, fig. 213.

As we have seen in cat. no. 71, as early as 1860 Richards was already highly proficient in the use of watercolor in Ruskinian study. He used the medium occasionally during the next decade, first exhibiting with the American Society of Painters in Water Colors at the third annual show in 1870. The summer before, he produced an interesting series of watercolor studies made along the New England coast, including cat. nos. 77 and 78. These reflect his increasing preoccupation with the coastal and marine subjects that would eventually dominate his work in both oil and watercolor.

Richards' focus upon the distinctive geology of the North American continent allied him not only with the interests of coastal specialists like William Haseltine (cat. no. 109), a friend of his youth, but also with the 1860s inland geological proclivities of David Johnson (cat. no. 113) and Martin Johnson Heade (cat. no. 110), as well as, of course, with the Pre-Raphaelite circle. Although the circle had by then disbanded as a formal entity, the collective Ruskinian impulse can still be traced in the parallels between these meticulously realized rock studies and those in the same medium, and probably the same period, by Charles Herbert Moore (cat. nos. 49 and 50). Both series, in their care to record the coloration and distinctive surface qualities of individual boulders and

77

faceted outcroppings, continued to pay homage to the watercolor virtuosity of Ruskin's famed *Fragment of the Alps* (cat. no. 125), extolled in *The New Path* as the epitome of devoted and careful study from nature. The isolation of cat. no. 78, on a field of barely penciled rocks, minutely realized as it is, aptly demonstrates Russell Sturgis's advice in *The New Path*:

> The requirements of a good study are that it shall have been undertaken with earnest and modest desire to learn, that it shall have been carried through without hurry or slovenliness, and that it shall have been left untouched from the moment when the student felt he had learned all that the subject could teach him. . . . ("Pictures and Studies," *The New Path*, vol. II, no. 3, July 1864, p. 38).   LSF

Francesca Alexander   1837–1917

Francesca Alexander, internationally acclaimed in her own time for her exquisite draftsmanship, was praised and exalted by John Ruskin (q.v.) as the perfect manifestation of the principles he advocated in *Elements of Drawing* (1857). Born Esther Frances Alexander on February 27, 1837, to a well-to-do Boston family, she was brought up in a proper and religious Protestant, Victorian home by a mother who dominated her life, and a father, Francis, a successful Boston portrait painter, who encouraged her precocious artistic talent. The family moved to Florence in 1853, and there, sheltered from the outside world, she devoted herself to drawing and to charitable endeavors such as aiding the sick and the poor.

During her family's summer vacations at Abetone in the Apennines, Alexander began to collect, record, and translate hundreds of folk songs and stories of the Tuscan peasants, transcribing many of them calligraphically in a format of two parallel columns on white folio-size sheets of paper and illustrating the texts with pen-and-ink line drawings of flowers. Between 1868 and 1882 she completed one hundred twenty-two folios of what was to become her most famous work, *Roadside Songs of Tuscany* (1884–85).

In 1882 Henry Roderick Newman (q.v.), who was by then living in Florence, introduced Alexander to John Ruskin, who was enchanted with her work, gave her the name Francesca, and formed a lasting attachment to both her and her mother, corresponding with the two of them until his death. Ruskin bought the *Roadside Songs* manuscript and went on to write the preface for it and two of her other books, *The Story of Ida* (1883) and *Christ's Folk in the Apennines* (1887–89). By publicizing her work in his lectures as Slade Professor of Fine Art at Oxford and distributing her drawings among various English museums, he brought her worldwide attention and helped make her an attraction for visitors to Florence.

Alexander's eyesight, which began to deteriorate as early as 1885, failed toward the end of her life. She died on January 21, 1917, about a year after her mother, and is buried outside of Florence.

REFERENCES
FA; DAB; M.H. Spielman, "The Roadside Songs of Tuscany," *Magazine of Art*, June 1895, pp. 295–298.

79
Woman Sewing   1860s

Oil on canvas
12½ × 9¼ (31.8 × 23.5)
Unsigned
Mr. and Mrs. Wilbur L. Ross, Jr.

PROVENANCE
Private collection, 1977; [Childs Gallery, Boston, 1980]; Mr. and Mrs. Wilbur L. Ross, Jr.
REFERENCES
Childs Gallery Bulletin, no. 7, Spring-Summer 1977, as *Self-portrait*; *Childs Gallery Painting Annual*, 1980, p. 13, as *Senora Pistolesi*.

Although Francesca Alexander is known to have begun painting in oil as early as 1862 and to have continued until at least 1878, only four of her works in this medium are now located. (I am indebted to Joan Esch, Curator of Education at The New Hampshire Historical Society, for this information.) *Woman Sewing* is one of these rare examples. Formerly known as a self-portrait, it has the

78

79

devotional mood and portrayal of feminine virtue so characteristic of Alexander's pen-and-ink drawings.

The figure represents a type—pale face, large eyes, and dark parted hair— favored by the artist, and may be based upon the features of a family friend, Lina Pistolesi, or the little seamstress, Ida, whose life story Alexander wrote in 1883 (*The Story of Ida: Epitaph on an Etruscan Tomb*, ed. John Ruskin, New York: John W. Lovell Co.). If the woman portrayed here is Ida, the picture in her sewing basket is probably of the military officer she loved, and the book next to it is the Bible, her favorite book. Ida, who posed for Alexander on numerous occasions, would have been an appropriate model for the figure in *Woman Sewing* because she was a seamstress and deeply religious. Alexander always chose "for the type of every personage in her imagined picture, someone whose circumstances and habitual tone of mind are actually like those related and described in the legend to be illustrated" (Alexander 1884, p. 12).

Deep in prayer, the sitter is shown simultaneously involved in household work; rather than looking at her sewing, her half-closed eyes produce a meditative expression of complete tranquility. The religious overtones are further enhanced by the prie-dieu and devotional tondo in the background. Although Alexander was never formally a part of an artistic circle, the attention to detail, the meticulous technique, and the reverential attitude towards subject matter found in *Woman Sewing* ally her with the American Pre-Raphaelites.   HPC

80
Per la Nativita di Nostro Signore
circa 1868–82

Pen and ink on paper
14⅛ × 10½ (35.9 × 26.6)
Unsigned
The Brooklyn Museum, Dick S. Ramsay Fund
PROVENANCE
John Ruskin, 1882; Joseph R. Goldyne, 1981; [Jeffrey Alan Gallery, New York, 1983]; The Brooklyn Museum.
EXHIBITED
Jeffrey Alan Gallery, New York, *Francesca Alexander 1837–1917*, April 7–30, 1983, cat. no. 19.
REFERENCES
Alexander 1897, pl. XCVII; Goldyne, cat. no. 44; FA, cat. no. 19.

81
S. Zita   1874–82

Pen and ink on paper
14⅜ × 10¾ (36.5 × 27.3)
Unsigned
The Brooklyn Museum, Dick S. Ramsay Fund
PROVENANCE
John Ruskin, 1882; Joseph R. Goldyne, 1981; [Jeffrey Alan Gallery, New York, 1983]; The Brooklyn Museum.
EXHIBITED
Jeffrey Alan Gallery, New York, *Francesca Alexander 1837–1917*, April 7–30, 1983, cat. no. 18.
REFERENCES
Alexander 1897, pl. LXX; Goldyne, cat. no. 33; FA, cat. no. 18.

80

These two pen-and-ink drawings from Francesca Alexander's *Tuscan Songs*, the 1897 American edition of her well-known publication *Roadside Songs of Tuscany*, illustrate not only the artist's prodigious graphic skill but also her strong interest in the folk songs, hymns, and ballads of the Tuscan peasants. Alexander's involvement with the Tuscan peasantry was so profound that she spent close to fourteen years creating the original manuscript for *Roadside Songs.* "I have wished to make my book all of poor people's poetry," she wrote. "I have done my best to save a little of what is passing away" (Alexander 1884, p. 6).

Alexander seems to have been particularly attracted to the story of the thirteenth-century Tuscan saint Zita, whom Ruskin described as "the type of perfectness in servant life to the Christian world" (Alexander 1884, p. 18). Thirteen illustrations (plates LXVIII-LXXX) in the original English edition (1884–85) of *Roadside Songs* are devoted to the story of this servant saint of Lucca, who, like the artist herself, was deeply concerned with the plight of the poor.

Alexander blended her flowing calligraphy with floral subjects—crocuses in *Per la Nativita di Nostro Signore* (cat. no. 80) and buttercups in *S. Zita* (cat. no. 81)—because "it seemed natural that road-side songs should have borders of road-side flowers." (Alexander 1884, p. 5. I am indebted to Dr. Stephen K-M. Tim, Director of Scientific Affairs, Brooklyn Botanic Garden, for identifying these flowers.) The exquisite detail and botanical accuracy of these drawings explain the immediate attraction Alexander's work held for Ruskin, who purchased the entire set of one hundred twenty-two drawings for *Roadside Songs.* Although he dispersed some of them among various British institutions, he kept a cache of them for himself. "In absolute skill of drawing and perception of all that is loveliest in human creatures and in the flowers that live for them," Ruskin wrote, "I think these works are in their kind unrivalled and that they do indeed represent certain elements of feeling and power peculiar to this age" (Ruskin, Introduction to vol. XXXII, p. xxi).   HPC

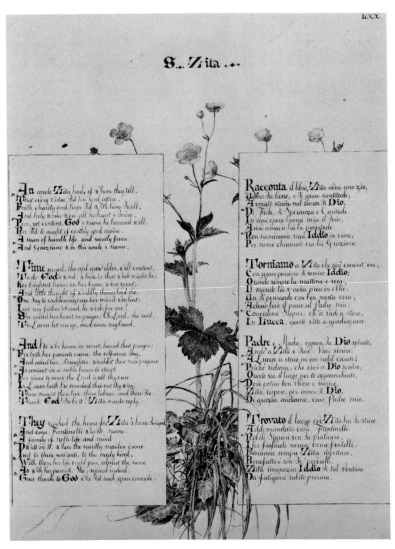

81

Albert Bierstadt   1830–1902

Albert Bierstadt, a painter of the American West whose large romantic paintings rivaled those of Frederic Church (q.v.) during the 1860s, was born at Solingen, near Düsseldorf, Germany, on January 7, 1830, and emigrated with his parents to New Bedford, Massachusetts, at the age of two. When he returned to Düsseldorf to study in 1853, he worked with Worthington Whittredge (q.v.) and was influenced by such local artists as Karl Friederich Lessing (1807–1880) and Andreas Achenbach (1827–1905). He toured Italy with Whittredge in 1856, spending a year in Rome before returning to America in 1857. He began exhibiting at the National Academy of Design in 1858 and became an Academician two years later.

Bierstadt's first trip to the West took place in 1859 when he joined Colonel Frederick J. Lander's expedition to Nebraska and Wyoming. Sketches and photographs from this trip became the basis for such later works as his painting *The Rocky Mountains* (1863, Metropolitan Museum of Art), which hung opposite Church's painting *Heart of the Andes* (1859) at the Metropolitan Sanitary Fair in 1864. Returning from the trip late in 1859, he took a studio in the Tenth Street Studio Building in New York which he kept until 1879, even after he had built Malkasten, his house and studio at Irvington-on-Hudson, New York, in 1866. This estate was destroyed by fire in 1882.

In 1863 Bierstadt went west a second time, touring Nebraska, Colorado, Utah, California, and Oregon with the writer Fitz Hugh Ludlow (whose wife Rosalie he married in 1866 after her divorce from Ludlow). Paintings resulting from this trip, such as The Brooklyn Museum's extraordinary *Storm in the Rockies: Mount Rosalie* (1866), brought him great success. He took a third trip west from 1871 to 1873—visiting Washington, Vancouver, and Yellowstone Park and living in California—and went west again in 1886 and 1889. From 1867 to 1869 and again in 1878, 1883, 1884, 1887, and 1891 he travelled in Europe as well.

The dry, tightly painted style that Bierstadt developed never really changed. Although in the sixties his work was praised by English critics for its Ruskinian observation of details and its Turnerian grandeur and movement, the popularity of his paintings waned in the seventies and by the eighties the demand had virtually ended. He suffered bankruptcy in 1895, but his second wife, whom he had married the year before, was independently wealthy and he was able to travel and live well until his death in New York City on February 18, 1902.

REFERENCES
Gordon Hendricks, *Albert Bierstadt: Painter of the American West* (New York: Harry N. Abrams, 1973); Richard S. Trump, *Life and Works of Albert Bierstadt* (Ph.D. dissertation, Ohio State University, 1963).

82
Niagara Falls   *circa* 1869

Oil on canvas
25 × 20 (63.5 × 50.8)
Inscribed lower right: "A Bierstadt"
Thomas Gilcrease Institute of American History and Art, Tulsa, Oklahoma
PROVENANCE
Roland McKinny, New York; [M. Knoedler and Co., New York, September 1949]; Thomas Gilcrease Institute of American History and Art, January 1950.
EXHIBITED
New Orleans Museum of Art, *The Waters of America*, May 1–November 18, 1984.
REFERENCES
Gordon Hendricks, *Albert Bierstadt* (New York: Harry N. Abrams, 1974), illus. CL-217; *The Waters of America* (exhibition catalogue, New Orleans Museum of Art, 1984), cover illus.

Although Richard Trump's dissertation on Albert Bierstadt (Ohio State University, 1963) records a lost *Niagara* dated 1863 (oil on canvas, 50 × 36 inches), this painting of *Niagara Falls*, as well as two others of the same title (one 19 × 27⅛ inches in The National Gallery of Canada, Ottawa; the other 13 × 18 inches in a private collection in Tulsa, Oklahoma) and a fourth titled *Niagara from The American Side* (oil on paper, 14 × 19½ inches, Museum of Fine Arts, Boston), probably dates from Bierstadt's visit to his sister at Niagara upon his return from Europe in August 1869.

That Bierstadt chose a point of view below the falls may indicate his desire to deviate from more conventional compositions and attempt something as distinct as Frederic Edwin Church's (q.v.) daring horizontal panorama of both the American and Canadian Falls, which eliminated the surrounding landscape entirely and drew the viewer vertiginously over the water itself. But Church's focus, praised by Ruskin in 1857, was clearly on the effects of light on water (even in other views closer in compositional structure to Bierstadt's), while Bierstadt's attention is centered on the foreground stone shelf protruding from the base of the American Falls (Tuckerman, p. 371). According to Frederick H. Johnson's *Guide to Niagara Falls and Its Scenery* (Buffalo, 1868), replete with descriptions by the eminent geologist Sir Charles Lyell, the American Falls "can be seen to advantage from below." Perhaps the artist stood on Prospect Point, where it is possible to stand within a few feet of the water without being sprayed.

Bierstadt's depiction of the foreground elements demonstrates both the technical facility and attention to detail resulting from his Düsseldorf training and the Ruskinian focus upon geological specifics prevalent during the 1860s. This latter interest was evident earlier in the selections he made for *Stereoscopic Views of the Hills of New Hampshire* (1862), a book of forty-eight close-up photographs of rocks, cascades, and mountains taken by his brothers Edward and Charles. Here, the strata of dolostone, shale, and limestone eroded by the formidable action of the water are differentiated in color and texture but with a broader stroke than that used by true Ruskinians (Irving Tesmer, ed., *Colossal Cataract: The Geological History of Niagara Falls*, Albany: State University of New York Press, 1981). The rainbow, a phenomenon so prevalent at the falls that it is mentioned in Johnson's guidebook, is depicted with similar scientific dedication as the reflection of the sun's rays in the watery mist, rather than as the traditional symbol of hope. Its inclusion, along with the Horseshoe Falls in the distance, only underscores Bierstadt's intent to subordinate such popular images to the craggy cliff that composes half the picture space.   AB

82

83

Ferns and Rocks on an Embankment

circa 1869

Formerly *Florida Rock Study*
Oil on canvas
19¼ × 13½ (48.9 × 34.3)
Inscribed lower left: "A. Bierstadt"
Private collection

PROVENANCE
[Kennedy Galleries, New York, early 1960s]; [Robert M. Fitzgerel, Newcastle Galleries, Newcastle, Maine, 1966]; [Kenneth Lux Gallery, New York, 1970–72]; private collection.

This work was once thought to be a scene in Florida, but because it contains botanical specimens native to the Northeast, such as Queen Anne's Lace and Christmas ferns, it is now believed to have been done during one of Bierstadt's many trips to the White Mountains of New Hampshire. (I am grateful to Dr. Stephen K-M. Tim, Director of Scientific Affairs, Brooklyn Botanic Garden, for verifying the location.) Bierstadt first visited the White Mountains in 1852 before going to study in Düsseldorf, returned several times between 1857 and 1862, and spent considerable time there at Glen House in Pinkham Notch in the fall of 1869 after his visit to Niagara Falls (Donald

83

Keyes, Catherine H. Campbell, et al., *The White Mountains*, exhibition catalogue, University Art Galleries, University of New Hampshire, Durham, 1980, p. 80). Although *Ferns and Rocks* could have been painted on any of these trips, its similarity in subject, touch, and color to other oil sketches painted during the 1869 period suggests that it is one of more than two hundred preparatory studies Campbell states Bierstadt did for *The Emerald Pool* (1870, Huntington Hartford Collection, p. 80).

Although such plein-air data gathering links Bierstadt to the Ruskinians in concern for site specificity, for him careful documentation was not an end in itself. Rather it was a step toward a more ambitious goal in which a group of sketches, broadly painted by Ruskinian standards, was transformed into a meticulously painted grand composite in the studio (Novak, p. 94). The large number of sketches made for *The Emerald Pool* was perhaps a subconscious response to criticism in *The New Path* to the effect that Bierstadt had attempted monumental paintings such as his 1863 work *The Rocky Mountains* before giving "years of study to the subject" (vol. I, no. 11, March 1864, p. 162).

Even in this seemingly conscientious effort to be true to nature, then, Bierstadt's vision was different from that of the Ruskinians. Criticism directed at James M. Hart (1828-1901) in *The New Path* of December 1863 is equally appropriate for him: ". . . it comes very near the truth, but always stops a little short. . . . Every part of it tempts us to look more carefully, and when we do so, disappoints us. . . . It is finished suggestion . . ." (vol. I, no. 8, p. 100). Nevertheless, *The New Path* critics never seemed to lose hope "that [Bierstadt] will recover himself before it shall be too late and that he will walk with nature . . ." ("The Mutual Art Association," *The New Path*, vol. II, no. 5, May 1865, pp. 74-77).

Robert Bolling Brandegee 1849-1922

Robert Brandegee was born April 1849 in Berlin, Connecticut. Before departing for extended study in France he produced a series of meticulously painted watercolors strongly influenced by the American Ruskinians. As a child, he received drawing lessons from a Miss Sarah Tuthill, who may be the S.S. Tuthill later associated with the Association for the Advancement of Truth in Art. He also studied with one of the Hills, probably John Henry Hill (q.v.), in Nyack, New York, and subsequently received instruction from Thomas Charles Farrer (q.v.) in New York. It comes as no surprise then that during the late 1860s, when he worked chiefly in watercolor and exhibited with the American Society of Painters in Water Colors, his nature studies as well as his figural work manifested the vivid colors and dedication to the minute details of nature characteristic of the American Pre-Raphaelites.

After three years in Hartford, Connecticut, where beginning in 1869 he gave drawing lessons based on Ruskin's teachings, Brandegee left for Paris on April 29, 1872, with Charles N. Flagg (1848-1916) and William Faxon (1849-?), two fellow artists from Connecticut. He supposedly remained there for nine and a half years, working in the studio of Louis-Marie-François Jacquesson de la Chevreuse (1839-1903) and enrolling in the École des Beaux-Arts on March 22, 1875. Nevertheless, in 1878 he gave a New York address for his one contribution to the National Academy of Design's annual exhibition, and two years later he listed himself as a resident of Berlin, Connecticut. His fellow students in Jacquesson's small academic atelier, which emphasized contour and shape, included such American painters as J. Alden Weir (1852-1919), William H. Coffin (1855-1925), and Samuel Isham (1855-1914). Although he visited the Louvre to study old master paintings, he preferred watercolor to oil and considered the work of William Henry Hunt "the finest thing I had seen so far." He also went on sketching trips in Europe but began to prefer portrait and figure painting.

Upon his return to America, Brandegee opened a studio in New York which he maintained for fifteen years. He concentrated his energy more on teaching than on painting, however, working at Miss Porter's School in Farmington, Connecticut, until 1903, and helping to found the Connecticut League of Art Students in Hartford. On May 17, 1898, at the age of forty-nine, he married the cellist Susan Lord. While continuing to paint portrait commissions, landscapes, and a few murals in and around Farmington, he took up writing, publishing his first book in 1901 and also producing the *Farmington Magazine*, a short-lived quarterly, that same year. He wrote his autobiography in 1918 and died on March 5, 1922.

REFERENCES
French; Jones; NAD; TB.

84

Anemones 1867

Pencil on paper
4¼ × 6⅝ (10.8 × 16.8)
Inscribed lower left (on mat): "(Robert Brandegee)
April 15th 1867"
The Brooklyn Museum, Charles S. Smith Memorial Fund
PROVENANCE
The artist, 1922; Robert L. Brandegee, Salisbury, Connecticut, 1982;
The Brooklyn Museum.

The depiction of wild flowers growing in a natural setting was one of the new categories of still life developed in the middle of the 1850s by artists influenced by John Ruskin's (q.v.) writings. As early as 1856, Aaron D. Shattuck (q.v.) exhibited a study of *Grasses and Flowers* at the National Academy of Design (see Gerdts 1969, pp. 31, 93), and the popularity of the subject among the American Pre-Raphaelites continued into the late 1880s with such works as Henry R. Newman's *Wildflowers* (cat. no. 64). The humble subject matter, low viewpoint, and realistic out-of-doors setting had all been strongly advocated by Ruskin, who wrote, " . . . the most beautiful position in which flowers can be seen is precisely the most natural one—low flowers relieved by grass or moss" (Ruskin, addenda of "A Joy Forever," vol. XIV, p. 116).

The direct visual inspiration for Brandegee's 1867 interpretation of this Ruskinian theme, however, is probably Thomas C. Farrer's (q.v.) *May in the Woods*, previously known as *Study of Anemones*, a work Brandegee would have known through the photograph issued by *The New Path* in 1864 (see fig. 7). Both drawings share similar subject matter—white Rue-anemones placed close to the picture plane among a tangle of vegetation—and both manifest an interest in botanical accuracy through the use of painstaking detail. (My thanks to Dr. Stephen K-M. Tim, Director of Scientific Affairs, Brooklyn Botanic Garden, for identifying these flowers.) Brandegee's work can also be related to John Henry Hill's (q.v.) 1866 engraving *Wild Flowers of the Genus Bidens*, another monochromatic treatment of white flowers viewed myopically, which was published in Hill's *Sketches from Nature*. Painted repeatedly by the American Ruskinians, anemones held a strong fascination for Brandegee. "But loveliest of all was the anemone, the Thalictrum Anenenordes," he wrote, "it is as delicate and fragile as a young girl. My delight in these flowers never changes even after many years" (manuscript autobiography of Robert Brandegee, Collection of Robert L. Brandegee, Salisbury, Connecticut).   HPC

84

85
Dead Bird *circa* 1867

Watercolor on paper
6⅞ × 10 (17.5 × 25.4)
Unsigned
Anonymous loan
PROVENANCE
The artist, 1922; Robert L. Brandegee, Salisbury, Connecticut, 1982;
private collection.

Brandegee's lifelong interest in ornithology, which
culminated in his making a complete collection of native
New England birds, is manifested in two of his early
notebooks (Collection of Robert L. Brandegee, Salisbury,
Connecticut), which are filled with detailed descriptions of
different birds and their distinctive songs, nests, eggs, etc.
Although one of these notebooks, entitled "A Collection
of facts about birds which have come under my own
observation," reveals that he owned stuffed specimens, this
watercolor is based on a dead bird found in the wild. John
Henry Hill's (q.v.) comments in *Sketches from Nature*
(1867) are therefore brought to mind: "Dead birds make
excellent studies; many of W. Hunt's (q.v.) most beautiful
watercolor drawings are of dead game; do not waste time
on stuffed specimen if you can get the real." In fact, *Dead
Bird* derives part of its inspiration from an engraving of a
black-capped titmouse in that publication.

The similarities between Hill's engraving and
Brandegee's watercolor are striking: both depict dead birds
lying with their beaks in the air against a dark, blank
background, and both have an extremely factual approach
to their subjects that borders on morbidness in the way the
eyes of the animals are shown clamped shut while the legs
are drawn up slightly from rigor mortis. Brandegee,
however, carries his scientific documentation even farther
than Hill in that he has isolated in the foreground precisely
rendered breast and tail feathers. Not only is each of these
feathers clearly differentiated with regard to color and
shape, but each is also carefully placed adjacent to that
part of the body from which it came. Although the
compositions of both *Dead Bird* and *Anemones* (cat.
no. 84) are modeled after engravings by Hill, Brandegee's
works are distinctive in their use of crisp, stark details,
recalling a contemporary writer's comment that "his style
was somewhat after his master's but expressed withal an
independence and individuality. It was fresh, strong and
vigorous" (French, p. 158).   HPC

85

86

Writing to Mother   1869

Watercolor on paper
10 × 9½ (25.4 × 24.2)
Inscribed lower right: "Writing to Mother/Farmington/
January 10, 1869"
The Brooklyn Museum, Charles S. Smith Memorial Fund
PROVENANCE
The artist, 1922; Robert L. Brandegee, Salisbury, Connecticut, 1982;
The Brooklyn Museum.
EXHIBITED
The Brooklyn Museum, New York, *Homer, Sargent, and the American
Watercolor Tradition*, May 11–September 3, 1984.
REFERENCES
Blaugrund, p. 19; Ferber and Blaugrund, p. 314.

By 1869 Brandegee was capable of handling more
sophisticated and complex compositions. *Writing to
Mother* is not only a touching portrait of the artist's
younger brother Henry but also a genre painting that
includes a domestic setting in which each object is
depicted with great clarity. Henry, who like the artist
himself was probably sent away to school in Farmington,
Connecticut, is shown here as a devoted son and a diligent
student. His well-worn copy of the popular children's
magazine *Our Young Folks* is prominent among the
foreground accessories. Deep in concentration, the young
boy pens his letter. The manual and mental exertions of
the sitter bring to mind the efforts of the artist, who
likewise must have bent to his craft in order to create this
intricate watercolor.

86

An important link to Ruskinian technique in general and to the watercolors of Brandegee's early mentors, the Hills (q.v.) and Thomas C. Farrer (q.v.), in particular, is the brilliant color and use of stippling found in *Writing to Mother*. Stippling, which allows for a high degree of finish and the inclusion of precise detail, had been popularized by William Henry Hunt (q.v.), John Ruskin's (q.v.) favorite still-life painter, who was also singled out for praise in the writings of both John Henry Hill and Brandegee. Commenting on his experiences in London in 1872, Brandegee wrote, "Watercolors are better than oils and a little watercolor by William Hunt was about the finest thing I have seen so far" (manuscript autobiography of Robert Brandegee, Collection of Robert L. Brandegee, Salisbury, Connecticut).

A drawing close in subject to this watercolor is found on the cover of one of Brandegee's early sketchbooks (Collection of Robert L. Brandegee, Salisbury, Connecticut). There the subject's appearance offers intriguing parallels to the *Portrait of John Henry Hill* attributed to Robert J. Pattison (cat. no. 65). *Writing to Mother* also has the same small scale, intimate details, and candid viewpoint found in the highly detailed portrait drawings by Brandegee's teacher, Thomas C. Farrer (see cat. nos. 1–5).   HPC

87
Apple Blossoms   *circa* 1869

Watercolor on paper
4¾ × 4¾ (12.0 × 12.0)
Unsigned
Anonymous loan

PROVENANCE
The artist, 1922; Robert L. Brandegee, Salisbury, Connecticut, 1982; private collection.

EXHIBITED
(Possibly) NAD, *Third Winter Exhibition Including the Third Annual Collection of the American Society of Painters in Water Colors*, 1869–70, cat. no. 221.

This might be the picture of apple blossoms by Robert Brandegee that was entered and then withdrawn from the *Third Winter Exhibition* at the National Academy of Design in 1869. Since so few dated paintings are known from Brandegee's early period, which began around 1867 and ended in 1872 when the artist left for Europe, it is difficult to discuss his stylistic development during those years. Nevertheless, a date of *circa* 1869 seems appropriate for *Apple Blossoms*, since it has a compositional unity lacking in *Anemones* of 1867 (cat. no. 84) and a brilliant color and circular format strongly reminiscent of the 1869 watercolor *Writing to Mother* (cat. no. 86).

Apple blossoms, a humble subject matter with the potential for a realistic setting, were a favorite motif among the American Ruskinians. During the 1860s and '70s, they were painted by John William Hill (q.v.), William J. Hennessy (q.v.), George C. Lambdin (q.v.), and Martin Johnson Heade (q.v.), as well as by a number of now obscure women artists. In Brandegee's work the blossoms are dramatically cropped at the edges of the picture plane and silhouetted against a bright blue sky, a format he was well known for as early as 1879. "The bright sunshine and bold relief were courted in his subjects," wrote H.W. French. "They will be good qualities if held in obedience, and developed through careful education" (French, p. 158). *Apple Blossoms*, with its jewel-like colors, circular shape, and small scale, is an intimate work of great beauty.   HPC

87

Fidelia Bridges 1834–1923

Fidelia Bridges, an artist known chiefly for her small-scale watercolors of plant life and birds, was born May 19, 1834, in Salem, Massachusetts. Both her parents died when she was in her teens, and in October 1854 she followed her sisters to Brooklyn, where she took a position as governess to the three daughters of William A. Brown. By this time she had probably read John Ruskin's *Modern Painters* and seen English art available in New York. In May 1860, at the suggestion of her friend the sculptor Anne Whitney, she went to Philadelphia to study painting at the Pennsylvania Academy of the Fine Arts and with William Trost Richards (q.v.). Richards became her lifelong friend and professional mentor, instilling in her an appreciation for Ruskinian attention to detail and close focus on subjects from nature.

Bridges made a commitment to follow a career as an artist and in 1862 exhibited her first paintings at the Pennsylvania Academy; the following year she exhibited at both the Brooklyn Art Association and the National Academy of Design. She was elected an Associate of the National Academy in 1873 and continued to exhibit there until 1908. In 1875 she became a member of the American Society of Painters in Water Colors, a group she exhibited with from 1871 to 1912. Between March 1867 and the fall of 1868 she travelled with friends to Europe, visiting Paris, Darmstadt, Geneva, and Rome. She does not seem, however, to have been influenced by contemporary art there.

Bridges sold her first work, a series of paintings representing the months of the year, to the publisher Louis Prang in 1875, and in 1881 Prang made her one of his permanent designers, a position she held until 1899. Although she painted meticulously rendered watercolors in a high-keyed palette at the height of her career, the freshness of her approach and her meticulous technique were eventually affected by her commercial work for Prang and her late works demonstrate a self-conscious decorative arrangement and a broader stroke. She moved to Canaan, Connecticut, in 1880 and died there on March 14, 1923.

REFERENCES
BAA; May Brawley Hill, *Fidelia Bridges, American Pre-Raphaelite* (exhibition catalogue, Berry-Hill Galleries, New York, November 15, 1981-January 3,1982); NAD; PAFA; Frederic A. Scharf, "Fidelia Bridges, Painter of Birds and Flowers," *Essex Institute Historical Collections*, vol. 104, no. 3, 1968, pp. 217-238.

88

88
Study of Ferns *circa* 1863

Oil on panel
10 × 12 (25.4 × 30.5)
Inscribed lower right: "F Bridges"
Collection of Jean E. Taylor

PROVENANCE
(Possibly) S. Mills, 1863; [Gallery New World, Darien, Connecticut, early 1970s]; Jean E. Taylor.
EXHIBITED
(Possibly) BAA, March 1863, no. 1; Philadelphia, *The Pennsylvania Academy and its Women: 1850 to 1920*, May 3–June 16, 1974, pp. 32, 33, cat. no. 11, fig. 9.
REFERENCES
Ferber 1980 (a), pp. 161, 425, 500, fig. no. 129.

Although oil paintings by Bridges are quite rare, she is known to have worked in this medium for close to two decades, if not longer. The exhibition records of the Brooklyn Art Association reveal that except for four years she contributed at least one of her oils annually from 1863 until 1881. Her first entry, in March 1863, was titled *Study of Ferns*, and this is probably that work, since the inscription on the back gives the same title and states that the piece was painted in Brooklyn. Although she is known to have exhibited three different paintings of ferns in the 1860s, the 1863 listing is the only one with this exact title.

This oil is clearly related to similar treatments of the subject by Bridges' teacher, William T. Richards (q.v.), from 1859 to 1860, particularly his *Ferns in a Glade* (cat. no. 68; Ferber 1980 [b], p. 161). Both works are small-scale studies of ferns growing around a central tree cropped at the top by an arched frame. Bridges' technique, however, is considerably looser and more feathery than that of her mentor. Demonstrating her early proficiency in oils, the work also brings to mind a contemporary writer's comment that "she is as happy in the handling of oil-colors as those mixed with water" (Clement and Hutton, vol. I, p. 95).

Despite its small scale, *Study of Ferns* depicts a microcosm of nature that refers to biological cycles in its combination of decaying wood and growing trees. Throughout her career, Bridges seems to have favored the format used in this early work: close focus on foreground plant life, little or no middle ground, and a glimpse of the distant horizon.

Ferns were a particularly popular theme among the American Ruskinians. Richards, Henry R. Newman (q.v.), Thomas C. Farrer (q.v.), and Robert Brandegee (q.v.) were all known to have treated this subject at least once.   HPC

89
Calla Lily 1875

Watercolor on paper
14 × 10 (35.5 × 25.4)
Inscribed lower left: "/75"
The Brooklyn Museum, Museum Collection Fund

PROVENANCE
The artist; Oliver I. Lay, Canaan, Connecticut; George C. Lay, Stratford, Connecticut; [Berry-Hill Galleries, Inc., New York, 1981]; The Brooklyn Museum.
EXHIBITED
The Brooklyn Museum, New York, *Homer, Sargent, and the American Watercolor Tradition*, May 11–September 3, 1984.
REFERENCES:
May Brawley Hill, *Fidelia Bridges: American Pre-Raphaelite* (exhibition catalogue, New Britain Museum of American Art, Connecticut, November 15, 1981–January 3, 1982), pp. 22, 24, cat. no. 3; Blaugrund, p. 19.

Bridges' continued preoccupation during the 1870s with the close observation of plant life especially favored by the American Ruskinians is clearly illustrated in *Calla Lily*. A single flower is set against a neutral background of gray wash; no indication of the setting detracts from our intense scrutiny of this intrinsically beautiful specimen. The meticulous attention to botanical detail characteristic of Bridges' early plant studies has been combined in this work with a new breadth of handling, a feature that distinguishes her paintings from about 1880 onwards. Through a fluid and painterly application of the wash, Bridges has achieved a dramatic silhouette whose intricacy belies the seeming simplicity of the overall design.

Calla lilies were a particularly popular subject in the 1860s. The exhibition records of the Pennsylvania Academy of Fine Arts and the American Society of Painters in Water Colors list nine different depictions of this flower during those years, including works by George B. Wood, Jr. (q.v.), William Mason Brown (q.v.), George C. Lambdin (q.v), John Henry Hill (q.v.), and Thomas C. Farrer (q.v.). Bridges' interpretation is closest to that of Lambdin's oil painting of 1874, *Calla Lilies* (Berry-Hill Galleries, New York), with a similar viewpoint, undifferentiated background, and cropping of stem and leaf. Bridges would have known Lambdin in the early 1860s, when both lived in Philadelphia, and Lambdin is thought to have been a pupil of William T. Richards (q.v.). In the mid-1870s, she might have been influenced by Lambdin, who was the best-known flower painter of his generation, and whose works were popularized through numerous chromolithographs.   HPC

89

90
Milkweeds 1876

Watercolor on paper
16 × 9½ (40.6 × 24.1)
Inscribed lower left: "F Bridges 1876"
Munson-Williams-Proctor Institute
PROVENANCE
Proctor Collection; Munson-Williams-Proctor Institute.
EXHIBITED
E.B. Crocker Art Gallery, Sacramento, California, *Works from the Munson-Williams-Proctor Institute Collection*, October 25–November 25, 1974; AFA 1976, cat. no. 88.
REFERENCES
Stebbins 1976, pp. 157, 159, 426, fig. no. 126; Ferber 1980 (b), pp. 71, 73.

In its precise technique, close focus, and accumulation of accurate botanical details, *Milkweeds* illustrates how thoroughly Bridges had absorbed the tenets of John Ruskin's (q.v.) writings. Bridges' choice of subject matter, a common weed in its natural setting, is particularly telling because the English critic in *Modern Painters* had strongly advocated painting wild rather than cultivated plants. One of the duties of the artist, according to Ruskin, was "to distinguish between the real works of nature and the diseased results of man's interference with her ... It must be the pure, wild volition and energy of the creation which

[the artists] follow—not persuaded into proprieties, nor pampered into diseases" (Ruskin, vol.III, p. 627). Ruskin's influence is also apparent in the low viewpoint, where "we seem not to be looking at a distant prospect, but lying on the ground with herbage and blossom directly under our eyes" (Tuckerman, p. 524). In following Ruskin's tenets, painters like Bridges and William T. Richards (q.v.) began to challenge the traditional boundaries between pure flower painting and landscape art, thereby creating a new category of still life.

Though distinctive in its luminous and harmonious color, *Milkweeds* is dependent upon Richards' early 1860s oil paintings in its use of crisp botanical details and plant forms silhouetted against the sky. As Linda Ferber was the first to note, there is a similarity between Bridges' watercolor and Richards' unlocated oil painting *And Some Fell Among Thorns*. The religious implications of the latter—which takes its title from Matthew 13:7—may be applicable to the former, because it too juxtaposes vigorous weeds flourishing in a cultivated wheatfield. Symbolic intent, however, plays a secondary role to Bridges' interest in precisely recording wheat, weeds, grasses, and ferns in a realistic outdoor setting.   HPC

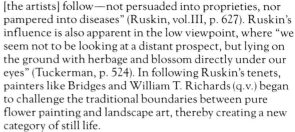

90

John George Brown 1831-1913

John George Brown is best known for his meticulously painted sentimental pictures of street urchins, but his earlier work, often of children outdoors, is characterized by a restrained sentimentality and a sensitivity to light, color, and natural details comparable to that of Winslow Homer (1836-1910) and Eastman Johnson (1824-1906).

Brown was born in Durham, England, on November 11, 1831, and at the age of fourteen was apprenticed for seven years to a glass cutter in Newcastle. When he was eighteen he began to study art at the local Government School of Design under William Bell Scott (1811-1890), a friend of Dante Gabriel Rossetti (1828-1882). Scott's work was somewhat influenced by the Pre-Raphaelite style, which paralleled his own meticulous topographical accuracy and use of stipple technique, and more than likely it was he who introduced Brown to Pre-Raphaelite painting at the inception of the Brotherhood.

Upon becoming a journeyman, Brown moved to Edinburgh to work in a glass cutting factory, studying in his spare time with Robert Scott Lauder (1803-1869) for a year at the Royal Scottish Academy. After winning a prize for drawing in 1853, he moved to London to try his hand at portraiture. Unsuccessful at that, he decided to emigrate to America, arriving in New York City on November 11, 1853, his twenty-second birthday. He soon found work in a Brooklyn glass factory where his employer, whose daughter he married in 1855, encouraged him to paint.

In 1856 Brown enrolled in Thomas Seir Cummings' class at the National Academy of Design and began his career as a professional artist by setting up a studio in Brooklyn. He began exhibiting at the Academy two years later and contributed pictures there almost yearly until the end of his life. By 1863 he was elected a National Academician. Between 1862 and 1869 he also exhibited at the Brooklyn Art Association, and at other times he exhibited at the Pennsylvania Academy and the Boston Athenaeum.

Brown rented a studio in the famous Tenth Street Studio Building in 1860 and remained in that space for fifty-three years. In addition to working six to ten hours daily, he found time to serve as Vice-President of the National Academy from 1899 to 1904, as President of the American Water Color Society from 1887 to 1905, and as President of the Artists' Fund Society in 1900. He also taught both privately and at the Academy school. A good businessman with a large family to support (after the death of his first wife he married her sister in 1867), he not only made money through his paintings, which brought high prices, but invested in New York real estate. Toward the end of his life he was earning from forty to fifty thousand dollars a year. He died in New York City on February 7, 1913.

REFERENCES
BA; BAA; S.G.W. Benjamin, "A Painter of the Streets" (*The Magazine of Art*), V, 1882, pp. 265-270; Philip Grim and Catherine Mazza, *John George Brown, A Reappraisal* (exhibition catalogue, The Robert Hull Fleming Museum, Burlington, Vt., The University of Vermont, April 14-May 10, 1975); NAD; PAFA; Sheldon; Obituary, February 9, 1913, *New York Times* and *New York Herald*.

91
Watching the Woodpecker   1866

Oil on canvas
18 × 12 (45.8 × 30.5)
Inscribed lower right: "J.G. Brown/1866"
Private collection

PROVENANCE
Private collection.
EXHIBITED
BAA, November 1867, no. 252.
REFERENCES
BAA, p. 136.

A paradigm of careful observation and meticulous painting, this work serves as a prime example of both Brown's technical skill and his capacity to introduce other levels of meaning into anecdotal genre. Trained in England by William Scott Bell (1811–1890), who wrote for *The Germ* in 1850, and by Robert Scott Lauder (1803–1869), Brown was well prepared for the Ruskinian approach to natural details. His concern for fidelity to nature is

91

revealed in his conscientious delineation of the lichen and moss on the rock, the furrows and texture of the bark of the tree, the particularization of the red-headed species of woodpecker, and the botanical exactitude of the vegetation. " ... [A]n artist should go direct to Nature and use his own eyes," he told his students (Sheldon, p. 143). One of his earlier pictures, *The Spring*, painted in 1864 with C.H. Moore (q.v.) and exhibited at the Brooklyn Art Association, testifies to his close connection with the American Pre-Raphaelites during this period.

Brown may have noticed a review in the November 1856 issue of *The Crayon* of John Everett Millais' *Autumn Leaves* (1855-56), by Frederick George Stephens (1828-1907), a Pre-Raphaelite who abandoned painting for writing (III, p. 324). Stephens commented on the picture's symbolic content at length; the season, the time of day, and even the children were all considered "senseless instruments of fate." Millais himself praised Stephen's sensitive analysis, saying that he "intended the picture to awaken by its solemnity the deepest religious reflection" (quoted in Malcolm Warner, "John Everett Millais's 'Autumn Leaves': a picture full of beauty and without subject," *Pre-Raphaelite Papers*, Leslie Parris, ed., London: The Tate Gallery, 1984, p. 127).

It is tempting to wonder whether Millais' work, painted ten years earlier, served as a prototype for Brown's *Watching the Woodpecker* or whether Brown was inspired by the work of Millais' followers, who utilized symbolic instead of narrative subjects. The fact is, Brown's painting echoes the melancholy mood and content of Millais'. The autumnal tone, the dying, half-chopped tree, the twilight hour, and the pensive state of the child—all suggest a meditation on the transience of life. Even the boldly colored bird, traditionally a symbol of the soul, adds to the iconography of mortality (James Hall, *Dictionary of Symbols in Art*, New York: Icon Edition, Harper and Row, 1974, p. 48).

Brown specialized in painting children in country settings during the 1860s and '70s but few of these paintings seem as laden with symbolic meaning as this work, although *Resting in the Woods* (Jo Ann and Julian Ganz, Jr. Collection), painted the same year, portrays a similarly pensive child. Here, the mood in the sun-dappled forest is evocative not of death but of spring, the nosegay in the girl's hand perhaps emblematic of the season. Later, in the allegorical *Picnic in the Woods* (1872), Brown treated the stages of life in a more direct fashion in genre form. "Morality in art? Of course there is. A picture can and should exert a moral influence," Brown said. But he expressed this concept more overtly in his moralizing pictures of city street urchins, which he painted with great success throughout his career, than in his rural genre scenes (Sheldon, p. 142). **AB**

William Mason Brown 1828–1898

William Mason Brown, principally remembered as a painter of fruit, was born in Troy, New York, in 1828. He studied with the area's leading portrait painter, Abel Buel Moore (1806-1827), and began his career as a portrait painter. When he moved to Newark, New Jersey, in 1850 he turned to landscapes, which although sometimes broadly painted reveal such traditional compositional components as meticulously painted foreground detail, water, and distant mountains. The tight painting and particularization of these elements of nature presage his change in the mid-sixties from romantic landscapes to crisply painted and meticulously detailed still lifes. Although little is known about his associations, given the number of fruit studies in which he used a natural setting instead of the conventional tabletop, it would seem that he was exposed to and affected by the Ruskinian dogma prevalent during the sixties, or at least by the work of artists who followed those tenets.

Brown moved to Brooklyn in 1858 and there achieved great success as a still-life artist, selling his work for as much as two thousand dollars. He exhibited annually at the National Academy of Design from 1859 to 1891 and at the Brooklyn Art Association from 1865 to 1886. His hard-edge compositions were well-suited to reproduction in chromolithography, and many of his paintings were published (including *Apples* by Currier and Ives in 1868), thus affording him a wide popular audience. For all his success he never became a member of the National Academy of Design and apparently never travelled abroad. He died in Brooklyn on September 6, 1898.

REFERENCES
BAA; Wilmerding, Ayres & Powell; Gerdts 1981; NAD.

92
Raspberries

Oil on canvas
20 × 16 (50.8 × 40.6)
Inscribed lower right: "WMB"
The J.B. Speed Art Museum, Louisville, Kentucky

PROVENANCE
[Fifth Avenue Art Galleries, New York, January 1907]; Mrs. Hattie
Bishop Speed, 1927; The J.B. Speed Art Museum.
EXHIBITED
Newark 1974; Hunt Institute for Botanical Documentation, Pittsburgh,
Pennsylvania, April–July, 1976; Philbrook 1981.
REFERENCES
Gerdts & Burke, p. 68, illus. p. 82 (fig. 5–24); Gerdts 1974, pp. 9, 63, illus.
p. 62; The J.B. Speed Art Museum, *A Checklist of Drawings, Paintings,
and Sculpture in the J.B. Speed Art Museum 1927–1977* (Louisville,
Kentucky: The J.B. Speed Art Museum, 1978), p. 38.

Raspberries stands as a prime example of the still-life
subject for which William Mason Brown is best known.
Immediately apparent here are the high color and
hard-edged detail that lent themselves well to the
chromolithographic process. Like his contemporary
George Henry Hall (cat. no. 108), Brown often employed
a natural setting as a backdrop, a practice which can now
easily be seen as a residual effect of Ruskinian influence.
There is detectable in this painting, however, a duality in
his approach to nature that is antithetical to Ruskinian
doctrine. The individual berries, the sheltering bush, the
wild flowers, and the grassy patch of earth are uniformly
executed in a fashion comparable to that of Ruskin's
closest followers. Yet the berries do not appear as they
would in nature; the artist's hand has intervened in order
to create a pleasing composition. This feature, along with
the stage-like setting and theatrical lighting, introduces
an artificial note which suggests that however veristic it all
may seem, this is a composition that originated in the
studio and not in nature.   BDG

92

Frederic Edwin Church 1826-1900

Frederic E. Church was one of the most successful artists of his day, producing highly popular monumental paintings ranging in subject from the tropical splendors of South America to the awesome icebergs of Labrador to the vast wilderness of the United States. Born in Hartford, Connecticut, on May 4, 1826, he received his first artistic training from Benjamin H. Coe (1799-after 1883) and Alexander H. Emmons (1816-?). With the aid of Hartford's leading patron, Daniel Wadsworth, he moved to Catskill, New York, to study with Thomas Cole (1801-1848) from 1844 to 1846 and began to exhibit his work, which at first showed Cole's influence, at the National Academy of Design in 1845. He opened a studio in New York in 1847 and had two students, William J. Stillman (q.v.) from 1847 to 1848 and Jervis McEntee (1828-1891) from 1850 to 1851. In 1849 he was elected a full member of the National Academy of Design. During this period his realistic landscapes contained carefully delineated foregrounds reflective of his knowledge of Ruskinian theories.

Caught up in the mid-nineteenth-century interest in travel and exploration and inspired by Alexander von Humboldt's *Cosmos*, among other scientific books, Church visited the Andes Mountains of Columbia and Equador in 1853. This trip produced a series of large paintings of tropical subjects including his famous *Heart of the Andes* (1852, Metropolitan Museum of Art). Realizing the potential of the oil sketch, he made a number of plein-air sketches (few of which survive) that recorded his observations of natural detail. After a visit in 1856 to Niagara Falls, a subject which became his first great success, he returned to Ecuador in 1857 with fellow artist Louis Remy Mignot (1831-1870).

Although Church maintained a room in New York's Tenth Street Studio Building from 1858 to 1887, he continued to travel in quest of new and exotic scenery. He sailed to Newfoundland and Labrador with the writer Louis Noble in 1859, went to Jamaica with the artist Horace Walcott Robbins, Jr. (1842-1904), in 1865, and took an extensive European and Near Eastern tour with his family from 1867 to 1869. His paintings from these journeys display the romantic and the spiritual aspects of his work with carefully observed botanical, geological, and atmospheric details.

In 1870 Church commenced work on a villa he called Olana overlooking the Hudson River in Hudson, New York, a project which occupied him for many years. By 1877 he began to suffer from inflammatory rheumatism, and his output declined. Until his death on April 17, 1900, in New York City, he spent his summers either at Olana or in Maine and his winters in Mexico.

REFERENCES
Frederic Edwin Church (exhibition catalogue, National Collection of Fine Arts, Washington, D.C., 1966); David Carew Huntington, *Frederic Edwin Church, 1826-1900: Painter of the Adamic New World Myth* (Ph.D. dissertation, Yale University, 1960).

93
Natural Bridge, Virginia 1852

Oil on canvas
28 × 23 (71.1 × 58.4)
Inscribed lower center: "F.E. Church, 1852"
University of Virginia Art Museum, Charlottesville, gift of Thomas Fortune Ryan, 1912

PROVENANCE
The artist; Cyrus W. Field; Thomas Fortune Ryan, 1912; University of Virginia.

EXHIBITED
RA 1852, no. 1089 as *Natural Bridge in Virginia, U.S.A.*; NAD, 1853, no. 105, lent by Cyrus W. Field; The Mint Museum of Art, Charlotte, North Carolina, *10th Anniversary Exhibition*, October 1946, no. 29; National Collection of Fine Arts, Smithsonian Institution, Washington, D.C., *American Landscape, A Changing Frontier*, April 28-June 19, 1966, unnumbered checklist, p. 3; The National Gallery of Art, Washington, D.C., *The Eye of Thomas Jefferson*, June 5-September 6, 1976, no. 582; duPont Gallery, Washington and Lee University, Lexington, Virginia, *So Beautiful an Arch: Images of the Natural Bridge*, January 4-29, 1982, no. 27.

REFERENCES
William Howard Adams, ed., *The Eye of Thomas Jefferson* (exhibition catalogue, The National Gallery of Art, Washington, D.C., 1976), illus. p. 337; William Howard Adams, "Thomas Jefferson and the Art of the Garden," *Apollo*, n.s. vol. 104 (September 1976), illus. p. 92; Pamela H. Simpson, *So Beautiful an Arch: Images of the Natural Bridge* (exhibition catalogue, du Pont Gallery, Washington and Lee University, Lexington, Virginia, 1982), p. 27, illus. cover.

"To behold it without rapture, indeed, is impossible; and the more critically it is examined, the more beautiful and the more surprising does it appear." This reaction to the great Natural Bridge of Virginia by the British traveller Isaac Weld, Jr., typifies the attitude toward this natural wonder that prevailed throughout the first half of the nineteenth century. Visitors, both foreign and American, were drawn to the Bridge, which, in its awesome sublimity, had as its only rival Niagara Falls (Isaac Weld, Jr., *Travels Through the States of North America and the Provinces of Upper and Lower Canada, during the Years 1795, 1796, and 1797*, London, 1807, 4th edition, vol. 1, p. 223).

Church visited the Natural Bridge in the summer of 1851 in the company of his friend Cyrus West Field (1819-1892). According to Field's daughter, Field asked Church to make a sketch of the Bridge from which a painting could later be made. Out of concern for accuracy, Field suggested that Church collect rock samples in order to have a model for color in the studio. Church declared this unnecessary, and when the finished painting was delivered the following winter, Field, who had retained the samples, discovered that the artist had indeed accurately reproduced the color from memory (Isabella P. Judson, *Cyrus W. Field, His Life and Work*, New York, 1896, p. 39).

Church's *Natural Bridge* falls within a period of transition in his work: he is emerging from the romantic, idealized landscape tradition embodied in the work of his teacher Thomas Cole (1801-1848) and taking the advice of the German naturalist Alexander von Humboldt (1769-1859), who advised his readers to focus "on the true image of the varied forms of nature" (Alexander von Humboldt, *Cosmos*, II, London, 1849, p. 452). The detailed treatment of the landscape formation on a small scale reveals that he had arrived at a vision close to the Ruskinian ideal for a brief moment before going on to paint his famous cosmic epics of the New World.   BDG

93

94
Century Plant April–August 1865

Oil and pencil on board
8½ × 11¼ (21.6 × 28.6)
Unsigned
The Cooper-Hewitt Museum, the Smithsonian Institution's
National Museum of Design

PROVENANCE
The artist; Louis P. Church, 1917; Cooper Union Museum for the Arts
of Decoration (now The Cooper-Hewitt Museum, the Smithsonian
Institution's National Museum of Design).
EXHIBITED
Graham Gallery, New York, *Frederic Edwin Church*, December 17,
1974–January 11, 1975; Smithsonian Institution Traveling Exhibition
Service, *Close Observation: Selected Oil Sketches by Frederic E. Church*,
1978–1980, no. 51 (Museum of Fine Arts, Boston, Massachusetts;
University Art Gallery, University of Pittsburgh, Pennsylvania; Ulrich
Museum of Art, Wichita State University, Kansas; University of
Michigan Museum of Art, Ann Arbor; Elvehjem Museum of Art,
University of Wisconsin, Madison; Corcoran Gallery of Art,
Washington, D.C.; Brunnier Gallery, Iowa State University, Ames;
Nelson Gallery-Atkins Museum, Kansas City, Missouri).
REFERENCES
Theodore E. Stebbins, Jr., *Close Observation: Selected Oil Sketches by*
Frederic E. Church (exhibition catalogue, Smithsonian Institution Press,
Washington, D.C., 1978), p. 35, illus., p. 76; Peggy D. Kutzen, "Frederic
Edwin Church," *Arts Magazine*, vol. 55, no. 1 (September 1980), p. 13.

95
Cardamum June 1865

Oil and pencil on board
11 × 8½ (27.9 × 21.6)
Inscribed lower left: "Jamaica/June '65"
(Although the date as it is inscribed appears to be 1867,
microscopic examination reveals that it is 1865.)
Inscribed lower left on leaf: "Cardamum"
The Cooper-Hewitt Museum, the Smithsonian Institution's
National Museum of Design

PROVENANCE
The artist; Louis P. Church, 1917; Cooper Union Museum for the Arts
of Decoration (now The Cooper-Hewitt Museum, the Smithsonian
Institution's National Museum of Design).
EXHIBITED
Graham Gallery, New York, *Frederic Edwin Church*, December 17,
1974–January 11, 1975; Whitney 1984.
REFERENCES
Novak, pp. 119, 122, illus. p. 126 (fig. 64); Foshay, p. 48, illus. p. 49.

94

Both of these studies belong to a body of work, remarkable for its variety, quality, and volume, which came out of the four months Church spent in Jamaica starting in April 1865. The artist's decision to explore the tropical island attests to his continued preoccupation with the New World landscape theme, an interest inspired by the writings of Alexander von Humboldt, which had spurred his South American expeditions of 1853 and 1857. Humboldt had called for artists to study all aspects of the New World and recommended as part of that process the preparation of separate studies of plant life taken directly from nature. Church was well aware of the methodology prescribed by Humboldt prior to his South American travels, just as he was also conversant with the writings of John Ruskin (q.v.). Yet neither trip in the 1850s resulted in studies that suggest an application of Humboldt's or Ruskin's advice in any but the broadest of terms.

Here, however, in his Jamaican studies, Church adopted the detail and format of the natural-setting still life to provide an unusually myopic view of the individual plant or blossom. While little effort was made to eliminate evidence of the brush stroke, the paint was applied smoothly and sparingly so as to permit the full expression of botanical detail. A possible explanation for the emergence of this intensified vision in some of Church's Jamaican studies may be that by 1865 Ruskinian attitudes had become part of the visual as well as theoretical currency in American art. Therefore, these studies may signify a response to the work of contemporary artists in addition to the often parallel ideas present in the writings of Humboldt and Ruskin.   BDG

95

John B. Duffey 1828/29–after 1876

In the world of art the name of John B. Duffey has until now been unknown. The elusive Duffey exhibited two paintings at the Pennsylvania Academy in 1866, both of which have been credited with question to his wife, Mrs. E.B. Duffey (1838–1898), the former Eliza Bisbee, another obscure artist mentioned in the annals of still-life painting, who exhibited eight paintings, mostly flower and fruit subjects, between 1865 and 1868 at the Pennsylvania Academy. Surprisingly, considering her limited output, Mrs. Duffey was made an associate member of that Academy in 1869.

New information about John B. Duffey's short-lived career, however, has now come to light in a letter Duffey wrote to the dealer-collector Samuel P. Avery on September 10, 1866. Avery had apparently bought one or two of Duffey's paintings, and when he sent payment he requested a biography of the artist. Duffey explained that "even as yet [he had] scarcely made up [his] mind to embrace art as a profession," but that his "fancy for art" had begun at age twelve when he had the privilege of watching the portrait painter and sculptor William Walcutt (1819–1882 or '95), who was then working in Columbus, Ohio. Duffey apparently spent part of his youth in Ohio during the mid-forties and may have met his wife there since she was born in Ohio. Lacking the perseverance to pursue a career as an artist, he had since the age of twenty held such varied positions in the literary field as newspaper editor, typesetter, and "book-maker."

Duffey is listed in the Philadelphia directory between 1861 and 1863 as an editor and in 1864, for the first time, as an artist as well as an editor. His earliest known work, painted in Woodbury, New Jersey, is dated 1860. Thus he must have moved to Philadelphia the following year, and according to his letter took up painting "with serious intentions" when he lost his employment during the second year of the Civil War, around 1863.

While painting Duffey persisted in his literary activities, working as a translator with the ambition "to convey with 'High Dutch' poetry into the vulgar tongue." Although he also indulged in some form of agriculture, which he declared a "hygienic necessity," he was most successful at painting. During this period he produced "little Pre-Raphaelite sketches" painted so "incredibly slow" that he could never be adequately compensated for his time. He was aware of the Ruskinian concept of rendering "a tolerably faithful transcript of Nature" and felt better equipped to handle this than subjects which required imagination. One of the paintings owned by Avery was titled *Nothing But Leaves* and was lent to the Artists' Fund Society exhibition in New York in 1866.

By 1867 Duffey had moved back to Woodbury, where his wife had bought a cottage and some land. The two of them remained there until 1872 when they sold the property back to its original owner. The 1870 census for Deptford Township, Gloucester County, New Jersey, lists Duffey as a forty-one-year-old New York-born artist with four daughters; Eliza is listed as a thirty-two-year-old Ohio-born housewife. The following year, however, she wrote in a letter that she was assistant editor of *Arthur's Home Magazine* and *Godey's Ladies Book*, and she is remembered for several popular books about women and etiquette. John Duffey also wrote for *Arthur's Home Magazine* and published one book, *Lives and Portraits of All the Presidents from Washington to Grant*, in 1876. Although

the Duffeys are not recorded in the Woodbury or Philadelphia directories in the seventies and eighties, they surely lived in that vicinity because all their literary activities centered around Philadelphia. No paintings by either artist dated after 1870 have been recorded or located, leading to the belief that they must have dedicated the rest of their lives to literary endeavors.

REFERENCES
I am grateful to May Hill for disclosing the existence and whereabouts of Duffey's letter to Avery in the Avery Autograph Collection of the Metropolitan Museum of Art Library and to William H. Gerdts for the use of the Gerdts Art Reference Library and Archive, City University Graduate Center; for the material in the National Union Catalogue; and for his generosity in leading me to a good deal of the new material in this biography. I am also indebted to Edith Holley, Librarian at the Gloucester County Historical Society for providing the following information: a letter da ed March 27, 1871, at the Society; the 1850 Burlington County census; the 1870 Gloucester County Federal census; the deed books at the Gloucester County Court House (G5, p. 83, August 9, 1867, and N5, p. 488, October 14, 1872); and *Allibone's Dictionary of Authors*, vol. 1, supplement, p. 519.

Columbus, Ohio, City Directories 1843-1846, information courtesy of Dennis East, Chief, Archives-Library Division of Ohio Historical Society; Christine Huber, *The Pennsylvania Academy and its Women* (exhibition catalogue, Pennsylvania Academy of Fine Arts, Philadelphia, May 3-June 16, 1974); *The National Union Catalogue*; PAFA.

96
October 1860

Oil on canvas
14⅛ × 12 (35.8 × 30.5)
Inscribed lower right: "J.B. Duffey/1860"
Cyrus Seymour

PROVENANCE
[George Guerry Gallery, New York, *circa* 1960]; Cyrus Seymour.
REFERENCES
Attributed to Mrs. E.B. Duffey in Gerdts 1964, pp. 108, 109; Gerdts 1969, pp. 81, 83.

Although Duffey wrote that "it was not until the 2nd yr of the 'rebellion' [*circa* 1862] that . . . I took up the pencil agn with serious intentions," he did paint this precisely rendered still life in 1860. He stated that he did "best in little Pre-Raph sketches" (Duffey to Samuel P. Avery, September 10, 1866, Avery Autograph Letters, Art Reference Library, The Metropolitan Museum of Art, New York), and *October*, his only known work, has the humble subject matter, meticulous technique, natural outdoor setting, and seemingly informal arrangement that characterize the still-life paintings of other American Pre-Raphaelites. Another stylistic connection between *October* and the works of this circle is the combination of a detailed and closely viewed foreground with the sort of distant view that John Ruskin (q.v.) discussed at length in *Modern Painters*. "[I]f, on the contrary, we look at any foreground object so as to receive a distinct impression of it," Ruskin wrote, "the distance and middle distance becomes all disorder and mystery. And therefore, if in a painting our foreground is anything, our distance must be nothing, and *vice versa*" (Ruskin, vol. I, p. 321). *October* aptly demonstrates this approach because the botanical accuracy of the foreground leaves and plants is in marked contrast to the loosely painted and abbreviated background.

In its mixture of growing wild flowers and dead leaves and branches, *October* evokes not only the month that signifies the passing of summer's vitality and the onset of winter's hibernation but also the entire seasonal progression. Such seasonal and cyclical motifs are also found in the works of William T. Richards and Fidelia

Bridges (see cat. nos. 70 and 88). Another compositional link is established with the paintings of these two Philadelphia artists in the way the form of the gentian in *October* is dramatically silhouetted against the sky. (Dr. Stephen K-M. Tim, Director of Scientific Affairs, Brooklyn Botanic Garden, kindly identified this plant.) Although the artist's inscription on the back states that *October* was painted in Woodbury, New Jersey, Duffey was probably familiar with the works of Richards and Bridges because, like them, he exhibited at the Pennsylvania Academy of the Fine Arts in the 1860s.   HPC

96

Robert Spear Dunning   1829–1905

Robert Spear Dunning, the leader of the Fall River School of still-life painting, was born in Brunswick, Maine, on January 3, 1829. When he was five, his family, reputed to be descendants of the Earl of Ashburton, moved to Fall River, Massachusetts, where his father built the first marine railway. He was educated in the local public schools and in his early years worked in one of the town's textile mills. He also spent three years working on coastal vessels before beginning his art studies with James Roberts in Tiverton, Rhode Island, around 1844.

In 1849 Dunning moved to New York, where he studied with Daniel Huntington (1816–1906) for three years. Under the influence of his teacher, he exhibited at the American Art-Union in 1850 a fairly large genre painting, *The Grandfather's Guide*, which was bought by John William Hill (q.v.). His other early works were portraits and genre subjects which he exhibited at the National Academy of Design in 1850 and 1851.

Dunning returned to Fall River in 1852 and remained there the rest of his life, marrying Mehitable D. Hill on December 6, 1869. Adding landscapes to his repertoire, he exhibited in Boston and Rhode Island and only once again at the Academy in 1880. In 1859 he entered into an artistic partnership with John Grouard (1824–1887), an artist about whom little is known, and in 1870 they founded the Fall River Evening Drawing School. He also taught privately, and according to one of his pupils, Mary L. Macomber, was a stickler for the highest quality materials, careful craftsmanship, and individuality.

Although Dunning began to specialize in still-life painting, the hallmark of the Fall River School, in 1865, he continued to paint portraits of many prominent Fall River citizens. In 1892, after raising one thousand dollars for the purpose by public subscription, the Washington Society of Fall River commissioned him to copy the Gilbert Stuart portrait of Washington that hung in the old State House in Newport, Rhode Island. He remained active and successful until the end of his life and died at his summer home in Westport Harbor, Massachusetts, on August 12, 1905.

REFERENCES
I am indebted to Michael Martins of the Fall River Historical Society for supplying much of the information about Dunning.

AA-U; Fall River Library Memorial Exhibition, December 14–28, 1905; Gerdts & Burke; *American Art Annual* 1905–06, vol. V, p. 120; Groce & Wallace; Letter from Dunning to Robert Vose, December 12, 1901, Vose Galleries, Boston; NAD.

97
Harvest of Cherries   1866
Formerly known as *Cherries in Basket and Hat*
Oil on canvas
20 × 26½ (50.8 × 67.3)
Inscribed lower right: "R.S. Dunning 1866"
Inscribed verso: "R.S. Dunning 1866"
Terra Museum of American Art, Evanston, Illinois
PROVENANCE
[William Doyle Galleries, New York, October 24, 1984]; [Berry-Hill Galleries, Inc., New York, October 1984]; Terra Museum of American Art.
EXHIBITED
Goupil & Co., New York, March 1866.
REFERENCES
Important 19th and 20th Century American Paintings and Sculpture (auction catalogue, William Doyle Galleries, New York, October 24, 1984), illus. no. 36.

Robert Spear Dunning's *Harvest of Cherries* occupies a unique position within his recorded oeuvre in that its combination of precise technique and natural-setting still-life motif suggests a pronounced Ruskinian orientation. Contrary to the visual evidence supplied here, Dunning's connections with John Ruskin (q.v.) appear to have been tangential. Although he was studying in New York with Daniel Huntington when *Modern Painters* experienced its first wave of popularity, there is nothing to indicate that he ever made Ruskinian theory a primary concern.

On the other hand, by 1866 Dunning is likely to have seen examples of American art whose inspiration from Ruskin was manifested in this particular type of composition. His move to Fall River, Massachusetts, in 1852 would not have precluded the occasional trip to New York to keep abreast of current trends, nor would it have prevented access to contemporary criticism in periodical literature. Furthermore, the fact he later encouraged his students to investigate all styles of art suggests that he was receptive to new ideas and therefore willing to experiment.

It is in the context of an experiment that this painting must be considered, for it stands apart from the tabletop compositions Dunning usually provided for his still-life subjects. In 1866 Dunning had been painting still lifes for only two years and, as a relative newcomer to the genre, would have been open to motifs of demonstrated popularity, or, in this case, the natural-setting format.

However, even if Dunning borrowed this motif with knowledge of its Ruskinian associations, he does not appear to have adopted the theory attached to it. The strong narrative elements introduced by the juxtaposition of the man's and woman's hats lying in the luxuriant grass are not strictly in keeping with Ruskin's advocacy of truth to nature: the philosophical commitment to the purity of the natural scene is absent, replaced by a content which reaches far beyond Ruskinian intentions. Stylistic sources aside, contemporary press notices contained generous praise for this painting. One writer declared it to be the finest still-life picture in New York, while another wrote, "A 'Harvest of Cherries' by Denning [sic] of Boston is a decided attraction . . . and is worth a journey from Trinity to Grace Church on foot to see, to the laziest among us. The basket and the hats and the cherries, as they lie upon the sward waiting the presence of their owners, are among the best representatives on canvas of chip and straw and the stony-hearted fruit we have seen for many days" (*New York Times*, March 12, p. 6, col. 3).

Interestingly, Dunning painted another unusual still life which, although set in a darkened interior, exhibits similar thematic aims and features the same man's straw hat found in *Harvest of Cherries* (private collection, reproduced in Gerdts & Burke, p. 168, plate xxi). While that work's facture and thematic approach correspond with those of the painting here, the elimination of the natural setting erases any hint of a Pre-Raphaelite connection. (I am grateful to James Berry Hill of Berry-Hill Galleries, Inc. for bringing the contemporary newspaper notices of this work to my attention.)   BDG

97

Asher Brown Durand   1796–1886

A leader of the Hudson River landscapists, Asher B. Durand was highly regarded for his paintings, his engravings, and his essays on painting. Born August 21, 1796, in what is now Maplewood, New Jersey, he began his career as an apprentice to Newark engraver Peter Maverick from 1812 to 1817, subsequently became a partner in the firm, and then moved to New York City. After being commissioned to engrave John Trumbull's (1756–1843) painting of the *Declaration of Independence* in 1820, he started his own business, establishing a reputation as a skillful engraver that brought him such other important projects as the engraving of bank notes, book illustrations, and portraits after paintings. In the 1830s, while beginning to concentrate on painting, he produced the engravings for *The American Landscape* with text by William Cullen Bryant, the plates for the *National Portrait Gallery of Distinguished Americans* (1832–40), and an engraving after John Vanderlyn's *Ariadne* (1835).

Portraits dominated Durand's early work, but towards the end of the 1830s, under the influence of Thomas Cole (1801–1848), he began to concentrate on landscape. From June 1840 to June 1841 he made the requisite grand tour of Europe with John F. Kensett (1816–1872), John W. Casilear (1811–1893), and Thomas P. Rossiter (1818–1871). After

Cole's death in 1848, he was acknowledged as the foremost American landscape artist. A founding member of the National Academy of Design in 1825, he served as its President from 1845 to 1861.

Durand, who was a deeply religious man, shared with John Ruskin (q.v.) a reverence for nature. He was one of the earliest American painters to give up conventional compositional models based upon European prototypes and to paint directly in response to what he actually saw in nature. His nine "Letters on Landscape Painting," published in *The Crayon* (co-edited by his son John), influenced many contemporary artists to draw and paint on the spot and to record nature realistically.

By 1875 Durand's health had declined and his output decreased. He died in the town in which he was born on September 17, 1886, and is buried in Greenwood Cemetery in Brooklyn.

REFERENCES
Montclair 1971; Lawall.

98
Landscape: Creek and Rocks   *circa* 1850s
Oil on canvas
17 × 26 (43.2 × 66.0)
Unsigned
Pennsylvania Academy of the Fine Arts

98

PROVENANCE
Charles Henry Hart, 1915; Pennsylvania Academy of the Fine Arts, Philadelphia.
EXHIBITED
Two Hundred Years of American Art, an exhibition organized by the Pennsylvania Academy of the Fine Arts, which travelled to seven museums in the southern United States, September 18, 1970–July 31, 1971; Pennsylvania Academy of the Fine Arts, Philadelphia, *Held in Trust*, June 23–August 26, 1973, no. 56; Cincinnati Art Museum, Ohio, *Masterpieces of American Painting from the Pennsylvania Academy of the Fine Arts*, October 5–November 10, 1974, no. 21; Pennsylvania Academy of the Fine Arts, Philadelphia, *In This Academy: The Pennsylvania Academy of the Fine Arts, 1805–1976*, special Bicentennial exhibition organized by the Pennsylvania Academy of the Fine Arts, 1976, no. 166.
REFERENCES
Pennsylvania Academy of the Fine Arts, *Check List: Paintings, Sculptures, Miniatures from the Permanent Collection* (Philadelphia, 1969), p. 15; Pennsylvania Academy of the Fine Arts, *Masterpieces of American Painting from the Collection of the Pennsylvania Academy of the Fine Arts* (Philadelphia, 1974), illus. p. 29; David B. Lawall, *Asher B. Durand: A Documentary Catalogue of the Narrative and Landscape Paintings* (New York and London: Garland Publishing, Inc., 1978), no. 345, fig. 188.

99

Study of Wood Interior *circa* 1850s

Oil on canvas
17 × 24 (43.2 × 60.9)
Unsigned
Addison Gallery of American Art, Phillips Academy, Andover, Massachusetts, gift of Mrs. Frederic Durand

PROVENANCE
The artist's family, 1932; Addison Gallery of American Art.
EXHIBITED
Whitney Museum of American Art, New York, *Loan Exhibition of 19th Century Paintings from the Addison Gallery of American Art*, March 28–April 27, 1933; Whitney Museum of American Art, New York, *A Century of American Landscape Painting, 1800–1900*, January 19–February 25, 1938, no. 15; The Baltimore Museum of Art, *Romanticism in America*, May 10–August 21, 1940; The Century Association, New York, *Exhibition of Paintings by Asher B. Durand, 1796–1886*, January 14–February 12, 1943, no. 8; Columbia Museum of Art, Columbia, South Carolina, *Landscape in Art: Origin and Development*, January 17–February 26, 1967, no. 50; Montclair 1971, no. 69.

REFERENCES
Addison Gallery of American Art, *Supplement to the Catalogue* (Andover, 1933), p. 4; Addison Gallery of American Art, *Handbook of Paintings, Sculpture, Prints and Drawings in the Permanent Collection* (Andover: Phillips Academy, 1939), illus. p. 18; Montclair 1971, p. 69, illus. p. 93; Lawall, p. 364, illus. fig. 120; David B. Lawall, *Asher B. Durand: A Documentary Catalogue of the Narrative and Landscape Paintings* (New York and London: Garland Publishing, Inc., 1978), no. 356, fig. 199.

Asher B. Durand's allegiance to the code of "truth to nature" is evidenced by the high degree of detail displayed by these oil studies. Credited with being the first American artist to make such studies directly from nature (having done so perhaps as early as 1832), Durand had already formulated the core of his landscape aesthetic by the time his "Letters on Landscape Painting" appeared in *The Crayon* in 1855. Yet because of the frequency of John Ruskin's (q.v.) writings in American publications—particularly in *The Crayon*—it is tempting to look to the English critic as a source of Durand's inspiration when he was faced with the challenge of putting his ideas into words.

Although Durand's awareness of Ruskin cannot be doubted, the question of Ruskin's impact on him remains open, since Durand is silent on the subject. Both men saw nature as a vehicle for attaining greater knowledge of the divine spirit, and, to this end, both emphasized the value of foreground study. The specificity required by Ruskin in *Modern Painters* (". . . and so a rock must be either one rock or another rock; it cannot be a general rock, or it is no rock") is mirrored in Durand's call for "portraiture" in representing rocks, tree trunks, grass, and banks of earth (Ruskin, vol. III, p. 33; Asher B. Durand, "Letters on Landscape Painting—No. V," *The Crayon*, vol. I, no. 10, March 7, 1855, p. 145). Durand adhered to this rigid approach to form in a limited way, however, seeing attention to minutiae as merely a step in accomplishing a true representation of the object in its most characteristic form and not as an end in itself. Because of this, his finished landscapes rarely exhibit the level of detail demonstrated in these studies.   BDG

99

Henry Farrer 1843–1903

Henry Farrer, younger brother of Thomas Charles Farrer (q.v.), was born in London on March 23, 1843, and is best remembered for his delicate watercolors and etchings. Little is known about his childhood or early training, but it is said that he was self-taught. At the age of nineteen he emigrated to the United States and opened a studio in New York City where he painted landscapes, predominantly in watercolor but occasionally in oil. He does not seem to have been a formal member of the Association for the Advancement of Truth in Art although his brother was its primary organizer. He was, however, a founding member of the American Society of Painters in Water Color in 1866 and was secretary of that organization for many years.

In 1867 Farrer exhibited for the first time at both the National Academy of Design and the Brooklyn Art Association. Influenced by Ruskinian principles via his brother, his early work demonstrates the characteristic attention to detail, close focus, and meticulous brushwork of the American Ruskinians.

Sometime around 1868, inspired by French etchings he saw exhibited in New York, Farrer built his own etching press and began his first attempts at etching by making precise topographical views featuring scenes of New York buildings. About 1871–72 these efforts resulted in a series of eleven pictures published under the title *Old New York*. Although financial necessity forced him to give up etching for a time, he later returned to it. He was one of the founders of the New York Etching Club and became its President in 1881. He was also elected a member of the Royal Society of Painter Etchers in London and an honorary member of the Philadelphia Society of Painter Etchers. About 1878 he returned to England for a visit.

During the 1880s Farrer maintained a studio in New York's Tenth Street Studio Building, there developing a freer, looser style. He lived in Brooklyn from about 1887 until his death on February 23, 1903, and was an avid collector of Oriental art objects.

REFERENCES
BAA; *Biographical Sketches of American Artists* (Lansing: Michigan State Library, 1924); S.R. Koehler, "The Works of the American Etchers. II Henry Farrer," *The American Art Review*, 1880, vol. 1, pp. 55–56; Koke; NAD.

100
Peaches and Plums *circa* early 1860s
Watercolor on paper
4½ × 6½ (11.4 × 16.5), sight
Inscribed lower right: "H.F."
Private collection
PROVENANCE
Private collection.

101
Carnations 1864
Watercolor on paper
3¾ × 7¾ (9.5 × 19.7), sight
Inscribed lower left: "H. Farrer. 1864"
The Brooklyn Museum, purchased with funds given by Mr. and Mrs. Leonard L. Milberg
PROVENANCE
The artist; William Collier Bross; William Warren Bross; Mr. and Mrs. Robert L. Thompson, 1984; The Brooklyn Museum.

100

102

Pink Rose 1871

Watercolor on paper
3⅝ × 7⅝ (9.2 × 19.4), sight
Inscribed lower left: "H. Farrer 1871"
*The Brooklyn Museum, purchased with funds given
by Mr. and Mrs. Leonard L. Milberg*
PROVENANCE
The artist; William Collier Bross; William Warren Bross;
Mr. and Mrs. Robert L. Thompson, 1984; The Brooklyn Museum.

In view of Henry Farrer's long-standing identification with
the American Pre-Raphaelite movement and the fact he
was the brother of Thomas C. Farrer (q.v.), it might seem
curious that he was not a member of the Association for
the Advancement of Truth in Art. Yet when the Association was founded, Henry Farrer was only twenty years old,
and doubtless still ranked as a student rather than as a
professional artist. Thus, youth and inexperience probably
account for his exclusion from membership.

Each of these three paintings represents a step along
Farrer's path to proficiency in the watercolor medium. All
exhibit his compliance with the Ruskinian imperative to
place objects originating in nature against a neutral
ground. The surface on which they rest acts as both a

support and a backdrop, a spatial ambiguity that may be
a result of Ruskin's direction to work with the drawing
paper on an incline. One of the most telling indicators of
Farrer's progress is the increasing refinement revealed in
the gradation of the background: the rough hatching
strokes found in *Peaches and Plums* ultimately give way
to the relatively uniform (and less distracting) patterning
displayed in the *Pink Rose* of 1871. Similarly, the muddied
transitions in color and shading that mark his early
attempt to convey precise detail are corrected in the tightly
controlled handling seen in *Carnations* of 1864. Farrer's
efforts to perfect his technique were rewarded. His *Study
of Apples*, shown at the first exhibition of the American
Water Color Society in 1867–68, prompted one critic to
point out its "astonishing force in color and photographic
fidelity in imitation" ("Art Notes: Exhibition of Water
Colors at the Academy of Design," *New York Herald*,
December 29, 1867, p. 8).

Farrer stopped exhibiting still-life subjects after the
American Water Color Society exhibition of 1872, when
one of his paintings, titled *Flying Peach* in the catalogue,
was apparently the butt of a joke. However, he continued
to paint still lifes, as demonstrated by his *Rose and Violets*
of 1876 (private collection).   BDG

101

102

103

Acorns and Barn   *circa* late 1860s

Pencil on paper
6 × 8 (15.2 × 20.3)
Unsigned
Mr. and Mrs. Wilbur L. Ross, Jr.
PROVENANCE
[Kennedy Galleries, Inc., New York, December 1983];
Mr. and Mrs. Wilbur L. Ross, Jr.

103

104
A Rocky Cliff   *circa* 1875

Graphite on paper
9 × 11¹⁵⁄₁₆ (22.9 × 30.3)
Unsigned
Harvard University Art Museums (Fogg Art Museum),
anonymous gift in honor of Professor Benjamin Rowland
PROVENANCE
Harvard University Art Museums (Fogg Art Museum).
EXHIBITED
Delaware Art Museum, Wilmington, *The Pre-Raphaelite Era 1848–1914*,
April 12–June 6, 1976.
REFERENCES
Rowland and Betty Elzea, *The Pre-Raphaelite Era 1848–1914* (exhibition
catalogue, The Wilmington Society of the Fine Arts, Wilmington, Dela-
ware, 1976), p. 66, illus. p. 67 (fig. 3-35).

105
Study of a Tree Trunk   1880

Pencil on paper
9 × 12 (22.8 × 30.5)
Inscribed lower right: "The light and shade should be
much stronger"
Lent anonymously
PROVENANCE
[The Old Print Shop, Inc., New York, 1965]; private collection.
EXHIBITED
Heckscher 1977, no. 17.
REFERENCES
Troyen, p. 42, illus. p. 43.

These drawings demonstrate the varying degrees to which
Farrer applied Ruskinian drawing principles over the
course of his career. *Acorns and Barn* is probably the
earliest of the three, and may date from the late 1860s,
when still-life and landscape subjects were of equal
concern to the artist. The extreme care taken in portraying
the subtle gradations of light on the finely grained surface
of the nuts conveys the feeling of a textbook exercise and,
in fact, conforms to the type of study recommended in the
early chapters of *The Elements of Drawing*.

A likely date for *Rocky Cliff* is 1875, the year in which
Farrer executed several large, carefully finished watercolors
featuring the rugged coast of Maine. The assignment of

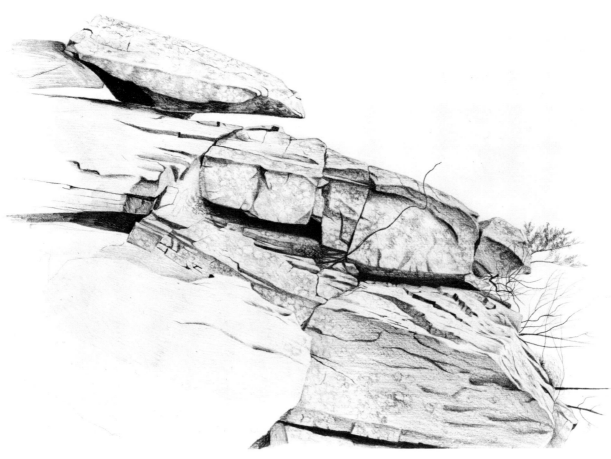

104

such a date is strengthened by the fact that the texture and surface configurations found here are also displayed in the boulders of Farrer's *Coastal Highlands* (cat. no. 106). Although this drawing conforms generally to the Ruskinian demands for economy of line, emphasis on masses, and the relief of contour outline through shading, there is an apparent freedom of execution which suggests that Farrer's approach to drawing had matured beyond total reliance on textbook formulae.

Study of a Tree Trunk may be assigned a relatively firm date of 1880 owing to the occurrence of the same tree motif in a larger, more elaborate drawing of 1880 (*On the Hillside*, see Troyen, p. 42). As Carol Troyen has indicated, both are probably preparatory drawings for an etching. This assumption is reasonable in view of Farrer's notation to himself regarding the heightening of contrast. Furthermore, by 1880 Farrer was known primarily for his work as an etcher rather than as a watercolorist. The anthropomorphic character with which he has invested this tree trunk gives form to Ruskin's phrase referring to "the woody stiffness hinted through muscular line" that is to be found in trees of the greatest interest (Ruskin, vol. III, p. 586).   BDG

105

106
Coastal Highlands   1875

Watercolor on paper
12 × 18½ (30.5 × 46.9)
Inscribed lower left: "H. Farrer 1875"
Mr. and Mrs. Wilbur L. Ross, Jr.
PROVENANCE
[Kennedy Galleries, Inc., New York, 1983]; Mr. and Mrs.
Wilbur L. Ross, Jr.
EXHIBITED
American Water Color Society, 1876, no. 10.
REFERENCES
Ferber 1980(a), p. 71, illus. p. 73.

While Farrer normally concentrated on scenes of the
waterways and countryside surrounding New York City,
several works dated 1875 confirm a trip to Maine that year.
This painting, which shows Monhegan Island in the
distance, can now tentatively be identified as *On White
Head, Coast of Maine*, one of twenty-two works Farrer
exhibited in 1876 at the American Water Color Society
exhibition. Among those paintings was another Maine
subject, *Portland Headlight*, which appears to have been
intended as a pendant for this work.

This body of watercolors drew the greatest amount of
criticism Farrer had ever earned at one time. It was noted
that "Mr. Farrar [sic] paints with almost photographic
minuteness, and, while this quality makes his pictures
sometimes a little hard, their stillness has a poetical
character of its own, and their minuteness even gives one a
sense that the artist must have cared very much for the
impression he wished to portray. . ." ("The Arts. The
Water-Color Exhibition. Second Notice." *Appleton's
Journal*, vol. XV, no. 361, February 19, 1876, p. 251). The
poetical stillness the critics found in Farrer's art suggests an
intersection of Ruskinian and Luminist aims at this time.

Farrer has engaged the full complement of Ruskinian
watercolor methodology, from the precise stippling
evident in the foreground detail to the broader application
of overlapping washes for the sky. He was judged to be at
his best when painting skies, and here his use of subtly
blended washes of color vividly illustrates the Ruskinian
axiom that the sky is the greatest example of gradation in
nature—gradation being one of the most important
technical skills for a watercolorist to achieve (Ruskin, *The
Elements of Drawing*, vol. XV, p. 34).   BDG

106

107
Sunrise, East River 1875
Also known as *Sunrise, New York Bay*

Watercolor on paper
12 × 18½ (30.5 × 46.9)
Inscribed lower left: "H. Farrer, 1875"
Private collection

PROVENANCE
Mr. and Mrs. Thomas L. Colville, New Haven, Connecticut; private
collection.

EXHIBITED
American Water Color Society, 1876, no. 101; International Exhibition,
Philadelphia, 1876, no. 153d; BAA, December 1876, no. 107 (possibly).

REFERENCES
United States Centennial Commission, *International Exhibition, 1876.
Official Catalogue. Department of Art* (Philadelphia: John R. Nagle and
Company, 1876), p. 18, where it is incorrectly listed as an oil painting;
"The Arts. The Water-Color Exhibition. Second Notice," *Appleton's
Journal*, vol. XV, no. 361 (February 19, 1876), p. 251; Stebbins, pp. 160,
162 (illus. p. 161 as *Sunrise, New York Bay*); Foster, vol. I, p. 120 (illus. vol.
II, p. 572, fig. R-26, as *Sunrise, New York Bay*).

Painted in 1875, *Sunrise, East River* signals the advent of a
transitional phase in Farrer's art that may be seen as
symptomatic of a general trend occurring within the
American watercolor movement at this time. (See Kathleen
Foster's essay, "The Pre-Raphaelite Medium: Ruskin,
Turner, and American Watercolor," contained herein.)
The golden tonality and softly modulated atmospheric
effects exhibited here indicate a growing preference for the
art of J.M.W. Turner (1775–1851) and a concomitant
rejection of that portion of Ruskin's (q.v.) teachings calling
for absolute fidelity to the minute details of nature.

This turnabout in stylistic vision did not, however,
embody a wholesale dismissal of Ruskinian notions.
Rather, it indicated a change in interpretation and
emphasis. Indeed, the approach to Turner was through
Ruskin; the critic's early championing of Turner not only
permitted this aesthetic conversion, but validated it as well.
Furthermore, Ruskin had always allowed for the eventual
release of the artist from the rigors of detailed facture,
providing the artist attained, to the greatest degree
possible, the requisite proficiency in combining visual
acuity and technical accuracy. Once properly trained, the
artist would then be free to exercise these skills in concert
with his imagination (or subjective vision) to achieve an art
of the highest order.

Critics welcomed this transformation in Farrer's work, a
process which evidently became more pronounced
following his trip to England (*circa* 1878), where he made
watercolor copies of Turner's paintings for the
chromolithographer Louis Prang. One critic's observations
made in 1880 apply equally well here: "He has learned from
Ruskin that pre-Raphaelitish slavery to Nature is not
necessary in order to be faithful to Nature" ("Fine Arts.
American Water-Color Society. 13th Annual Exhibition,"
Independent, vol. 32, February 19, 1880, pp. 9–10).   BDG

107

George Henry Hall 1825-1913

George Henry Hall was born in Manchester, New
Hampshire, on September 21, 1825, and moved with
his family to Boston in 1829 after the death of his father.
He began to paint as early as 1842, seemingly without the
benefit of formal instruction. In 1846-47 he listed himself
in the Boston directory as an artist and began to submit
work to the Boston Athenaeum, continuing to exhibit
there intermittently through the sixties.

In August 1849 Hall sailed to Europe with his friend
Eastman Johnson (1824-1906), stopping in Holland on
the way to Germany. He had been advised by the American
Art-Union, where he exhibited in 1848, that the finest
training available was at the Düsseldorf Academy, but he
found the painting there dull and dry and left within the
year to go to Rome and Paris. Returning to New York in
1852, he became active in the art community, was elected
an Associate of the National Academy of Design that year
(a position he apparently resigned in 1855, possibly due to
frequent travel), and exhibited there fairly regularly until
1908. A sale of his work at the Academy in February 1860
enabled him to go to Spain that year, and he became an
Associate Academician again in 1863 and a full member in
1868. He also exhibited at the Pennsylvania Academy of
the Fine Arts in the fifties and sixties and at the Brooklyn
Art Association from 1861 to 1881.

As a bachelor Hall travelled frequently, eventually
spending more than twenty years abroad, including
another trip to Spain in 1867-68, one to Italy in 1872,
to Egypt in 1875, and to Italy again on and off during the
eighties with visits to France as well. In Europe he was
friends with such expatriates as Elihu Vedder (1836-1923)
and Charles Caryl Coleman (1840-1928). His last trip
was probably in 1895. Between travels the Tenth Street
Studio Building in New York was his home base from
1874 to 1883.

Hall painted both genre and still life throughout his
career, incorporating objects, figures, and sites from
his travels. Among his work from the sixties, however,
still lifes in natural settings predominate, suggesting that
the all-pervasive influence of Ruskin and his followers had
affected him. He died in New York City on February 17,
1913.

REFERENCES
DAB; Wilmerding, Ayres & Powell; Clement and Hutton; NAD; Patricia
Hills, *Eastman Johnson* (exhibition catalogue Whitney Museum of
American Art, New York: Crown Publishers, 1972); Barbara Groseclose,
Emanuel Leutze 1816-1968: Freedom is the Only King (Washington D.C.:
Smithsonian Institution Press, 1975).

108
Raspberries in a Leaf 1861

Oil on canvas
12½ × 15½ (31.7 × 39.4)
Inscribed lower left: "G.H. Hall '61"
William Nathaniel Banks

PROVENANCE
[Victor D. Spark, New York]; Paul Magriel, *circa* 1965; [Coe Kerr Gallery,
New York]; William Nathaniel Banks.

George Henry Hall considered himself to be primarily a
painter of figure subjects and explained that when he
turned to flower and fruit still lifes he did so because the
work pleased him for its color. The title of the first still life
he exhibited at the National Academy of Design in 1857,
Sweet Peas, A Study from Nature, is perhaps the best
evidence of his awareness of the trend in American still-life
painting that was elicited by Ruskinian attitudes.

As shown by *Raspberries in a Leaf*, Hall was flexible in
his interpretation of the natural-setting still-life aesthetic.
Granted, the setting is out-of-doors, but the raspberries
are cradled in a "plate" of leaves (tentatively identified as
rhubarb, a leaf which frequently occurs in Hall's still-life
subjects), in a contrived manner that hardly would have
gained Ruskin's (q.v.) approval. The painterly use of the oil
medium also separates this work from that of Ruskin's true
disciples. These differences in technique and approach to
subject are doubtless manifestations of Hall's cosmopolitan
artistic experience. They should not be interpreted as
indicators of a failure to understand Ruskinian tenets,
but rather as evidence of his decision in favor of a broader
European artistic tradition over the exacting English style
from which he borrowed a popular motif.   BDG

108

William Stanley Haseltine 1835–1900

William Stanley Haseltine, an artist well known for the carefully delineated New England coastal scenes he painted before his expatriation to Italy, was born in Philadelphia on June 1, 1835, into an artistic family. In 1850, at the age of fifteen, he studied with the German painter Paul Weber (1823–1916) and entered the University of Pennsylvania. He transferred to Harvard University in 1852 and graduated two years later, returning to Philadelphia to continue his studies with Weber.

Accompanied by his teacher, Haseltine went to Düsseldorf to study in 1854, and in the summer of 1856 travelled with Worthington Whittredge, Albert Bierstadt, and Emanuel Leutze (1816–1868) through Switzerland to Italy. Returning to the United States toward the end of 1858, he opened a studio at New York's Tenth Street Studio Building which he maintained until 1870, the year he moved to Rome permanently. In 1866 he went to Paris with his second wife and there became friends with such important French academic painters as Adolphe William Bouguereau (1825–1905) and Jean-Léon Gérôme (1824–1904); he also studied at Barbizon. Subsequent years were spent between the United States and Europe.

While in America Haseltine often painted on the East Coast, one of his favorite haunts being Nahant, Massachusetts. He exhibited frequently at the National Academy of Design, the Pennsylvania Academy of the Fine Arts, and the Boston Athenaeum, and was a member of the Century Association and the Salmagundi Club. In 1861 he was elected a National Academician.

Three years after he moved to Italy, in the summer of 1873, Haseltine came back to America and rented a studio on East 15th Street in New York to exhibit his work. When he returned to Rome the following June, he settled into an apartment at Palazzo Altieri, his family residence for the next twenty-five years and the meeting place for visiting artists and writers. He lived comfortably and was a noted collector of, among other things, Pre-Raphaelite work. Active in the American community in Rome, he was a founding member of the American Academy and a benefactor of the Episcopal Church there. He travelled extensively throughout Europe and returned to the States several times toward the end of his life, touring the Pacific Northwest and Alaska. He died in Rome on February 3, 1900.

REFERENCES
BA; NAD; Helen Haseltine Plowden, *William Stanley Haseltine* (London: Frederick Muller, Ltd., 1947); PAFA; John Wilmerding, *William Stanley Haseltine* (exhibition catalogue, Davis and Langdale Co., New York, March 5–April 2, 1983).

109

109
Rocks at Nahant 1864

Oil on canvas
22⅛ × 40 (56.2 × 101.6)
Inscribed lower left: "W.S. Haseltine 1864"
The Brooklyn Museum, Dick S. Ramsay Fund and
A. Augustus Healy Funds
PROVENANCE
The Mosely Family, Nahant, Massachusetts, 1982; [Adams Davidson
Galleries, Washington, D.C., 1982]; The Brooklyn Museum.

Closely observed paintings of coastal rock formations
constituted an important subject for Haseltine during his
American years, before he moved permanently to Italy in
1870. *Rocks at Nahant* is a fine example of what art critic
Henry T. Tuckerman referred to as his "rock-portraits set
in the deep blue crystalline of the sea" (pp. 556–557).
Like others of its type, including *Castle Rock, Nahant*
(1865; Corcoran Gallery of Art) and *Rocks at Nahant,
Massachusetts* (1864; Lano Collection), it combines a softly
lit atmospheric distance with a sharply focused delineation
of the foreground boulders. The roots of this style can
perhaps be traced to Haseltine's early study with the
German artist Paul Weber (1823–1916), a study he shared
with fellow Philadelphian William T. Richards (q.v.), and
to his two-year stay in Düsseldorf. Returning to New York
in 1858, Haseltine found an enthusiasm among his fellow
landscapists for the ideas of John Ruskin (q.v.) that would
have fortified the tendency for tight, detailed handling he
had practiced in Europe. In a manner like that taken by
Fitz Hugh Lane (1804–1865) in his contemporary series
of Brace's Rock, Gloucester, he repeatedly essayed the
Nahant shoreline from different angles in the meticulous
linear pencil drawings advocated by Ruskin and later
transferred these to canvas.

Given the many sites along the New England coast
painted by his fellow artists, Haseltine's choice of Nahant
as his most frequent subject takes on particular interest.
Nahant, situated just north of Boston, had something of
a local reputation in these years as the location of an
informal summer school of the great Harvard naturalist
Louis Agassiz. Agassiz worked in a laboratory set up for the
study of local sea life and minerals and discussed
philosophy with his assistants and with his neighbor
Henry Wadsworth Longfellow. His presence must have
had special relevance for Haseltine, who had studied at
Harvard in the years of the scientist's greatest popularity
(Edward Lurie, *Louis Agassiz: A Life in Science*, Chicago:
University of Chicago Press, 1960, pp. 167, 171, 192). From
Agassiz's lectures and writings, known to every student in
the university, he would have developed an appreciation
for the geological forces that had shaped every fissure and
surface irregularity he so faithfully delineated. Like their
mentor Ruskin, Haseltine and other American
landscapists endeavored to reconcile their deep interest in
natural science with the aims of their art. Paintings such as
Rocks at Nahant were not intended as mere records of the
rocky shore but, rather, as probings into the deeper
questions that Ruskin, like Agassiz, continually kept
before their readers: How were they formed? What was
their origin? Tuckerman perhaps put it best when he wrote
that Haseltine's rock pictures "speak to the eye of science,
of a volcanic birth and the antiquity of man. . ."—an
interpretation of which both Agassiz and Ruskin would
have approved. KM

Martin Johnson Heade 1819–1904

Martin Johnson Heade never earned more than a modest
reputation during his lifetime. Although he regularly
exhibited at the National Academy of Design through
most of the 1860s and '70s, he never became a National
Academician. He was, however, an accomplished artist
who in addition to painting portraits, landscapes,
marines, and still lifes also specialized in more
unconventional subjects such as marsh scenes,
orchids with hummingbirds, and magnolias.

Born in Lumberville, Pennsylvania, on August 11, 1819,
Heade began his artistic training in 1837, working briefly
with the folk painter Edward Hicks (1790–1849). The
following year he went abroad to study, spending two
years in Rome and visiting England and France. The
portraits he painted on his return show little technical
advance; nevertheless he began to exhibit his work at the
Pennsylvania Academy of the Fine Arts in 1841 and at
the National Academy in 1843.

Heade was on the move in the forties, working in
Philadelphia, New York, and Brooklyn—probably in
search of portrait commissions—and changing the spelling
of his name from Heed to Heade. After a second trip to
Rome in 1848 his style became more sophisticated and he
added genre and history subjects to his repertoire. During
the fifties he continued his peripatetic ways, working in St.
Louis, Chicago, Trenton, and Providence. From 1859 to
1860 and again from 1866 to 1877 he worked in New York
in the Tenth Street Studio Building, where he formed
a lasting friendship with Frederic E. Church. The
intervening years were spent partly in Boston (1861 to
1863), where he produced his first still life, and partly
in Brazil (1863), where he painted a series of small
hummingbird pictures for an unrealized publication
called *The Gems of Brazil*.

Heade returned to South America (and also visited
Central America) in 1866 and 1870, and several tropical
landscapes and his orchid-and-hummingbird pictures,
which he continued until his death, resulted from these
trips. In 1883, at the age of sixty-four, he married and
moved to St. Augustine, Florida, where he continued to
produce flower still lifes and landscapes until his death
on September 4, 1904.

REFERENCES
NAD; PAFA; Theodore E. Stebbins, Jr., *The Life and Works of Martin
Johnson Heade* (New Haven: Yale University Press, 1975).

110

Lake George   1862

Oil on canvas
25 × 49¾ (66.0 × 126.3)
Inscribed lower left on rock: "M.J. Heade 1862"
Museum of Fine Arts, Boston, bequest of Maxim Karolik

PROVENANCE
The artist; [S.M. Vose, Providence, Rhode Island]; Sumner Robinson;
[Vose, Galleries, Boston, 1948]; Maxim Karolik, 1964; Museum of Fine
Arts, Boston.

EXHIBITED
Worcester Art Museum, Massachusetts, *19th-Century American
Painting*, 1952, no. 18; American Federation of Arts, *19th-Century
American Paintings* (circulated to Stadelsches Kunstinstitute, Frankfurt;
Bayerische Staatsgemaldesammlungen, Munich; Kunsthalle, Hamburg;
Charlottenburger Schloss, Berlin; Kunstsammlungen der Stadt
Düsseldorf; Galleria Nazionale d'Arte Moderna, Rome; Villa
Communale, Milan; Whitney Museum of American Art, New York),
1953-54, no. 22; M. Knoedler and Company, New York, *Heade and
Lane*, May 3-28, 1954, no. 16; Smithsonian Institute, Washington, D.C.,
19th Century American Paintings (circulated to J.B. Speed Art Museum,
Louisville, Kentucky; Museum of Art, Toledo, Ohio; Lowe Gallery,
University of Miami, Coral Gables, Florida; Museum of Fine Arts,
Richmond, Virginia; Wilmington Society of Fine Arts, Delaware;
Museum of Art, Baltimore, Maryland; Carnegie Institute, Pittsburgh,
Pennsylvania), 1954-56, no. 27; Museum of Fine Arts, Boston,
Massachusetts, *American Paintings 1815-1865*, 1957-59, no. 157;
Museum of Art, Ogunquit, Maine, *8th Annual Luminist and Trompe
l'Oeil Painters*, 1960, no. 12; State University College, Geneseo, New
York, *Hudson River School*, February 27-April 6, 1968; The High
Museum of Art, Atlanta, Georgia, *The Beckoning Land*, April 17-June
13, 1971, no. 28; Dallas Museum of Fine Arts, Texas, *The Romantic
Vision in America*, October 9-November 28, 1971; Cultural Education
Center, New York State Museum, Albany, *New York, New York: The State
of Art*, October 8-November 27, 1977; The National Gallery of Art,
Washington, D.C., *The Luminist Movement, 1850-1875: Paintings,
Drawings and Photography*, February 10-June 15, 1980.

110

Lake George is a unique subject in Heade's oeuvre, although it is one that was favored by other mainstream nineteenth-century landscape painters, especially John F. Kensett (1816–1872), who painted the lake many times. While Heade's choice of the location reflects the influence of Kensett and others who were attracted to this scenic area, his use of bright color, linear clarity, and detailed delineation of foreground rocks suggests that he was also looking at the work of Frederic E. Church (q.v.), his neighbor and mentor in New York's Tenth Street Studio Building. The most compelling inspiration for such sharp focus at this time, however, was probably the English Pre-Raphaelites, and Heade had possibly seen their work early in 1858 when the American Exhibition of British Art traveled to the Boston Athenaeum after being shown in New York and Philadelphia (Theodore E. Stebbins, Jr., *Life and Works of Martin Johnson Heade*, New Haven: Yale University Press, 1975, p. 28). Two paintings in particular, John Brett's *Glacier of Rosenlaui* (Tate Gallery, London) and John Ruskin's *Study of a Block of Gneiss, Valley of Chamouni, Switzerland* (cat. no. 125), would have served as appropriate models of Ruskinian concern for geological accuracy. The planar construction, accumulation of detail, and anonymity of stroke in *Lake George* also resemble William Dyce's 1858 painting *Pegwell Bay, Kent—A Recollection of October 5, 1858* (Tate Gallery, London), a work Heade could not have seen but one that demonstrates a shared sensibility on both sides of the Atlantic at this time and serves to underscore the pervasiveness of Ruskinian dogma. Pre-Raphaelite inspiration closer to home may have come from essays in *The Crayon* (1855–61), which reiterated Ruskin's writing and championed Pre-Raphaelite art, and from Charles H. Moore (q.v.), a contemporaneous tenant in the Studio Building. Heade may even have seen some of Moore's meticulous rock studies.

Except for his *Rocks in New England* (Museum of Fine Arts, Boston), painted in 1855, Heade's other landscapes focusing on foreground rocks date from 1858, testifying to the influence on him of both British art and the American Pre-Raphaelites (*Rhode Island Landscape*, 1858; *Rhode Island Shore*, 1859; *Storm Clouds on the Coast*, 1859; *Lake Study*, 1860; *Low Tide*, 1860; *Two Hunters in a Landscape*, 1862; *The Lookout, Burlington, Vermont*, circa 1862; and others). The use of high-key colors, crisp painting, and equal emphasis of foreground and background detail is characteristic of Luminism as well as Ruskinianism and illustrates the compatability of the two modes in his work at this moment (Barbara Novak, *American Painting of the Nineteenth Century*, New York: Praeger Publishers, 1969, chap. 7). His interest in the meticulous depiction of rocky foregrounds seems to have diminished by the second half of the sixties as he turned his attention to the new subject of coastal marshes.   AB

William John Hennessy   1839–1917

William John Hennessy, a painter-illustrator who specialized chiefly in genre scenes, was born in Thomaston, County Kilkenny, Ireland, on July 11, 1839. Joining his father, who had emigrated earlier, he and his family moved to New York in 1849. For several years he worked at an English import house, and later he took a job with a wood-engraving firm. Having been privately tutored in Ireland, he made his first studies in art independently, but then, in 1855, enrolled in the Life and Antique class at the National Academy of Design, taking some classes with Thomas Seir Cummings (1804–1894). By 1860 he had set up a studio in the University Building, remaining there until his permanent departure from the United States. By this time he was acquainted with T.C. Farrer (q.v.).

Hennessy began to exhibit at the Academy in 1857 and was elected an Academician in 1863. He was invited to join the Century Association in 1865 (a membership he later resigned). He helped found the Artists' Fund Society and was made an honorary member of the American Society of Painters in Water Colors. From 1864 to 1882 he exhibited periodically at the Brooklyn Art Association.

While Hennessy is little known today, his sentimental narrative genre subjects were praised by Henry T. Tuckerman in his *Book of the Artists* (1867). The illustrations he made during his New York period, which are better remembered than his Victorian genre pieces and landscapes, appear in books by Elizabeth Barrett Browning, Charles Dickens, and William Cullen Bryant. He also drew for the children's monthly *Our Young Folk*, which gave an account of his University Building studio in 1866, and in 1872 his sketches were engraved for a folio about Edwin Booth called *The American Experience*.

Hennessy left America in 1870 with a married woman, and until 1875 he lived in Ireland and exhibited at the Royal Academy. Upon the woman's divorce, they married, spending summers in Normandy, France, and eventually settling near Honfleur. William Merritt Chase's informal "Artist's Club" made him an honorary member in 1878. By 1882 he had moved to Saint Germain-en-Laye, but after a tour of Italy in 1891 he returned to England. He died on December 26, 1917, in Sussex.

REFERENCES
Thomas Baily Aldrich, "Among the Studios," *Our Young Folk*, September 1866, pp. 573–576; DAB; Koke; Letter from Lady Clark to Barbara Gallati, The Brooklyn Museum, October 26, 1984, outlining biographic details of the artist's life; Tuckerman; Clement.

111
Woman in an Autumn Landscape   1868

Oil on board
12 × 16½ (30.5 × 41.9), sight
Inscribed lower right (initials in monogram):
"WJ Hennessy Oct 1868"
Graham Williford

PROVENANCE
Estate of Thornton Chatfield Thayer, 1983; [Christie, Manson
& Woods, New York, 1983, as *Woman Gazing Out Over a Marsh*];
Graham Williford.
EXHIBITED
(Possibly) NAD, 1869, no. 176, as *An October Day*.

This image of a solitary female figure silhouetted against a
darkening autumn landscape is characteristic of Hennessy's
paintings from the mid- to late 1860s. Noted especially
for the mood of poetic melancholy that infused his compositions, Hennessy was looked upon by contemporary
reviewers as a young artist of promise, and his work occasionally drew comparisons with that of another Anglo-
American artist, George H. Boughton (1833–1905).
Ironically, a few months before this picture was painted
Hennessy had received criticism for his inability to render
the human face in correct proportion ("Forty-Third
Exhibition of the National Academy of Design. Second
Notice," *The Nation*, vol. VI, no. 149, May 7, 1868, p. 377),
and this negative commentary may account for the figure's
averted face.

The extent of Hennessy's involvement with the
members of the inner circle of Ruskin's American followers is not known, but his close relationship with one of
the Farrers (q.v.) is documented by a letter (date illegible)
in the Gordon Lester Ford papers (GLF/NYPL). Although
Woman in an Autumn Landscape cannot be said to have
originated out of a specific aesthetic doctrine, intimations
of certain Ruskinian concerns are revealed in the detailed
portrayal of the natural environment and in the subject
itself—a woman gathering autumn leaves.   BDG

112
Mon Brave   1870

Oil on board
12 × 8⅞ (30.5 × 22.5)
Inscribed lower left (initials in monogram):
"W.J. Hennessy—1870."
The Brooklyn Museum, gift of the Rembrandt Club

PROVENANCE
[Mrs. Frank, London]; Lord Glendevon, 1976; [Christie, Manson
& Woods, London, May 1976]; [Kurt Kalb Kunst Handlung, Vienna];
[Shepherd Gallery Associates, New York, 1980]; Graham Williford,
1980; [The Washburn Gallery, New York, 1980]; The Brooklyn Museum.
EXHIBITED
Exhibition in Aid of the French Peasantry, London, 1871.
REFERENCES
Louis Aragon, *Les Collages* (Paris: Hermann, 1965), p. 26 (illustrates Max
Ernst's *L'Autel de la patrie*, which is based on *Mon Brave*); Ferber 1980(a),
p. 71, illus. p. 69.

111

Because Hennessy painted *Mon Brave* for the Exhibition in Aid of the French Peasantry which opened in London in January 1871, it is possible to place the narrative within the context of the Franco-Prussian War. Contained in this ostensibly simple picture of a young woman mourning her dead soldier-lover is a rich matrix of symbolic detail and literary allusion that puts the work firmly within the vernacular of Pre-Raphaelite figure painting. The laurel leaves above the soldier's photograph confirm his heroic death, and the symbolic meanings of the flowers on the small table (which functions as an informal, domestic altar) underscore the basic theme of lost love. The white rose signifies chastity and love; the blue forget-me-nots, lasting devotion; and the iris, the sacrifice of a loved one. The iris carries an additional meaning, for, as the fleur-de-lis, long a symbol of the French nation, it can be read as a reference to the patriotic cause for which the young soldier died.

While the trancelike state of the young Pre-Raphaelite beauty and the necrophilic content of the painting demonstrate a general correspondence with Pre-Raphaelite concerns, the work appears to have a specific connection with John Keats' "Isabella; or The Pot of Basil," a poem which enjoyed great popularity on both sides of the Atlantic during this period. Hennessy seems to have set up an associational reference to Keats' pot of basil by juxtaposing the empty vase and the portrait head. Evidence of this iconographic connection lies in the significant compositional parallels between *Mon Brave* and George Scharf's 1854 illustration for the poem (*The Poetical Works of John Keats*, London: Moxon, 1854, p. 209), which Hennessy is likely to have known. Although William Holman Hunt's famous painting of Keats' Isabella predates *Mon Brave* by two years, it cannot be looked to as a primary source of Hennessy's inspiration, since, according to Henry T. Tuckerman, writing in 1867, Hennessy had used this motif for an earlier version of *Mon Brave* (now unlocated) which expressed similar sentiments in a Civil War context (Tuckerman, p. 454).   BDG

112

David Johnson   1827–1908

David Johnson, a second-generation Hudson River School painter who produced precise landscapes in a style consistent with the philosophy of John Ruskin and Asher B. Durand, was born in New York City on May 10, 1827. He had little formal training except for a few lessons with Jasper Cropsey (1823–1900), with whom he painted side by side in West Milford, New Jersey, in 1850.

Johnson's formal career began in 1849 with the exhibition of works at both the American Art-Union and the National Academy of Design. His earliest subjects, in addition to landscapes, included rocks, which he painted with a precision that suggests some familiarity with the Ruskinian emphasis on geological detail and exacting technique. He often spent his summers either in the Catskills or in the White Mountains at North Conway, New Hampshire, the latter of which he first visited in 1851 in the company of several artists including John William Casilear (1811–1893) and Benjamin Champney (1817–1907). He married in 1856 and in 1857 and 1859 he visited Lake George. In 1860 he was drawn to Virginia, perhaps to paint the spectacular Natural Bridge, of which he did two full-scale versions.

Although Johnson sometimes experimented with a broader style of painting, he always seemed to return to the crisp realism which allies his paintings stylistically to those of the American Pre-Raphaelites. He continued to paint landscapes (some of which, in the late sixties and seventies, revealed a Luminist sensibility) until his output diminished in 1880. One of his works won an award at the Philadelphia Centennial Exposition in 1876. He remained a resident of New York City until 1904, when he moved to Walden, New York. He died in Walden on January 30, 1908.

REFERENCES
AA-U; John I. H. Baur, "'. . . the exact brushwork of Mr. David Johnson,' An American Landscape Painter, 1827–1908," *American Art Journal*, 12:4 (Autumn 1980); NAD.

113
The Natural Bridge of Virginia   1860

Oil on canvas
24 × 20 (60.9 × 50.8)
Inscribed lower right: "D. Johnson. 1860"
Jo Ann and Julian Ganz, Jr.

PROVENANCE
[Ortgies & Co., New York, 1890]; Charles F. Gunther, Chicago; Y.M.C.A., Chicago; [Sally Turner Gallery, Plainfield, New Jersey, 1975]; Jo Ann and Julian Ganz, Jr.
EXHIBITED
National Gallery, 1981.
REFERENCES
John I.H. Baur, "'. . . the exact brushwork of Mr. David Johnson,' An American Landscape Painter, 1827–1908," *The American Art Journal*, vol. 12 (Autumn 1980), p. 46, illus. (fig. 23), p. 48; Wilmerding, Ayres & Powell, pp. 17, 18, 145, illus. pp. 19, 146; Pamela H. Simpson, *So Beautiful An Arch: Images of the Natural Bridge* (exhibition catalogue, duPont Gallery, Washington and Lee University, Lexington, Virginia, 1982), p. 38.

David Johnson, who visited Virginia's renowned Natural Bridge in 1860, here shows the towering rock formation from a vantage point similar to that taken by Frederic E. Church in 1852 (cat. no. 93) and John Henry Hill in 1876 (cat. no. 26). Seen from a short distance at an angle accentuating the vertical rise of the great arch, the Bridge fills the picture surface, allowing only small patches of sky to be revealed. Human figures are included not only to emphasize the massiveness of the structure but perhaps also to indicate the prevalent atmosphere of cultural nationalism, which affirmed man's place in the New World. Although as John I.H. Baur notes, Johnson had for the most part abandoned his tight, detailed early style by 1860 in favor of a freer application of paint and more general approach to form, here he returned to it, no doubt in response to the rock formations (John I.H. Baur. "'. . . the exact brushwork of Mr. David Johnson,' An American Landscape Painter, 1827–1908," *The American Art Journal*, vol. 12, Autumn 1980, p. 48).

Johnson's 1860 trip yielded other views of the Bridge. One painting, also dated 1860, provides a panoramic view with the Natural Bridge in the middle distance (Reynolda House, Inc., Winston-Salem, North Carolina), and there is a drawing thought to be a study for it in a private collection. A third painting, a miniature oval in the collection of Mr. and Mrs. Wilbur L. Ross, Jr., is believed to be the one once owned by Samuel P. Avery, or a variation thereof, upon which an oval engraving by Samuel Valentine Hunt (1803–1893) is based (Pamela H. Simpson, *So Beautiful an Arch: Images of the Natural Bridge*, exhibition catalogue, duPont Gallery, Washington and Lee University, Lexington, Virginia, 1982, p. 39).   BDG

113

George Cochran Lambdin 1830–1896

George Cochran Lambdin spent most of his life painting anecdotal genre subjects and flower still lifes that were found in the best American collections of the nineteenth century, including those of George Whitney, Samuel P. Avery, and John Taylor Johnston. Born in Pittsburgh in 1830, he studied with his father, the successful portrait painter James Reid Lambdin, and exhibited at the Pennsylvania Academy of the Fine Arts as early as 1848, continuing to exhibit there through 1868 and being elected a member in 1863. In 1855-56 he went to Paris and Munich to study and upon his return began to exhibit at the National Academy of Design, where he was elected an Academician in 1868. He rented a studio in the Tenth Street Studio Building in New York for about two years in 1868 and in 1870 visited Europe again.

Lambdin established his reputation with anecdotal pictures of children and with Civil War themes such as *Consecration*, an 1861 painting of a young volunteer parting from his sweetheart that is reminiscent of such English Pre-Raphaelite subjects as John Everett Millais' *A Huguenot* (1851-52), which may have served as its inspi-

114
Roses on the Wall 1874

Oil on canvas
19¾ × 15¾ (50.2 × 40.0)
Inscribed lower left: "Geo. C. Lambdin 1874"
Mr. and Mrs. William C. Burt

PROVENANCE
Mr. and Mrs. William C. Burt.
EXHIBITED
The American Federation of Arts, New York, *A Century of American Still-Life Painting 1813–1913*, travelled to ten institutions from October 1, 1966 to November 12, 1967, no. 31; Newark 1974; Philbrook 1981; Montclair 1983.
REFERENCES
Gerdts & Burke, p. 93, illus. p. 88 (fig 6-1); Gerdts 1974, p. 91, illus. p. 90; Gerdts 1981, pp. 124–125, illus. p. 124 (fig. 6.3); Gerdts 1983, p. 20, listed p. 136, illus. p. 72.

114

ration. There is little doubt that he saw the American Exhibition of British Art at the Pennsylvania Academy in February 1858, since his father was chairman of the exhibition committee. In 1863 he is said to have studied with W.T. Richards (q.v.), and about this time occasional still-life paintings of flowers appeared among his exhibited work.

After 1870 Lambdin settled in the Germantown section of Philadelphia, where he became a skillful gardener and devoted himself primarily to painting flowers. Roses were his favorite, and he even wrote a short essay entitled "The Charm of the Rose" for the *Art Union Magazine* in 1884. While the flowers growing against his garden wall gave a natural appearance in keeping with Ruskinian principles, he also presented flowers dramatically and decoratively silhouetted against a black ground. The best-known flower painter of his generation, he published many of his works in chromolithography, thereby spreading his fame and popularity. He continued to exhibit yearly at the National Academy of Design until 1886 and died ten years later in Germantown on January 28, 1896.

REFERENCES
Gerdts 1981; NAD; PAFA; Wilmerding, Ayres & Powell.

It may be assumed that George Cochran Lambdin was aware of Pre-Raphaelitism, if only because his father was Chairman of the Exhibitions Committee of the Pennsylvania Academy of the Fine Arts at the time the Exhibition of British Art travelled to Philadelphia. This assumption is strengthened by the possibility that Lambdin studied with William T. Richards (q.v.) while Richards was affiliated with the Association for the Advancement of Truth in Art.

Yet beyond the strong affinity for the Victorian narrative mode displayed in his genre paintings, there is no evidence pointing to Lambdin's conscious adoption of a particular aesthetic during the course of his career. When he added the "growing still-life" format to his repertoire of compositions in the 1870s, it was well after John Ruskin's (q.v.) impact on American art had reached its zenith, and although he was probably cognizant of the composition's Ruskinian origins, he used the format without engaging a Pre-Raphaelite technique.

It was doubtless Lambdin's avocation as a cultivator of roses that prompted his choice of composition, for it afforded a fine means to portray the species which, for him, was unmatched in its combination of "beauty of form and color with such exquisite delicacy of texture and such delicious perfume" (George Cochran Lambdin, "The Charm of the Rose," *The Art Union Magazine*, vol. 1, June–July 1884, p. 137). Here, he presents two varieties of roses as he would have seen them flourishing in his own garden. Each stage in the development from bud to fully opened bloom is included in a manner that balances the desire for botanical accuracy with the wish to capture the "exquisite delicacy" of which he wrote. That he elected to use this idiomatic brand of realism, which finds its source in Ruskin, indicates the degree to which it had become absorbed into the mainstream of late nineteenth-century American flower painting. BDG

Nina Moore   (active 1857–1875)

Nina Moore, alternately listed as G. Nina Moore and Mrs. Nina Moore, or incorrectly as Nora Moore, is one of the many nineteenth-century women artists whose careers were short-lived and about whom almost nothing is known. Moore could be dubbed the Master of the Autumn Leaves since one third of her recorded paintings were titled *Autumn Leaves*, a favorite Ruskinian still-life subject, and in her only known work she used a meticulous technique to carefully scrutinize a selection of leaves similar to those seen in pressed arrangements.

Moore may have been allied to a family of artists, or may have learned to paint as a hobby. But by the 1860s serious art classes for women were available at institutions like the Pennsylvania Academy, and she may have studied at one. She exhibited at the National Academy of Design in 1857 and again in 1866, when she gave an Orange, New Jersey,

address. In 1864, listed as Nora Moore, she contributed one of her *Autumn Leaves* to New York's Metropolitan Sanitary Fair. Under the auspices of the Women's Art Association she submitted two paintings to the Pennsylvania Academy in 1867 when she was living in Lexington, Kentucky. She entered three watercolors in the American Watercolor Society's exhibition of that same year and more in its exhibition of 1869. Her last recorded submission was to an exhibition at the Essex Institute in Salem, Massachusetts, in 1875.

Like Annie McLane, a member of the Association for the Advancement of Truth in Art, whose artistic career seemingly ended with her marriage to T.C. Farrer, she may have had her professional life curtailed by marital commitments.

REFERENCES
William H. Gerdts Art Reference Library and Archive, City University of New York Graduate Center; NAD; PAFA.

115
Autumn Leaves   1858

Watercolor on paper
8⅝ × 7³/₁₆ (21.9 × 18.3)
Inscribed lower right (along contour of leaf):
"Mrs. Nina Moore 1858"
Inscribed upper left (upside down along contour of leaf):
"Mrs. N.M. Moore"
The Walters Art Gallery, Baltimore
PROVENANCE
John Taylor Johnston Collection, December 1876; The Walters Art Gallery.
REFERENCES
Edward S. King and Marvin C. Ross. *The Walters Art Gallery. Catalogue of the American Works of Art* (Baltimore: Trustees of The Walters Art Gallery, 1956), p. 24, no. 92; Gerdts & Burke, pp. 98, 113, illus. p. 114 (fig. 8–2).

By virtue of subject, medium, and botanical accuracy, Nina Moore's *Autumn Leaves* suggests a direct response to Ruskinian ideas. There is, however, another important factor to be considered, and that is the genteel pastime of collecting and pressing leaves. The popularity of this hobby at the time can, perhaps, be interpreted as an expression of the teachings of Henry David Thoreau (1817–1862) and John Ruskin (q.v.) in broader cultural terms. In 1857, the year Moore began to exhibit at the National Academy of Design, a small volume entitled *Leaf and Flower Pictures and How to Make Them* was published in New York (Anson D.F. Randolph, publisher). In it, the anonymous woman author (known only by the initials "H.B.") provided step-by-step instructions for the collection and preservation of leaves and flowers to be used to create, among other things, pictures with which to adorn the walls of the home.

With this in mind, Moore's *Autumn Leaves* seems to represent one stage in the process of making a pressed-leaf picture. Here, a selection of leaves is placed on an apparently clean page, ready for pressing. The careful arrangement meets with the anonymous author's dictum that "a variety of outline is as essential as variety in color for the highest beauty of the picture" (p. 13). Interestingly, Moore has included shadows, thereby emphasizing that the leaves are not yet fixed to the page, that this is a leaf picture still in the making. The curious presence of two signatures leads to the discovery that the composition functions equally well when the painting is turned upside down.   BDG

115

Thomas Moran 1837–1926

During his lifetime Thomas Moran was highly regarded for his Western landscapes, his etchings, and his illustrations. Born January 12, 1837, at Bolton, Lancashire, England, one of four brothers to become artists, he emigrated to the United States with his family in 1844, first living in Baltimore before settling in Philadelphia. In 1853 he was apprenticed as a draftsman in an engraving firm, but by 1856 he began to paint in watercolor and oil. He shared a studio with his older brother Edward, from whom he received advice and instruction, and was encouraged by Edward's teacher, the noted marine painter James Hamilton (1819–1878).

In 1860 Moran travelled to Lake Michigan's Upper Peninsula with the artist Isaac L. Williams (1817-1895) to see the Pictured Rocks, spectacularly eroded cliffs on the south shore of Lake Superior. The following year he visited England, where the works of J.M.W. Turner (1775-1851) made a lasting impression on him. Returning to the States in 1862, he married the painter-etcher Mary Nimmo, by whom he had two children. With his wife he visited England, France, and Italy in 1866-67 and in 1871 joined the United States Geological Survey under F.V. Hayden in the Yellowstone region.

Moran was one of the first artists to see and paint the American West. His first trip resulted in a large panoramic picture, *The Grand Canyon of the Yellowstone*, while a second trip two years later produced the *Chasm of the Colorado*. (Both paintings were bought by Congress to hang in the Capitol.) On assignment from Appleton's to illustrate *Picturesque America*, he agreed to accompany Hayden and photographer William H. Jackson (1843-1942) down the Colorado River during the summer of 1873, subsequently joining forces with Major John Wesley Powell for further exploration of the river through the Grand Canyon. He continued to visit the West for many years and was instrumental in establishing Yellowstone National Park.

In 1878 Moran made his first visit to Long Island, and in 1884 he built a studio there in East Hampton. On an 1882 trip to England he met Ruskin, who bought a set of chromolithographs of his watercolors of American scenery. Elected a member of the National Academy of Design in 1884, he continued to travel throughout the United States and Europe, making important sketching trips to Venice in 1886 and 1890 and exploring the British Isles in 1906 and 1910. In 1916 he moved to Santa Barbara, California, where he died on August 26, 1926.

REFERENCES
BAA; Carol Clark, *Thomas Moran: Watercolors of the American West* (Fort Worth: Amon Carter Museum, 1980); DAB; Fritiof Fryxell, ed., *Thomas Moran, Explorer in Search of Beauty* (New York: East Hampton Free Library, 1958); NAD.

116
Butterfly and Irises 1862

Pencil on paper
11⅞/₁₆ × 5 (29.4 × 12.7)
Inscribed lower right: "Water Lilly/T. Moran/1862"
Museum of Fine Arts, Boston, bequest of Maxim Karolik

PROVENANCE
Maxim Karolik; Museum of Fine Arts, Boston.
REFERENCES
William H. Truettner, "'Scenes of Majesty and Enduring Interest:' Thomas Moran Goes West," *The Art Bulletin*, vol. LVIII, no. 2 (June 1976), p. 251, illus. p. 252 (fig. 19).

This delicately wrought pencil study could have been executed while Moran was on his 1861–62 trip to England or shortly after his return to the United States. On the basis of facture and the placement of the floral subject in a natural setting it may be suggested that Moran was indeed influenced by the Ruskinian outlook. However, his interest in achieving scientific accuracy is counterbalanced by a decorative lyricism that is seldom apparent in a composition observed solely from nature. Since neither plant comprising the main motif is a water lily, the "Water Lily" inscription may be a compositional notation referring to the summarily sketched leaves at the base of the drawing.   BDG

116

117
Under the Trees 1865

Oil on canvas
40 × 35 (101.6 × 88.9)
Inscribed lower left: "T. Moran 1865—op. 17"
Private collection
PROVENANCE
Mr. Baird by 1866; [Alexander Galleries, New York, April 1980];
private collection.
EXHIBITED
NAD 1866, no. 474.

It is generally accepted that Thomas Moran's knowledge
of John Ruskin's (q.v.) theories dates to his student days
in Philadelphia in the 1850s. His English heritage, his
early encouragement from British-born marine painter
James Hamilton (1819–1878), and his admiration for the
work of J.M.W. Turner point to the likelihood of an
inherent predisposition toward British art. Even more
pertinent to the issue at hand, however, are the probable
influences Moran derived from the Exhibition of British
Art shown in Philadelphia in 1858, the art of fellow
Philadelphian William T. Richards (q.v.), and Moran's
first trip to England in 1861–62, which he made
especially to study the work of Turner (an endeavor that
would necessarily include an investigation of Ruskin's
attitudes). Not to be ignored is the Hudson River School
aesthetic, which had maintained its position as the
dominant strain in nineteenth-century American
landscape painting to this point.

Under the Trees (Opus 17) demonstrates Moran's
application of the lessons learned from these varied
sources. He has painted a quiet forest interior on a scale
that is simultaneously both intimate and grand.
Although he seldom allowed for evidence of man's
presence in his landscapes, in this instance he included a
small male figure (possibly a self-portrait) in the
foreground, perhaps in reference to his frequent
sketching forays along the banks of the Wissahickon
River. The figure is both an observer and a part of the
natural scene unfolding before him, which is painted
with the pristine clarity and chromatic brilliance
customarily associated with English Pre-Raphaelite
landscape painting. The artist's choice of a wooded
setting finds a parallel in the contemporaneous forest
interiors of William T. Richards, such as *Woodland
Interior* (cat. no. 74) and *In the Woods* (cat. no. 73). But
Moran was even less successful than Richards in
rendering spatial recession convincingly; the
Turneresque view of the distant hills framed by the
precisely executed foliage is jarring and indicates the
artist's inability to resolve the major stylistic influences
working in his art at this time.

Moran painted a number of forest subjects during the
1860s and drew more critical praise for precisely painted
autumnal scenes like this than he did for the
Turneresque renderings of English landmarks he was
exhibiting at the same time ("Philadelphia Art Notes,"
The Round Table, vol. 1, no. 22, May 14, 1864, p. 344).
The designation "Opus 17" was part of a numerical
system Moran used for a five-year period starting in 1863
to signify his more important works.   BDG

117

Aaron Draper Shattuck 1832–1928

Aaron Draper Shattuck, a successful second-generation Hudson River School painter, lived to the age of ninety-seven, but his artistic career spanned only one third his life due to an illness of 1888 that affected his vision. Shattuck was born March 9, 1832, in Francestown, New Hampshire, the seventh of nine children. He studied portrait and landscape painting under Alexander Ransom (active 1840s–60s) in Boston in 1851 and continued to study with him in New York City the following year even after enrolling in the Antique and Life Class at the National Academy of Design. He was one of a small group of American artists who never travelled to Europe.

In 1859 Shattuck became a tenant in the Tenth Street Studio Building, where his neighbors included such major figures of the landscape school as Frederic Church (q.v.) and Albert Bierstadt (q.v.), and for a short time C.H. Moore (q.v.). Inspired by the doctrines espoused by John Ruskin (q.v.) in *Modern Painters*, he produced a number of detailed, closely observed nature studies and landscapes in the 1850s and early 1860s, spending his summers gathering material for his paintings in Maine, New Hampshire, Vermont, western Virginia, and New York State. He was elected a National Academician in 1861 and exhibited regularly at both the Academy and the Brooklyn Art Association while also occasionally contributing to the Boston Athenaeum and the Maryland Historical Society.

118

Shattuck married Marion Colman, sister of the painter Samuel Colman, Jr., in 1860, and they had six children. Although he moved his family to Granby, Connecticut, in the late sixties, he maintained his Tenth Street studio until 1896. His illness, combined with changing tastes in landscape painting, led him to develop new interests. As an inventor he developed and patented a metal stretcher key which brought him financial success, and in his later years he made violins and experimented with animal breeding and horticulture. He died on his farm in Granby on June 30, 1928, then the oldest living Academician.

REFERENCES
BAA; Charles B. Ferguson, "Aaron Draper Shattuck, White Mountain School Painter," *American Art Review*, 3 (May–June 1976); John Myers, *Aaron Draper Shattuck* (Ph.D. dissertation, University of Delaware, 1977); NAD.

118
Leaf Study with Yellow Swallow Tail

circa 1859

Oil on canvas
18 × 13 (45.7 × 33.0), arched top
Unsigned
Jo Ann and Julian Ganz, Jr.

PROVENANCE
Estate of the artist; Eugene and Katherine Emigh, 1973; [Hirschl & Adler Galleries, Inc., New York, 1973]; Jo Ann and Julian Ganz, Jr.
EXHIBITED
The New Britain Museum of American Art, Connecticut, *Aaron Draper Shattuck, N.A., 1832–1928: A Retrospective Exhibition*, March 17–April 26, 1970, no. 13; Santa Barbara Museum of Art, California, *American Paintings, Watercolors and Drawings from the Collection of Jo Ann and Julian Ganz, Jr.*, June 23–July 22, 1973, no. 66; National Collection of Fine Arts, Smithsonian Institution, Washington, D.C., *America as Art*, April 30–November 7, 1976, no. 141; National Gallery 1981.
REFERENCES
Charles B. Ferguson, *Aaron Draper Shattuck, N.A., 1832–1928: A Retrospective Exhibition* (exhibition catalogue, The New Britain Museum of American Art, Connecticut, 1970), illus. n.p.; Taylor 1976, p. 120 illus.; Charles B. Ferguson, "Aaron Draper Shattuck, White Mountain School Painter," *American Art Review*, vol. 3 (May/June 1976), pp. 72–74, illus. p. 73; Taylor 1979, p. 97 illus.; Ferber 1980(b), pp. 139, 423, 486 illus. (fig. 101); John Walker Myers, *Aaron Draper Shattuck, 1832–1928, Painter of Landscapes and Student of Nature's Charms* (Ph.D. diss., University of Delaware, 1981; Ann Arbor: University Microfilms International, 1981), pp. 66–67, illus. p. 215 (fig. 31); Wilmerding, Ayres & Powell, p. 21, illus.; p. 165, illus.

Shattuck did not decide to become a landscape painter until 1855, the year his first notice appeared in *The Crayon* with the remark that his "studies of rocks, grasses and field flowers are truthful as well as earnestly painted" ("Domestic Art Gossip," *The Crayon*, vol. II, no. XXI, November 21, 1855, p. 330). By the time he painted *Leaf Study with Yellow Swallow Tail* around 1859, he had fully embraced the tenets advanced by John Ruskin (q.v.) and aligned himself with the newly emerging landscape-as-still-life aesthetic. Here, in this small, vibrant canvas, he offers the narrow yet intensely detailed view of living nature for which he was admired.

In the years immediately prior to the painting of this work, Shattuck had the opportunity to absorb Asher B. Durand's (q.v.) landscape philosophy through the "Letters on Landscape Painting" published in *The Crayon*, as well as through personal contact with Durand. John Ruskin's *Modern Painters* had become firmly established as the theoretical authority for the group of artists with whom Shattuck associated, and the important Exhibition of British Art had occurred in 1857. In this light, *Leaf Study with Yellow Swallow Tail* can be seen as the culmination of the variety of factors that contributed to the development of the American Pre-Raphaelite style.   BDG

119

The Shattuck Family, with Grand-mother, Mother, and Baby William

1865

Oil on canvas
20 × 16 (50.8 × 40.6)
Unsigned
The Brooklyn Museum, given in memory of Mary and John D. Nodine, by Judith and Wilbur Ross

PROVENANCE
The artist; William Shattuck; Granville Shattuck; Katherine and Eugene Emigh, 1980; The Brooklyn Museum.
EXHIBITED
The New Britain Museum of American Art, New Britain, Connecticut, *Aaron Draper Shattuck, N.A., A Retrospective Exhibition*, March 17–April 26, 1970, no. 88; *Aaron Draper Shattuck, N.A.–1861: 19th-Century New England Artist* (The Shattuck Collection, a condensed version of the 1970 retrospective exhibition that travelled to sixteen venues from 1970 to 1976).
REFERENCES
Charles B. Ferguson, "Aaron Draper Shattuck, White Mountain School Painter," *The American Art Review*, vol. 3 (May/June 1976), p. 78, illus. p. 79; Edgar de N. Mayhew and Minor Myers, Jr., *A Documentary History of American Interiors from the Colonial Era to 1915* (New York: Charles Scribner's Sons, 1980), illus. p. 187 (fig. 97); John Walker Myers, *Aaron Draper Shattuck. 1832–1928. Painter of Landscapes and Student of Nature's Charms* (Ph.D. diss., University of Delaware, 1981; Ann Arbor: University Microfilms International, 1981), pp. 40–41; Eunice Agar, "Aaron Draper Shattuck," *Art and Antiques*, vol. 7, no. 5 (September/October 1982), illus. p. 54.

119

This painting is one of a series of family portraits that Shattuck executed during the 1860s. Although care was taken to achieve facial likenesses, the emphasis here is not on portraiture. Instead Shattuck placed his subjects within the context of the conversation-piece genre, which, by definition, consists of a group portrait within a domestic or otherwise familiar setting. The scene is the parlor of the Shattucks' summer home in Great Barrington, Massachusetts. In a playful exchange, the artist's wife holds a glittering fish bowl just out of reach of their infant son, William, who is tenderly restrained by his grandmother.

By using a set of "disguised" symbols, an iconographic device popular with the English Pre-Raphaelites, Shattuck establishes this work as a private tribute to the sanctity of family life. The arrangement of the figures recalls the traditional motif of the Virgin and Child with Saint Ann, and the deliberateness of the composition is confirmed by the prominence with which the print of Paul Delaroche's *Madonna and Child* is positioned on the wall directly above the group. The light streaming through the window not only unites the figures compositionally but also reads as a metaphor for the divine love of God binding the family unit. The rays illuminate the infant's head before passing through the transparent glass bowl (here a symbol of the Christian sacrament of baptism) to the mother's face, finally reflecting in her wedding ring. Further corroboration of the baptismal theme is found in the fact the child is wearing a christening gown (John Walker Myers, *Aaron Draper Shattuck. 1832–1928. Painter of Landscapes and Student of Nature's Charms*, Ph.D. diss., University of Delaware, 1981, pp. 40–41). The religious theme is reinforced by the placement in the upper right corner of an engraving of Sir John Everett Millais' (1829–1896) *Huguenot Lover* (fig. 4), a painting that is itself rich in associations linking spiritual and earthly love.

Shattuck's use of familiar works of art to support the thematic content of his own painting is indicative of an iconographic convention frequently relied upon in Victorian genre subjects featuring domestic interiors. These "paintings within paintings" not only amplified specific themes, but, as signposts of taste, also helped to establish the narrative in a general way by suggesting the moral values, economic position, and social rank of the persons whose homes they decorated. Additional examples of this convention may be seen in Thomas C. Farrer's *Gone! Gone!* (cat. no. 8), in which Millais' *Huguenot Lover* augments the theme of separation, and in Farrer's *Woman Sewing* (cat. no. 2), wherein Raphael's *Madonna della Sedia* sets the tone for the quiet atmosphere of domestic respectability.   BDG

William James Stillman 1828-1901

William James Stillman, artist, journalist, and diplomat, was born June 1, 1828, in Schenectady, New York. His artistic career began after his graduation from Union College in 1848 and lasted until 1860, bracketed by his study of landscape painting with Frederic E. Church (q.v.) and a counterproductive sketching tour in Switzerland with John Ruskin (q.v.). In reaction to Ruskin's critical interference his vision became temporarily impaired and he abandoned regular painting, although he made various attempts throughout his life to paint again.

In December 1849 Stillman travelled to England briefly, meeting J.M.W. Turner (1775-1851) and beginning his long friendship with Ruskin. After exhibiting at the National Academy of Design for the first time in 1851 he met the Hungarian patriot Lajos Kossuth and went on a secret mission to Hungary. He returned the following year and was elected an Associate of the Academy in 1854. In January 1855 he launched the first American art magazine, The Crayon, with John Durand, son of the artist Asher B. Durand (q.v.). It proved to be a great literary success, attracting poems and articles by such notable writers as William Cullen Bryant, James Russell Lowell, Charles Eliot Norton, and William Rossetti. The magazine lasted until 1861, but Stillman, due to exhaustion from overwork, severed his connection with it in 1856. In that one year, he wrote much of the magazine's material, making a lasting contribution to American art by preaching Ruskinian principles and championing Pre-Raphaelite work.

After recovering from his fatigue, Stillman moved to Cambridge, Massachusetts, and began to paint again. In 1858 he helped form the Adirondack Club, which brought together men like Lowell, Ralph Waldo Emerson, and Louis Agassiz to enjoy nature and exchange ideas. After going abroad in the winter of 1859, he never again resided permanently in the United States, though he did return in November 1860 to marry Laura Mack, with whom he had three children. John Ruskin was godfather to his firstborn son.

In 1862 Stillman was appointed American consul in Rome, and in 1865 he was transferred to Crete, where he remained until he moved his family to Athens in 1869. When his wife committed suicide in 1870, he moved to London, where the following year he met and married Marie Spartali, an aspiring painter associated with the Pre-Raphaelite circle.

Stillman's career as a reporter began around 1873 when he worked as a free lance for the New York Tribune, the London Times, and the New York Herald. In 1886 he became the permanent reporter for the Times in Greece and Italy while residing in Rome. He remained in that position until 1898, when he retired to Surrey, England, where he died on July 6, 1901. While few of his paintings have survived, his autobiography provides detailed information about his career as an artist.

REFERENCES
DAB; Francis Miller, with introduction by Barbara Rotundo, Catalogue of the Union College William James Stillman Collection (Schenectady, New York: Friends of the Union College Library, 1974); NAD; Edgar P. Richardson, "William James Stillman: Artist and Art Journalist," Union Worthies, 1857, no. 12, pp. 9-15; Stillman.

120
Saranac Lake, Adirondack Mountains
1854

Oil on canvas
30½ × 25½ (77.5 × 64.8)
Unsigned
Museum of Fine Arts, Boston
PROVENANCE
Charles Eliot Norton; Miss N. Norton; Dr. J. Sydney Stillman, 1977; Museum of Fine Arts.
EXHIBITED
NAD 1855, no. 134, as Study on Upper Saranac Lake.

Stillman read the first volume of John Ruskin's (q.v.) Modern Painters during the winter of 1848-49 while studying with Frederic E. Church (q.v.). As he confessed in his autobiography, "I received from it a stimulus to nature worship, to which I was already too much inclined which made ineffaceable the confusion in my mind between nature and art" (The Autobiography of a Journalist, Boston: Houghton Mifflin and Co., 1901, vol. 1, p. 116). He painted his first careful outdoor studies in the summer of 1849 and by selling one of them to the American Art-Union partly financed a trip to England, where he met Ruskin himself. During a second trip in 1853, he visited the Royal Academy and saw John Everett Millais' Proscribed Royalist, a work whose unorthodox treatment of landscape inspired him to paint The Forest Spring. According to Stillman, when The Forest Spring was shown in the 1854 exhibition of the National Academy of Design, "the old stagers did not know what to say of a picture which was all foreground. . . . The picture gave rise to a hot discussion . . . , the old school of painters denouncing such slavish imitation of nature" (Autobiography, pp. 177-179).

At the same time Stillman was making a careful study of nature's appearance, he undertook a systematic investigation of spiritism, or the manifestation of a spirit world through particularly sensitive persons. In quest of both nature and spirit, he visited the Adirondack wilderness in the summer of 1854. As he recounted in his autobiography, "Under the stimulus, in part, of the desire for something out of the ordinary line of subject for pictures, and in part from the hope that going into the 'desert' might quicken the spiritual faculties . . . I decided to pass the next summer in the great primeval forest in the northern part of New York State" (p. 198).

Following the suggestion of the landscape painter Sanford R. Gifford (1823-1880), Stillman boarded with a family on Upper Saranac Lake. There he found a subject that, as had The Forest Spring, occupied him for three months. The resulting Study on Upper Saranac Lake, a view of the lake seen through meticulously defined tree trunks and foreground rocks, was exhibited at the National Academy the following spring.

The poet James Russell Lowell, in a letter to Stillman dated May 21, 1855, discussed this painting. After quoting from an unfavorable review that had characterized it as "an unpleasingly grouped assemblage of unpleasing natural objects," Lowell wrote, "Is a hemlock trunk unpleasing? Is the silvery-grey bole of a sloping birch unpleasing? Is the beech stem splashed with wavering pools of watery sunshine unpleasing? And pray tell me how in a picture, a thing can be 'literally rendered' . . . Anyhow, I like your picture and the idea of it; only you must make interest with Aquarius to water your lake a little" (quoted in Stillman,

The Old Rome and the New and Other Studies, Boston, 1898, pp. 143–144).

Stillman would return to the Adirondacks each summer through 1859. In the summer of 1858 he led a party of Cambridge friends, including Ralph Waldo Emerson, into the wilderness. Two fascinating documents of this trip are Emerson's poem "Adirondacks," which extolls Stillman as woodsman and artist, and Stillman's painting *The Philosopher's Camp* (Concord Free Library), which shows all those present engaged in characteristic activities.   MBH

120

(Thomas) Worthington Whittredge
1820–1910

Although he was primarily a landscape painter, Worthington Whittredge, as he called himself from 1855 on, painted a variety of subjects. Born May 22, 1820, on a farm near Springfield, Ohio, he began his artistic training as a house and sign painter in Cincinnati at the age of seventeen. Between 1837 and 1849 he worked as an artist in Indianapolis, Charlestown, West Virginia, and Cincinnati, painting both portraits and landscapes. In 1849 commissions from Cincinnati patrons allowed him to travel to Europe, where he visited England, France, and Belgium before settling in Düsseldorf, Germany.

Whittredge spent seven years mastering the carefully detailed technique of Johann Schirmer and other members of the Düsseldorf Academy. While there, he lived in the house of Andreas Achenbach (1815–1910) for a year and was also befriended by Emanuel Leutze (1816–1868), the leader of the American artist community. He posed as George Washington in Leutze's monumental 1851 history painting *Washington Crossing the Delaware* (now in the Metropolitan Museum of Art) and belonged with Leutze to Malkasten, an international group of artists who gathered to discuss art, literature, philosophy, and music. In the summer of 1856 the two of them went on a sketching trip to Switzerland with William Stanley Haseltine (q.v.) and John B. Irving, Jr. (1825–1877). Later, joined by Albert Bierstadt (q.v.), they all travelled to Italy, where Whittredge spent the next three years in Rome with Bierstadt and Sanford Robinson Gifford (1823–1880) as his constant companions, supporting himself by painting souvenir pictures for tourists.

The artist returned to the United States in 1859, first visiting Cincinnati but afterward settling at the Tenth Street Studio Building in New York. He maintained rooms there from early 1860 until the turn of the century, concentrating on landscapes but also painting occasional still-life subjects. The National Academy elected him an Associate in 1860 and a full Academician the following year, and the Century Association made him a member in 1862. During the early sixties, while teaching at The Cooper Union, he came into contact with T.C. Farrer (q.v.).

In 1866 Whittredge joined General John Pope on a government inspection tour of Colorado and New Mexico, obtaining important new subject matter for his paintings. He returned to the West three years later with Sanford Gifford and John F. Kensett (1816–1872) and made a third trip there in 1871. In between, he married Euphemia Foot, with whom he had three children.

From 1874 to 1877 Whittredge served as President of the National Academy of Design. After moving to Summit, New Jersey, in 1880 he remained active, and in 1896 he took a trip to Mexico with Frederic E. Church (q.v.). He wrote his autobiography in 1905 and died five years later in Summit on February 25, 1910.

REFERENCES
Whittredge; Cheryl A. Cibulka, *Quiet Places, The American Landscapes of Worthington Whittredge* (exhibition catalogue, Washington, D.C.); Anthony F. Janson, "The Development of a Hudson River Painter, 1860–1868," *American Art Journal*, 2, no. 2 (April 1979), pp. 71–84; Janson, "The Western Landscapes of Worthington Whittredge," *American Art Review*, November-December 1976, pp. 58–69; Jones, p. 47.

121

Apples 1867

Oil on canvas
15¼ × 11¾ (38.2 × 29.9)
Inscribed lower right: "W. Whittredge/1867"
Museum of Fine Arts, Boston, M. & M. Karolik Collection

PROVENANCE
The artist; John Cushing Whitridge, Baltimore (the artist's cousin); [Plaza Art Galleries, New York]; A.F. Mondschein, New York, 1945–48; Museum of Fine Arts, Boston.
EXHIBITED
Knoedler Gallery, New York, organized by Public Education Association of New York, *The American Vision*, October–November, 1968, no. 32; Munson-Williams-Proctor Institute (Utica, New York), Albany Institute of History and Art, Cincinnati Art Museum, *Worthington Whittredge (1820–1910), A Retrospective Exhibition of an American Artist*, October 12, 1969–March 8, 1970, no. 23; Brockton Art Center, Massachusetts, *The Good Things in Life: Nineteenth Century American Still Life*, March 8–April 29, 1973; Philbrook 1981.
REFERENCES
Wolfgang Born, *Still-Life Painting in America* (New York: Oxford University Press, 1947), p. 40; *M.& M. Karolik Collection of American Paintings 1815–1865* (Cambridge, Mass.: Harvard University Press, 1949); Knoedler Gallery exhibition catalogue, 1968, no. 32; Edward H. Dwight, *Worthington Whittredge (1820–1910), A Retrospective Exhibition of an American Artist* (exhibition catalogue, Munson-Williams-Proctor Institute, Utica, New York, 1969), no. 23; Gerdts 1981, p. 109.

Apples, probably painted during the artist's honeymoon in the autumn of 1867, depicts not a whole tree but a single branch silhouetted against the sky, as prescribed by Ruskin. It is not a landscape *per se* because of its magnification of a portion of a tree, nor is it a conventional still life, since the fruit is still growing on the branch.

Whittredge was not alone in choosing to depict this duality of landscape and still life. Robert Brandegee in *Apple Blossoms* (cat. no. 87), John William Hill in a treatment of the same subject (cat. no. 39), and Martin

121

Johnson Heade (q.v.) in several pictures of apple tree branches in the 1870s all concentrated on a single bough. For Whittredge, however, this was an unusual subject, perhaps painted for his private enjoyment, since as far as can be determined it was never exhibited publicly. He did occasionally paint other still lifes, including *Peach Tree Bough* (Munson-Williams-Proctor Institute) and *One Peach*, exhibited at the Century Association, and a watercolor entitled *Laurel Blossoms in a Blue Vase* (private collection, Pennsylvania).

That Whittredge was aware of the Ruskinians is evident in the high-keyed colors he used in this work, a departure from the somber autumnal colors associated with his forest scenes. He was acquainted with several English artists in Düsseldorf and Rome, and his training in Düsseldorf prepared him to paint in a meticulous manner easily adaptable to the subject matter characteristic of the American Pre-Raphaelites. As Henry T. Tuckerman wrote, "Whittredge unites to the American fidelity to nature in feeling, much of the practical skill derived from foreign study . . ." (Tuckerman, p. 515).

After his return to the States from Europe in 1860, Whittredge worked in New York's Tenth Street Studio Building, where he most likely met Charles Herbert Moore (q.v.). Still lifes by Martin Johnson Heade (q.v.) and the close-focus nature studies of Frederic E. Church (cat. nos. 94 and 95) and Albert Bierstadt (cat. no. 83), who were also his neighbors in that building, would have been available influences, and while teaching at The Cooper Union during the early 1860s he would have known fellow teacher Thomas C. Farrer (q.v.). While Farrer used flowers and leaves as models, Whittredge is said to have used "old boots and shoes, powder flasks and empty game bags" ("Art: The Cooper Institute School of Design for Women," *The Round Table*, n.s. no. 6, October 14, 1865, p. 93). Despite the negative feelings that he expressed about Ruskinian "literal transcripts" years later in his *Autobiography*, his close contact with those affected by American Pre-Raphaelitism may have inspired him to paint this particular kind of subject at this particular moment (Whittredge, p. 55).   AB

George Bacon Wood, Jr.   1832–1909

George B. Wood, Jr., a relatively obscure painter of genre scenes and portraits of interiors and specific streets, was born into a Quaker family in Philadelphia on January 6, 1832. He studied at the Pennsylvania Academy of the Fine Arts and probably saw the American Exhibition of British Art there in February 1858.

Wood's works of the early sixties, primarily landscapes, reflect a Ruskinian exactitude in representing nature. This heightened perception of natural details was probably encouraged by William Trost Richards, his friend and neighbor in the Germantown section of Philadelphia. Richards' patron, George Whitney, also favored his work.

Wood spent the Civil War years painting mainly the area surrounding Philadelphia, but judging from the titles of his paintings, he also took a few longer trips. In 1866 he rented a studio in central Philadelphia, and the following year he moved downtown. About this time he began summering—and even spending an occasional winter in the early '70s—in the Adirondacks in Elizabethtown, New York. By 1870 he had married and was well established as an artist.

Wood exhibited at the Pennsylvania Academy from 1858 to 1869 and again from 1876 to 1887, after the opening of its new building designed by Frank Furness. He also exhibited at the National Academy of Design in New York from 1861 to 1885 and at the Brooklyn Art Association in 1866 at the height of his Ruskinian activity. A member of the Philadelphia Artists' Fund Society, he was generally part of the artist community in that city.

By the seventies Wood had turned from landscapes to documenting Philadelphia streets and interiors, but at the end of the decade he switched his focus to photography, concentrating on both landscape and genre. According to a biography written by one of his daughters, his work in photography won several prizes.

In 1883 Wood travelled abroad, recording the sights in carefully rendered watercolors. Some of these sketches served as sources for later, more highly finished work he submitted to the Pennsylvania Academy in 1884 and 1887. From then on he dabbled in photography but does not seem to have painted professionally again. He died in Ipswich, Massachusetts, on June 17, 1909, while visiting his daughter, and is buried at West Laurel Hill Cemetery in Philadelphia.

REFERENCES:
I am indebted to Donelson Hoopes for providing me with information leading to correction of material in his article.

BAA; Donelson F. Hoopes, "George B. Wood, Jr., A Student of Nature," *American Art and Antiques*, vol. 2 no. 5 (September/October 1979), pp. 118–125; NAD; Obituary, *Philadelphia Inquirer*, June 19, 1909; PAFA.

122
Leaf and Berry Study   1864

Oil on paper
7¼ × 6¾ (18.2 × 17.1)
Inscribed lower right: "G.B. Wood Jr/Philad. 1864"
Mr. and Mrs. Wilbur L. Ross, Jr.
PROVENANCE
The artist, 1864; Charlotte Cushman, possibly until her death in 1876;
[Kennedy Galleries, New York, 1975–81]; Mr. and Mrs. Wilbur L. Ross,
Jr.

122

123
Study from Nature   *circa* 1866

Oil on canvas
10¼ × 15 (25.7 × 38.1)
Inscribed lower left: "Geo B Wood Jr"
Jeffrey R. Brown Fine Arts, Inc.
PROVENANCE
Jeffrey R. Brown Fine Arts, Inc.
EXHIBITED
BAA, March 1866, no. 160 (possibly).
REFERENCES
Donelson F. Hoopes, "George B. Wood, Jr., A Student of Nature," *American Art and Antiques*, vol. 2, no. 5, September/October 1979, p. 122.

Although both of these paintings are faithful transcriptions of a fragment of a natural setting, they differ in their degree of magnification. *Study from Nature* is an unadulterated record of a particular spot that includes lichen-covered rocks, a growing herb of the geranium family, and a cobweb. It may have been the cobweb spun across the plant life that attracted Wood to this microcosm, which, although it includes all the aspects of natural still lifes that John Ruskin (q.v.) advocated, differs from the work of true Ruskinian followers in its lack of brilliant color.

Leaf and Berry Study is more microscopic in focus and precise in treatment, a botanically accurate rendering of sheep laurel, trailing arbutus, and partridgeberry *in situ* (plant identification courtesy of Dr. Stephen K-M. Tim, Scientific Director, Brooklyn Botanic Garden). Such leaf-by-leaf pursuit of the truth links Wood generally to the pervasive influence of Ruskin during the 1850s and '60s and more specifically to contemporary painters working in this manner in the Philadelphia area. He was probably most influenced by the work of William T. Richards (q.v.), a Germantown neighbor whose work was available to him at the Pennsylvania Academy of the Fine Arts. Also working in the genre of informal growing still lifes and exhibiting at the Academy were George Cochran Lambdin (q.v.), Richards' student Fidelia Bridges (q.v.), and both Eliza B. and John B. Duffey (q.v.).

Leaf and Berry Study was among the paintings bound in Moroccan leather that Abraham Lincoln presented in 1864 at Philadelphia's Great General Sanitary Fair to America's foremost actress, Charlotte Cushman (1816–1876), for her outstanding service during the Civil War. Since it is painted on paper and dated 1864, it was probably made specifically for the occasion.   AB, HPC, LSF

William Henry Hunt   1790–1864

William Henry Hunt, the son of a tinsmith who lived near Covent Garden, London, was born in 1790. Crippled from birth, he was apprenticed to the watercolor painter John Varley (1778–1842) in 1804 and studied side by side with John Linnel (1792–1882) and William Mulready (1786–1863). In 1808 the latter persuaded him to study at the Royal Academy schools where he had exhibited three oils the year before. The following year he worked on scene paintings at the Drury Lane Theatre. Although he did some drawings for Dr. Thomas Munro, a patron of the arts, as early as 1806, the greater part of his work for the doctor, copying earlier English drawings, was done during the teens.

Hunt specialized in watercolor for most of his life, becoming a member of the Old Water Colour Society in 1826. He did topographical views at first but had to stop about 1820 because of infirmity. He did, however, continue to paint interiors and genre subjects of rural figures and anecdotal drawings of children, all in the eighteenth-century tradition of pure watercolor over pencil or pen outlines. From 1827 he favored still lifes and began to use a stipple technique with Chinese-white highlights. After 1848 his work was limited mostly to small drawings of fruit, flowers, and bird's nests. He seems to have been the first English watercolorist to make frequent and regular use of bird's-nest subjects, having begun painting them in 1830, the year he married. They were exceedingly popular and earned him the nickname "Bird's-nest Hunt."

With age, Hunt began producing work that was minutely detailed, so technically controlled that he could capture textural effects with his stippled use of prismatic color. He achieved these effects by his invention of placing pure watercolor on a ground of Chinese white mixed with gum. Ruskin admired his work greatly and advised artists in *The Elements of Drawing* to "study the work of William Hunt." In 1850 he commissioned Hunt to make sample drawings to be placed in provincial art schools, and at various other times he bought works for his own collection. In 1879 Ruskin sponsored a posthumous retrospective of Hunt's work, an exhibition which also included the paintings of Samuel Prout (1783–1852), another favorite of Ruskin, and some of the sponsor's own drawings.

Although Hunt was never formally part of the Pre-Raphaelite Brotherhood, his work was admired by them. His techniques and subject matter served as models for American artists both through the writings of Ruskin and through the nine Hunt watercolors that were shown at the American Exhibition of British Art in 1857–58. From 1851 until his death in 1864 his output diminished but did not cease.

REFERENCES
Cummings, Rosenblum & Staley; John Ruskin, *The Elements of Drawing* (New York: Dover Publishers, 1971), p. 152; Andrew Wilton, *British Watercolours 1750–1850* (Oxford: Phaidon Press Ltd., 1977); John Witt, *William Henry Hunt (1790–1864), Life and Work* (London: Barrie and Jenkins, 1982).

123

124
Hedge-sparrow's Nest with Primroses and Violets *circa* 1840–50

Watercolor on paper
7½ × 9⅝ (19.0 × 24.5)
Unsigned
David Daniels

PROVENANCE
[Thomas Agnew and Sons, London, 19th century]; [Jeremy Maas, London, 1960s]; David Daniels.
EXHIBITED
The Emily Lowe Gallery, Hofstra University, Hempstead, New York, *Victorian Art*, October 29–December 17, 1972, no. 73.
REFERENCES
John Witt, *William Henry Hunt: Life and Work* (London: Barrie and Jenkins, 1982), p. 201, no. 622.

Although William Henry Hunt was never part of the English Pre-Raphaelite circle, he was often associated with them on account of his similar devotion to truth to nature and the quality of high finish that characterizes the small watercolors to which he devoted his life after 1825. Hunt was very close to John Ruskin (q.v.) in the 1850s, and Ruskin's writings, particularly *The Elements of Drawing* (1857), praised his color technique. Ruskin, who recognized the difficulties of using pure watercolor, urged

his readers to "study the works of William Henry Hunt of the Old Water-Colour Society" (Ruskin, vol. XV, pp. 152–153) and hung examples of Hunt's work at his art school in Oxford.

After about 1840 bird's nests became Hunt's signature subject, so much so that he carried the nickname "Bird's Nest" Hunt in later life. *Hedge-sparrow's Nest with Primroses and Violets* is a typical example of Hunt's exquisite nest pictures. Meticulously detailed, the nest lies as if abandoned against a mossy bank with a delicately rendered group of flowers. Such naturalism was judged unusual— even unique—and in an essay tribute to the work of Hunt and Samuel Prout (1783–1852), Ruskin contrasted Hunt's style with the artificiality and formality of Dutch flower painting (Witt, p. 52).

Hunt was not the only British artist painting nests at the time, but a comparison of John William Hill's 1867 *Bird's Nest and Dogroses* (cat. no. 31) with *Hedge-sparrow's Nest with Primroses and Violets* suggests that his nest pictures were the most imitated. Hunt's work paralleled Ruskin's theories on painting nature, and the American Pre-Raphaelites, who had an opportunity to see nine of his watercolors in the British Exhibition of 1857–58, learned much from his example.   MC

124

John Ruskin 1819-1900

John Ruskin's books on aesthetics strongly influenced several generations of English and American artists, and his criticism changed the direction of several painters he knew personally, such as William J. Stillman (q.v.). Although not a professional artist himself, he was a prolific draftsman who sometimes exhibited his work and illustrated his own books. He also wrote and lectured widely throughout his life on architectural, political, and social matters.

Born in London on February 8, 1819, to prosperous middle-class parents, Ruskin was richly educated but severely repressed at home. His interest in art began with childhood drawing lessons and an attraction to the work of J.M.W. Turner (1775-1851), whose paintings he saw as early as 1832. He attended Oxford University from 1837 to 1840 but did not graduate until 1842.

An attack on Turner in *Blackwood's Magazine* in 1836 prompted Ruskin to write a defense which, although unpublished, marked the beginning of an obsession with that artist that culminated in the publication of the first volume of his five-volume work *Modern Painters* (1843-59). He first met Turner in 1840, subsequently purchased some of his paintings, and went on to become his friend and ultimately the executor of his estate. In 1842, inspired by Turner's Alpine sketches, he gave up more conventional methods and turned to factually recording nature with fanatical precision.

Ruskin's recommendations paralleled certain American spiritual and artistic interests and thus, in varying degrees, appealed to many of this nation's artists. His *Seven Lamps of Architecture*, published in 1848, and his *Stones of Venice*, published in 1851, influenced such American architects as Peter Bonnett Wight (1838-1905) and Russell Sturgis (1836-1909), both of whom were members of the Association for the Advancement of Truth in Art. Wight designed the National Academy of Design Building (1863-65) using Ruskin's favorite model, the Doge's Palace in Venice.

Although he was not yet acquainted with them at the time, Ruskin came to the defense of the English Pre-Raphaelites in 1851. A short time later he met John Everett Millais (1829-1896) and William Holman Hunt (1827-1910), and from 1854 to 1858 he taught elementary drawing at the Working Men's College with Dante Gabriel Rossetti (1828-1882). Among his students at the college was T.C. Farrer (q.v.).

After the publication of his books *The Elements of Drawing* and *The Elements of Perspective* in 1857, Ruskin's writing about art diminished and he devoted his energy to political, social, and scientific affairs. He maintained an interest in American art, however, writing short pieces first for *The Crayon* and later for *The New Path*, and often commenting on American paintings shown in England, such as those of Frederic Church (q.v.).

In 1876 Ruskin met C.H. Moore (q.v.) through a letter of introduction from their mutual friend, the scholar and writer Charles Eliot Norton, who had modeled the position he offered to Moore as the first Professor of Fine Arts at Harvard in 1874 after Ruskin's tenure from 1869 as the first Slade Professor of Fine Arts at Oxford. Moore, who shared Ruskin's interest in architecture, travelled with the English critic and in 1877 introduced him to the work of H.R. Newman (q.v.), which Ruskin bought. In 1879 Newman and Ruskin met, and they, too, travelled

together, drawing European architecture. Newman in turn introduced Ruskin to the work of Francesca Alexander (q.v.) in 1882, and Ruskin ended up promoting her work and developing a lifelong friendship with her and her mother. In 1884 Ruskin met yet another American artist, Thomas Moran, and bought some chromolithographs of his watercolors.

Ruskin's emotional life was unbalanced, and in 1878, just prior to his trial on charges of slandering J.A.M. Whistler (1834-1903), he suffered a mental breakdown. He continued to have attacks and ceased writing entirely by the end of the eighties, living the life of a recluse at Brantwood, his home in the English Lake District, until his death on January 20, 1900.

REFERENCES
Bowness 1984; Cummings, Staley & Rosenblum.

125
Fragment of the Alps *circa 1854-56*

Watercolor and gouache over graphite on cream wove paper
13 × 19½ (33.0 × 49.5)
Inscribed in graphite, verso, in Charles Eliot Norton's hand: "Don't cut off this strip, put it in frame just *as it is.*"
Harvard University Art Museums (Fogg Art Museum), gift of Samuel Sachs

PROVENANCE
Charles Eliot Norton; the Misses Norton; Samuel Sachs, 1919; The Fogg Art Museum.
EXHIBITED
National Academy of Design, New York, *American Exhibition of British Art* (travelled to Philadelphia and Boston), 1857-58 as no. 155, *Study of a Block of Gneiss, Valley of Chamouni, Switzerland*; Noyes and Blakeslee Gallery, Boston, Massachusetts, *Drawings by Mr. Ruskin Placed on Exhibition by Professor Norton*, 1879; Fogg Art Museum, Cambridge, Massachusetts, *Ruskin, in Memory of Charles Eliot Norton*, 1909-10; Sophie Newcomb Galleries, New Orleans, Louisiana, *Drawing and Architecture*, 1965; Staatliche Kunsthalle, Baden-Baden, West Germany, *Präraffaeliten*, 1973-74; Fogg Art Museum, Cambridge, Massachusetts, *Wash and Gouache*, 1977; National Museum of Western Art, Tokyo, Japan, *European Master Drawings in the Fogg Art Museum*, 1979; Fogg Art Museum, Cambridge, Massachusetts, *Drawings of John Ruskin*, 1979.
REFERENCES
Marjorie B. Cohn, *Wash and Gouache* (exhibition catalogue, Fogg Art Museum, Cambridge, Massachusetts, May 12-June 22, 1977), frontispiece and pp. 107-108; *Präraffaeliten* (exhibition catalogue, Staatliche Kunsthalle, Baden-Baden, West Germany, November 23, 1973-February 24, 1974), p. 32.

During one of his tours of the Alps, in the summer of 1854 or 1856, Ruskin stopped in Chamonix and made this watercolor study of boulders. The work was first shown

125

in the American Exhibition of British Art that opened at the National Academy of Design in New York in 1857, and after travelling with the exhibition to Philadelphia and Boston in 1858 it became the property of Charles Eliot Norton, Ruskin's good friend in Boston. Although Ruskin wrote to Norton in October 1858 expressing dissatisfaction with the drawing, by 1886 he had changed his mind and concluded, "There is no drawing of stone by my hand as good as your boulder" (*Letters of John Ruskin to Charles Eliot Norton*, Boston: Houghton Mifflin, 1905, vol. 1, pp. 62, 563).

Stone was extremely important to Ruskin as a subject that challenged both the knowledge and the technical skill of the artist. In volume four of *Modern Painters*, published in 1856, in the section titled "Of Mountain Beauty," he outlined its importance: "For stone, when it is examined, will be found a mountain in miniature. The fineness of Nature's work is so great that in a single block . . . she can compress as many changes of form and structure, on a small scale, as she needs for her mountains on a large one . . ." (Ruskin, vol. VI, p. 368). For Ruskin, it was through drawing that one could best scrutinize what was to be revealed in rocks to the deserving "patient observer" (Ruskin, vol. VI, p. 368). Through the close study of nature's objects, particularly stone, he felt that an artist could begin to ascertain the laws of beauty.

American reaction to *Fragment of the Alps* was predictably enthusiastic. Ruskin's writings had been revered in artistic circles for over a decade, and this was his first work to be shown in America. A reviewer in the November 1857 *Crayon* wrote, "This sketch is masterly, and said to be one of the most complete studies he has ever made" (*The Crayon*, vol. IV, part XI, November 1857, p.343). Neither the exhibition nor the drawing was quickly forgotten. In 1863, an article in *The New Path* entitled "Naturalism and Genius" included a lengthy discussion of the gneiss boulder. Impressed by the drawing's thoroughness and usefulness as a study as well as by its coloration, the author wrote, "There is no attempt at 'general effect.' The truth is told about the whole." A few paragraphs later the writer included a note that the boulder seemed "photographed in color" (*The New Path*, vol. I, no. 6, October 1863, p. 66).

As Gail S. Weinberg has pointed out, this purity of color was achieved by laying color side by side in the manner of Tintoretto (1518-1594), and it enhanced Ruskin's technical study of the rock (G.S. Weinberg, *Drawings of John Ruskin*, Fogg Art Museum, unpublished catalogue, 1979, p. 9). The concern for geological specificity appealed to such Americans as Charles Herbert Moore (q.v.) and William T. Richards (q.v.), whose own watercolor rock studies—such as the former's *Rocks By the Water* and *Landscape: Rocks and Water* (cat. nos. 49 and 50) and the latter's *Study of a Boulder* (cat. no. 78)—follow Ruskin's program.   MC

126
A Cluster of Oak Leaves   1856

Ink, pencil, wash, and tempera on blue paper
8½ × 11 (21.6 × 27.9)
Inscribed lower right: "J. Ruskin 1856"
Pierpont Morgan Library, Purchase E. J. Rousuck Fund, 1977

PROVENANCE
L.C. Duke; [Duke Sale, Sotheby's London, 1970]; Stephen Spector; Pierpont Morgan Library.

A Cluster of Oak Leaves clearly relates in visual terms the primary concerns of Ruskin's writings in *The Elements of Drawing* (1857) and the last volume of *Modern Painters* (1860). In *The Elements of Drawing*, Ruskin sets forth a program of exercises for learning drawing that parallels the system he used as a teacher at the Working Men's College in London. As he outlines the importance of sketching from nature, he particularly directs the reader's attention to foliage, not only for its easy access but also mainly because "its modes of growth present simple examples of the importance of leading and governing lines. It is by seizing these leading lines, when we cannot seize all, that . . . grace and a kind of vital truth are given to the rendering of every natural form" (Ruskin, vol. XV, p. 91). This point is well demonstrated by *A Cluster of Oak Leaves*, a carefully rendered sketch on blue paper in which the end of a branch, silhouetted to imply its placement against the sky, blows in the wind, its graceful lines drawn with absolutely truthful delineation.

In volume five of *Modern Painters*, which includes a section entitled "Of Leaf Beauty," Ruskin reiterated the importance of studying leaves for their natural form and instructiveness, writing, ". . . any group of four or five leaves . . . consists of a series of form not only varied in themselves, but every one of them seen under a different condition of foreshortening" (Ruskin, vol. VII, p. 51). Whereas a rock presented Ruskin with a "mountain in miniature," a leaf or a flower provided him an avenue for his lifelong study of form and perspective in nature.

How the American Pre-Raphaelites applied Ruskin's approach to their own graphic investigations of American foliage can be seen in such works as Charles Herbert Moore's *Pine Tree* of 1868 (cat. no. 48) and John Henry Hill's *Plant Studies* of 1866 (cat. no. 21). The latter artist wrote in his *Sketches from Nature* (cat. no. 18), "I would say, drawing a single flower, leaf, or bit of rock thoroughly well is something better worth doing than conjuring up pictures in the studio . . ." (Hill 1867).   MC

126

127
Self-portrait 1861

Watercolor and gouache over pencil on paper
6¼ × 4⅝ (15.9 × 11.8)
Unsigned
The Pierpont Morgan Library, gift of the Fellows
PROVENANCE
The artist; Joan Ruskin Agnew Severn (Mrs. Arthur Severn); Violet
Severn (sister of Arthur Severn); Frederick James Sharp; Mrs.
M. Holmes; Pierpont Morgan Library.
EXHIBITED
Arts Council of Great Britain, London, *Ruskin and his Circle*, 1964.
REFERENCES
Ruskin, vol. XVII, pp. cxiv–cxv and frontispiece; vol. XXXVIII, p. 205.
James S. Dearden, "Further Portraits of John Ruskin," *Apollo*, June 1961,
p. 174

Ruskin probably painted this self-portrait in the fall of
1861. It was, after that, widely circulated as a chromolitho-
graph with a facsimile signature and was also used as the
frontispiece for volume seventeen of *The Complete Works
of John Ruskin*, which included writings mostly on political
economy from 1860 to 1873.

In early November 1861, Ruskin sent the picture to his
father from Lucerne with a letter describing it as "very
sulky . . . but has some qualities about it better than a

photograph" (Ruskin, vol. XVII, pp. cxiv–cxv). He had
presented himself with his head turned right, but looking
to the left with a somewhat ambivalent glance. His face is
evenly lit; the hair and sideburns are delineated with line
and color as carefully as his earlier botanical subjects. The
bust-length portrait is finished with only a sketchy suggestion of his collar and the outline of his coat in a manner
similar to the way in which the surroundings of his studies
in nature are intimated.

Ruskin applied to his own likeness the principles for
drawing and methods of study he set forth in *The Elements
of Drawing* and *Modern Painters* for other subjects. His
features have undergone the same close scrutiny he gave
rocks and flowers to reveal through the study of the parts
the complicated character of the whole.

Similarly, Thomas Farrer's carefully rendered *Self-
portrait* (cat. no. 1) demonstrates Ruskin's approach. Also,
Farrer's *Portrait of John William Hill* (cat. no. 5) shows how
Farrer appropriated Ruskin's principles for a portrait: Hill's
face, meticulously rendered, is placed on only the suggestion of a body sitting in a room. This latter work is a testa-
ment to Ruskin's influence on two of his greatest
admirers.   MC

127

128
Twig of Peach Bloom   *circa* 1874

Watercolor and gouache on paper
8¼ × 6⅜ (21.0 × 17.0)
Inscribed lower right: "JR"
Harvard University Art Museums (Fogg Art Museum),
bequest of Mrs. Alfred Mansfield Brooks
PROVENANCE
The artist; William Ward; Arthur H. Brooks; Alfred H. Brooks; Alfred
M. Brooks; Fogg Art Museum.
EXHIBITED
Fogg Art Museum, Cambridge, Massachusetts, *Drawings of John Ruskin,*
1979.

Ruskin's *Twig of Peach Bloom* is typical of his flower
studies of the 1870s and shows a further development of
the approach he took in his earlier flower drawings. Like
his *Cyclamen* (1873, Fogg Art Museum) and his *Study of a
Wild Strawberry Blossom* (Ashmolean Museum), it depicts
a single branch of flowers rendered carefully in color and
placed on a solid background. The branch stands alone,
isolated as a study, but the blue background suggests that
it is seen against the sky.

Ruskin wrote in *Proserpina* (1875–81) that there are
"two main facts . . . you have to study in every flower: the
symmetry or order of it, and the perfection of its substance
. . ." (Ruskin, vol. XV, pp. 463–464). Contrary to his earlier
writings, in which he emphasized the importance of
studying flowers in their natural setting, this isolated
specimen attests to his search in the individual object for
an understanding of order in the natural universe.
Although *Twig of Peach Bloom* shares the careful, detailed
drawing and definition of form through color that were
Ruskin's trademarks in all his botanical studies—as well as
a natural setting—the degree of intensity paralleling his
own philosophical explorations distinguishes this drawing
from the earlier ones.

It is these trademarks that American artists responded to
most strongly in the 1850s, '60s, and '70s. Charles Herbert
Moore's *Lilies of the Valley* (cat. no. 45), John William Hill's
Apple Blossoms and *Peach Blossoms* (cat. nos. 39 and 40),
and Henry Roderick Newman's *Anemone* (cat. no. 59) all
demonstrate how closely the Americans absorbed Ruskin's
aesthetic.   MC

128

Index to Lenders

The Addison Gallery of American Art, Phillips Academy, Andover, Massachusetts   99
The Art Institute of Chicago, Department of Architecture, Chicago, Illinois   6, 7
The Art Museum, Princeton University, Princeton, New Jersey   2, 45, 47, 48, 51, 52, 54

William Nathaniel Banks, Newnan, Georgia   108
Bowdoin College Museum of Art, Brunswick, Maine   73
The Brooklyn Museum, Brooklyn, New York   26, 29, 39, 67, 69, 80, 81, 84, 86, 89, 101, 102, 109, 112, 119

Mr. and Mrs. William C. Burt, Montclair, New Jersey   114

The Cooper-Hewitt Museum, The Smithsonian Institution's National Museum of Design, New York   94, 95

David Daniels, New York   124

Peter A. Feld   14

Jo Ann and Julian Ganz, Jr., Los Angeles, California   113, 118

Harvard University Art Museums (Fogg Art Museum), Cambridge, Massachusetts   21, 46, 49, 50, 55, 59, 62, 104, 125, 128
Hirschl & Adler Galleries, Inc., New York   4

The J. B. Speed Art Museum, Louisville, Kentucky   92
Jeffrey R. Brown Fine Arts, Boston, Massachusetts   58, 123

Maier Museum of Art, Randolph-Macon Woman's College, Lynchburg, Virginia   61
The Metropolitan Museum of Art, New York   17, 36, 40
Mr. and Mrs. Leonard L. Milberg, Rye, New York   20, 63
Munson-Williams-Proctor Institute, Utica, New York   90
Museum of Fine Arts, Boston, Massachusetts   9, 15, 53, 56, 57, 64,* 76, 110, 116, 120, 121

The New-York Historical Society, New York   5, 30, 31, 34, 42
The New York Public Library, Print Collection, Astor, Lenox, and Tilden Foundations, New York   18, 19

Pennsylvania Academy of the Fine Arts, Philadelphia, Pennsylvania   98
The Pierpont Morgan Library, New York   3, 126, 127
Private collections   1, 8, 13, 22, 28, 32, 33, 37, 38, 43, 66, 68, 70, 74, 77, 78, 83, 85, 87, 91, 100, 105, 107, 117

Mr. and Mrs. Wilbur L. Ross, Jr., New York   10, 11, 23, 24, 35, 60, 65, 75, 79, 103, 106, 122
Stephen Rubin, New York   41

Cyrus Seymour, New York   96
Sheldon Memorial Art Gallery, University of Nebraska, Lincoln   27
Sleepy Hollow Restorations, Tarrytown, New York   16
Smith College Museum of Art, Northampton, Massachusetts   12

Jean E. Taylor, Norwalk, Connecticut   88
Terra Museum of American Art, Evanston, Illinois   97
Thomas Gilcrease Institute of American History and Art, Tulsa, Oklahoma   82

Vassar College Art Gallery, Poughkeepsie, New York   44
University of Virginia Art Museum, Charlottesville, Virginia   93

The Walters Art Gallery, Baltimore, Maryland   71, 115
Washburn Gallery, New York   25
Graham Williford, New York   111

Yale University Art Gallery, New Haven, Connecticut   72

*Exhibited at the Museum of Fine Arts, Boston, only